Ruby on Rails Enterprise Application Development

Plan, Program, Extend

Building a complete Ruby on Rails business application from start to finish

Elliot Smith

Rob Nichols

PUBLISHING

BIRMINGHAM - MUMBAI

Ruby on Rails Enterprise Application Development
Plan, Program, Extend

Copyright © 2007 Packt Publishing

First published: November 2007

Production Reference: 1011107

Published by Packt Publishing Ltd.
32 Lincoln Road
Olton
Birmingham, B27 6PA, UK.

ISBN 978-1-847190-85-7

www.packtpub.com

Cover Image by Rob Nichols

Credits

Authors

Elliot Smith

Rob Nichols

Reviewer

Keynan

Senior Acquisition Editor

David Barnes

Development Editor

Mithil Kulkarni

Technical Editor

Swapna V. Verlekar

Editorial Manager

Dipali Chittar

Project Manager

Abhijeet Deobhakta

Project Coordinator

Sagara Naik

Indexer

Monica Ajmera

Proofreader

Cathy Cumberlidge

Chris Smith

Production Coordinator

Shantanu Zagade

Cover Designer

Shantanu Zagade

About the Authors

Elliot Smith has worked in IT since 1996: at OpenAdvantage (an open-source solutions center) as a business analyst, as a learning technologist and web developer at the University of Birmingham, England, and as a technical writer for Armada Computer Publications. He runs his own training and consulting company, mooch labs, when he gets a chance. He has an M.Sc. in Artificial Intelligence and a Ph.D. in Computer Science from the University of Birmingham.

He thanks Nicola, his wife, for giving him the time and space to write a book; Madeleine, his daughter, for keeping him sane while doing it; and Rob Nichols for giving him the opportunity in the first place.

Rob Nichols first started using computers during his apprenticeship at Rolls-Royce in the early 1980s. At 23, he decided to change direction and started a degree in Geology and Geography at Cardiff University. By 1995 he had gained a Ph.D. from Bristol University, studying the behavior of quicksand.

During his time in Bristol and in a subsequent lectureship at Leeds University, he started using the fledgling Internet to communicate with co-workers, gather information, and present Geological information in the form of his first web pages. Following his return to Britain from a lectureship in U.S.P. Fiji, Rob found himself without another lectureship position to go on to. So, changing direction again, he started working for a U.K. computer manufacturer, where he rose to the position of Engineering Manager, managing a team of seventy maintenance and networking engineers, and support staff.

Following the collapse of the U.K. computer market in 2002 he moved on to the role of IT manager for a small business providing products and services to the water industry. In this role, Rob has had great success developing intranet-based business applications that streamlined business processes, saved time, and increased efficiency. In doing so, he transformed the IT department from a business cost to a profit generator by reducing costs and thereby increasing margins.

When not working with computers, Rob and his wife reside happily in a small Midlands town in England, where he writes scripts for the local movie-makers club and photographs the local wildlife.

Thank-you Diane, for putting up with my disappearances into the study to "work on the book".

Table of Contents

Preface

Ruby on Rails is a development framework designed to make the creation of web applications straightforward, well structured, and productive. By using convention over configuration, it reduces the work needed to set up an application and leaves the developer to concentrate on the components that address the problem at hand. That is, the common repetitive basic tasks are dealt with seamlessly and easily, and therefore most effort can be concentrated on creating the particular elements required for the current solution.

The strengths of this framework, that make it such an excellent tool to create Internet applications, also make it an excellent system to create business applications within private networks. It allows a developer to efficiently create distributed applications. Thereby users throughout a company are able to enter, manipulate, and report on data. This is done in a way that is easy to roll out and maintain; the resulting applications are easy to expand and extend.

This book describes both how to create business applications using Ruby on Rails, and how to create the complete creative environment. This includes how to support the development process with systems such as version control and integrated development environments, and deploy the final product on efficient web and database servers.

What This Book Covers

Chapter 1 provides an overview of the book. You will learn why Ruby on Rails should be used in preference to the multitude of other programming and scripting frameworks for developing database-driven web applications.

Chapter 2 here you will learn about some of the conventions used in Rails, and the Rails framework will be introduced. We describe some methods of controlling and logging user access and discuss their merits and limitations. We also discuss data validation and user input control via form design in this chapter.

Chapter 3 outlines how to lay some firm foundations for a sustainable Rails development project. The core of this is obviously the Rails stack itself. You will learn how to install and configure this in some detail. The chapter recommends a few of the technologies closest to the heart of Rails, which can readily be used to support your development work.

Chapter 4 will help you build from an idea and an initial Rails installation to a fully-fledged data model, populated from an external data source, with full validation and unit test suite. This chapter also provides examples of how to integrate the application with external data sources, and how to share code development across a team.

Chapter 5 describes how to build a web interface on top of the models developed earlier. You will learn about creating a controller from scratch, how to add style sheets, writing complex controller actions to update multiple models simultaneously, and using pagination.

Chapter 6 describes how to set up a Rails production environment. In particular, it covers the decisions you will need to make to successfully get your business application up and running. Some coverage of error handling is presented, and we describe some systems that will make it easier to back up and restore your application.

Chapter 7 concentrates on the tools you can use to improve the user experience. These include providing links into the application, providing search tools, enhancements to the user interface, and providing help to the users.

Chapter 8 aims at showing more of the depth and usefulness of Rails, while at the same time demonstrating how to extend an existing application with new functionality.

Chapter 9 discusses advanced deployment of your application. You will learn how to deploy your application with Capistrano. You will also learn about troubleshooting deployment and optimizing your Rails applications.

Chapter 10 covers how you can improve your Rails skills further, and suggests alternative skills that complement Ruby on Rails, thereby broadening your skill set.

What You Need for This Book

You need prior knowledge of Ruby on Rails, as this book helps developers to find out how to rapidly build easily-deployed, easily-supported business applications.

Who is This Book for

Developers who have completed on-line Ruby on Rails tutorials and perhaps have built their first basic application are a key group this book is aimed at, especially those who like what they have seen in the basic tutorials, and now want to know how to create an environment in which they can most efficiently develop new applications and improve their understanding of the Rails framework.

This book is also aimed at developers who particularly want to create data-centric applications within a private network, those who want to leverage the best of intranet applications to provide distributed easily maintained applications.

On completion of the book the reader will not only know how to write better Ruby on Rails code, but also how to create a development environment and roll out completed applications onto production systems.

Conventions

In this book, you will find a number of styles of text that distinguish between different kinds of information. Here are some examples of these styles, and an explanation of their meaning.

There are three styles for code. Code words in text are shown as follows: "We can include other contexts through the use of the `include` directive."

A block of code will be set as follows:

```
[default]
exten => s,1,Dial(Zap/1|30)
exten => s,2,Voicemail(u100)
exten => s,102,Voicemail(b100)
exten => i,1,Voicemail(s0)
```

When we wish to draw your attention to a particular part of a code block, the relevant lines or items will be made bold:

```
[default]
exten => s,1,Dial(Zap/1|30)
exten => s,2,Voicemail(u100)
exten => s,102,Voicemail(b100)
exten => i,1,Voicemail(s0)
```

Any command-line input and output is written as follows:

```
# cp /usr/src/asterisk-addons/configs/cdr_mysql.conf.sample
    /etc/asterisk/cdr_mysql.conf
```

New terms and **important words** are introduced in a bold-type font. Words that you see on the screen, in menus or dialog boxes for example, appear in our text like this: "clicking the **Next** button moves you to the next screen".

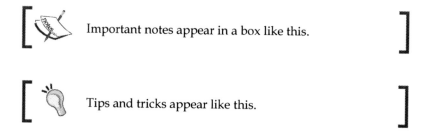

> Important notes appear in a box like this.

> Tips and tricks appear like this.

Reader Feedback

Feedback from our readers is always welcome. Let us know what you think about this book, what you liked or may have disliked. Reader feedback is important for us to develop titles that you really get the most out of.

To send us general feedback, simply drop an email to feedback@packtpub.com, making sure to mention the book title in the subject of your message.

If there is a book that you need and would like to see us publish, please send us a note in the **SUGGEST A TITLE** form on www.packtpub.com or email suggest@packtpub.com.

If there is a topic that you have expertise in and you are interested in either writing or contributing to a book, see our author guide on www.packtpub.com/authors.

Customer Support

Now that you are the proud owner of a Packt book, we have a number of things to help you to get the most from your purchase.

Downloading the Example Code for the Book

Visit http://www.packtpub.com/support, and select this book from the list of titles to download any example code or extra resources for this book. The files available for download will then be displayed.

The downloadable files contain instructions on how to use them.

Errata

Although we have taken every care to ensure the accuracy of our contents, mistakes do happen. If you find a mistake in one of our books—maybe a mistake in text or code—we would be grateful if you would report this to us. By doing this you can save other readers from frustration, and help to improve subsequent versions of this book. If you find any errata, report them by visiting http://www.packtpub.com/support, selecting your book, clicking on the **Submit Errata** link, and entering the details of your errata. Once your errata are verified, your submission will be accepted and the errata added to the list of existing errata. The existing errata can be viewed by selecting your title from http://www.packtpub.com/support.

Questions

You can contact us at questions@packtpub.com if you are having a problem with some aspect of the book, and we will do our best to address it.

1
Introduction

This book describes how the web development framework, Ruby on Rails, can be used to create small applications and, in particular, applications that form the key components within business solutions. It uses the example of a customer contact application to work through the process of solution creation; also providing a practical description of the steps required. This book not only covers the coding techniques, but also explains how to build a development environment, configure host servers, and develop the application over and above its original scope.

Why this Book?

One could ask when picking up this book: "Why another book on Rails?". In the last couple of years there have been a number of excellent books published, describing this new web development framework. There are books that introduce the framework and walk people through developing their first Rails applications. Other books describe how to add specific functionality to existing applications. References for the language and syntax also exist. So why do we need another book?

There are two answers to that question. The first is that there is a lack of material in the middle ground. That is, there is a wealth of material on how to get started with Rails, both in print and on the Internet. Then there are the latest books that address the needs of the experienced developer, who requires information to supplement the online source code documentation. What is less obvious is where a developer finds the information to move them from the beginner who has built his first application, to the experienced Rails aficionado who can get the most from the detailed advanced literature.

This book is aimed at developers who have just started out with Rails, have worked through the basic tutorials, and built their first applications. These developers, who feel pleased with the achievement of building their first Rails application, now ask the question, "What do I do next?"

However, there is another target audience; developers who are looking for more than just another book describing a 'web development tool'. These are the developers who recognize and want to exploit the unique attributes of Rails that make it the ideal tool to address a vital business requirement.

[Rails is the ideal framework to develop small business applications.]

This book, therefore, is also aimed at developers who want to find out how to rapidly build small, easily deployable, easily supportable, business applications. They come to this book not because they necessarily want to write Rails applications, but because Rails is the ideal framework to build their business applications.

Why Develop?

Traditionally, there are two ways to implement an IT solution in a business process.

1. Buy an off-the-shelf solution.
2. Pay a developer to build a bespoke solution.

For many problems these are still the best options. However, when dealing with specific, small, everyday problems, both have drawbacks.

Off-the-shelf solutions tend to be plentiful when trying to address the usual run-of-the-mill problems. However, when it comes to overcoming a small, specialized problem it can be difficult to find an appropriate off-the-shelf solution. They are often designed to work for *everyone*, but do not seem to work for you. The result is change in the working procedures to fit the application, instead of being able to find the solution that neatly slots into your existing business process.

Another issue with buying an off-the-shelf solution to address every small problem, is a proliferation of applications that do not communicate with one another. Often, data that may be useful elsewhere in the business is locked up and inaccessible within a number of independent applications.

Bringing in a specialist developer to create an application also brings in its own problems, the most obvious of which is *cost*. For major business developments, this cost is justifiable, but for many small problems it is not. Another problem is supporting and developing the application after it has been rolled out. Often further development requires bringing the developer back in at additional cost or finding an alternative developer, who will spend much of their time working out how the bespoke application works. As for fixing faults—custom applications tend to have custom faults. The knowledge bases available for off-the-shelf applications will not exist for your unique application.

If you can develop the application yourself, with a framework that is easy to use and encourages you to follow good practice, you can overcome these problems. You will be able to rapidly develop and deploy solutions that are tailor-made to address the current issues. Working to a clear, well defined framework, will make it easier to write a code that you can return to six months later and understand. This makes support and future development easier. As the development staff used is in-house, costs will tend to be lower, and it will be more likely that the developer will be available to fix problems.

Why a Client/Server based Web Application?

The common response to the problem of gathering, tracking, or manipulating data within an active business is to use spreadsheets. These bring their own problems, particularly apparent when one tries to share the resulting files with multiple users spread around the company. Trying to control data change and user updates is difficult. The usual result is multiple copies of files spread about the company, with some not being the same as others.

Attempts to manage these separate copies tend to add complication to the spreadsheets, making them more likely to fail and more difficult to support. For example, you might add a macro to automate a process within a spreadsheet, only to find that the macro does not run on all the computers because of a missing dependent file.

The answer is to centralize the data and then distribute tools that allow users to view, manipulate, add, and report on the data. In networking terminology, the central resource is the *server*, and the distributed end-user interface, the *client*.

The server part of the solution is a database: a central data storage system. In many ways, this part is easy. There are many database systems available, from personal desktop databases like Access and Open Office's "Base", to large corporate systems such as Oracle and Microsoft's SQL server. Many such as MySQL, PostgreSQL, and SQLite sit in the middle ground, providing excellent low cost database solutions for most everyday requirements, and are particularly suited to web applications. They are easy to find, and many are easy to install and use. Effective solutions can be created with the minimum of customization.

The client part is more problematic: provide a user with an input and output tool that is available wherever the information is required within the business. The output from the system needs to be tailored to the user's requirements, if they are to use the data most efficiently. The input must be controlled to maintain the quality and integrity of the data. "Rubbish in, rubbish out", is a cliché, but a useful one that highlights the fact that a data system is only as good as the data it holds. Without input control, a database can rapidly lose its value as it gets filled with data that cannot be searched nor compared easily. For example, it is surprising to see that the problems can be caused by entering the alphabetic character "o" where a zero should be added.

Most databases have administration interfaces that afford a user the ability to retrieve and input data, but by their nature they do so in an uncontrolled manner that is unsuitable for most end-user requirements. Instead a user interface is required.

The control of input and output is likely to be unique to the business requirement, and therefore, this element usually requires the most customization. This raises a problem that on first appearance may not seem to be too important, but on closer inspection has a fundamental effect on the performance and stability of the resulting application. The server part of the system will be located on a small number of easily controlled servers. The distributed client part will be spread around the business' desktop computers.

In many businesses (especially smaller businesses), desktop computers are often varied, with new computers added as they are needed. There is often a wide range of end-user computing hardware in place throughout a business. Servers, on the other hand tend to be small in number and are brought in to address a limited number of requirements.

Therefore, the straightforward server application (the database) is being held on the most easily controlled and defined area of the network; *the server*. The complicated client user interface is hosted on the most diverse part of the network; *users' computers*. So there is a problem in that the part of the system that needs most customization, and therefore is most likely to require maintenance, is located on the most diverse part of the network. This is a recipe for failure.

Deploying the client side of the system via a web service overcomes this problem. With a web service, the client application is split between a central web server, and a distributed web interface (the users' web browser). The two are connected over the network via a well-defined standard based protocol (HTTP). The majority of computation and logical operations are carried out at the web server. The user's web browser is used to display information and provide simple forms for user input.

In their simplest form, both the information display and input forms are presented via standard languages (HTML or XHTML). This reliance on simple defined open standards means that the work of the user's web browser is kept to a minimum, with most of the complicated work being carried out at the web server.

The result is that the least controlled part of the network (end user workstations) now hosts the simplest part of the system (receiving and displaying the HTML information). The more complicated parts of the system resides on the most easily controlled parts of the network: *the web* and *database servers.*

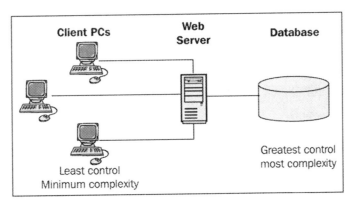

Extra functionality can be added to the web pages presented to the user, by the use of JavaScript (which allows logical operations to be carried out at the browser), XML (as either an alternative to HTML or as part of custom data transfer operations), and CSS (Cascading Style Sheets provide a way of improving the appearance of web pages without significantly increasing the complexity of the HTML code. In essence, the best way to convert drab web pages into attractive media experiences). These three systems are combined into a framework called AJAX, which is used to greatly enhance the user experience. There is a tradeoff between the addition of this extra functionality, and the additional complication that results, but with care the tradeoff is manageable, and resulting systems are still simpler than alternative solutions.

Therefore, a client/server based web application provides the ideal platform to store, manipulate, and present data throughout a dispersed business environment.

But why Ruby on Rails?

There are a number of alternative programming and scripting frameworks that can provide a web application to present data stored in a central database. So why use Ruby on Rails rather than JSP, ASP.Net, or PHP?

Rails Handles Menial Tasks

An underlying principle of Ruby on Rails is that of convention over configuration. Basically, this means that the designers of the framework have broken the workings of a web application into its core components. Conventions have allowed the core components to be standardized, and thereby access to them is greatly simplified.

For example, if you want to save data comprising details of a list of bags, the Rails convention is to save the list in a database table called bags. The convention then prescribes that each line of data can be represented by an object that is the singular of the table name. So if our table is bags, the object that can hold data from the tables is a Bag object. Fields in the table are automatically converted to properties of the object. So if there is a color field, the object will have this property; that is, bag.color. All you need is to create the database schema, define the database connection in a single configuration file, and your application will be able to create your bags table and use the data in the table as Bag objects. Saving a new bag to the database will be as simple as:

```
next_bag = Bag.new
next_bag.color = "Black"
next_bag.save
```

In three lines you've created a Bag object, defined the color as black, and saved it to the database. Thanks to the Rails conventions, the system knows automatically to save the data into a table called bags, and to enter the text Black into the color field. Programmatically, you do not have to open the connection to the database, define the database command that will input the data for you, and close the database connection; all of that is taken care of, for you.

By keeping to the conventions, the application developer is able to concentrate on the logic of an application and is freed from having to worry about the underlying nuts and bolts. So rather than wasting time repeating the code required for all the web applications, the developer can devote most of his time to work on the logic that makes the new application different from the rest, and address the problem at hand.

With the use of convention, everyday tasks such as page pagination, data validation, and search ahead AJAX tools, that can take tens of lines of code to write in other frameworks, can be added in two or three lines of code.

Clear Code

Underlying everything is Ruby. Ruby is an elegant language with syntax that is easy to understand and use.

The best way to demonstrate this is with an example:

```
this_day = Time.now
next_week = 1.week.from_now
seconds_between = next_week - this_day
seconds_in_day = 24 * 60 * 60
days_between = (seconds_between / seconds_in_day).to_i
print "There are " + days_between.to_s + " days between today and the
day next week"
```

The code creates two times a week apart, and returns a short report describing the number of days between the two. It appears very simple, but in fact, there is a lot of work being done by Ruby:

- First off, it has created five named objects. It was able to create these objects on the fly without the programmer having to pre-define them.

- Ruby has created objects of four different classes: `this_day` and `next_week` are Time objects; `seconds_between` is a Float [decimal number]; `seconds_in_day` and `days_between` are Fixnums [an integer type]; and the final output text is a String.

- In creating `days_between`, Ruby compared two different types of objects, worked out the required class type to store the result (a Float), and then allowed that object to be converted to a Fixnum Integer, thereby discarding the unwanted decimal content (that is what the `.to_i` is doing).

- When printing, Ruby has converted an Integer to a String (the .to_s tells Ruby to do the conversion) and combined it with two strings to create a new String object. The new object is then output to the console.

This ease of use means that the code is easy to write, but perhaps (more importantly) it is easy to read. It means that you can easily understand code you wrote a year ago, and another developer can read your code, modify it, or fix bugs.

The other aspect of Ruby that plays an important role in defining the coding used in Rails, is that it is an Object Orientated Programming (OOP) language. Without going into details, the consequence is that sections of code are separated into discrete blocks each with well defined inputs and outputs. This helps to prevent spaghetti code with code pathways being difficult to follow. This does not mean that it is impossible to write gobbledygook in Ruby, but rather the structure of Ruby encourages the programmer to write well formed code. Well formed code is easy to read, understand, and modify. The creation of well formed code is the object of every competent developer.

Text Based File

Ruby on Rails applications are built using three types of text files: Ruby code files (`.rb`), HTML templates (typically `rhtml` files, but can also be `rxml`), and YAML configuration files. Being text files, they are easy to edit, move, deploy, and back up. No complicated development environment is required. Code does not require compiling before use. You can create these files in Notepad on a Windows system, edit them in Textmate on a Mac, and then deploy them on a Linux server, should you so desire.

Open Source

Typically, open source software is considered a low cost option, though there is some argument as to the on-going support costs. Certainly open source solutions are not expensive and tend to be of good value. However, while the cost aspect is attractive, there are other features of open source software that have more compelling benefits to a business application developer.

- **Open access to source code**: This allows you to read the underlying coding to gain better understanding of how the system: works, thereby making it easier to optimize your solution and more easily extend and customize the functionality. With Ruby on Rails, this is even easier as much of the underlying framework code is written in Ruby itself.

- **No vendor locks in:** There are no hidden costs such as extra charges for upgrades and bug fixes. Your choice of software solution is not reliant on the status and expected longevity of the vendor. However, you are reliant on the life of the open source project. If the community moves onto something else, the project development can dry up. However, even in this case, the code is still available and there is nothing to stop you further developing it. If a vendor goes out of business, the code usually disappears too.

- **Written by and for the people using the software:** Open Source applications are written by the people who use the software. OK, not all the people who use it, but a wide group of different users. This means that the resulting applications work the way a lot of people who use them, want them to work. They do not work the way a corporation has decided they should work and more importantly they do not require you to work the way some faceless corporate entity dictates, to get the best out of the application. This is one of the key reasons why open source software is so often user friendly and why so many people find using open source applications such a liberating experience.

Plentiful Documentation

As already mentioned, there is a rapid increase in literature base available for both Ruby and Rails. Online resources are plentiful too. For example, the site `http://api.rubyonrails.com` lists the frameworks, classes, and methods used by Ruby on Rails, allowing a developer to find the classes and methods they need, and dig into the underlying code to see how they work.

Being open source, the manuals are also written by the people who use the system. Too many manuals for commercial software seem more to be a list of functions, rather than a guide on how to use those functions. Good examples of these are instructions on how to install software. Help systems written by developers tend to skimp on this area, as the developers do not install very often and tend to install in a fairly limited environment. End users on the other hand have a wide range of installation issues. As users tend to write open source documentation, the resulting manuals often have the solutions to a range of installation issues. Such is the case for Ruby on Rails with there being guides and assistance to installing in a range of environments.

Built-in Safe Test Environment

The test environment is built into the Rails framework, can be configured to populate a test database, and then run test procedures on that data, reporting back on their success. This means that you can safely test an application without adding live data to it, whether at the creation stage, while modifying, or further developing a production application, and during bug fixing. These tests are stored with the application code and therefore can be used to test the application after moving code to a new environment.

The test system encourages a developer to create test procedures early in the development process, and use the resulting test code throughout the life of the application. To detect system malfunction, test systems are used to help developers identify when the code they have created does not quite work the way they expect it to work.

The integrated test system can be used to ensure that applications are tested effectively and often.

Ruby on Rails in Detail

Often when developing applications, the most difficult part is not creating the application, but getting it to work with other systems. This can also be the case with Ruby on Rails, particularly during the early stages of development.

In the early years of Rails, it was a common experience for new developers to be creating useful Rails code within hours of their first introduction to the framework. Then, it would take them days of research, head scratching, and many reconfigurations to get their chosen web server to work well with their new Rails application. Getting the connection to work between the Rails application and the web server was often more difficult than writing the Rails code. Fortunately, the web server connection headaches are a thing of the past, but this example illustrates that a guide, which simply described how to write Rails code would leave a developer with some difficult problems to solve before they could roll out a complete solution. Therefore, some effort is made here not only to describe how to create a Rails application, but also how to get it to work with the operating system that will host it and the services that will interact with it.

There are a number of tools that aid the developer to both generate and maintain a good development environment. For example, an integrated development environment (IDE) can make writing and working with code easier. Version control systems provide many useful tools for a developer; especially if the developer works in a team. This book is not a guide to these tools, but does describe how to configure the tools and the Rails environment so that they work together.

Summary

This book is aimed at developers who are new to Ruby on Rails, but have some familiarity with the framework and who want to move on from the basic tutorials. In particular, the book is aimed at those who wish to use the unique attributes of Rails to develop and roll out small applications. These applications will be straightforward to develop, easy to roll out, and simple to maintain. The developer will also be provided with guidance in creating a development environment where code can be created, stored, and shared easily.

2

The Initial Problem

In this chapter, an example of the type of problem that often leads to the development of a small business application is introduced. That is, to make available to many the data currently restricted to a small number of people. Some of the decisions and processes that a developer needs to consider and complete, before starting to create a new application is described. In particular, how to organize the data, define named objects, and start considering how users will interact with the data. Whilst developing small business applications, I have found it important to involve the end users throughout the development process and therefore user involvement is introduced here too. At the end of this chapter, we will be ready to move on to the creation of the application itself.

A Normal Day in the Office

Rory thinks this Monday is going to be a straightforward day in the office. A problem in the email log needs investigation and the production team needs a spreadsheet fixing. Ken, the company's Managing Director, appears at the door:

"Rory, Mary in sales has just shown me her contacts list. That list is dynamite. She's got all sorts of business contacts in there. I need the rest of the sales team to be able to access that list. Get it sorted. I'll be back at the end of the week and will expect to see something in place." With that Ken was gone.

This is a typical problem for an IT manager to face while managing a company's computer systems. A small application is required on a short time scale. Often budgets are limited and the scope of the project is poorly defined. We will use the above example to describe the process of building a simple business application to address this kind of a problem.

So, what are Rory's options? Two options spring to mind immediately, but both have issues:

- First, he could use a groupware email server such as Microsoft Exchange and then use the functionality in the server to share Mary's contact list with others in the company. If the company was already using a groupware email server, this would probably be the simplest solution, but they have a basic email server that does not provide this functionality. Upgrading to a groupware email server would require work to prepare the server as well as carry out the upgrade. As the upgrade will also require upgrading or reconfiguring everyone's email clients, and migrating existing email data, the process would need careful planning. It is not the sort of job to carry out in a week. Also, these products usually have a significant cost, especially when client licenses are taken into account. So this option's main problem would be cost, and the difficulty of getting the solution in place within a week.

- Second, the contact list could be exported out of Mary's email software and published as a static web page. For example, it is fairly straightforward to export a contact folder in Outlook as a tab delimited text file, and then import that into a spreadsheet such as OpenOffice's Calc and then use the spreadsheet application to tidy the data and publish it in an HTML format. It is then simply a case of copying the resulting file to a web server. This is probably the quickest solution to implement. However, the resulting data would be static; the process would need to be repeated to keep the online version up-to-date with any changes. The data would also be in a format that is not easy to use elsewhere. If the data really is "*dynamite*", Rory is sure that making it available to everyone is only the first thing that Ken will want to do with it. Rory needs a solution that he can develop as Ken's requirements grow. Therefore, conversion into a static web page is a dead end that will sort the immediate problem, but leave Ken in the position of having to re-invent a solution when Ken moves the goal posts. Rory's worked with Ken before — he is confident the goal posts will change, and at a short notice.

Fortunately, there is another option providing the flexibility that the static web page lacks; and unlike the groupware email solution, it would neither break the bank nor take long to create it. That is, to export the data and build a Ruby on Rails application to publish the data and allow that data to be managed.

So, Rory decides upon the Ruby on Rails option. How would he go about developing a Ruby on Rails application to publish a list of sales contacts?

Examining the Data

The first task is to examine the data, identify how it is organized, and how it can best be structured within a database. The initial data will consist of a single list of people and their contact details such as postal and email addresses, and telephone numbers. There will also be other information about each contact, including the name of the company they work for.

The simplest solution is to convert the data list into a single database table with each column in the list being mapped to a table field. This is the approach Rory initially considers. However, as he looks through the list of contacts, he notices that there is a lot of duplication. In particular, a number of contacts work for the same companies. If a company has three of its employees in the contacts list, information about the company (its address for example) is held in three places; that is once with each contact's details. It means that if the company moves location, all three contact details will need to be updated at the same time. It can also be difficult to ensure consistency of data if the same entries have to be matched in three places. For example, a user may spot that company A's post code is wrong and correct it in the entry for the contact which the user is working on at that time, but fail to realize that there are other employees of that company whose details also have to be corrected. The result is inconsistency in the data.

The best way to overcome the issues associated with multiple contacts working for the same company is to split the company information out into a separate area. That is, to have separate contact data and company data. Then all the contact data requires is a pointer to tell the system, which of the entries in the company data relates to this contact.

In the contact list data, there are three address types: Home, Business, and Other. When Rory examines the data, he realizes that the "Other" address type is not used, but contacts have both Home and Business addresses. Some contacts have only a Home or a Business address, and some both. It is a fairly straightforward step to assume that the Home address applies to the contact, and the Business address applies to the company. It seems, therefore, that both the company and contact tables require address information.

Is there an issue with having a duplication of address information in contacts and companies data, and therefore should addresses have their own data area? There is a possibility that two people who live together could appear in the contact list (a husband and wife working for the same company, for example), or two companies could share the same premises. However, the instances are likely to be uncommon; and it seems excessive to base a major design decision like separating out addresses, just on dealing with these occasional instances.

On the other hand, there is another reason why separating addresses may be an advantage. The relationship between different parts of an address is special. For example, a post code usually refers to a small number of properties within a small geographical area. These special relationships can be used to carry out actions such as verification. For example, a simple lookup process could be created to check that the town in the address is valid for the given post code. Carrying out this processing will be easier if all the addresses are together, so that their format is easy to control, and all the data can be examined in one pass.

As Rory continues to examine the data, he notices more duplication and specially formatted data. For example, some contacts have multiple email addresses and, of course, email addresses have a special format themselves, with an ampersand in the middle and a root level domain name at the end. The format of telephone numbers conform to simple rules; would these be easier to validate and check if they were separated. There are also dates within the data. For example, Birthdays and Anniversaries. Other dates that would be useful to track are those for events such as meeting dates, contract start and end, and project milestones. However, at the moment, the data does not include this information.

Separating out all these data groups would result in the data being separated into many locations, and a complicated inter-relationship between groups of data would be required to create a meaningful output from the system. There is a tradeoff between the benefits gained from separating data into groups and the added complication that results from having to maintain many relationships between the data groups. Often there is no right answer to this dilemma, and the solution designer's task is to choose the best compromise. How can we tackle this dilemma?

Data Objects

Ruby, the programming language underlying Ruby on Rails, is an Object Orientated Programming (OOP) language. OOP's use of objects to store and manipulate data can point to a useful approach to use when deciding how to group data. That is, to consider the real world entities you are modeling with your application and then mapping the data objects to those entities. Groups of data are then defined as objects.

Let us use this approach to address Rory's problem on how far to separate his data down into object groups, by considering how the data relates to the real business entities he is trying to model.

- **People** — the core real entities within the contact data are the people the list is being used to track.

- **Companies** — in simplistic terms, these are the business groups people in the contact list belong to.

- **Addresses** — the labels that allow us to identify the geographical location of the premises where companies and people reside, and that we can send information and materials via the postal system.
- **Email addresses** — the labels used to identify and locate people within the Internet space and to which we can send messages and data to via email.
- **Telephone numbers** — the labels used to identify the telephone a person uses and its location within the telephone network.
- **Dates** — Key dates tracked so as to allow the sales team to develop their relationship with current and potential customers.

So, how do we use this breakdown of data objects to decide how the data should be split? The best approach is to create a simple set of rules and then use those rules to test each data object to see if it passes or fails. The rules need to describe the features of a data object that makes it worthwhile separating them from the rest of the data and treating them separately.

Database Table Design Rules

Rory looks at his data, considers what he is trying to achieve by separating the data into objects, and comes up with the following rules:

1. A data object must comprise more than one piece of data. There is little point in separating out the data if all you achieve is to add a pointer to a unique piece of data.

2. The data within an object must relate directly to the entity described by the object. Data has to be grouped logically or you may as well just group it by the position within the list or not group it at all.

3. Separating the data object must provide a benefit that is not available or as easily achieved if the data is not separated.

Using these rules, Rory is able to remove email addresses, telephone numbers, and dates as candidates for separating into objects. Each of these items is a self-contained single entity within Rory's data, and therefore, fails both rule 1 and 3. With each of these, it is easiest to store them as single fields within the data and no obvious benefit is apparent from separating them out. They will need individual methods to handle them and carry out processes such as validation, but that is easy to handle at the field level.

This leaves people, companies, and addresses.

Separating the Data

The next process is to consider which columns/fields in the original data belong to which data objects. In OOP, each individual data column or field is described as a property of the host data object. So this process is actually mapping the original data fields to object properties.

The data will already be separated in the process of defining the data objects, but it is a good idea, at this stage, to work through each property and check that the best fit is used to associate it with its data object. As with choosing which objects to use, there can be some ambiguity in choosing which object a property is best associated with, and again it is a designer's task to choose the best association to suit the case at hand.

Rory's rules 2 and 3 help here again. For example, the city that has a company belonging to it may be useful when trying to group companies together. So it could be held within the company data. However, the city is more closely related to *addresses* (rule 2). Rory thinks the benefits of having the city property in the company area is far outweighed by the significant benefits in associating city with the rest of the components that go together to make an address (rule 3). Therefore, the city property is put with the address object.

Considering the data objects in relation to the real objects that they represent, also helps to choose where to hold telephone data. For example, mobile telephones belong to individual people, and therefore the mobile telephone numbers should be stored within the people object. On the other hand, switchboard telephone numbers relate to a company and therefore need to be within the company object.

Naming Conventions

Rory has identified the data entities and separated them into separate objects with each entity being defined as a property of the object. The next issue is what he will call these objects and properties. There are a number of things that need to be considered when choosing names.

Use Meaningful Names

The more meaningful names we use in code, the easier it is to understand what the code is doing when we return to the code months or years later (to debug or develop further). If the code is easier to understand later, it will also be more understandable for someone else who works on the code at a later date. Also, meaningful names allow the code to do its own commenting; the clearer the names, the fewer comments are required to remind ourselves what objects and properties do.

For example, when I was taught trigonometry at school, I was taught the following equation to describe the relationship between the lengths of the sides of a right angled triangle:

```
a² = b² + c²
Where a is the length of the longest side (the hypotenuse),b, and c are
the lengths of the other two sides.
```

While writing the equation, it made it easier to simplify the length parameters into the single letter representations a, b, and c. However, when learning the equation, not only had I to remember the form of the equation, but also what each letter represented. So, remembering one equation required two memory processes: remember the *equation* and remember the *where statement* that described how each parameter was mapped to the right letter. In isolation from the where clause, it can be difficult to determine what the equation represented.

In coding, the benefit of shortening a parameter name is not as great as it is when making calculations on paper. In fact, the advantages of lengthening the name usually outweigh those of shortening it, if the lengthening is used to make the name clearer. Look at how the representation below of the same equation is easier to understand without defining a where statement:

```
long_side_length^2 = medium_side_length^2 + short_side_length^2
```

As the parameter names now describe the parameter itself, we no longer need a where clause.

The names also demonstrate how the simple use of underscores can be used to combine a series of words into a single text string in a way that makes them easy to read. An alternative is to use "camel case" where a capital letter indicates the start of each sub-word, so long_side_length becomes LongSideLength.

Use a Consistent Naming Convention

As names are often made up from a combination of words, it is always a good idea to develop a simple set of rules to help keep each name of a consistent structure. For example, if in the triangle equation the sides were labeled side_1, side_2, and three_side, someone else reading the code would have to wonder what it was about the third side that led to it being named using a different convention to the first two sides. Being haphazard in naming objects and parameters leads to unnecessary confusion.

A naming convention will also allow you to take a few shortcuts in names. For example, someone describing objects on a map of London may want to describe both Green Park (an area of London) and some parks that are green. They could use long names of *green_park_the_district* and *park_that_is_green*. However, if they used a convention that:

- place names always used `camel case`
- descriptive text always followed the main description and was separated by an underscore they could have names of GreenPark and Park_green as simpler names.

Ruby on Rails Naming Conventions

Ruby on Rails has a set of its own naming conventions and complying with these conventions simplifies many tasks. Therefore, this is a good point to introduce some of these conventions as they can be used here to demonstrate some of the advantages of using a consistent naming convention. Also, it is probably not a good idea to describe many more naming conventions if they do not comply with the Ruby on Rails conventions and have to be abandoned later.

Constants and Classes

In Ruby, constants are written in `camel case`. The form and function of an object is defined by its Class. As Class names are constants, they always use `camel case`. So a Class that describes hairy bikers would be the HairyBiker Class.

Variables

In Ruby, variables are lowercase and use underscores to separate sub-words (for example, `longest_side`). Constant variables are by convention written in uppercase with underscores to separate sub-words (for example, `ABSOLUTE_ZERO`). Prefixes to variable names are used to define the scope of a variable with a single ampersand (@name) signifying that a variable is an instance variable and Class variables start with two ampersands (@@name)

Methods and Properties

Methods and Properties form sub-objects of a Class. They are treated as instance variables and therefore always use lowercase and underscores to separate sub-words. When used with the parent Class name, properties follow the Class name and are separated from it by a full stop. So if a bag object of the Class Bag has a property color, this would be written as `bag.color`.

Special Method and Property Suffixes

Some key ending words have special significance.

- _id is used to denote a foreign key. So in a Class Named Products, the foreign key property that ties each product to a particular supplier would be called `supplier_id`.

- _at and _on denote times and dates, respectively. So, `sold_at` is the time something was sold, and `visited_on` the date when a visit took place.

- ?, a question mark at the end of a Method name signifies that the Method will only return true or false. So, if you want a Method that tests whether an item is in stock or not, you would call it `in_stock?` and you could then use this test:

  ```
  if item.in_stock?
  ```

- !, an exclamation mark at the end of a Method name indicates that the Method operates on the object it's raised on. If you have an array and you want a Method that sorts the array you could call the Method `sort!`. This usage is probably easier to demonstrate in an example:

  ```
  # this method returns a copy of array "items" as a new object
  sorted_items = items.sort
  # whereas this method alters the object "items" itself
  items.sort!
  ```

Please note that these are conventions. For example, adding a question mark to the end of a Method you create, does not automatically force the Method to only return true or false. The Method `hello?` shown below, will return the string *Hello* even though the Method name ends with a question mark.

```
def hello?
return "Hello"
end
```

Conforming to these conventions makes it easier for others to understand your code. Ruby naming conventions are not shortcuts to a particular functionality. Changing a method name is not enough to change its functionality. You must also change the underlying code.

Notice also that there are Rails Methods that do not conform to these conventions. Some Methods operate on the object that raised them, but the Method name does not end with an exclamation mark. For example, the Method `model.save`.

Reserved Words

The following are reserved words that cannot be used as object names:

BEGIN	class	ensure	nil	self	when
END	def	false	not	super	while
alias	defined	for	or	then	yield
and	do	if	redo	true	
begin	else	in	rescue	undef	
break	elsif	module	retry	unless	
case	end	next	return	until	

This information was obtained from
`http://www.ruby-doc.org/docs/ProgrammingRuby/`, where further information on reserved words can be found.

Back to the Data

Using the information that Rory has gathered, his next step is to separate the data from Mary's contact list into the data object groupings of people, companies, and addresses. To do this, he carries out the following:

- The contact list is in Microsoft Outlook and Rory uses the Export feature of this program to create a single tab delimited text file. He then imports that into a spreadsheet which gives him a single table with all the field names across the top.

- On a large sheet of paper, he creates three tables, each with two columns. He labels the three tables: People, Companies, and Addresses, respectively.

- He then works through each of the field names, decides which data object the field belongs to, and enters that on his sheet of paper in the appropriate table in the left column. He starts with the first field `Title` that relates to the title a person uses, and is therefore a property of the person. So Rory enters `Title` in the left column of the `People` table. The next four fields follow `Title` into the `People` table. However, `Company` holds the contact's `company name` that is a Property of the company and therefore is the first entry in the `Company` table. In this way, Rory works through all the fields.

- Once all the Outlook field names are separated into three tables, Rory goes through each one and in the right column of the table, he enters a new name for the field that will match Ruby on Rails' naming conventions. As he does this, he is able to identify some fields that will not be required in the new applications, and for these fields he skips the step of adding a Ruby on Rails name.

The address table requires a little extra thought. When Rory gets to this table, he sees that there are three sets of Address fields listed (business, home, and other). Each set of addresses has the same types of components (Street, Street 2, Street 3, City, State, and Postal Code). Therefore, the three addresses can be entered into a database as three separate entries in the same table.

Outlook data		Three Address data objects			New common fields names
Single Contact		Address 1	Address 2	Address 3	
Business Street		Business Street	Home Street	Other Street	street_1
Business Street 2		Business Street 2	Home Street 2	Other Street 2	street_2
Business Street 3		Business Street 3	Home Street 3	Other Street 3	street_3
Business City		Business City	Home City	Other City	city
Business State		Business State	Home State	Other State	state
Business Postal Code		Business Postal Code	Home Postal Code	Other Postal Code	post_code
Home Street					
Home Street 2					
Home Street 3					
Home City					
Home State					
Home Postal Code					
Other Street					
Other Street 2					
Other Street 3					
Other City					
Other State					
Other Postal Code					

The end result is shown below.

Outlook	RoR
Companies	
Company	name
Department	department
Business Address	address_id
Business Fax	fax
Company Main Phone	telephone
ISDN	
Business Phone	business_phone
Telex	
PO Box	po_box
Organizational ID Number	org_id
Account	account
Billing Information	
Web Page	url

Outlook	RoR
People	
Title	title
First Name	first_name
Middle Name	middle_name
Last Name	last_name
Suffix	suffix
Job Title	job_title
Home Address	address_id
Other Address	address_id
Assistant's Phone	
Callback	
Car Phone	
Home Fax	home_fax
Home Phone	home_phone_1
Home Phone 2	home_phone_2
Mobile Phone	mobile
Other Fax	
Other Phone	
Pager	pager
Primary Phone	
Radio Phone	
TTY/TDD Phone	
Anniversary	
Assistant's Name	
Birthday	birthday_on
Children	
E-mail Address	email_1
E-mail Display Name	email_name_1
E-mail 2 Address	email_2
E-mail 2 Display Name	email_name_2
E-mail 3 Address	
E-mail 3 Display Name	
Gender	gender
Government ID Number	gov_id
Hobby	hobby
Profession	profession
Language	language
Referred By	referred_by
Initials	
Keywords	keywords
Notes	notes
Manager's name	manager
Spouse	spouse

Outlook	RoR
Addresses	
Business Street	street_1
Business Street 2	street_2
Business Street 3	street_3
Business City	city
Business State	state
Business Postal Code	post_code
Home Street	street_1
Home Street 2	street_2
Home Street 3	street_3
Home City	city
Home State	state
Home Postal Code	post_code
Other Street	street_1
Other Street 2	street_2
Other Street 3	street_3
Other City	city
Other State	state
Other Postal Code	post_code

When exporting data into comma delimited text files, commas within the source data can cause a lot of problems when processing data later. Using a tab delimited text file output format usually leads to fewer problems and I recommend using tab delimited files rather, than comma delimited files, whenever possible.

Review the Result

Rory feels pleased with his results; so pleased that he takes them to Mary to show her. He is rather disappointed when she looks at it and says, "I don't think that will work."

This is not an uncommon occurrence for a developer. It is very easy to get so intensely focused on a vision of what an application should look like that we fail to appreciate that chosen options do not actually suit the end user's requirements.

There are two methods to deal with this. The first requires that we get the users to create a detailed specification of what they want before we start, and then we develop to that specification. The second, is to start with a rough outline of what is required and then to involve the end user with the project development, showing them mock-ups, prototypes, and pre-production versions. At each stage, we take into account the user's comments and modify the design to suit them.

When creating applications for a separate organization, the first method has a lot of benefits, especially where contracts and payments for work are concerned. However, in the environment Rory finds himself, two things make the second method more appropriate.

1. One, to create a specification with the level of details required to provide all the information needed through the development, takes time and Rory's tight deadline makes it difficult to set aside time to create a detailed specification.

2. Two, probably more importantly, the end users are not sure themselves of what they want and therefore would be unable to create a detailed initial specification.

It is my experience that when developing small business applications, it is uncommon for the end users to have a very clear vision of what they want. They also commonly have a poor appreciation of what functionality can and cannot be provided by a small application. On the rare occasions when detailed specifications have been available, working with the user throughout the development has led to variation away from that initial specification and a better application as a result.

A problem with this method is that development can become aimless and meander, achieving little that is useful. The developer needs to ensure that they work towards a goal. We may not need to have a detailed map of how to get there, but we do need to know where we are going.

Fortunately, there is one thing that end users are always clear about. They know the problem they need a solution to. Always keep in mind the users' problem that is being addressed and make the solution to that problem the key goal. Put that goal at the top of your task list and remind yourself of it throughout the development process.

Project Preparation Steps

In Rory's situation he should do the following on starting a new project:

1. Determine as clearly as possible the nature of the problem or issue the application will address. Write this and place it somewhere that will remind him of that goal throughout development.

2. Initially, he should create a rough outline of the solution and discuss it with the users before starting development.

3. Endeavour to create mock-ups and prototypes as early as possible so that users can see and understand how the final application will appear at an early stage in development. This will allow them to provide useful feedback early on in the process.

4. Prepare him for the occasions when users will decide that what has been done so far does not suit their requirements.

It is always more fruitful to start development and then have to modify it as the specification develops, than to postpone development until we have an ideal specification. Therefore, the developer needs to be ready for review meetings that do not go as expected, and changes in the specification that were not foreseen.

How Good is the Source Data?

The main problem Mary points out to Rory is that the separation of address types is not as clear cut as he thought. Some of Mary's contacts are home workers, and for them she has put their "*home*" address in the "*business*" address fields. Other contacts are self-employed and for them their "*home*" is also their business address. In fact, as they review the data, it becomes clear to Rory that Mary's allocation of addresses has been fairly haphazard.

A previous solution's inability to control or correctly organize the data presented to it, is often a key reason for replacing it with a new solution. For instance, one of the problems with using a spreadsheet to store information is that they usually allow free text entry of data. Users are often inconsistent with their entries, especially if more than one person enters the data and free text entries put no control in place to prevent this behavior.

As an example, a company whose business systems created a works order for each product they manufactured. Each works order contained a unique number that was used to track the product through manufacture, sales, and after sales support. The number comprised the first letters of the words "Works Order " and then an incremental number. So the number of the first product produced by this system had the form: "WO0001". Once in use, a problem became apparent in that users commonly failed to appreciate that the second character was the letter "O" and would often enter these product numbers as: "W00001". Less commonly, they would enter all the round characters as: "O", including the zeros: "WOOOO1". The result was that in reports a single product could appear as three separate products: "WO0001", "W00001", and "WOOOO1".

The problem was fairly easy to deal with in the main applications. The problem was more difficult to deal with in the small spreadsheets managers and supervisors created for their teams to track progress and problems. These were often put together simply and had no validation of input. The result was misreporting, and wasted time tracking problems that had already been dealt with but logged with a different form of the works order number.

Therefore, it is extremely likely that existing data will require processing before it is input to an application. To do this successfully, the user and developer must work together to create a set of rules to deal with any inconsistencies. Some processing can be automated. In the works order example, it would be easy to process works order numbers so that all zeros at the second character position were converted to "O" and all O's in the following positions were converted to zeros. A simple batch script could be created to carry out this processing. It could even be incorporated into the data import process for the new application. However, some data inconsistencies require manual correction and there can be little alternative than to have someone go through the data and correct any inconsistencies.

Rory realizes that the address problem is not systematic. That is, there is nothing within the data itself that would allow an automation script to detect that the data needs to be altered. Therefore, he is unable to create a script to correct the problem. However, when he suggests to Mary that she go through all her contacts and correct the inconsistencies, she states that she cannot give in the time required to do that. Therefore, Rory suggests a compromise—he prints out a listing of the contacts and addresses, and then asks Mary to skim through these and mark any address she spots as being incorrectly assigned. He suggests that if it is a home address that should be a business address, she mark it with a "B", and if it is a business address that should be a home address, she mark it with an "H". Self-employed workers should be marked with "HB", which means that the same address is used for both home and business. As this is a lot easier to do than manually move each one within

Mary's email application, and she readily agrees to do this. When she is finished, Rory is able to process the raw data and move the addresses as marked.

However, even after going through this process, Rory realizes that some erroneous address allocation has not been corrected. It becomes apparent that the new application will need to have the facility to easily move addresses from the person to the company so that inconsistencies within the data can be corrected as the data is used.

Assume errors will get through from the source data and provide tools within your application to easily correct those errors.

You can waste a lot of time and effort tracking down and correcting every error in source data. To compound the problem, errors can often be hard to identify within raw data, yet be only too obvious once the application goes into production. A pragmatic solution to that problem is to accept that some errors will get through, despite your best efforts. Make a best effort to correct errors before and during the import process. Then make sure you build in processes and methods that allow users to correct errors easily as they find them. The key to success of this strategy is to make it easy for the users of the application to identify and correct errors as they find them.

Tracking Who does What

As Rory discusses the data processing with Mary, another issue is raised. Mary becomes concerned that other people will start altering her data. She asks how she would be able to find out who had over-written her entries.

System logs can be used to search for and correct errors that occur within an application. However, often they are not so useful for tracking an individual user's use of the system. Another thing to consider is that with web applications, it is not straightforward to track who has accessed the application. To preserve anonymity on the Internet, web systems tend not to pass user information back and forth unless specifically configured or requested to do so.

To track and control who can access and change data we must both, log activity and identify end-users. To do this, the solution is usually to force users to log onto the application and thereby identify themselves. However, there are two issues with this. First, providing a log-on utility and systems to prevent unauthorized access to the application adds complication. Second, there can be resistance from users to log on as it can be seen as an unnecessary inconvenience. Therefore, it is worth identifying levels of authentication and user access logging, and then selecting the level that is most appropriate to the current need.

No Log-On and No Authentication

There are two main reasons why this level of authentication is appropriate. First, the application is very basic and ease of development outweighs the requirement for monitoring user activity. Second, total refusal of key users to having a log on process (for example, if in spite of your best arguments, the person who pays your wages insists that there is no user log-on process, you have little choice but not to have one).

There are three things to consider in this situation, to provide a minimum of logging information with the minimum impact on development and use of the application.

- Log the creation and last update of a data entry. Ruby on Rails has automated systems that will update `"created_at"` and `"update_at"` fields with appropriate times if these fields exist in a data table. Therefore, always include these fields in your tables. Knowing when a problem occurred is far better than having no information about a problem. In fact, it is surprising how much easier it can be to track down the source of a problem if you know precisely when it happened.

- If users refuse to use a log-on, consider tracking usage via their IP address. IP addresses are passed from a user's browser to the server within the HTTP header and therefore are fairly easy to detect and to use in a web application. Within the confines of a company network, it is straightforward to identify a user's computer from its IP address (even when dynamic addressing is in place) and to track the user from there. IP address tracking is not perfect (for example, if two users use the same computer, the system will not be able to differentiate between the two), but it is far better than having no information to track user activity.

- Add either a free text entry (if users vary a lot) or a selection drop down (if you can maintain a list of all users) that allows a user to simply identify themselves when they enter or alter data. Include a `"last_user"` field in each table and store the user's entry in that field and/or include the user information in any log entry. Without a password or similar authentication process, it will be impossible to rely on the integrity of this input, but in my experience most users will use such a system and the resulting entries can be useful when tracking down problems. If you use the selection option, you can use cookies to remember a user's last selection. This makes the system easier to use for the user, and therefore can encourage them to use it properly, rather than just pick the first selection item they come to.

With this system, you will not be able to provide different levels of access to different users. If different levels of access are required (for example, to allow data update access, or higher level reporting), the users must identify themselves, and a log-on system is the best way to do that.

This level of authentication is workable within the restricted area of a company intranet. However, exposing a Ruby on Rails application to Internet access with no authentication in place would be extremely unwise.

Simple Password Access

The simplest authentication system is to add a password field to all data entry and update forms. When the form is submitted, the password is checked against the stored password and data is only entered into the system if the passwords match.

In its simplest form, everyone with "create" or "update" access uses the same password. In this case, the use of a password would not allow the system to identify and log who had edited the data. However, you could give each user his/her own password and then identify the user by the password added, or add a simple user selector as described above.

If you use this system, consider these recommendations:

- It is a good practice to change the password regularly and enforce a minimum level of complexity to passwords. For example, a policy may ensure that passwords are at least eight characters long, contain numbers, and both upper and lower case letters.

- Always create a system that allows either you or a designated user to securely change the password. At some point, you will need to change the password. If you do not, most users will come to learn the password and it will become redundant.

This is the simplest system to create two level access rights: those two levels being *read-only* for those who do not know the password and *full access* for those who do.

It is worth considering that if data is entered and updated often, this authentication method is actually more inconvenient than a log-on system, as the password has to be entered every time a form is submitted. Therefore, its use is best restricted to simple systems that are rarely updated.

As the application does not need to track the logged-on user, this system is simpler to create than a proper log-on system. Therefore, it can be useful to use if you need to get an application in place in a hurry, or as a quick way to add simple password protection to a system that previously had none. Especially, as a temporary stage to provide some protection while a log-on system is developed.

User Log-On

In most circumstances, the best way to control access and log activity is to use a log-on system. A log-on system comprises three elements: a storage area — containing a list of all users together with their authentication credentials (typically their password); a log-on system — where a user can enter their log-on credentials and thereby log-on, and a way of tracking and maintaining the logged-on status so that the user is not continuously asked to log-on.

This system is more complicated than the other systems, but the extra effort is worthwhile. Maintaining the logged-on status and controlling access based on that status is usually the most difficult part of a log-on system. However, tools built into the Rails framework help make this option relatively straightforward.

- If users are allowed to change or specify their own passwords, consider enforcing basic password conditions such as forcing a minimum password length of 8 characters and use of upper and lower case characters, and numbers.

- Log-on status can be stored within the session. This allows a user only to log on once each time they use the application. We can use cookies to remember the user so that log-on screens have that user's name preselected next time they access the system. Then they only have to enter their password to log on. That will make the process easier for the user and they will be happier to log on more often.

- Think about what you want to protect with a log-on system. For many systems, we only need to log and control adding, editing, and deleting data. Therefore, if a user only wants to read some data, they may not need to log on.

I strongly recommend that you create and use a log-on system!

One of the best things about Ruby on Rails is how easy it is to reuse processes and simplify common tasks. A good example of this is how easy it is to reuse a log-on system once it is created. All it takes is a couple of lines of code in a new part of an application, for that new part to implement the log-on functionality.

Recording Access History

To get the most out of a log-on system, we need to record some activities that users carry out. We may not want to create a log entry every time a user views data, but with most applications we will need to log when people add, change, and delete data. For most cases, we probably do not want to record everything. What we want is to be able to audit the use of the system, both to track down problems and to provide reports to managers.

To achieve this, we need to create a new data object: *the access history*. As a minimum, this data object should include the following:

- The identity of the user who carried out the action

- The time the action occurred

- A description of the action

- The condition of any status after the action occurred. For example, in a project tracking system, we will want to log when the status changed to "project completed" and "customer billed".

We will also want to consider how to display this information and who should have access to it. Fortunately, a dynamic access-controlled web page is a splendid way of displaying such information. Therefore, Ruby on Rails provides an ideal platform to provide information on the access history.

Often, we need to be able to report on the access history of both individual objects and overall access history. For example, a team manager will want to see a report that keeps them up-to-date on how their team has been using the system. They will want reports based on all activity. For them, systems that generate period totals will help them create reports for their superiors. On the other hand, a project manager will only want to see the history of access to specific projects. Therefore, consider who will need activity reports from a system and be prepared to provide different information to different groups.

The person managing the system (in small businesses that is often us, the developers) will need a set of tools that lets them pull out the information needed to track down problems. Therefore, we need to be able to follow individual processes through, whether that is by following a user's progress, isolating changes to a specific area, or view data for a specific small period of time. We could do this by viewing the underlying data, but if we can create report and search systems that easily aid us in these tasks, this time will be very well spent. Also never forget, that while we may be the person managing the system now, it may be someone with less intimate knowledge of the system who manages it in the future. Leverage Ruby on Rails to make the administration job easier and we will all have more time to concentrate on more interesting tasks.

Access Control for Rory's Application

As speed is of the essence in Rory's project and most users will require read-only access, he decides to implement simple password access for the application, prior to his deadline.

For the immediate requirement this is a satisfactory solution. However, Rory is conscious that once the system goes live and people start using it, more people will want to add and update data. Upgrading access control to a log-on system will be a requirement for the likely second stage of development.

Rory discusses this with Mary and explains why he is developing access control in this way. She readily agrees to Rory's strategy.

However, Mary also asks Rory a question that makes him realize there is something he's missed: "How do we stop users putting in invalid data?".

Data Validation

There is another control system that Rory needs to consider. That is, *data validation*. Data validation provides a system whereby a user's data entries can be tested against a series of rules. Only if the rules are passed, is the data entered into the database. Rails, has a series of methods that make validation a straightforward task to set up and maintain.

As with so much of Ruby on Rails, validation methods do much of the nuts and bolts work for us. Two important processes are mostly taken care of: intercepting the user's input of data before it gets to the database; and then if the validation tests are failed, returning the data input form to the user (with a relevant warming message) so that the user can correct their input and resubmit the form. Very few additional lines of code are needed to set this up. We can then concentrate on deciding what needs validating and the logic needed for those validations.

The next step is to ask what we need to validate or consider when setting up the validation tasks.

The Minimum Required Data is Entered

The most basic level of data validation, tests whether the user has actually entered some data. At a basic level, it means ensuring that at least one field has data in it. However, we also need to consider if there is a minimal amount of data that needs to be entered with each input. For example, if an application is a price list of products, each product probably needs to have a price entered.

Each Record can be Uniquely Identified

Often this means having enough data to allow for the unique identification of the new data. For example, when considering a list of people, there may be a number of people with the surname *Smith*, and therefore it is likely that we would want to validate that both a surname and first name are entered. We may also need to ensure that a particular field entry is unique within the table or that a combination of fields is unique. For example, we may want to ensure that addresses have a combination of house number and zip code (or postal code) that is unique within the table.

However, it is also worth pointing out that the default behavior of Rails is to add an ID field as the primary key. By definition, each ID must be unique within each table. Therefore, all data records will be individually identifiable within the database. If validation was turned off and a user entered ten records with no data, each would have a different ID and therefore each of the ten empty entries could be identified and manipulated individually.

It is considered bad practice to have identical records within a relational database. Having an independent ID field allows a developer to do just that (see the empty record example that I have described in the previous paragraph). Occasionally, we may find ourselves creating tables of data with series of entries that are identical to one another. Pragmatically, this may be the simplest solution to get an application up and running. However, it is always indicative of a system that could be better designed. Instead we should consider doing the following:

- Test to see if the data already exists and reference the existing data rather than adding a duplicate entry. For example, if we were importing a set of orders and each order had a status, we may want to store the statuses in a separate table. If we simply store each status in the statuses table, we will have as many entries in the statuses table as there are in the orders table. Instead, we should test to see if the current status already exists and then set the order `status_id` to the id of the existing status; only adding a new status where the current one does not already exist.

- Add a field that uniquely identifies the entry. For example, we may want to allow partial data to be entered while more data is gathered. A list of leads in a Customer Relationship Management system may consist of very limited information for new contacts that need to be validated manually at a later date. In this case, adding fields that identify when, how, or why the data was added (for example, a data import reference or "entered by George on 12-Jun-07") or what the next action will be (for example, "assigned to Henry to validate on 12-Jun-07") will make it easier to identify and manage each data set at a later date.

Log information

There are two ways of entering information like "entered by George on 12-Jun-07". You can either generate the text string and then enter it into a text field, or create new fields that store the information programmatically. For example, by adding an updated_by field to store the user id for George and an updated_at field to store the date/time when the update was made.

 In most circumstances you will want to use the second method. However, there are circumstances where a text entry is better. The advantage a text field entry has is that it can be read independently of any other data. Therefore, if you export the data away from the user table, the information will still be easy to read. It also stores the data as it is at the time of entry. For example, you may find that George is deleted as a user from the system at a later date. It can be easier to store the name as a string, than to ensure that a system is in place to handle this situation. Therefore, text field entries can be useful for activity logs where the log entry is not to be altered once it has been created.

Identify Fields that Need to Have a Particular Format

Some data must have a particular format for it to be correct. Email addresses are a good example. Therefore, it makes sense to test the format of such data at the point of input, and validation tasks are perfect for this task.

 There is a trap here: it is a mistake to think of validating data input as a way of controlling the user input. Rather, I strongly believe that we should think of it as a way of helping the user detect and correct mistakes that they have made. If we need to control input, we should use the design of the input form to provide control and not the validation task.

Consider telephone numbers; a developer may have a preferred format for telephone numbers. However, each of these three UK-style telephone numbers is a valid representation of the same number: 0111 111111, (0111) 111111, and 0111111111. So how do we handle the fact that a user may use any of the three given formats? There are four options:

1. **Provide a free text field and allow any of the formats to be used.** This will overcome the problem of different formats being entered, but add complication later when we try to compare telephone numbers. For example, 0111 111111 and (0111) 111111 will appear to be different even though they represent the same telephone number.

2. **Configure validation so that it only allows through data formatted as we prefer.** When users enter an incorrect format, the entry is rejected and they are prompted to re-enter the data. The result is likely to be annoyed users. Users do not like having their entries rejected, especially when their mistake was simply not to choose the format we prefer. At the very least, we should provide, on the input form, a guide to correct usage.

3. **Design the input form to closely match our desired format and provide visual clues as to the correct format to use.** For example, if we want credit card entries to be entered as four sets of four characters, provide four text boxes, four characters long rather than a single text box, where we expect users to insert spaces into the appropriate places. Validation is then used to check that the input data is likely to be correct.

4. **Anticipate the formats that may be entered and process the data so that the format used is detected and the entry reformatted to match our desired format.** Regular Expressions are ideal for detecting and modifying data entries into a preferred format. Validation is then used to check that the input data is likely to be correct.

Options 1 and 2 are both unsatisfactory and likely to result in poor data in the database and a bad user experience, respectively.

Options 3 and 4 will help the user enter valid data. Option 3 makes it easy for the user to enter data in the right format, and Option 4 allows users to use their preferred format without upsetting the integrity of the data. Which one we use, depends on how easily we can distinguish the different formats without compromising the validation. If it is easy to distinguish between the alternative input formats, use option 4. If it is difficult to distinguish between the formats use option 3.

Dates are a good example of where we should always use option 3. Living outside of the U.S.A., I am very aware of the confusion between the dd/mm/yyyy and mm/dd/yyyy formats. Programmatically, we cannot detect the difference between the two, unless the day is greater than twelve. That is, it is impossible to tell whether a single entry of 01/07/1916 refers to the day the Battle of the Somme started (1st July 1916), or 7th January of the same year. Therefore, always avoid allowing users to enter dates in these two formats. To do this, use a named month drop-down within a date selection. In that way, the confusion is avoided.

This brings us onto another point. If there are only a small number of options for data entry (for example, the statuses: "Requested", "Processing", "Completed", and "Shipped") do not use validation to control user input. Instead, use drop-downs or a selection list to restrict user entry to only the valid entries. Validation can then be put in place to detect errors when this system has been bypassed, but most of the time the validation will be redundant.

References to Data in Other Tables Point to Actual Data

Within the database, data in separate tables are linked via foreign keys. In Ruby on Rails, these are usually between the ID field of one table and a link field of another table. The link field has a name comprising the singular name of the first table and ending with the suffix _id. When data is entered or altered, a validation process can be used to make sure that the entries in any link fields match an existing ID field entry in the target table.

Therefore, if a people table contains a link to an addresses table, each person will have an `address_id` field. The validation process would take the number in the `address_id` field and check that there is a corresponding address record with a matching ID.

Rory's Data

Having considered how he needs the contact data to be separated into tables and validated, his data structure consists of three tables as shown below.

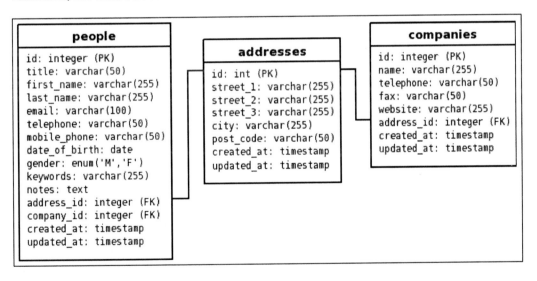

After considering his validation options, he makes the following decisions.

Person

- `First_name` and `last_name` should not be empty.
- Email should be a valid email address (matches regular expression) and unique to this person.
- Gender should be set to "M " or "F".
- `Address_id` and `company_id` should reference records in the appropriate tables.

Company

- must have a name

Address

- must have a `street_1` entry
- must have a valid `post_code` (regular expression match)
- `street_1` + `post_code` must be valid on creation of the address

A single regular expression is to be used to check and reformat telephone numbers.

Rory is now ready to start the practical steps of building his application.

Summary

In this chapter, a description of how to group data into separate data objects has been presented, including the decisions made as to how many data objects are required and how to allocate data to the appropriate object. The benefits of using a consistent naming convention have been described, and some of the conventions used in Ruby and the Rails framework have been introduced. In most real world cases, it can be impossible to avoid data errors, and therefore, the need to ensure that we design systems to cope with and manage data errors has been highlighted. Some methods of controlling and logging user access have been described and their merits and limitations discussed. Data validation and user input control via form design was also discussed.

As many small business applications arise from the imprecise requirements of users, methods to best manage this have been presented. These methods involve the end users throughout the process, creating mock up and prototypes early in the process, and setting clear goals.

3
Laying the Foundations

Any sustainable software development project needs good foundations. While it is possible to write a Ruby on Rails application with nothing more than Ruby, a few libraries, and a text editor; this approach does not lend itself well to a team project where multiple authors may be working on the same code base. In addition, deployment and maintenance of the application once it reaches production becomes problematic if there is no supporting infrastructure in place.

This chapter outlines how to lay some firm foundations for a sustainable Rails development project. The core of this is obviously the Rails stack itself: we'll see how to install and configure this in some detail. But you also need some good infrastructure under this to ease development, deployment, and maintenance. Rails developers have faced the same issues all web developers face, and have integrated Rails with a variety of supporting technologies; things like database servers, graphics generation libraries, IDEs, version control systems, and web servers. Throughout the chapter, we'll encounter a few of the technologies closest to the heart of Rails, which can readily be used to support your development work.

Supporting Rails Development

In the preceding chapters, the example of the Acme development team was used to illustrate the initial stages of a Rails project. In this chapter, we'll see how such a team can set up its infrastructure for Rails development, using Acme as a case study. As is typical of small companies, Acme has limited cash to pay for software, and makes extensive use of open source software. We'll take the same approach, utilizing several best breed of open source technologies which can accelerate your Rails development.

We'll also focus on setting up Rails development infrastructure on limited hardware. In the case of Acme, they are again typical of many small companies and have the minimum hardware setup they can get away with. The hardware they use for their projects looks like the following screenshot:

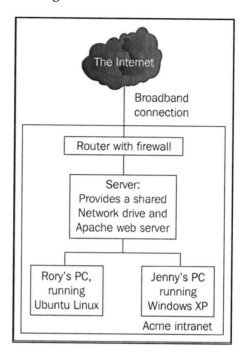

Zooming in, the development environment looks like this:

- Developer machine
  There are two developer machines, belonging to Rory and Jenny, respectively. Rory refuses to use Windows, and insists on Ubuntu Linux for his machine; Jenny uses Windows XP Pro.

- Server
  Runs Apache for the Acme web site, a shared network drive, and handles local email (including spam filtering). Acme currently uses the shared network drive for its ad hoc code repository. The plan is to deploy Rails applications to this machine for use on the intranet by Acme staff.

There are other machines on the network, but they are used by administrators and other company employees rather than for development work. However, they do make use of the shared network drive on the server.

This kind of heterogeneous environment is fairly typical where hardware has been added as a company grows, and where developers get to install and manage their own machines. It introduces extra challenges where the aim is to introduce infrastructure to support new technologies, as it makes it harder to provide a consistent environment for the team.

Another issue is that small teams tend to work in a single room where they can manage projects verbally. In the case of Acme, if Jenny and Rory both need to work on a single file, they make an ad hoc arrangement to prevent potential synchronization problems, for example, "I'm working on library X, so stay off it for a while". However, they are thinking of hiring contractors for some of their new projects, who could potentially be working off-site, making ad hoc arrangements like this unwieldy and slow. They have also been stung a few times when their ad hoc *verbal locking* of files has failed, and they have both ended up simultaneously editing a single file: important changes made by Jenny were overwritten by Rory when he saved his copy of the file. Consequently, they have been considering using some kind of **version control system** to manage their code better. This will also allow an arbitrary number of developers in geographically-dispersed locations to work on a single body of code. They also see the value of having a mechanism for *rolling back* to previous versions of an application or individual files.

Addressing the Challenges

Acme's challenges are not unique, and we'll follow them throughout the chapter to inform the process of building a Rails development infrastructure. Generalizing, they boil down to the following:

- The software choices need to support any operating system (as far as possible). We'll concentrate mainly on Ubuntu Linux version 6.06 (Dapper Drake), but will also cover Windows in some detail. Mac OS X is briefly touched on, though not explored in depth as it is treated thoroughly in other books.

- The software needs to be low cost and should not lock a company into proprietary systems (as discussed in Chapter 1).

- The infrastructure should support collaborative project work (i.e. it should have a version control system).

- The infrastructure should enable the company to do solid deployments of applications into production (i.e. provide them with a web/application server).

- The infrastructure should help the team work with Rails, not make their lives harder.

Keeping these points in mind, we'll cover two broad groups of software:

1. The Rails stack
   This is the set of components that you need to develop a Rails application. Each developer needs a stack of his/her own, so that they can work on the code from their own desk.

2. A team server
   The server needs a Rails stack of its own, to enable it to run the Rails applications. It will also need some additional software to support team development and live deployments.

Green field infrastructure

In some halcyon situations, you will be working from scratch and will be able to buy new hardware and source new software for your development.

If you have this luxury, Rails, places no restrictions on your choice of hardware. You have free reign to use any of the major hardware platforms (Intel, AMD, Power PC) for your machines. You should get as much RAM as you can afford, both for the server and the developer machines, aiming for a minimum of 512Mb on the developer machines and 1 Gb on the server machine. Rails can be quite RAM intensive (even while developing a small application) and having a decent amount of RAM can make the development process far more pleasurable.

Similarly, Rails places no restrictions on your choices of the operating system. However, Linux is an excellent choice for the server. It is very stable, powerful, fast, and flexible, and runs Rails beautifully. If you choose to develop on Windows, XP Pro is the preferred choice; for the server, Windows Server 2003 is a good choice.

Setting Up a Rails Stack

A Rails stack is the set of components you need to develop and run a Rails application. The Rails stack on each of our preferred operating systems is fairly similar and consists of the following:

- **Ruby**
  Ruby is a general purpose programming language. It is open source, making it free to use, modify, and distribute. This means that you won't have to pay a license fee to use it. We'll be using Ruby version 1.8.4 throughout the book.

- **Rubygems**
  This is the packaging system used for the majority of Ruby libraries (packaged Ruby libraries are called *gems*). The version used in this book is 0.9.3 .

- **Rails**
  Rails is actually composed of several related gems (see previous bullet point), each of which needs to be installed to get a working Rails environment. Note that this book is based on version 1.2.3 of Rails (current at the time of writing, with version 2 still under development).

- **Other libraries**
  There are several other libraries which are useful for Rails development, for example:
  - **Capistrano** (to help with deployment)
  - **Mongrel** (for serving Rails applications); note that other servers such as **Lighttpd** can be used as an alternative to Mongrel.

- **A database**
  This can either be a file-based database (like SQLite) or a database running on a server (like MySQL or PostgreSQL). **MySQL** is used here, as it is thoroughly integrated with Rails and is extremely stable. It is also worth installing the **MySQL bindings for Ruby** for better performance.

- **An editor**
  A programmer's editor or Integrated Development Environment (IDE) will make your life easier. We will be using **EasyEclipse**, but you can use whichever editor or IDE you prefer. Some popular alternatives are covered in the section: *Installing an IDE* later in this chapter.

The easiest route to setting up a Rails stack is to use a **bundle—an integrated package which provides all of the pieces you need in a Rails development environment**. This option is described briefly in the next section.

However, it is a good idea to learn how to install the components of the Rails stack yourself, rather than using a bundle. This gives you maximum flexibility and an insight into what makes your Rails applications tick. This is the approach we'll be taking.

At the end of this section, we'll see how Acme sets up their Rails development machines, as an example of how to put these recommendations into practice.

Installing a Rails Stack Using a Bundle

An easy-to-install *bundle* exists for each of the operating systems we are considering (Windows, Mac OS X, and Linux), handily packaging an entire Rails stack. If you already have one or more components installed (e.g. you already have a web server or database server), they can make things more complicated and create conflicts, which are difficult to troubleshoot. We are not going to spend much time covering installation of these packages (they're supposed to be easy, and are covered extensively elsewhere), but here are some pointers.

- **InstantRails**

  The easy way to install Rails on Windows. It packages Ruby, all the Rails libraries, plus some extras into a single zip file. Installing it is as easy as unpacking the package and running an executable. You can get it from the following link: `http://rubyforge.org/projects/instantrails`.

- **Locomotive**

  A *one-click installer* for Mac OS X, with a similar set of features to InstantRails. However, it also provides capabilities for running multiple versions of Ruby and Rails simultaneously. You can get it from the following link: `http://locomotive.raaum.org/`.

- **AxleGrease**

  An add-on for XAMPP on Linux. XAMPP itself is an Apache, MySQL, PHP, and Perl installer for Mac OS X, Linux, or Windows. It is available at `http://apachefriends.org/en/xampp.html`. AxleGrease extends XAMPP by providing Ruby, the Rails gems, and various useful libraries, plus scripts to ease deployment of Rails applications to the XAMPP Apache server. It should be installed on top of a valid XAMPP installation. You can get it from the following link: `http://rubyforge.org/projects/rorox/`.

While Rails bundles provide low-friction installation, you can gain complete control over your environment by understanding a bit more about how to install the components yourself. This approach is covered in the following sections. (You'll still need to install an editor or IDE of some kind, so you may need to refer to that section even if you are using a bundle.)

Installing a Custom Rails Stack

If you want to go it alone and install the components of a Rails stack yourself, you gain the advantage of being able to precisely tailor the pieces of software installed on your system. For example, even if you don't want MySQL to be installed, it is difficult to avoid if you use AxleGrease or InstantRails, which both bundle MySQL (Locomotive uses SQLite). A custom installation means you can remove any of the items that you don't need.

Another advantage of this approach is that you can sometimes leverage the package management provided by your operating system (if it is Linux or Mac — the Ruby packages are not a part of the mainstream Windows, and aren't covered by Windows Update). This makes it easy to keep up with bug fixes and feature enhancements. By contrast, the bundles described in the previous sections require you to manually upgrade when a new version is released (though all, except AxleGrease, provide an upgrade script to make this relatively simple).

One final benefit of a custom installation is that the package manager will track dependencies for you, ensuring that all the parts work nicely together. While the bundles do some of this work for you, you may find that adding new libraries to them (e.g. new Ruby gems) may lead to dependency issues you have to resolve yourself.

 You will need to have administrator access on the machine to perform the following installations.

Installing Ruby and Rubygems

The first step is to get a working Ruby installation. In this section, We will also look at Rubygems, as it is included with Ruby on some platforms.

Ruby on Windows

The easiest approach is to get the One-Click Ruby Installer from:
`http://rubyforge.org/projects/rubyinstaller/`. It is a good way to install
Ruby and Rubygems; ignore the text editors that it prompts you to install (**FreeRIDE**
and **SciTE**) by unticking the boxes on the options screen:

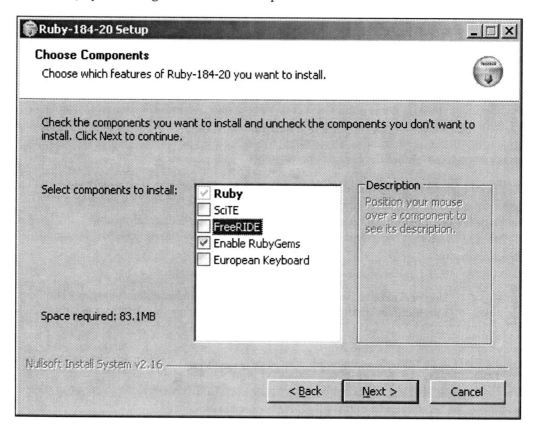

Ruby on Linux

Most distributions (e.g. Ubuntu, Debian, and Fedora) provide packaged versions of Ruby and its libraries, which can be installed via package management (e.g. **apt**, **yum**, and **synaptic**). On Ubuntu, for example, you can use Synaptic:

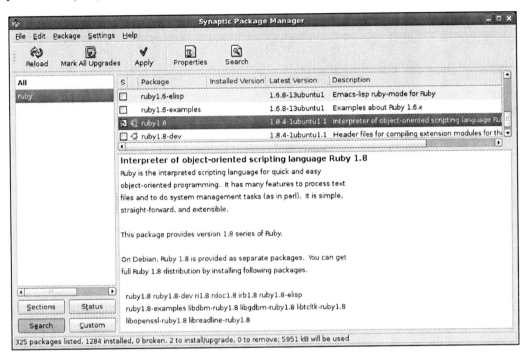

Alternatively, you can install from the command line with:

```
$ apt-get install ruby ri rdoc irb
```

However, if you install Ruby on some wholly-free Linux distributions (like Debian), you may find that Rubygems is not provided through the package management system. This is because Rubygems is a package management system itself, and the gem packaging approach is at odds with the Debian Filesystem Hierarchy Standard (FHS—see: http://www.pathname.com/fhs/). The FHS specifies how files relating to a piece of software are distributed across the system—configuration files in /etc, documentation in /usr/share/doc, and so on. Rubygems, by contrast, installs software libraries into a single directory, documentation and all, which is incompatible with how Debian packages are organized and built.

Consequently, the best approach for installing Rubygems is to download the source and compile it yourself. This is easier than it sounds. First, you compile it yourself. This is easier than it sounds. First, you need to get hold of the Rubygems source from: `http://rubyforge.org/projects/rubygems/` (you need the file with the `.tgz` suffix).

Next, you need to install the tools for compiling the source. On Ubuntu Dapper, you would do:

```
$ apt-get install build-essential
```

You are now in a position to install Rubygems from the command line. The examples below use version 0.9.0:

```
$ tar xzf rubygems-0.9.0.tgz
$ cd rubygems-0.9.0
$ ruby setup.rb
$ gem update
```

Verify that gem is working by running the gem-v command and you should see something like this:

```
$ gem -v
0.9.0
```

(The gem command is used to manage all the gems on the system: you use it to install, uninstall, and list them.)

Ruby on Mac OS X

Ruby can be installed on Mac by first installing the DarwinPorts (`http://darwinports.opendarwin.org/`). Once this is in place, you can install the Ruby port and then the Rubygems port. Full instructions on using ports can be found on the DarwinPorts website.

Installing Rails

You can install Rails from a command line:

```
$ gem install rails -y
```

The -y on the end of this command tells gem to install all of the Rails dependencies. If you leave this off, gem will prompt you to install them anyway: adding the switch just automatically answers *yes* to installing the dependencies.

If this doesn't work for you, the most likely cause is a failure to install Rubygems. If you are using the *Windows One-Click Installer*, try reinstalling it and make sure the **Enable RubyGems** option is ticked as shown in the screenshot in the earlier section *Ruby on Windows*. If you are using Linux, check that you have installed Rubygems correctly by following the instructions given above.

When you use gem to install Rails, you are actually installing six separate gems. If you prefer (the gem update site can be horrendously slow at times), you can download them from `http://rubyforge.org/projects/rails/` and install them individually, provided you do so in this order:

1. rake
2. activesupport
3. actionpack
4. activerecord
5. actionwebservice
6. actionmailer
7. rails

Installing from downloaded gems (rather than from the network) can be particularly useful if you have a whole load of developer machines you want to keep in sync—setup a central repository holding the Rails gem files, make it available over the network (e.g. via HTTP), and download and install the gems on the developer machines from this repository. In this way, you can ensure that you are using the same versions of the same gems. You can also extend this approach to cover other non-Rails gems. See Appendix A for more details about running your own gem server

A Note on Rails Documentation

While this book provides a thorough reference for using Rails, there are cases where you really need to dig into the Rails API documentation to get all the information you need. Fortunately, this is included with the Rails gems.

The simplest way to find the Rails documentation is to run the gem documentation server with the following command:

```
$ gem_server
```

The gem_server command runs a local web server, (on port 8808), which serves up all your Ruby gem documentation, making it accessible via a web browser. Browse to http://localhost:8808/ and you should see the front page of the installed documentation:

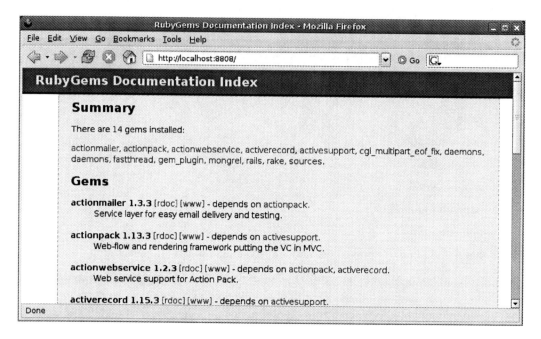

Click on the **[rdoc]** links to see the local documentation for your gems.

To find the Rails documentation manually (e.g. if gem_server doesn't work):

- On Windows, if you used the *Ruby One-Click Installer* (see the section *Ruby on Windows*, earlier in this chapter) and installed it into C:\ruby, the gem documentation is installed in:
  C:\ruby\lib\ruby\gems\1.8\doc
- On Linux, if you installed using *apt-get*, the documentation is installed in:
  /usr/lib/ruby/gems/1.8/doc

Within the main documentation directory, you should see a directory for each installed gem, for example:

actionmailer-1.3.3

actionpack-1.13.3

actionwebservice-1.2.3

```
activerecord-1.15.3
activesupport-1.4.2
rails-1.2.3
rake-0.7.2
```

To get to the documentation for a given gem, go to the appropriate directory (e.g. `activerecord-1.14.4`). Next, go to the `rdoc` directory. Then load the `index.html` file in your browser.

Other Libraries

At this point, you may not be sure about what exactly your application is going to do, and you may not have a fully-formed idea about which libraries you'll require. However, there are a few libraries that are very useful when building practically any Rails application (particularly if you build them how we're going to build them).

Many of the libraries are available using gem and are simple to install. Others require a bit more work, but typically use the `make` build tool and Ruby's `extconf` to compile and install Ruby extension code

Libraries vs. plugins

When you're developing with Ruby on Rails, there are two sources of *add-ons* you may need to make use of.

Libraries are extensions to Ruby itself and can be used for writing command line scripts or GUI applications in Ruby, as well as from within Rails applications. These are the add-ons I'll be describing in this chapter.

Plugins are Rails-specific extensions. They have little meaning outside of Rails, as they typically alter the behavior of classes specific to Rails. They are covered in Chapter 8.

Capistrano for Easier Deployment

Capistrano is a deployment tool which is tightly integrated with Rails. It allows you to do things like check out your application code from a version control system and deploy it to production servers, restart application servers, etc. It can be installed from the command line with:

```
$ gem install capistrano -y
```

We'll be covering Capistrano in some detail in Chapter 9.

Mongrel: A Better Way to Run Rails Applications

Mongrel (`http://mongrel.rubyforge.org/`) is a great way to run Rails applications in either a development or production environment. It provides a Ruby-centric application server, specifically designed for running Ruby web frameworks (as well as Ruby on Rails, it also supports **Nitro** and **Camping**). Additionally, Mongrel can be fronted with Apache, enabling you to leverage Apache's awesome power when serving static files (images, static HTML) while farming out dynamic pages to your Rails application. You can even cluster Mongrel instances for higher performance. By starting out with Mongrel, you are kitting yourself out with all the tools you need to run applications efficiently once they get to production.

On Linux, you will need the development libraries for your version of Ruby to install Mongrel. This is because Mongrel is compiled by gem for the architecture you are using. The development library has the same name as the main library, with `-dev` appended to it. In the case of Ruby 1.8.x, where the Ubuntu library is called `ruby1.8`, the development library is `ruby1.8-dev` and can be installed with:

```
$ apt-get install ruby1.8-dev
```

Mongrel can now be installed via gem:

```
$ gem install mongrel -y
```

One, slight complication is that there are many versions of Mongrel, which can be confusing. Here's a fraction of the list shown when installing it on Ubuntu:

```
Select which gem to install for your platform (i686-linux)
 1. mongrel 1.0.1 (ruby)
 2. mongrel 1.0.1 (mswin32)
 3. mongrel 1.0 (mswin32)
 4. mongrel 1.0 (ruby)
 5. mongrel 0.3.13.4 (ruby)
 6. mongrel 0.3.13.3 (ruby)
 7. mongrel 0.3.13.3 (mswin32)
. . .
```

Some guidelines for choosing which version to install:

1. Get the one with the highest version number (and nearest to the top of the list). At the time of writing, this was version 1.0.1.

2. If you are installing on Windows, choose the **mswin32** gem; on any other system, use the gem marked **ruby**.

The Mongrel dependencies are also installed by this command: `daemons`, which enables you to run Ruby programs as background processes and manage them through start/stop scripts; `gem_plugin`, which enables loading of 3rd party Mongrel extensions; `fastthread`, which provides a faster threading implementation for Ruby; and maybe others, depending on the version of Mongrel you are installing. If you are prompted for a version of any of the dependent libraries you want to install, select the one nearest to the top. Choose the **mswin32** version if installing on Windows, and the **ruby** version for other platforms.

It is also worth installing `mongrel_cluster`, which makes it easier to manage multiple Mongrel instances for scaling your application gracefully. We won't be using it for now, but it doesn't hurt to have it around:

```
$ gem install mongrel_cluster
```

If you are installing on Windows, it is a good idea to install the Windows services support for Mongrel. With this, you can run Mongrel as a service on a Windows server, so it starts when the machine boots. Install it with:

```
C:\> gem install mongrel_service
```

Mongrel configuration is described in Chapter 6, and again in more depth in Chapter 9.

Choosing a Database Platform

Most Rails applications depend on a database for storing their data (though, you can write a Rails application without a database, of course). Rails supports a variety of databases, including most of the main open source ones (**MySQL**, **PostgreSQL**, **SQLite**), as well as proprietary ones (**Oracle**, **SQL Server**).

If you work in a small development team with complete control over your environment, you could do worse than choose MySQL as your database server. You can use MySQL for internal development work with no cost whatsoever, no strings attached, on as many machines as you like. If you want to, you can also roll it out into production with little or no cost, and it will scale phenomenally well. When you do want support, you can get it from MySQL AB (the company which originated MySQL and owns the intellectual property): their support contracts are reasonably priced (cheaper than those for many proprietary databases), and scale from two-incident to 24-7 phone support. Aside from the cost angle, it is also easy to learn and administer and is very stable, too. For these reasons and others, MySQL is recommended as a database server for development work.

Another database platform you will commonly encounter is SQL Server, as it's part of Microsoft's Small Business Server, a ubiquitous piece of software in small businesses. If you are building applications for a client who controls the production platform, you may be required to use this for your database. Fortunately, Rails cleanly separates the development and production environments, so it is eminently plausible to develop on MySQL (for example), and deploy to SQL Server for production.

In fact, because of how Rails is designed, your choice of database server at this point is less important than it could be. For example, Rails lets you define your database schema in a platform-agnostic fashion (via **migrations**, covered in the next chapter). This means you can reproduce the same structure on a variety of database platforms with little effort.

Personally, I like *SQLite* for my development work, because I can move a whole application and its database between machines very easily; while I prefer *MySQL* for production deployments.

Throughout the book, we'll be using Rails with MySQL. However, if you need to use a different database, you can find information on configuring Rails to work with your choice of database here: `http://wiki.rubyonrails.com/rails/pages/Howtos`.

Installing MySQL

MySQL is included with several of the Rails bundles mentioned earlier: for example, if you use InstantRails on Windows, you get MySQL for free. If you are installing MySQL in standalone mode, installation is still straightforward. Recommendations for the different platforms are given below.

MySQL on Windows

To install MySQL on Windows, download the Current Release for Windows from the MySQL website (`http://mysql.com/downloads/#downloads`). Your best bet is to get the Windows Essentials package, which includes all the binaries and command line tools you need to run MySQL on Windows. (The larger Windows package adds extra support for developers who need to get further into MySQL's internals.)

MySQL comes with a full Windows installer, which takes you through the installation process step-by-step. The Typical setup installs both the server and command line utilities we need.

Configuration is also accomplished through a graphical wizard. During installation, you will be asked whether you want to configure the server immediately, and should do this.

The configuration wizard is slightly confusing (at least for me, as it uses terms like OLAP and OLTP which are kind of irrelevant), so here are some recommendations for each step of the configuration process:

1. Select **Detailed Configuration**.

2. Select **Developer Machine**. This prevents MySQL from hogging memory.

3. Select **Multifunctional Database**. This gives you the option to use the InnoDB table type (if you want to), which supports transactions and foreign keys.

4. Leave the **InnoDB Tablespace Settings** at their defaults.

5. Select **Decision Support** as you are unlikely to be pushing hundreds of connections onto a developer's server.

6. Un-tick the **Enable TCP/IP Networking** setting. If installing for a developer, the MySQL server doesn't need to be accessible to other machines over the network. However, if you want to remotely manage MySQL from another machine on the network (either from the command line or using the MySQL Administrator GUI tool), you need to enable TCP/IP Networking here.

7. Set the default character set to the one you are most likely to work with. **utf-8** is a good choice, as it is suitable for general-purpose work.

8. Check **Install as Windows Service** (so MySQL starts and stops automatically with the machine) and **Include Bin Directory in Windows PATH** (so the command line tools are readily accessible).

9. Set a **New root password** to secure the administrative user account.

10. Click on the **Execute** button.

If everything has worked correctly, the MySQL server should start up and you should see a window like this:

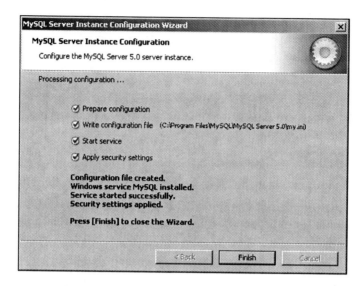

See section *Checking Your MySQL Installation* (later in this chapter) for instructions on how to verify your installation.

 When you are installing MySQL on a production server, some of these settings may not be appropriate. For example, you may want to increase the number of concurrent connections allowed, or turn on TCP/IP networking (e.g. if you have multiple web servers which need to talk to a single MySQL server).

MySQL on Linux

The easiest way to install MySQL on Linux is via package management, e.g. on Ubuntu:

```
$ apt-get install mysql-server
```

On Ubuntu, this installs a standard MySQL server and command-line client. The server is installed with InnoDB support and networking enabled (on the local interface only), comparable to the Windows installation outlined in the previous section. However, there is no root password set, which needs fixing. Run this command from a prompt:

```
$ mysqladmin password <new password>
```

Where <new password> is the new password you want to apply.

MySQL on Mac OS X

A binary distribution of MySQL is available for Mac OS X, from the same location as the Windows downloads (http://mysql.com/downloads/). Alternatively, you can install it via DarwinPorts (http://darwinports.opendarwin.org/). The MySQL site has some hints on installation at http://dev.mysql.com/doc/refman/5.0/en/mac-os-x.html.

> MySQL is already installed on the server edition of Mac OS X, so you shouldn't have to do any extra work to set it up on a Mac server.

Checking Your MySQL Installation

To check that your MySQL installation is working, the simplest approach is to use the mysql command line program. It can be used to access every part of your MySQL installation, from creating and managing databases, to configuring user permissions and system settings. You can test whether your server is working and is available with the following command line:

```
$ mysql -u root -p
```

Enter root's password when prompted. You should see something like this if you logged in successfully:

```
Welcome to the MySQL monitor.   Commands end with; or \g.
```

Your MySQL connection id is 11 to server version: 5.0.22-Debian_0ubuntu6.06-log

```
Type ''help;'' or ''\h'' for help. Type ''\c'' to clear the buffer.
mysql>
```

If this doesn't work, it could be that you typed the wrong password, or that the password was not correctly set. Try to run the mysqladmin tool again to reset the password. Alternatively, it may be that MySQL is not running, in which case you might see this message:

```
$ mysql -u root -p
```

```
Enter password:
ERROR 2002 (HY000): Can''t connect to local MySQL server through socket
''/var/run/mysqld/mysqld.sock'' (2)
```

In this case, ensure that the MySQL server has started, e.g. on Linux:

```
$ /etc/init.d/mysql start
```

If all else fails, it could be that the machine is not accessible over the network (try pinging the machine), or it could be a configuration problem. Check the MySQL manual for more troubleshooting tips (`http://mysql.com/doc/`).

MySQL GUI Tools

It is possible to control MySQL entirely from the command line. But if you prefer using GUI clients in your day-to-day work, several are available:

1. **MySQL Query Browser** is the official MySQL AB GUI client. You can use it to manage your server and its databases. It is open source and is easy to install, either using `apt-get` on Ubuntu, or by installer on Windows or Mac (from: `http://www.mysql.com/products/tools/query-browser/`).

2. **MySQL Administrator** is another official MySQL AB GUI client, a desktop application which runs on Windows, Linux, and Mac OS X. It provides an easy-to-follow wrapper around the MySQL configuration files.

3. **phpMyAdmin** is a web-based (PHP) MySQL management tool. It is extremely widespread, often provided in shared hosting environments as the end-user interface to a shared database server. It can be particularly useful if you have multiple-developer teams, each of which needs different levels of access to a shared server or their own private set of databases. One gripe is that the interface is a bit clunky (like many web interfaces), but it is perfectly functional and stable.

4. **MySQL Workbench** is a graphical database design tool, again from MySQL AB. You can use it to generate graphical database models and synchronize them to a database; or to reverse engineer the structure of an existing database (e.g. if you wanted to migrate it to a different database platform). It also supports Access, SQL Server, and Oracle database servers, so it could be useful for projects where you are working with legacy database systems.

Ruby-MySQL: Making Ruby and MySQL Work Better Together

The MySQL Ruby binding library is optional but useful. Rails will happily talk to MySQL without this library using Ruby code (see below for one caveat); but the conversation will be more efficient with it, as it uses faster C code. If you are using Mac or Linux, it is well worth installing.

At the time of writing, installation of the Ruby-MySQL is *essential* on Ubuntu: if you do not install the bindings, Rails will fail to connect to the database correctly and throw out an error, which looks something like this:

```
Mysql::Error: Lost connection to MySQL server during
query: ...
```

Follow the instructions in the next section to perform the installation.

On Windows, the installation is extremely troublesome and not worth attempting: your Rails application will still work with MySQL without the bindings.

If you insist on attempting to install Ruby-MySQL on Windows, you may be able to get a pre-built binary from http://raa.ruby-lang.org/project/mysql-ruby-win/ (none was available for Ruby 1.8.4 at the time of writing).

Ruby-MySQL on Linux

On Linux, you can either install the MySQL Ruby bindings through package management or by compiling it from source.

If using package management (the easiest approach) you can do:

```
$ apt-get install libmysql-ruby
```

Alternatively, to install from source, first download the .tar.gz file from http://tmtm.org/downloads/mysql/ruby/. Get the highest version number compatible with your version of Ruby: in my case, this was version 2.7. Then install, (as root), using the command line:

```
$ tar zxvf mysql-ruby-2.7.tar.gz
$ cd mysql-ruby-2.7
$ ruby extconf.rb
$ make
$ make install
```

Note that if the MySQL database server is in a non-standard location, you will need to specify this when running ruby extconf.rb. For example, to install with XAMPP, you would do:

```
$ ruby extconf.rb --with-mysql-include=/opt/lampp/include/mysql/ \
--with-mysql-lib=/opt/lampp/lib/mysql/
```

Ruby-MySQL on Mac OS X

The easiest approach to installing is to use one of the Ruby-MySQL ports (for the DarwinPorts package manager—see `http://darwinports.opendarwin.org/`). Search at `http://darwinports.opendarwin.org/ports/?by=name&substr=mysql` for the port appropriate for your version of MySQL.

Installing an IDE

Using a decent **Integrated Development Environment** (IDE) can make a big difference to your productivity as a programmer. While you can code a Rails application with nothing more than a text editor, an IDE gives you several benefits over a basic editor:

- *Syntax highlighting*
  An IDE will color your code by highlighting different data types, control constructs (if...else...end, while...end, etc.), and variable names. This makes it easier to spot places where you have made syntax errors, like missing a closing quote character when defining a string.

- *Detecting syntax errors*
  In cases where syntax errors occur, an IDE can help you navigate to the location of the error.

- *Automatic code indentation*
  Good indentation is very important in making code legible. While it is possible to do this in a text editor, pressing the space bar can get tedious. An IDE will provide facilities to customize indentation (e.g. tabs or spaces, N spaces per indent), indent whole blocks of code consistently, and may also help with auto-formatting of code.

- *Code templates*
  IDEs can help by generating boilerplate code for common tasks (e.g. a skeleton for new HTML files).

- *Integration with external tools*
  Development is not just about coding: it's also about working with databases, build tools, running batch scripts, copying files to servers, and so on. A good IDE will provide support for common development tasks, but also enable you to customize interactions with external applications.

- *Source code repository integration*
  Any serious coding project needs a source code repository, and your IDE should support interaction with this repository. While this is related to the previous point, your IDE should make version control easy and integrated into the fabric of coding.

A good text editor will provide some of these facilities, though not all. However, any text editor is better than the Windows default, **Notepad**: Notepad can be very problematic, as it doesn't handle line breaks on different operating systems that well. So, if you are looking at code written on a UNIX machine, Notepad may very well make it unintelligible.

One alternative is **SciTE for Windows** (`http://www.scintilla.org/SciTE.html`), which supports syntax highlighting for a variety of languages; it is also a part of the InstantRails bundle for Windows. However, it doesn't provide integration with source code repositories. Other good choices are **TextPad** (`http://textpad.com/`) and the **Programmer's Notepad** (`http://www.pnotepad.org/`).

Eclipse

One tool which provides all of the above facilities is **Eclipse** (`http://eclipse.org/`). This is rapidly becoming the de facto development environment for many programming languages, including Java and PHP, and is an excellent environment for Rails development. Here's what it looks like in action on Linux, editing some Rails code:

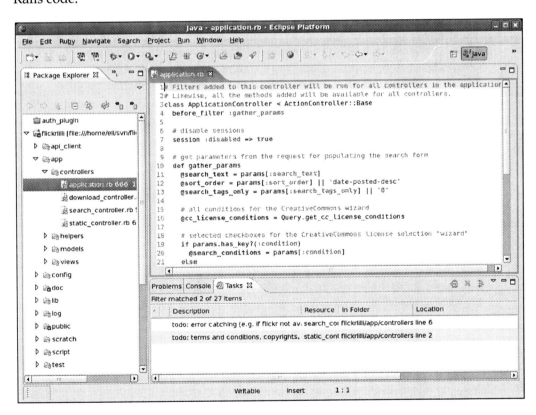

Here, you can see the Ruby syntax highlighted (right-hand pane), plus the resource view (left-hand pane) which shows the files and folders in the project. Also note the icons on the files and folders: these indicate the relationship between the local file system and a Subversion repository, enabling you to identify where you have made changes to your code which aren't yet committed to the repository. Also note the **Tasks** tab (bottom right) which you can use to leave yourself *to dos*.

Pros and Cons of Eclipse

Eclipse is a great development environment. However, some people see some cons with using it:

- *It requires Java*
  This used to be an issue, as it meant you had to install Java, which had no decent open source implementations. However, it is now possible to run Eclipse using `gcj`, a complete open source Java implementation.

- *It is a big download*
  Getting everything you need for your development work requires around 100Mb of download. This is big, granted, but less important as bandwidth soars into the stratosphere.

- *It is overkill*
  Many projects are small and don't need the overhead of a massive, complicated IDE. Butyou don't have to use Eclipse for everything: you can still use vim or a graphical text editor for quick edits or for tiny projects.

- *It is slow*
  This used to be more of an issue when RAM was expensive. However, while startup is still a bit painful at times, once Eclipse is up and running it is very responsive.

- *The interface is intimidating*
  However, it is highly customizable, so you can turn off the bits you don't like.

On the pros side:

- *It is cross platform* (Windows, Mac OS X, and Linux)
  This means you can use it in a mixed OS environment, and everyone will have the same tool, which lowers training costs and makes sharing application knowledge easier.

- *It is multi-purpose*
  While we are going to use Eclipse in the context of Rails development, you can use it to develop in many other languages (e.g. C, Java, PHP, Perl, and Python). This means that if a team develops using a variety of languages, they can use a single piece of software and a consistent interface for all their development work.

- *It is extensible through plugins*
  Eclipse is multi-purpose because of its plugin architecture: potentially anyone can extend Eclipse's functionality by writing their own plugin. This means that a wealth of tools has emerged, using Eclipse as a base, and practically any development task you might want to perform has an Eclipse plugin available.

- *It is freely available*
  You can use Eclipse, with no charge or restrictions, on an unlimited number of machines.

I believe the pros outweigh the cons, and that Eclipse is an ideal IDE for small teams with smaller budgets. From now on we're going to code in Eclipse throughout the rest of the book.

 A couple of caveats about requirements: Eclipse is *very* RAM hungry and won't perform brilliantly on machines with less than 512Mb of RAM: 1 GB of RAM will give good performance. You will also need about 200Mb or so of hard disk space.

EasyEclipse

EasyEclipse is a nice packaging of Eclipse for Windows, Mac OS X, and Linux. It includes a **Java Runtime Environment (JRE)**, Eclipse, plus some stable and useful plugins. The plugins included are dependent on the distribution you choose. Each distribution bundles plugins for a particular development situation: for example, there is an **EasyEclipse for PHP**, which includes PHP support, HTML editing tools, and Subversion integration; and an **EasyEclipse for Python**, which includes support for the Python language.

For our purposes, the best choice is Easy Eclipse for Ruby on Rails, which includes:

- **Eclipse,** itself.

- A **Java Runtime Environment** (in the Windows and Linux versions; Mac OS X has its own JRE). This is required to run Eclipse.

- **Ruby Development Tools**, for highlighting and syntax checking of Ruby files, integrated testing, code hints, source formatting, and a debugger.

- **RadRails**, for Rails-specific Eclipse features, such as convenient buttons to run automated tests and extra controls for activating the Rails code generators.

- **QuantumDB**, for interacting with database servers. You can use it to run SQL queries against databases and view tables and data graphically.

- **Subclipse**, for working with Subversion repositories. Code can be saved back to the repository or checked out of it (more information about Subversion is available in the Version Control section section towards the end of this chapter).

Easy Eclipse for Ruby on Rails downloads are available at:

```
http://www.easyeclipse.org/site/distributions/ruby-rails.html
```

EasyEclipse is very simple to install, as described next.

Installing EasyEclipse on Windows

The download is an executable file which contains an installer. Double-click on the downloaded file and follow the instructions; it's OK to accept all the default settings.

 The best location for installing EasyEclipse is outside your `Program Files` directory: If you install inside `Program Files`, you may find that EasyEclipse won't run at all, as Java dislikes spaces in filesystem paths

Once installed, you should have a new item called **EasyEclipse for Ruby on Rails** in your **Start** menu (under **Programs**).

Installing EasyEclipse on Linux

Download the EasyEclipse tarball for Linux (`.tar.gz` file). Unpack this file where you want to install EasyEclipse, e.g. to put it in your home directory:

```
$ cd ~
$ tar zxvf easyeclipse-ruby-rails-1.0.2.tar.gz
$ ln -s ruby-rails-1.0.2 easyeclipse
```

The `last` command creates a symlink from the full directory name to an easier-to-remember path.

It is easy to create a launcher for Eclipse on your Desktop. In Ubuntu, right-click on the desktop and select **Create Launcher...** from the context menu and fill in the options in the **Create Launcher** dialog box. This is what the dialog box looks like when complete:

(You can browse to the icon in the EasyEclipse installation directory.)

The important part of this is the **Command** text box, which should reference the correct path to your Eclipse start script, e.g. for the demo user this might be something like:

```
/home/demo/easyeclipse/eclipse
```

where /home/demo/easyeclipse/ references the symlink to the EasyEclipse installation directory, and eclipse is the name of the Eclipse start script.

Note that you can pass extra arguments to Eclipse on the end of this command. Modify the command line to make sure Eclipse has enough memory by passing these arguments:

```
-vmargs -Xms256M -Xmx512M
```

What's actually happening here is that we are passing extra arguments to the Java Runtime Environment (the -vmargs flag tells Eclipse "Here come some arguments for Java"); the two arguments we're passing are: -Xms256M ("Claim a minimum of 256Mb of RAM") and -Xmx512M ("But don't claim more than 512Mb of RAM"). You can set these higher if you like, but these values should be fine.

Click on the Launcher to start Eclipse. During the first startup, you are prompted to select a **workspace**: a default location for Eclipse to save projects to. Accept the default location or set a custom path. Also tell Eclipse to **Use this as the default and do not ask again**:

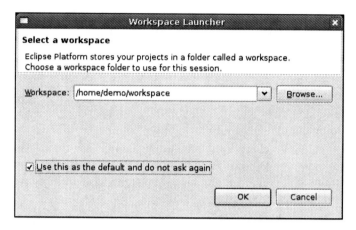

Once, the startup is complete, click on the Workbench icon to go to the main Eclipse interface.

The last piece of configuration is to tell Eclipse where the Ruby binary is located (which it uses to do syntax highlighting and the like.) First, locate the Ruby binary using the command line:

```
$ which ruby
```
```
/usr/bin/ruby
```

Then, in Eclipse, set the Ruby interpreter under **Window | Preferences | Ruby | Installed Interpreters**. Click on the **Add** button and fill in the dialog box with the path to Ruby, e.g.

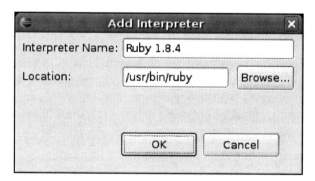

Installing EasyEclipse on Mac OS X

EasyEclipse is provided as a disk image file (`.dmg` suffix) for Mac OS X. Download this file, then double-click it to open up the **Volume**. Once inside, double-click on the **Installer Package** to install to the `/Applications` folder. Use the **Finder** to locate the EasyEclipse icon and double-click to run it. (You can drag and drop the icon into the **Dock** to make it easier to find.)

Instructions for Masochists

If you really enjoy making life hard for yourself, it is feasible to install every component of a Rails stack (more or less) from source code. This will really give you an insight into how Rails stack ticks, but it is not for the faint-hearted.

The definitive instructions for doing this on a Mac are available at: `http://hivelogic.com/articles/2005/12/01/ruby_rails_lighttpd_mysql_tiger`

Some Linux instructions are available on the Rails wiki: `http://wiki.rubyonrails.com/rails/pages/RailsOnUbuntu`

(This approach could be tricky on Windows, as it would require addition of large amounts of open source software before the compilation could even begin.)

As it is always the case with these sorts of how-to, they are continuously changing, so the above URLs may have vanished by the time you are reading this. The **Rails wiki** (`http://wiki.rubyonrails.com/`) is a good place to start looking for the most up-to-date instructions.

In the Back Rooms at Acme...

Following the recommendations from the previous sections, the developers at Acme decide on the following approach:

- They first agree on MySQL as the database for development and production deployment.
- On the Windows XP machine (Jenny's), they install MySQL Windows Essentials, Ruby (using the One-Click Installer, which includes Rubygems), Mongrel and Capistrano (via gem), and EasyEclipse for Ruby on Rails.
- On the Linux machine, Rory installs Ruby using Ubuntu's package management system, compiles Rubygems, then adds the gems for Rails, Capistrano, and Mongrel. Next, he installs MySQL using Ubuntu package management and compiles Ruby-MySQL. He installs MySQL Query Browser and MySQL Administrator to manage his MySQL server. Finally, he installs EasyEclipse for Ruby on Rails.

The Acme developers are now ready to start development. The next step is to setup the infrastructure for their project, to enable them to work collaboratively on the code and deploy live applications to their intranet.

Setting Up a Team Server

In this section, we'll see how to set up a team server for Rails development. We'll only cover the key software for supporting Rails development and assume you can install and configure the core of the operating system yourself. If you don't have the resources to run your own server, several ways of outsourcing this function are covered at the end of the chapter.

Another assumption we make is that this is not a publicly-available server exposed to traffic from the Internet. Instead, the intranet server is sitting behind a firewall, similar to the hardware setup at Acme, described in the Supporting Rails Development section. We also assume that the only people with access to the server are internal staff: no public or anonymous access. The configuration described below is the bare minimum you can get away with in this situation, and will need tweaking on public servers or servers open to the public at large.

Space prohibits covering how to setup a server for each of the main operating systems (Linux, Windows, Mac OS X), so we'll be using Linux, a reliable and stable platform for Rails team infrastructure. Having said this, all of the software covered in this section will also run on Windows or Mac OS X, with installation being similar to installation on Linux. For example, Subversion can run on Windows, and be configured using the techniques described below. Differences between Linux and these two operating systems are highlighted where appropriate.

In the next two sections, we'll see how to configure a team server for three core functions:

- **Remote access**, for deploy of Rails applications to the server using Capistrano.
- Storing Rails source code using a **version control** system.
- Running Rails code in production using an **application delivery** platform (i.e. a web server and/or application server).

If you have a separate servers for the code repository and web server, the instructions below should be adaptable to your circumstances.

The software covered in these sections *is not* specific to Rails. However, any Rails-specific issues involved in using this software are highlighted later in the book.

For reference, here's a list of the software needed on the team server:

- Rails stack, comprising:
  - Ruby
  - Rubygems
  - Rails
  - Mongrel and mongrel_cluster
  - MySQL
  - Ruby-MySQL

  Installing these components is covered in previous sections, and it is the same for client machines. (Note that we don't need Capistrano on the server, only on the developer machines.)
- Server-only software:
  - SSH
  - Subversion

Installation of the server-only software is covered in the following sections.

 We are not going to look at running Apache with Mongrel in the first instance. Mongrel on its own is a perfectly viable deployment platform for the first version of the application. Combining it with Apache is covered later, in Chapter 9.

Quick Gem Installation

The default behavior of gem is to include documentation for each gem you install. This slows down the installation process significantly, as gem generates the documentation from the source code.

When you are installing gems on the server, you don't really need the documentation. You can considerably speed up the installation progress by telling gem to dispense with the documentation using the --no-rdoc and --no-ri switches on the gem command. For example:

```
$ gem install rails -y --no-rdoc --no-ri
```

Remote Access via SSH

Secure Shell (SSH) is a vital tool for remote administration. It is included by default with practically every Linux distribution, and is very useful for Rails development, as it enables automated deployment of applications via Capistrano. We are also going to use it as the method of access to the Subversion repository.

The installation procedure on Ubuntu is simple:

```
$ apt-get install openssh-server
```

You can configure the port and various other options in `/etc/ssh/sshd_config`. For more information, see the SSH website at, `http://www.openssh.com/`.

> It is also possible to install an SSH server on Windows, and several SSH Windows installers exist such as, OpenSSH for Windows (`http://sshwindows.sourceforge.net/`) or the commercial WinSSHD (`http://www.bitvise.com/winsshd.html`).

Adding Users

To enable access to the team server, you will need to add user accounts for each developer on the team server. Use whichever tool you are most comfortable with. To do this on Linux, you can either use one of the GUI user management tools, or add the required users from the command line, e.g. for Rory:

```
$ sudo useradd --create-home --home-dir /home/rory -g users rory
$ sudo passwd rory
Enter new UNIX password:
Retype new UNIX password:
passwd: password updated successfully
```

Once, Rory is setup as a user on the team server (with IP address `192.168.13.129`), he can try to login using the Linux command line client:

```
$ ssh rory@192.168.13.129
The authenticity of host ''192.168.13.129 (192.168.13.129)'' can''t be
established.RSA key fingerprint is 61:7a:6a:0e:5d:c5:0b:45:24:08:44:
f0:06:eb:07:c0.
Are you sure you want to continue connecting (yes/no)? yes
Warning: Permanently added ''192.168.13.129'' (RSA) to the list of known
hosts.
rory@192.168.13.129''s password:
Linux demo-server 2.6.15-23-386 #1 PREEMPT Tue May 23 13:49:40 UTC 2006
i686 GNU/Linux

...
```

Note that the first time Rory logs into the server, he is prompted to accept the authenticity of the certificate presented by the server. Once he's done this, providing the server IP address doesn't change, he will not have to do it again.

If you're using Windows, you could use a tool like **PuTTY** (`http://www.chiark.greenend.org.uk/~sgtatham/putty/`) to test whether you can login to the SSH server.

Later in the chapter, we'll see how to use SSH to access a Subversion repository from Eclipse.

Version Control with Subversion

Most companies need some way to share electronic files between the members of staff: for example, timesheets, holiday forms, project documentation, etc. The typical approach taken is to setup what's colloquially called a **shared drive**. This is often as simple as a shared directory on a Windows machine in the corner of the office; or if the company has the money, they may stretch to a dedicated server or Network Attached Storage (NAS) appliance on their intranet.

Programmers working in these environments will often use the same approach, reading and writing source code files from the shared drive, resolving locks and conflicts manually (e.g. by email or verbally). In the Supporting Rails Development section, we saw how Acme staff used their server in this way. However, this brings with it a variety of problems, the most painful being accidental overwriting of other people's modifications.

The best solution in this situation is a **version control system**. Using this approach, developers each have their own local version of the code or **working copy**, checked out from a central **repository**. When they make changes to the code, they can save (**commit**) these changes back to the repository. Every other developer then has access to the changes and can **update** their working copy to incorporate them.

In situations where two developers working on the same file make conflicting changes, the version control system does its best to resolve the conflict and automatically merge in both sets of changes. In cases where this is not possible, the system will highlight conflicts and ask developers to manually resolve them. This makes it nearly impossible for two developers to overwrite each other's work.

The next section describes **Subversion**, the de facto standard open source version control system. This is a core part of a successful team infrastructure for Rails developments, as it provides:

- Control of submissions to the repository so that one person cannot accidentally overwrite another person's changes.
- A historical record of changes made to the code (it keeps a record of every modification).
- The ability to take snapshots of released versions.
- The ability to simultaneously develop multiple versions of a single application.
- And more...

Rails integrates nicely with Subversion via **Capistrano** (see the section *Capistrano for Easier Deployment*). Capistrano can radically simplify application deployment, making it easy to roll out a new version of an application, or to roll back if a new version causes problems.

This will only give a brief overview of how to install and configure Subversion, and will concentrate on showing how to integrate it with EasyEclipse. If you are interested in exploring Subversion in more depth, get hold of the free online book *Version Control with Subversion* from `http://svnbook.red-bean.com/`.

Installing Subversion

The simplest approach to installing Subversion on Ubuntu is via the command line (as root) with:

```
$ apt-get install subversion
```

That's all there is to it.

 If you want to install Subversion on Windows, a one-click installer is available at, `http://svn1clicksetup.tigris.org/`.

The command line Subversion client application is called **svn**. Type the following at a command line to see which version you are running and which subcommands are available:

```
$ svn help
usage: svn <subcommand> [options] [args]
Subversion command-line client, version 1.3.1.
Type ''svn help <subcommand>'' for help on a specific subcommand.
. . .
```

The administrative application is called **svnadmin**. We'll be using this in a moment to setup our source code repository. But first, we'll cover some standard practices for organizing team work around a Subversion repository.

Subversion Standard Practices

At its simplest, a Subversion repository is a place to store multiple parallel versions of files relating to a project. These files will typically be code, but could also include images, documentation, PDF files, and directories; in fact, any type of file you like. (Unlike **CVS**, an older version control system which predates it, Subversion is easily able to cope with binary files.)

One way to think of a Subversion repository is as a tree structure, similar to a filesystem. It's not really a filesystem, and in fact it is more like a database, but this is a useful analogy for understanding its structure. At the top of the tree, you have the "root" of the repository; inside that, you have a separate "directory" for each project in the repository. Assuming a repository with two projects, addressbook and calendar, its layout can be visualized like this:

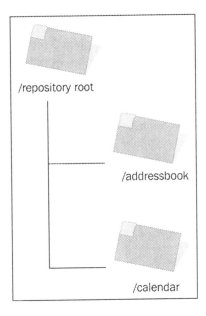

/repository root

/addressbook

/calendar

Within individual project directories, the standard Subversion layout involves three "subdirectories", representing three different aspects of a project:

- *Trunk*
  This represents the most up-to-date, mainstream version of the project's files. If you are adding new features to the latest release of an application, you will typically do so using trunk as a base.

- *Branches*
  This contains alternative, parallel versions of the project files. Each parallel version has its own subdirectory inside the branches directory called a **branch**. Each branch must have been derived from some other version of the project files at one time, whether from trunk or another branch.

  The most common use of branches is as a way of storing individual versions of an application, such as version-0.2, version-0.3 etc. (the naming of branches is flexible). Another, legitimate use is to create arbitrary branches like *dodgy-experimental-branch*, where someone can try out new ideas without affecting *trunk*. Any useful changes made in that branch could then be merged back into *trunk* when ready.

  Subversion's mechanism for creating branches is to copy some part of the repository: usually, a branch is a complete copy of the application *trunk* at some point of time. (You can think of this as equivalent to a literal directory copy on a standard filesystem.) Once the copy is made, the source of the branch (where the branch was copied from) and the branch itself are logically separated from each other: any changes to the branch do not affect the source unless a developer explicitly merges the changes in.

- *Tags*
  Tags are similar to branches, in that they are created by the same method (by copying a section of the repository tree). However, they are not intended to be worked on: they are static snapshots of the project files at a specific point of time. A typical approach might be to label them release-0.2, release-0.3 etc., maintaining them as historical copies of the code base when new versions are released.

Focusing on the *addressbook* project, the three subdirectories can be visualized like this:

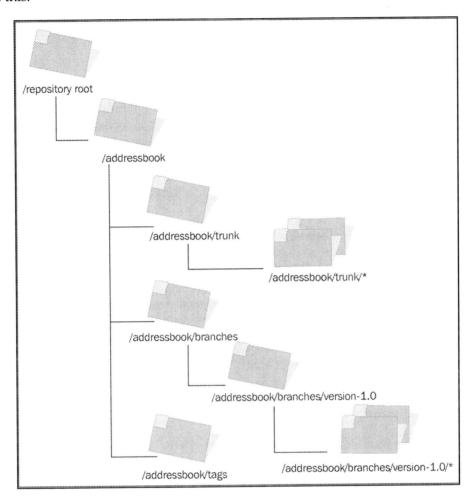

/repository root

/addressbook

/addressbook/trunk

/addressbook/trunk/*

/addressbook/branches

/addressbook/branches/version-1.0

/addressbook/branches/version-1.0/*

/addressbook/tags

The main development of the addressbook project goes on in the trunk of the repository. There is also a single branch called version-1.0 in the branches directory, which was copied from trunk when the first version of the application was released. Development can be carried out in the version-1.0 branch without affecting the content of trunk, as the former is logically isolated from the latter.

Note that version-1.0 is logically equivalent to a subdirectory inside the branches directory and contains all the files in that version of the application. A developer could check out the whole of version 1.0 by checking out that one branch. The asterisk is used to denote the multiple files and subdirectories making up a version of the application.

We'll follow this standard structure for the projects in the rest of the book, creating a "directory" for each project, with three subdirectories (trunk, branches, and tags) inside it. This isn't the only way you can structure a repository, but you will find that it is fairly standard among publicly-accessible projects.

Revisions and Working Copies

The final complication we've hidden until now is the concept of a **revision**. A revision is roughly comparable to a "third dimension" of the repository: time. A revision is basically a snapshot of the state of the entire repository at a particular point in time. Each time anyone makes a change to any part of the repository (e.g. adding or deleting a file, modifying a file), they create a new revision of the whole repository. This is not a literal copy of all the files in the repository, but in some ways can be thought of as a "virtual" copy of it.

What does this mean for an individual project? When you do a "default" checkout of a project from a repository, you get the project files as they appear in the **HEAD revision** of the repository. The HEAD revision corresponds to the most recent revision number of the repository. So, if the HEAD revision is 10, you get the project files as they appear in revision 10. This is true even if the project files haven't changed since revision 5 (or even earlier) of the repository.

When you checkout a project, you create a working copy of some subtree of the repository. This is typically from trunk, but could also be from a branch. You then work on your working copy until you are ready to commit your changes back. At this point, Subversion compares your working copy to the part of the repository you checked out in the first place. For each file, there are four possible outcomes:

1. The local file is unchanged and identical to the version in the repository. Subversion does nothing.

2. The local file has not been modified, but it has been modified in the repository since it was checked out. Subversion will not commit the file. You need to modify the local copy to make sure it is up to date with the repository.

3. The local file has been modified and no changes have been made in the repository since it was checked out. In this case, the local file changes are copied to the repository.

4. The local file has been modified, but it has been modified in the repository since it was checked out. Subversion will not commit the file to the repository. If you run an `update` operation, Subversion will attempt to merge changes in the repository version into your local copy of the file. Hopefully, you can subsequently commit your changes.

Armed with this knowledge of some Subversion terminology, we are now in a position to set up and start using a repository.

Setting Up a Subversion Repository

A Subversion repository is simply a specially-formatted directory structure on a server. Inside the root directory of the repository are a series of subdirectories and control files, which define the content of the repository and how it operates. The command line tool svnadmin can be used to initialize and maintain this structure on the team server.

> You will need to login as the root user to perform the following operations.

As the Subversion repository is part of the filesystem, all of the developers on the project who need to write to the repository will need write permissions on the repository directory. The easiest way to do this is to create a special group (e.g. svn) to which all of the developers belong. The repository directory can be owned by this group and made writable by it.

The svn group can be added using the Linux GUI user management tools (in Ubuntu, under **main menu | System | Administration | Users and Groups**), or via the command line:

```
$ groupadd svn
```

In Acme's case, Rory and Jenny will both need to be members of the svn group (as will anyone else who needs to write into the repository). The easiest way to accomplish this is to use the GUI user management tools available in Linux, or via the command line with:

```
$ usermod -G svn -a rory
```

The above command adds Rory to the svn group, retaining his existing group memberships.

Next, create the directory which will become the repository. This can be located anywhere, but we'll use /repository:

```
$ mkdir /repository
```

Now that the directory is in place, initialize the repository structure inside it:

```
$ svnadmin create --fs-type=fsfs /repository
```

The `--fs-type=fsfs` flag tells `svnadmin` to use the *fsfs* filesystem to store the repository structure. This is the recommended filesystem, as it is faster, more stable, and more efficient.

Set the group ownership of the `/repository` directory to `svn`, make the directory writable by that group, and set the group ID on the directory. The latter step means that any new folders or files added to the repository are also owned by (and writable by) the `svn` group:

```
$ chgrp -R svn /repository
$ chmod -R g+sw /repository
```

For testing purposes, add a normal user account to the `svn` group. Then login as this user, get a command line up and try this:

```
$ svn mkdir file:///repository/test -m ''testing''
Committed revision 1.
```

The message above (`Committed revision 1`) shows that the Subversion repository is working correctly. The `mkdir` command created a directory called `test` inside the repository; it also associated the comment `testing` with the revision (via the `-m` flag).

Use this command to view the first revision:

```
$ svn list file:///repository
```

You should get this in return:

```
test/
```

Once you have this up and running, you can delete your test directory with:

```
$ svn del file:///repository/test
```

Setting Up a Project in Subversion

A Rails project can be treated just like any other project in a Subversion repository, adhering to the standard layout outlined in the Subversion Standard Practices section. For now, we'll set up a blank project, ready to be populated with a Rails application in later chapters.

The first step is to create the project directory structure. Once the directories have been created, this structure can be imported into the repository. We'll use the project name Intranet. Enter these commands at the command line:

```
$ mkdir tmp
$ mkdir tmp/Intranet
$ mkdir tmp/Intranet/trunk
$ mkdir tmp/Intranet/branches
$ mkdir tmp/Intranet/tags
```

The `tmp` directory is a temporary store for the project structure (it can be deleted later). The aim is for the content of the `tmp` directory to be copied to the root of the repository, so the Intranet application will reside at `/Intranet` (relative to the repository root).

Import the project structure into the repository with this command:

```
$ svn import tmp file:///repository/
```

Once this is done, the `tmp` directory can be removed. Check the project structure is correctly setup by running this command:

```
$ svn list file:///repository/Intranet/
branches/
tags/
trunk/
```

From this point on, we'll interact with the repository through Eclipse rather than the command line. However, in its current state, the repository is not easily available to the team. We're going to access it over SSH, which is simple and secure to setup.

Browsing Subversion from Eclipse

EasyEclipse includes both Eclipse and the **Subclipse** plugin. The latter enables Eclipse to communicate with Subversion repositories over SSH. This is the approach we're going to use.

The best way to set this up is to first create a new Eclipse project based on a checkout from a repository. We've already seen how to configure the Subversion repository for the Intranet project, setting up a trunk, branches and tags for it. In this section, we will start a new project by checking out the content of the Intranet trunk.

To make this as realistic as possible, I will be accessing the server from a separate developer machine. The steps below will still work if the Subversion server and Eclipse are on the same physical machine.

Get EasyEclipse up and running on the developer machine, then follow these steps:

Select **File | New | Project**. In the dialog box, select **SVN | Checkout Projects from SVN** as shown below:

Click on **Next >**.

The next dialog box asks for the location of the repository:

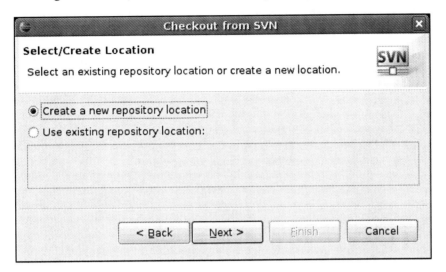

Select **Create a new repository location** and click on **Next**.

 On the Linux version of EasyEclipse that I was using, the **Next** button was disabled when I entered this dialog box (a bug). To fix this, I clicked on the other option (**Use existing repository location**), then came back to **Create a new repository location**. The **Next** button was now enabled.

In the **Url** text box of the next dialog box, enter the URL to the repository. It will look like this:

```
svn+ssh://user@x.x.x.x/repository/path/to/project/
directory
```

Where x.x.x.x is the IP address or hostname of the server, /repository is the path to the repository, and /path/to/project/directory is the path to the project directory in the repository, relative to the repository root. Note that we are using svn+ssh as the scheme for the URL: this makes use of SSH to connect to the server and start an svnserve process, which presents the repository to the user.

In our case, the client and server are on an internal network, and the client can reach the server at IP address 192.168.13.129. The repository is located on the path / repository on the team server; in addition, we want to work on the *Intranet* project, so the last part of the path should read /Intranet. Putting this all together gives the URL shown below:

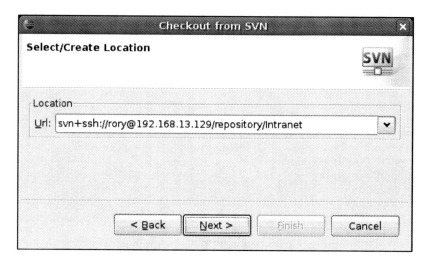

EasyEclipse now contacts the server and prompts you for the username and password for accessing the repository. Use the username and password set up in section earlier in this chapter (covering how to setup SSH users on the team server):

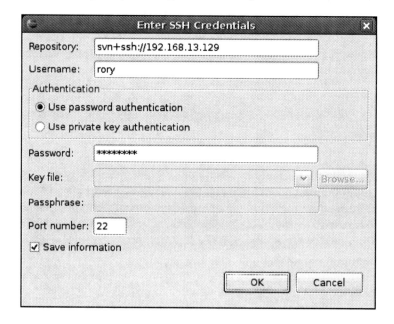

Note that the **Save information** checkbox: tick this so that there is no need to enter the password every time you check code back into the repository.

A list of the subdirectories for the *Intranet* project are now displayed. Select **trunk** and click on **Next >**.

Now, complete the final dialog box with the project details. A simple approach is to give the project a name matching the one in the repository:

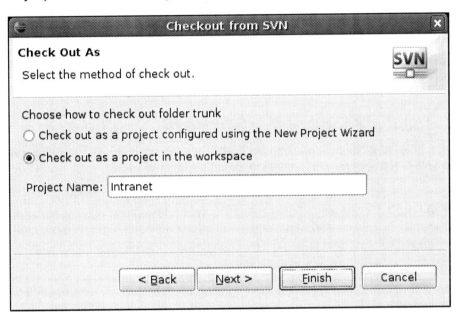

If this went smoothly, there should now be a new project in the left-hand sidebar of EasyEclipse.

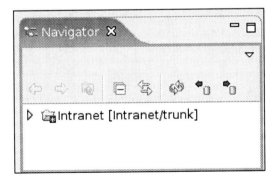

There's nothing inside the project yet, but we will be adding content over the following chapters.

Other Subversion Clients

If you are not convinced that EasyEclipse is the right Subversion client for you, or if you have non-programmers who need access to the repository, **TortoiseSVN** (`http://tortoisesvn.tigris.org/`) is a great alternative client tool for Windows. It integrates very cleanly with Explorer and makes it easy for non-technical users to work with version control.

If you are looking for a TortoiseSVN-style client for Linux, **Meld** is well worth a look (`http://meld.sourceforge.net/`).

Using Other People's Servers

If you don't have access to your own dedicated server, there is still the possibility of using external services for your development and deployment.

If you are looking for a Subversion repository, **RubyForge** (`http://rubyforge.org/`) is the main repository of Ruby and Rails related projects. Teams developing open source software can make use of their facilities to manage the project and host their code in a Subversion server. However, if you are developing proprietary code, your project will not be eligible for inclusion.

There are also commercial hosted project management solutions which may be suitable if you are not developing open source software. Try googling for *hosted subversion*.

If you are looking for a place to deploy your applications to, there are a variety of companies either providing Rails support as part of a larger offering, or providing dedicated Rails-only hosting. **Ruby On Rails Webhosting** (`http://www.rubyonrailswebhost.com/`) is one site which maintains a list of Rails-enabled hosting, along with user reviews.

Back at Acme

Acme already has a Linux server, housing a shared directory, with SSH installed for remote administration. First, they install a Rails stack, mirroring Rory's Ubuntu Linux developer machine setup. Next, they install Subversion set up user accounts for each member of the team. That's all they need to do to get up and running.

Rory and Jenny setup the repository structure for the Intranet project and configure their instances of EasyEclipse to talk to the new repository over SSH. They are now ready to start development of the Intranet application.

Summary

While Rails is easy enough to set up for a single user, there are many more choices to make when configuring Rails infrastructure for a small team. Having to cope with multiple operating systems and find productive and consistent developer tools, while catering for collaborative code development, makes requirements considerably more complex.

By choosing the proven, cross-platform, open source technologies recommended in this chapter, many of these requirements can be met at low cost and with high levels of reliability. Beyond meeting requirements, the deep integration between Rails and the suggested tools makes development more rapid and of higher quality. These are the reasons why it pays to get this right from the start.

In the next chapter, we'll start developing the *Intranet* application using these tools, demonstrating how they provide a smooth Rails development experience

4
Working with Rails

It's now time to get our hands dirty and start developing a Rails application. In Chapter 2, we saw the data structure for the *Intranet* application, which Acme plans to build. In this chapter, we'll start building this application: in effect, we will be looking over Rory's shoulder as he develops *Intranet*. For the purposes of this chapter, Linux will be used as the development platform; but as all of the tools used are cross-platform, the instructions should port easily to Windows and Mac.

Specifically, we'll focus on turning the abstract data structure for *Intranet* into a Rails application. This requires a variety of concepts and tools, namely:

- The structure of a Rails application.
- Initializing an application using the rails command.
- Associating Rails with a **database.**
- The built-in **utility scripts** included with each application.
- Using **migrations** to maintain a database.
- Building **models** and validating them.
- Using the Rails **console** to manually test models.
- Automated testing of models using **Test::Unit.**
- **Hosting a project** in a Subversion repository.
- Importing data into the application using **scripts.**

You may have noticed that we haven't mentioned much about the application's user interface. That's because we can build a large part of the application without having to code HTML. We'll see how to add a front-end in the next chapter, but for now we will concentrate on the data side of things.

The World According to Rails

To understand how Rails applications work, it helps to get under its skin: find out what motivated its development, and the philosophy behind it.

The first thing to grasp is that Rails is often referred to as *opinionated software* (see `http://www.oreillynet.com/pub/a/network/2005/08/30/ruby-rails-david-heinemeier-hansson.html`). It encapsulates an approach to web application development centered on good practice, emphasizing automation of common tasks and minimization of effort. Rails helps developers make good choices, and even removes the need to make choices where they are just distractions.

How is this possible? It boils down to a couple of things:

1. *Use of a default design for applications-*
   By making it easy to build applications using the **Model-View-Controller** (MVC) architecture, Rails encourages separation of an application's database layer, its control logic, and the user interface. Rails' implementation of the MVC pattern is the key to understanding the framework as a whole.

2. *Use of conventions instead of explicit configuration-*
   By encouraging use of a standard directory layout and file naming conventions, Rails reduces the need to configure relationships between the elements of the MVC pattern. Code generators are used to great effect in Rails, making it easy to follow the conventions.

We'll see each of these features in more detail in the next two sections.

Model-View-Controller Architecture

The original aim of the MVC pattern was to provide architecture to bridge the gap between human and computer models of data. Over time, MVC has evolved into an architecture which decouples components of an application, so that one component (e.g. the control logic) can be changed with minimal impact on the other components (e.g. the interface).

Explaining MVC makes more sense in the context of "traditional" web applications. When using languages such as PHP or ASP, it is tempting to mix application logic with database-access code and HTML generation. (Ruby, itself, can also be used in this way to write CGI scripts.) To highlight how a traditional web application works, here's a pseudo-code example:

```
# define a file to save email addresses into
email_addresses_file = 'emails.txt'
# get the email_address variable from the querystring
email_address = querystring['email_address']
```

```
# CONTROLLER: switch action of the script based on whether
# email address has been supplied
if '' == email_address
  # VIEW: generate HTML form to accept user input which
  # posts back to this script
  content = "<form method='post' action='" + self + "'>\
<p>Email address: <input type='text' name='email_address'/></p>\
<p><input type='submit' value='Save'/></p>\
</form>"
else
  # VIEW: generate HTML to confirm data submission
  content = "<p>Your email address is " + email_address + "</p>"
  # MODEL: persist data
  if not file_exists(email_addresses_file)
    create_file(email_addresses_file)
  end if
  write_to_file(email_addresses_file, email_address)
end if
print "<html><head><title>Email manager</title></head>\
<body>" + content + "</body></html>"
```

The highlighted comments indicate how the code can be mapped to elements of the
MVC architecture:

- **Model** components handle an application's state. Typically, the model does
  this by putting data into some kind of a long-term storage (e.g. database,
  filesystem). Models also encapsulate business logic, such as data validation
  rules. Rails uses **ActiveRecord** as its model layer, enabling data handling in a
  variety of relational database back-ends.

  *In the example script, the model role is performed by the section of code which saves the
  email address into a text file.*

- **View** components generate the user interface (e.g. HTML, XML). Rails uses
  ActionView (part of the **ActionPack** library) to manage generation of views.

  *The example script has sections of code to create an appropriate view, generating either an
  HTML form for the user to enter their email address, or a confirmation message acknowl-
  edging their input.*

- The **Controller** orchestrates between the user and the model, retrieving data
  from the user's request and manipulating the model in response (e.g. creating
  objects, populating them with data, saving them to a database). In the case
  of Rails, **ActionController** (another part of the **ActionPack** library) is used to
  implement controllers. These controllers handle all requests from the user,
  talk to the model, and generate appropriate views.

In the example script, the code which retrieves the submitted email address, is performing the controller role. A conditional statement is used to generate an appropriate response, dependent on whether an email address was supplied or not.

In a traditional web application, the three broad classes of behavior described above are frequently mixed together. In a Rails application, these behaviors are separated out, so that a single layer of the application (the model, view, or controller) can be altered with minimal impact on the other layers. This gives a Rails application the right mix of modularity, flexibility, and power.

Next, we'll see another piece of what makes Rails so powerful: the idea of using conventions to create associations between models, views, and controllers. Once you can see how this works, the Rails implementation of MVC makes more sense: we'll return to that topic in the section *Rails and MVC*.

Convention over Configuration

In the previous section, we met the MVC framework, used to define the general design of every Rails application. The MVC framework naturally breaks an application into three groups of components (models, views, and controllers). In the "olden" days, a web application framework would typically define relationships between these components using a configuration file (e.g. an XML file in the Struts framework). Writing this configuration file was often a laborious and error-prone task, and could take the same amount of time as writing the application code itself.

The Rails developers recognised that, most of the time, the relationships between the parts of an MVC application are obvious, repetitive, and shouldn't require configuration. There tends to be a common set of actions associated with each controller ("show a list of model instances"; "show a single model instance"; "create, update, or delete a model instance"); and developers will tend to give them similar names (list, show, delete, update, create). This realization prompted the Rails developers to create a set of conventions around how common application components are implemented: standards for class names and locations, controllers and actions, file names, and directory structure.

Rail uses these conventions to minimize the need for configuration, automatically generating much of it when the application is bootstrapped. As well as simplifying configuration, the conventions also remove the need for a developer to make certain decisions. In classical web applications, a developer would often have to decide where to put files and directories, and then have to define relationships between application elements (e.g. which views are used by which controller). By contrast, every Rails application has a familiar directory structure, automatically generated by tools; each file added to the project usually adheres to a naming standard; classes follow a similar naming convention; and there are conventions for naming and locating supporting files, like Javascripts and images. By making choices for the developer, Rails can save time (and sometimes arguments), leading to its much-touted productivity gains.

 If you need to, you can step outside the Rails conventions. Mostly, though, there is no need to, and you can greatly reduce development time by embracing the conventions instead.

Rails and MVC

At its core, the architecture of Rails is standard MVC; however, unlike older forms of MVC for the web, Rails minimizes the effort needed to maintain the MVC pattern. This is because the conventions inherent in Rails, as described in the previous section, reduce the need for configuration. The diagram, below, gives a graphical representation of how Rails implements MVC, and also summarizes how conventions are used to define the workflow of an application. Our fledgling *Intranet* application is used as an example; specifically, the page which displays a list of people:

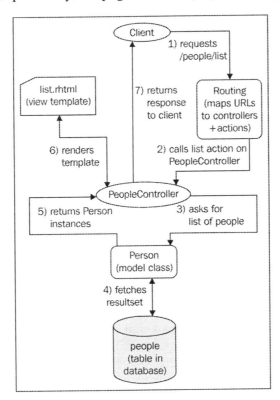

Fleshing out the steps in the diagram, here's what happens when a client requests a list of people:

1. The client asks for the URL:**/people/list**.

2. Rails' **routing** code parses the URL into a request for a particular controller, and a particular method on that controller. In this case, Rails uses a typical route to fragment the path into a controller name (*people*) and the name of a method on that controller (*list*). In this case, the following sequence is executed:

   a. An instance of the **PeopleController** class is created. Rails knows to generate an instance of this class, as it uses the first part of the path (= *people*), capitalised (= *People*), and with the string 'Controller' appended (= *PeopleController*), to determine the correct controller class to use. This returns a **PeopleController** object (which will be referred to as "the controller" from now on). This is followed by:

   b. A call to the `list` method (a.k.a. an *action*) of the controller. Again, the path is used to determine, which method to call: in this case, the second fragment of the path is **list**; hence Rails calls the **list** method.

   The routing facilities in Rails are covered in more detail in the section on *routing* in Chapter 7.

3. The `list` action of the controller uses the **find method** of the **Person** model class to query the database. Each model class provides a `find` method, which enables querying of the table associated with the model. Find methods are covered in more detail in the section on find methods in Chapter 5.

4. The **Person** class is, by convention, associated with a table called **people**. The **Person** class, therefore, generates the SQL required to retrieve a set of records from the **people** table in the back-end database.

   Note how the table name is the *pluralized, lowercase* equivalent of the model class name: *Person* associates with *people*; *Address* associates with *addresses*; *Company* associates with *companies*; etc. These relationships don't have to be specified: they are configured solely through consistent names. (It is also possible to turn pluralization off, if you want to buck these conventions.)

5. The set of records is converted into an array of `Person` instances and returned to the controller.

6. The controller uses a **view template** to create the output for the client. This output will typically be based on an HTML outline, filled out with data from the model. In our example, the template might produce an HTML table from the array of `Person` instances, one row per person, showing the name of the person and a link to their full details.

The name of the template to render for a given action is derived by convention (again), and is based on the name of the action: in this case, the action is called `list`, so Rails uses a template called **list.rhtml**. If there is no appropriate `.rhtml` file, Rails will look for a `.rxml` (Builder XML template) file instead. Views are covered in more detail in chapter.

7. The controller returns the generated HTML to the client.

As you can see, the Rails conventions enable some powerful connections between aspects of the model, view, and controller components, with no need for configuration.

The Rails "power tools" are the keys to leveraging its conventions, namely:

*   The `rails` command. This creates the "skeleton" for an application, including the directory structure, public files (like error pages and Javascripts), stubs for automated testing, plus several utility scripts. The created directories and files follow the conventions described previously.

*   The Rails *generators*. These are included with the utility scripts, and added to every new Rails application created using the `rails` command (see above). They are used to add new components to the application, such as new models or controllers, again following the naming conventions.

We'll see how to use these tools in the following sections, as we start building the *Intranet* application.

Setting Up a New Rails Application

Every Rails application looks basically the same. Each has the same directories, and even files with the same names. The reason for this is that Rails provides a command (`rails`) for creating a stock set of directories and stub files as a starting point for any new application, to be fleshed out as development progresses. These files and directories are arranged in such a way that the different parts of Rails (in fact, it is a framework of frameworks) can work together effectively. When starting a new application, running the `rails` command is the first step.

If you followed the tutorial sections in Chapter 3, you will have checked out the *Intranet* project from Subversion. This means, you already have an empty `Intranet` directory inside your Eclipse workspace, "connected" to the code repository. Rather than create a new directory for your application, you can use this existing one for your application as shown below:

```
$ cd workspace
$ rails Intranet
```

(Note that you may need to replace *workspace* with the directory you are using for your Eclipse workspace.)

More generally, use this command from a prompt to start a new Rails application in situations where you haven't created a project directory yet:

```
$ rails /path/to/application
```

Where */path/to/application* is the path to the directory where you want your application to live. If the directory doesn't exist, or if any directories in the path are missing, they are created too. If you use a non-absolute path, the directories are created below the current working directory.

Note that you must use operating-system-specific path separators, so on Windows you would do:

```
$ rails c:\path\to\application
```

When you run the `rails` command, you should see something like this:

```
$ rails Intranet
exists
create   app/controllers
create   app/helpers
create   app/models
create   app/views/layouts
create   config/environments
create   components

...

create   log/server.log
create   log/production.log
create   log/development.log
create   log/test.log
```

(This has been truncated for brevity: the `rails` command generates a *lot* of stuff.)

The absolute path to the top-level directory containing the application is referred to inside Rails as the `RAILS_ROOT` directory. In our case (as we're developing with Rory), this directory is:

```
/home/rory/workspace/Intranet
```

Rather than going into too much detail, below is a summary of what is contained in a fresh `RAILS_ROOT` directory. Directories which are particularly important are marked with an asterisk, as we'll be spending most of our time inside them:

- *app contains the core MVC classes of the application (s̶ ̶
  Rails and MVC), separated into four subdirectories:
  - ○ controllers contains controller definitions, which ha̶
    control flow of the application.
  - ○ *models hold model definitions, which act as the layer
    between the controllers and the database.
  - ○ views contains templates for generating interface elements,
    such as XHTML or XML output.
  - ○ helpers are companions to views. They are intended to move
    heavy lifting out of view templates and into "helper" methods,
    which (generally) generate HTML elements.
- Components is largely deprecated, and remains for historical reasons.
  Originally, components were intended to encapsulate reusable chunks of
  code, which could be shared across applications. They were superseded by
  plugins (see the section on plugins in Chapter 8). You can safely delete this
  directory.
- *config holds the application's configuration. Most of the time, you only
  need to worry about setting up the connection to the database (which we'll
  do in the section *Setting Up a Database Connection*, later this chapter).
- *db holds all database-related files and scripts. This includes dumps of
  the database and schema definitions. We'll be working in this directory
  throughout the chapter.
- doc holds an auto-generated API documentation for your application. This is
  covered briefly in the section introducing Rdoc in Chapter 5.
- lib holds library files, which are not necessarily Rails-specific, e.g. generic
  Ruby libraries. Any Ruby file you drop in here (anything ending in *.rb) is
  automatically loaded during your application's startup. It is most often used
  as the location for new Rake task definitions, which are added to the tasks
  sub-directory (see the bullet point below on the Rakefile).
- log holds log files for your application.
- public contains static files, such as images and Javascripts.
- *script contains helper scripts for your application, such as the interactive
  console and code generators. We'll be using these later in this chapter.
- test contains test cases for your code. Each time you auto-generate a new
  model or controller, tests are added here. Testing is covered later in
  this chapter.
- tmp contains temporary files, namely cached output, session data, and
  server sockets.

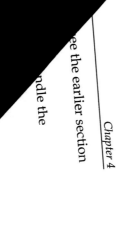

...is directory (for plugins, naturally — see the section
...is also used to store the libraries you haven't
...xternal gems).

...of your application directory contains generic
...may be installing your application. The
...doc directory is probably a better place to add
...comes part of any auto-generated documentation.

...your arsenal, enabling you to automate
...s. The `Rakefile` defines the set of tasks available
...hese include things like running your test suite,
...and clearing temporary data. You can add your
...asks.

...hopefully give some idea of what all that stuff

If you switch to Eclipse to browse your new Rails application, you might wonder where the files have gone. This is because Eclipse doesn't monitor changes to the filesystem. When we added our application files outside Eclipse (by running the `rails` command), Eclipse didn't know anything about it.

The solution is to refresh Eclipse's view of the filesystem. Right-click on the name of the project and select the **Refresh** option from the context menu. You should now be able to see your files.

Now we have a skeletal application, we are finally ready for some magic.

Using Mongrel to Serve Your Application

I expect you're dying to see your first Rails application up and running? It turns out this is no work at all. Connect into your application's directory using the command line, and run the following command:

```
$ ruby script/server
```

Or, on Windows:

```
$ ruby script\server
```

We'll be using the Linux-style syntax throughout the book when running the scripts, with forward slashes as path delimiters.

This command runs one of the Rails **built-in scripts**, located in the `script` directory, which starts a Mongrel server whose single purpose is running your Rails application.

If the server starts correctly, you should see:

```
=> Booting Mongrel (use 'script/server webrick' to force WEBrick)
=> Rails application starting on http://0.0.0.0:3000
=> Call with -d to detach
=> Ctrl-C to shutdown server
** Starting Mongrel listening at 0.0.0.0:3000
** Starting Rails with development environment...
** Rails loaded.
** Loading any Rails specific GemPlugins
** Signals ready.  TERM => stop.  USR2 => restart.  INT => stop (no
restart).
** Rails signals registered.  HUP => reload (without restart).  It might
not work well.
** Mongrel available at 0.0.0.0:3000
** Use CTRL-C to stop.
```

Note that the application is served on port 3000 by default and is accessible at the URL `http://localhost:3000/`. If you open this URL in a browser, you should see something like this:

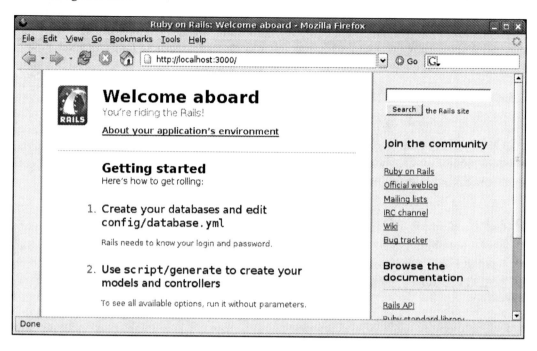

Click on the **About your application's environment** link to see some information about the versions of Ruby and Rails you are running with.

On Linux, you can dispense with the `ruby` command and just use this command to run the server:

```
$ script/server
```

The only requirement for this to work is that the script should be able to find your Ruby binary. This is defined in the shebang line (the first line of the file). Usually, the default line works correctly:

```
#!/usr/bin/env ruby
```

However, if your Ruby installation isn't in your PATH environment variable, you may have to modify the *ruby* part of this line to point at its location. For example, if your Ruby installation is in `/opt/ruby1.8.4` you would use the shebang:

```
#!/usr/bin/env /opt/ruby1.8.4/bin/ruby
```

Our application isn't too exciting so far, we can't interact with it very much, and it has little data to serve. In the next sections, we're going to build it up, taking a data-centric approach.

 As of Rails 1.2, if Mongrel is installed on your machine, it is used as the default web server for your application. However, if you don't have Mongrel installed, Mongrel isn't on your path, or you are using an older version of Rails, WEBrick is used instead. The only difference is that WEBrick is significantly slower, and not suitable for running Rails applications in a production environment. Other than that, you can happily develop an application using either.

Connecting Rails to a Database

Throughout decades of client-server computing, the architecture of database-driven applications has been designed by database administrators working in the "enterprise". This architecture places the responsibility for managing data squarely in the database itself. Applications are considered "dumb", not to be trusted with vital tasks like data validation and formatting, or managing relationships between different tables. Using this traditional architecture, we might manage our *Intranet* application's data structures (see Chapter 2) like this:

- *Stored procedures* could be used to manage complex operations on the database. For example, inserting a new person, company, and associated addresses might be done using a single call to a stored procedure. This would insert new records into the appropriate tables, manage foreign key relationships between the new records, and perform validation of data.

- *Cascade* operations could be used to manage dependencies between records in related tables. For example, if the id field of a record in the companies table changed, any references to that in the people table would be updated.

- *Views* could be used to retrieve, sort, and format data from one or more tables using a single query. In our case, a view might be used to retrieve the names, phone numbers, and website addresses from the companies table, ordered by company name.

By contrast, in the Rails view of the world, the application is king, and the database is its servant. This is due to Rails being the product of web developers: in the web development environment, databases are typically unsophisticated buckets for holding "stuff" (because they are often designed by people who aren't full-time database administrators).

However, beyond this, performing database operations through model classes simplifies database access considerably: making a change to an application can be done in the high-level application code, rather than by modifying low-level SQL code in the database layer. Therefore, operations, which would be delegated to the database in the traditional client-server architecture (such as the ones in the bullet points above) are instead handled by **ActiveRecord** in a Rails application.

ActiveRecord is a so-called **object-relational mapping (ORM) layer** (also known as a **relational persistence layer**), similar in scope to Hibernate (Java) or ADODB (PHP). Instead of dealing with the database through SQL statements, an ORM layer presents records in a database table as a series of objects; it also provides class-level methods for creating database connections, querying tables, and so on. The fields in a record are not read or written directly, but accessed through instance methods on an object. This reduces the complexity and tedium of working with a relational database, as the onus for creating database connections, correctly formatting SQL statements, escaping quote marks in strings, etc. is moved into the ORM layer, away from the developer.

Bruce Tate and Curt Hibbs call ActiveRecord an Object Relational *Wrapping* layer, rather than a *Mapping* layer: their view is that as there is no explicit configuration of the relationship between the model classes and the database tables, it doesn't count as a "mapping". They have a point, but the exact semantics aren't too important. Here, I'm treating "mapping" in the sense that objects can be mapped onto records in the database tables.

An ORM layer is one way to implement the model part of the MVC architecture, and this is the role ActiveRecord fulfils in a Rails application: it acts as the intermediary between the controller and the database, retrieving, validating, updating, and deleting records on behalf of the controller.

Before we can see how this works, we need a database to use as the back-end for our application. Setting this up is covered in the following sections.

Creating a Database and System Account

As described in Chapter 2, we're going to use MySQL as the database back-end for the *Intranet* application. If you followed the installation instructions, you should have MySQL available on your machine.

These instructions cover how to setup a database and user in MySQL. However, if you have an alternative database back-end (Oracle, SQL Server, PostgreSQL, etc.), create a database and a user with whichever tools that are appropriate for your database instead.

The first step is to initialise the MySQL database. You could use one of the MySQL GUI clients to do this, but we'll use the command line as this works the same regardless of your platform. Use this command to login to the database server on your local machine:

```
$ mysql -u root -p
```

Note that -u root specifies we are logging in as the root user: you need to use an account with sufficient privileges to create a new database. -p indicates that we intend to use a password to login. If your login is successful, you should see:

```
Welcome to the MySQL monitor.  Commands end with ; or \g.
Your MySQL connection id is 1 to server version: 5.0.24a
Type 'help;' or '\h' for help. Type '\c' to clear the buffer.

mysql>
```

Once you've logged in successfully, create a database called *intranet_development* with:

```
mysql> CREATE DATABASE intranet_development;
Query OK, 1 row affected (0.05 sec)
```

This is the database we'll be using during the development of our application. The next step is to create a user account for our Rails application. This is a good practice: instead of using a real person's account (or even worse, the *root* account) to connect our Rails application to MySQL, we will use a dedicated **system account**. This gives us a handful of security advantages:

- The system account can be given minimal permissions: just the ones the application needs to work with the database. If our application never needs to create temporary tables, we don't need to give the system account the CREATE TEMPORARY TABLES permission, for example. MySQL allows us to refine permissions further, down to the individual table and row level if required.

- We can restrict the system account's access to the Rails application's database. If the account's were compromised, the cracker's vandalism would be limited to just that database.

- We can restrict the load that the system account can put on the database service, such as the number of queries, updates, and connections the system account can make per hour. If the Rails application were hit by a denial of service attack, these settings could help limit the damage that the application can cause.

- The system account can be limited to accessing the database from a single IP domain name, IP address, or IP range. Any attempt to access the database from a machine outside the range automatically fails, further tightening our setup.

Again, you can use either a GUI tool or the command line to create the system account. Here's how to do it on the command line (once you are logged in to MySQL):

```
mysql> GRANT ALL ON intranet_development.* TO intranet@localhost
IDENTIFIED BY 'police73';

Query OK, 0 rows affected (0.01 sec)

mysql> FLUSH PRIVILEGES;

Query OK, 0 rows affected (0.00 sec)
```

This simultaneously creates the *intranet* user account and gives that user all permissions (known as *privileges* in MySQL) on the *intranet* database. The IDENTIFIED BY clause specifies the account password ('police73'). @localhost specifies the host name from which this user can access the database. If the database server is on a separate physical box from the application server, the application server's IP address or domain name should be used here. FLUSH PRIVILEGES applies the permissions to the server.

A note on permissions

In the example above, the system account is given all permissions on the database. You may not want to give your application this level of access to the database, once it is in production. MySQL makes it trivial to restrict permissions on individual tables or columns within tables and/or by SQL operation (e.g. the production system account could just be given SELECT permissions if the application just reads from the database tables).

Setting Up a Database Connection

The database connection settings for a Rails application are stored in a single file called database.yml, inside the config directory (which is in turn inside the RAILS_ROOT). The freshly-minted database.yml file (produced by the rails command) can seem a bit confusing, mainly because it contains a lot of examples and hints. However, after removing comments, it boils down to this:

```
development:
  adapter: mysql
  database: Intranet_development
  username: root
```

```
      password:
      host: localhost
    test:
      adapter: mysql
      database: Intranet_test
      username: root
      password:
      host: localhost
    production:
      adapter: mysql
      database: Intranet_production
      username: root
      password:
      host: localhost
```

This is a **YAML** (rhymes with "camel") file, which configures the database settings for each of the three Rails' environments: development, test, and production—which is explained in the next section).

YAML, ("YAML Ain't a Markup Language"), is officially described as a "data serialization language" (see, http://yaml.org/). Its purpose is comparable to that of XML: both YAML and XML are used to define configuration settings, log file formats, or other kinds of structured data. However, YAML has the following benefits over XML:

- Concise
- Easy to parse
- Easy to implement
- Human-readable

The YAML syntax used in the database.yml file defines a YAML **mapping** from keys to values. (If you've ever worked with a configuration file, the key-value concept should be familiar.) When the file is read by Rails, it is converted into a Ruby **hash** (c.f. a dictionary or associative array in other languages). The words which are flush with the left of the file ('development', 'test', 'production') are the *keys* of this top-level hash; in Ruby syntax, the hash looks like this:

```
{
  'development' => {...},
  'test' => {...},
  'production' => {...}
}
```

Underneath each of these top-level keys is a series of name-value pairs; each series is also converted into a hash. The parent key has this hash as a value. In Ruby syntax, the resulting "hash of hashes" looks like this:

```
{
  'development' => {
    'adapter' => 'mysql',
    'database' => 'Intranet_development',
    'username' => 'root',
    'password' => nil,
    'host' => 'localhost'
  },
  'test' => {...},
  'production' => {...}
}
```

(The 'test' and 'production' sections are truncated for brevity.)

Each sub-hash specifies a database configuration for one of the Rails **environments**, as described in the next section.

Configuring the Rails Environments

Rails can run an application in different modes; each mode is known as an *environment*. Each environment is kept isolated from the others, uses a different database, and handles logging and error checking differently. This makes it possible to develop your code without breaking the live application, run tests without wiping records from the live database, and run your application more efficiently in production (amongst other things).

The three environments have different purposes and characteristics:

1. **Development**
   This is the environment you use when building your application. Logging and error reporting are at their most verbose, making it simpler to track down bugs. This environment uses its own database which is kept isolated from the production database.

2. **Test**
   This environment is only normally used when running automated tests. The database for this environment is regenerated from scratch each time tests are run, by cloning the structure (not the data) of the development environment.

3. **Production**

   Rails does a lot of work behind the scenes creating classes and their methods on the fly (which is how it does the clever database reflection discussed later in this chapter). In the production environment, this work is done once when the application starts and cached to save work later (by contrast, in development, it is done on each request). Debugging and logging are also set to a minimum in this environment.

You can configure database settings by editing the section of the `database.yml` file named after the environment. For now, we'll just edit the settings for the *development* environment:

```
development:
  adapter: mysql
  database: 'intranet_development'
  username: intranet
  password: police73
  socket: /var/run/mysqld/mysqld.sock
```

> You must use spaces, not tabs, in a YAML file: attempting to use tabs in a YAML file will break it completely. For reference, so that you can recognize it in case it happens to you, here's a YAML error caused by an errant tab:
>
> ```
> /usr/lib/ruby/1.8/yaml.rb:133:in 'load': syntax error on
> line 13, col 11:
> '    adapter: mysql' (ArgumentError)
> ```

There is no need to configure the *test* and *production* databases at this point: we can leave the default settings as they are until we need these environments.

Each line of the configuration is described in more detail in the table below:

Configuration option	Example setting	Description
adapter	`mysql`	The type of database to which the application is connected.
database	`'intranet_development'`	The name of the database to use in this environment. The Rails convention is to use the suffix `_development` for the development database, and `_test` for the test database. (Note: quote marks are used around the database name as it contains an underscore: MySQL is sometimes a bit funny about underscores...)
username	`intranet`	The username for the system account.
password	`police73`	The password for the system account.
host	`localhost`	If the application needs to connect to the database server over a network, this is the hostname or IP address of the database server. Where the Rails application and the database server are running on the same machine, localhost can be used.
socket	`/var/run/mysqld/mysqd.sock`	This is an interesting setting, and one which is often overlooked. It is mainly used on *nix machines, where the database connection is made using a Unix-style socket, rather than a network (TCP) connection. In some cases, it may not be possible to create a network connection at all (TCP can be switched off on MySQL on *nix); in this case, specifying a socket location is the only option. The example setting shown here points at the default socket location on Ubuntu. See the section *Troubleshooting a MySQL Connection* for more details about sockets.

Although we are using MySQL as our database server, *ActiveRecord* supports a range of other back-ends. You can specify which by changing the `adapter` configuration option to one of these values:

- db2
- firebird
- frontbase
- oci (Oracle)
- openbase
- postgresql
- sqlite
- sqlserver
- sybase

Each adapter has its own set of configuration options: see the Rails documentation for adapter-specific details. (Chapter 3 explains how to locate the Rails documentation on your machine.)

> Some adapters have specific requirements, such as the installation of additional Ruby or native libraries. This may restrict your choice of server operating system for running your Rails application. For example, the sqlserver adapter requires the use of ODBC, which may in turn require you to install a variety of ODBC software on your application server (see `http://wiki.rubyonrails.org/rails/pages/HowtoConnectToMicrosoftSQLServerFromRailsOnLinux`). Make sure you are aware of all the pre-requisite software you need for some of the Rails database adapters.

Testing the Database Connection

It is useful to check that the database connection is working before going any further. There's an easy way to do this. Start up a Rails console session using another of the built-in scripts Rails adds to your application called the **console**. Do this using the command line, by connecting into RAILS_ROOT and running:

```
ruby script/console
```

You should see:

```
Loading development environment
>>
```

If you do, Rails has loaded your application's components correctly. The command prompt can now be used to enter commands, which directly manipulate your Rails application, without having to use a browser: very useful for general testing and tinkering. (We'll come back to the console throughout this chapter.) For now, enter this command to test your database connection:

```
>> ActiveRecord::Base.connection
```

If the database connection is working correctly, you should see:

```
=> #<ActiveRecord::ConnectionAdapters::MysqlAdapter:0xb74dbe34  ...>
```

This has been truncated, as you get a lot of detail back from the console. But providing an `ActiveRecord::ConnectionAdapters::MySQLAdapter` instance has been successfully created, you can be happy that the database connection is working.

If the database connection fails, you might see this instead:

```
Mysql::Error: Can't connect to local MySQL server through socket '/var/
run/mysql/mysqld.sock' (2)
```

...which means *the socket location is wrong.*

Or:

```
Mysql::Error: Access denied for user 'intranet'@'localhost' (using
password: YES)
```

...which means *the system account does not have access to the server and/or the database.*

The next section covers what to do if one of these errors occurs.

Troubleshooting a MySQL Connection

If you discover that your MySQL connection isn't working (see the previous section), check the following:

1. Test whether you can login to MySQL using the `mysql` command line client and the system account, as specified in your `database.yml` file. If you can login, it's likely that your `database.yml` file contains a typo in the username and/or password.

2. If you can login with the `mysql` command line client using the system account, try the command:

   ```
   USE intranet_development;
   ```

If you get an error at this point, it means the system account doesn't have the correct level of access to the database. Check the permissions granted to the system account.

3. Check that you are using the correct MySQL socket location. If you are unsure where your socket is located, login using the MySQL command line client and run this query:

```
| mysql> SHOW VARIABLES LIKE 'socket';
```

You should get back something like this:

```
+-------------------+-----------------------------------------+
| Variable_name | Value                              |
+-------------------+-----------------------------------------+
| socket       | /var/run/mysqld/mysqld.sock |
+-------------------+-----------------------------------------+
```

Now, make sure that the `socket` setting in `database.yml` matches the value of the socket variable reported by MySQL.

4. If you are connecting using a `host` option, ensure that you can connect from the application server to the database server using the `mysql` command line client. If you can connect successfully, but your Rails application can't, it may be that the `host` setting is wrong in `database.yml`.

Hopefully, you should be able to fix pretty much any MySQL connection error by following these steps.

ActiveRecord, Migrations, and Models

ActiveRecord is the ORM layer (see the section *Connecting Rails to a Database*) used in Rails. It is used by controllers as a proxy to the database tables. What's really great about this is that it protects you against having to code SQL. Writing SQL is one of the least desirable aspects of developing with other web-centric languages (like PHP): having to manually build SQL statements, remembering to correctly escape quotes, and creating labyrinthine join statements to pull data from multiple tables.

ActiveRecord does away with all of that (most of the time), instead presenting database tables through classes (a class which wraps around a database table is called a **model**) and instances of those classes (**model instances**). The best way to illustrate the beauty of ActiveRecord is to start using it.

Model == Table

The base concept in ActiveRecord is the **model**. Each model class is stored in the app/models directory inside your application, in its own file. So, if you have a model called Person, the file holding that model is in app/models/person.rb, and the class for that model, defined in that file, is called Person.

Each model will usually correspond to a table in the database. The name of the database table is, by convention, the pluralized (in the English language), lower-case form of the model's class name. (There are a few exceptions: see the section, *Many-to-many Relationships* for details.) In the case of our Intranet application, the models are organised as follows:

Table	Model class	File containing class definition (in app/models)
people	Person	person.rb
companies	Company	company.rb
addresses	Address	address.rb

We haven't built any of these yet, but we will shortly.

Which Comes First: The Model or The Table?

To get going with our application, we need to generate the tables to store data into, as shown in the previous section. It used to be at this point where we would reach for a MySQL client, and create the database tables using a SQL script. (This is typically how you would code a database for a PHP application.) However, things have moved on in the Rails world.

The Rails developers came up with a pretty good (not perfect, but pretty good) mechanism for generating databases without the need for SQL: it's called **migrations**, and is a part of ActiveRecord. Migrations enable a developer to generate a database structure using a series of Ruby script files (each of which is an individual *migration*) to define database operations. The "operations" part of that last sentence is important: migrations are not just for creating tables, but also for dropping tables, altering them, and even adding data to them.

It is this multi-faceted aspect of migrations which makes them useful, as they can effectively be used to version a database (in much the same way as Subversion can be used to version code). A team of developers can use migrations to keep their databases in sync: when a change to the database is made by one of the team and coded into a migration, the other developers can apply the same migration to *their* database, so they are all working with a consistent structure.

When you **run** a migration, the Ruby script is converted into the SQL code appropriate to your database server and executed over the database connection. However, migrations don't work with every database adapter in Rails: check the *Database Support* section of the `ActiveRecord::Migration` documentation (see Chapter 3 for instructions on how to locate it) to find out whether your adapter is supported. At the time of writing, MySQL, PostgreSQL, SQLite, SQL Server, Sybase, and Oracle were all supported by migrations.

> Another way to check whether your database supports migrations is to run the following command in the console (the output shown below is the result of running this using the MySQL adapter):
>
> ```
> >> ActiveRecord::Base.connection.supports_migrations?
> => true
> ```

We're going to use migrations to develop our database, so we'll be building the *model first*. The actual database table will be generated from a migration attached to the model.

Building a Model with Migrations

In this section, we're going to develop a series of migrations to recreate the database structure outlined in Chapter 2.

First, we'll work on a model and migration for the `people` table. Rails has a `generate` script for generating a model and its migration. (This script is in the `script` directory, along with the other Rails built-in scripts.) The script builds the model, a base migration for the table, plus scripts for testing the model. Run it like this:

```
$ ruby script/generate model Person
      exists   app/models/
      exists   test/unit/
      exists   test/fixtures/
      create   app/models/person.rb
      create   test/unit/person_test.rb
      create   test/fixtures/people.yml
      exists   db/migrate
      create   db/migrate/001_create_people.rb
```

Note that we passed the singular, uppercase version of the table name ("people" becomes "Person") to the generate script. This generates a Person model in the file app/models/person.rb; and a corresponding migration for a people table (db/migrate/001_create_people.rb). As you can see, the script enforces the naming conventions, which connects the table to the model.

The migration name is important, as it contains sequencing information: the "001" part of the name indicates that running this migration will bring the database schema up to version 1; subsequent migrations will be numbered "002...", "003..." etc., each specifying the actions required to bring the database schema up to that version from the previous one.

The next step is to edit the migration so that it will create the people table structure. At this point, we can return to Eclipse to do our editing. (Remember that you need to refresh the file list in Eclipse to see the files you just generated.)

Once, you have started Eclipse, open the file db/migrate/001_create_people.rb. It should look like this:

```
class CreatePeople < ActiveRecord::Migration
  def self.up
    create_table :people do |t|
      # t.column :name, :string
    end
  end

  def self.down
    drop_table :people
  end
end
```

This is a migration class with two class methods, self.up and self.down. The self.up method is applied when migrating *up* one database version number: in this case, from version 0 to version 1. The self.down method is applied when moving *down* a version number (from version 1 to 0).

You can leave self.down as it is, as it simply drops the database table. This migration's self.up method is going to add our new table using the create_table method, so this is the method we're going to edit in the next section.

Ruby syntax

Explaining the full Ruby syntax is outside the scope of this book. For our purposes, it suffices to understand the most unusual parts. For example, in the `create_table` method call shown above:

```
create_table :people do |t|
  t.column :title, :string
  ...
end
```

The first unusual part of this is the **block** construct, a powerful technique for creating nameless functions. In the example code above, the block is initialized by the do keyword; this is followed by a list of parameters to the block (in this case, just t); and closed by the end keyword. The statements in-between the do and end keywords are run within the context of the block.

Blocks are similar to lambda functions in Lisp or Python, providing a mechanism for passing a function as an argument to another function. In the case of the example, the method call `create_table :people` is passed to a block, which accepts a single argument, t; t has methods called on it within the body of the block. When `create_table` is called, the resulting table object is "yielded" to the block; effectively, the object is passed into the block as the argument t, and has its `column` method called multiple times.

One other oddity is the **symbol**: that's what the words prefixed with a colon are. A symbol is the name of a variable. However, in much of Rails, it is used in contexts where it is functionally equivalent to a string, to make the code look more elegant. In fact, in migrations, strings can be used interchangeably with symbols.

Converting a Data Structure into a M'

Referring back to the data structure in Chapter 2, we can b this `self.up` method:

```
def self.up
  create_table :people do |t|
    t.column :title, :string
    t.column :first_name, :string, :null
    t.column :last_name, :string, :null
    t.column :email, :string, :limit =
    t.column :telephone, :string, :li
    t.column :mobile_phone, :string
    t.column :job_title, :string
    t.column :date_of_birth, :dat'
    t.column :gender, :string, :'
```

```
        t.column :keywords, :string
        t.column :notes, :text
        t.column :address_id, :integer
        t.column :company_id, :integer
        t.column :created_at, :timestamp
        t.column :updated_at, :timestamp
    end
  end
```

Arguments to the `column` method specify the *name* of the column, the *type* of the column, and some optional parameters. For example:

```
    t.column :name, :string
```

The above line of code specifies that the table (`t`) should contain a column called *name*, which should be of data type *string*.

The extra `:limit` option passed in some of the `column` method calls, plus the various column data types, are discussed in the next section. There are a few of things to note first, though:

- There's no need to specify the `id` column for the table: Rails will infer that we need this and invisibly add the column definition for us.

- `first_name`, `last_name`, and `email` are the only columns which cannot contain null values: together they represent the minimum amount of data we need to record about a contact. We mark this by passing `:null => false` to prevent the insertion of null values into those columns.

- The `gender` column was specified in the data structure as having the MySQL data type ENUM. However, to keep the code database-agnostic, we'll create this as a one character `:string` field in the migration. We will leave management of the content of the column (i.e. it should contain "M" or "F") to the model: see the section *Checking for Inclusion in a Range of Values* for details of how we'll implement this.

- The `address_id` column references the ID column of records in the `addresses` table; the `company_id` column references the ID column of records in the `companies` table. We'll be creating the migrations for these tables and discussing how to define table-to-table relationships later in this chapter (see the section *Associations between Models*, later in this chapter).

- The `created_at` and `updated_at` columns have a special meaning in Rails: box below.

If you add a column to a table called *created_at, created_on, updated_at,* or *updated_on,* Rails will automatically record a timestamp against records in that table without you having to do any extra work:

*_on: When a record is created or updated, the current date is automatically recorded in this column. Give a column with this name a data type of `:date`.

*_at: When a record is created, the current date and time are automatically recorded in this column. Give a column with this name a data type of `:timestamp`.

Defining Columns in Migrations

When using migrations, bear in mind that a migration is (by design) a *database-agnostic representation* of a database. It uses generic data types for columns, like `:binary` and `:boolean`, to define the kind of data to be stored in a column.

However, different database servers implement the migration column types in different ways. For example, MySQL doesn't have a boolean data type; so any migration columns you define as `:boolean` are actually converted into `TINYINT(1)` fields in the resulting MySQL database table (0 = false, 1 = true). Each migration column type also has a range of extra options you can set, which again modify the definition of the resulting field in the MySQL database.

The table below summarizes the migration column types, how they map to MySQL field data types, and the extra options available.

Migration column type...	Converts to MySQL field type...	Available options[1]
:binary	TINYBLOB, BLOB, MEDIUMBLOB, or LONGBLOB[2]	:limit => 1 to 4294967296 (default = 65536)[2]
:boolean	TINYINT(1)	-
:date	DATE	-
:datetime	DATETIME	-
:decimal	DECIMAL	:precision => 1 to 63 (default = 10) :scale => 0 to 30 (default = 0)[3]
:float	FLOAT	-
:integer	INT	:limit => 1 to 11 (default = 11)

Migration column type...	Converts to MySQL field type...	Available options[1]
:primary_key	INT(11) AUTO_INCREMENT PRIMARY KEY	-
:string	VARCHAR	:limit => 1 to 255 (default = 255)
:text	TINYTEXT, TEXT, MEDIUMTEXT, or LONGTEXT[2]	:limit => 1 to 4294967296 (default = 65536)[2]
:time	TIME	-
:timestamp	DATETIME	-

All column types accept a :null or :default option:

- :null
  The default value for this is *true* (i.e. the field's value can be null in the database). Set :null => false if you don't want to allow nulls in the database field, e.g.

  - t.column :first_name, :string, :null => false

Note that if you allow nulls in a field (:null => true or not specified), you don't need to specify :default => NULL: NULL is already the default for a field, which allows null values.

- :default
  Specify the default value for the database field when new records are added to the table. The value you specify should be of the correct data type for the *column*, e.g.

  - t.column :completed, :default => true (for a :boolean column)

  - t.column :size, :default => 1 (for an :integer column)

  - t.column :name, :default => 'Unknown' (for a :string column)

  - t.column :reminder_on, :default => Time.now (for a :datetime, :date, :time or :timestamp column)

Note that the default value should match the data type of the *column* (not the *field*). For example, if you were using MySQL and had a :boolean column, even though boolean fields are represented internally in MySQL as 1 digit TINYINT fields, you would specify the :default as *true* or *false* (not 1 or 0). This keeps your migrations portable to other database back-ends (for example, while MySQL just emulates booleans, some database back-ends have a native boolean data type, and a value of 1 or 0 might not make sense).

The :limit option on a :blob or :text column specifies the size of the database field in bytes. You can set this directly in bytes, or use a convenience method to specify the size, e.g. 2.kilobytes, 2.megabytes, 2.gigabytes(!). Note that MySQL will actually create a field with a data type, which encompasses the size you specify, i.e.

- 1 to 256 bytes: TINYBLOB or TINYTEXT
- 257 to 65536 bytes (64KiB): BLOB or TEXT
- 65537 to 16777216 bytes (16 MiB): MEDIUMBLOB or MEDIUMTEXT
- 16777217 to 4294967296 bytes (4 GiB): LONGBLOB or LONGTEXT

The :precision option specifies the number of digits to store before the point in a decimal; the :scale option specifies the number of digits to store after the decimal point.

Here are some examples of how to use these options:

```
# column to store uploaded images up to 2Mb in size
t.column :image, :blob, :limit => 2.megabytes

# column to store prices (6 digits before decimal point, 2 after)
t.column :price, :decimal, :precision => 6, :scale => 2

# column to store whether someone's account is active (defaults to
false)
t.column :account_active, :boolean, :default => false

# column to store someone's birth date (must not be null)
t.column :birth_date, :date, :null => false
```

Other Operations Available in a Migration

Migrations can be used to perform operations other than table creation. A complete list is available in the documentation for ActiveRecord::Migration, but here are examples of the more useful ones:

- `create_table(table_name, options)`
  We've already used `create_table`; but it's worth mentioning here that you can optionally pass extra arguments to this method, for example:

  ```
  # drop any existing people table and recreate from scratch
  create_table(:people, :force => true)

  # create a table with table type "MyISAM" (Rails defaults to InnoDB)
  # using a UTF-8, case-insensitive collation (NB this is
  # MySQL-specific, but the :options argument can be
  # used to pass any other database-specific table creation SQL)
  create_table(:people, :options =>
                          'ENGINE MyISAM COLLATE utf8_unicode_ci')

  # rename the primary key to pid (if you don't want or haven't
  # got an ID field in the table)
  create_table(:people, :primary_key => 'pid')
  ```

- `rename_table(old_table_name, new_table_name)`
  Change the name of the table called `old_table_name` to `new_table_name`.

- `add_column(table_name, column_name, column_type, column_options)`
  This command is similar to the column method we've used already: `column_name`, `column_type`, and `column_options` follow the principles described in the section Defining Columns in Migrations.

- `remove_column(table_name, column_name)`
  Remove the column `column_name` from the table `table_name`.

> As mentioned in the sample code above, the default engine used for a table is **InnoDB** (which supports foreign keys and transactions). However, InnoDB is not supported by default on all MySQL servers; or it may be that you want to use **MyISAM** tables (which are optimised for many-read situations) instead. In these situations, you can use the `:options` argument to `create_table` to force the table type to MyISAM (see the sample code above).

Running a Migration

A complete migration can be applied to the development database from the command line (inside your application's RAILS_ROOT directory):

```
$ rake db:migrate
```

When you run this command, Rails does the following:

1. It checks the current version of the database. This is stored in an auto-generated table called schema_info in the database, containing a single record with a single field, version. The value of this field is the current version of the database. If the schema_info table doesn't exist, it is created the first time you run a migration.

2. The migrations available in db/migrate are checked. Any migrations with version numbers higher than the version stored in the schema_info table are applied, lowest-numbered first.

3. The database version number is updated in schema_info.

If the command completes successfully, you should see this:

```
$ rake db:migrate
(in /home/rory/workspace/Intranet)
== CreatePeople: migrating ===========================================
-- create_table(:people)
   -> 0.5130s
== CreatePeople: migrated (0.5158s) ===================================
```

You can check the table looks right using the command line MySQL client:

```
mysql> describe intranet_development.people;
```

Field	Type	Null	Key	Default	Extra
id	int(11)	NO	PRI	NULL	auto_increment
title	varchar(255)	YES		NULL	
first_name	varchar(255)	NO		NULL	
last_name	varchar(255)	NO		NULL	
email	varchar(100)	NO		NULL	
telephone	varchar(50)	YES		NULL	
mobile_phone	varchar(50)	YES		NULL	
job_title	varchar(255)	YES		NULL	
date_of_birth	date	YES		NULL	

```
+--------------+--------------+------+-----+---------+----------------+
| Field        | Type         | Null | Key | Default | Extra          |
+--------------+--------------+------+-----+---------+----------------+
| gender       | varchar(1)   | YES  |     | NULL    |                |
| keywords     | varchar(255) | YES  |     | NULL    |                |
| notes        | text         | YES  |     | NULL    |                |
| address_id   | int(11)      | YES  |     | NULL    |                |
| company_id   | int(11)      | YES  |     | NULL    |                |
| created_at   | datetime     | YES  |     | NULL    |                |
| updated_at   | datetime     | YES  |     | NULL    |                |
+--------------+--------------+------+-----+---------+----------------+
16 rows in set (0.01 sec)
```

Finally, we have a database table our application can work with!

Rake

Rake is a Ruby build tool used extensively in Rails. It is similar in scope to *Ant* for Java or *make* for C/C++ etc.: a tool designed for automating repetitive tasks around software development. In the case of Rake, this includes running tests, deploying code, maintaining the database, generating documentation, and reporting code statistics.

Rather than attempting to list everything Rake does, we will introduce individual tasks (that's what db:migrate is, a task) as they become useful. If you are incurably curious about what Rake can do for your Rails application, you can see a list of all the available tasks with the command rake -T.

Rolling Back to a Previous Version of the Database

If your table looks wrong, you can roll back to a table-free database with this command:

```
$ rake db:migrate VERSION=0
```

Once you get working with migrations, you can replace the "0" in the above command with another version of the database, to either roll forward or back to that version. For example, if you are at version 2 and you run `rake db:migrate VERSION=4`, Rails will upgrade the database schema from version 2 to 4.

The Scaffold

Rails is supposed to be a rapid application development environment, but so far we just have a back-end database. To get some instant front-end delight, we'll use another Rails feature called **scaffolding**.

Scaffolding is a monstrously fast and terribly tempting short-cut to create an interface for a model. It can be used to near-instantly (literally) generate some boiler plate pages for performing **CRUD** (Create, Retrieve, Update, Delete) operations on a database table (via a model). The code is basic and crude, and the interface is ugly as sin; but with minuscule effort, the scaffold enables you to knock together a simple administrative back-end for a database table within seconds.

The scaffold is also a useful learning tool, as it demonstrates the minimum amount of code you need to write in your own controllers. It is also useful in situations where you might be the only person who ever administers the database: if it doesn't need to be fancy, the scaffold plus a few tweaks is a great way to quickly create the administrator views.

To generate a scaffold, you simply need to specify the name of the model you want to scaffold for. In our case, the model is called *Person*. Therefore, from inside RAILS_ROOT, we would run:

```
$ ruby script/generate scaffold Person
```

This produces quite a few files, including controller classes and view templates for all the CRUD actions on that model. Using this generated interface, we can now add records to the `people` table in our database.

To do this, we need to start our application:

```
$ ruby script/server
```

Then browse to `http://localhost:3000/people` to see the application in its full glory:

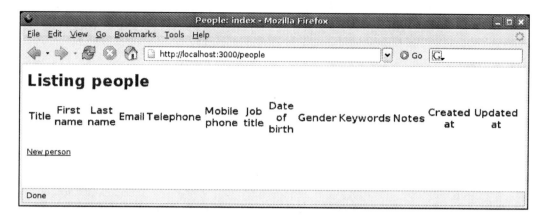

I warned you it would be ugly. But the point is, we now have a working administrative interface, which (with a bit of spit and polish) Rory could show to his colleagues at Acme.

Feel free to play around, but bear in mind we are in the development database, and will likely be destroying all the data at some point by running migrations backwards and forwards.

Alternatives to the basic scaffold

If the scaffold is simply too ugly for you to look at, you could try one of the prettier (but more complicated) alternatives:

The **Ajax Scaffold Generator** (`http://ajaxscaffold.com/`) provides virtually the same functionality as the default scaffold, but wraps it in a more responsive interface. It also has enhanced facilities for editing records in one table which are associated with another table (see the section *Associations Between Models*).

Streamlined (`http://streamlined.relevancellc.com/`) is a framework for generating an administrative back-end for a set of Rails model classes. The resulting interface is very rich in functionality and much smoother to use than the scaffold. Streamlined also provides a declarative language for specifying the layout of the administrative interface, how relationships between models are displayed in the interface, plus an authentication framework. On the negative side, the documentation is practically non-existent, and it may well be difficult to figure out how to configure the generated code.

We'll go into scaffolding in more detail in the next chapter. Through the rest of this chapter, we'll see how to build up the models associated with our new database tables.

Completing the Database

The migration we created previously in this chapter built just one of the tables in our database. Referring back to the data structure we designed in Chapter 2, there are two more database tables to add: companies and addresses. The next two sections give a brief overview of how to create these using migrations. In both cases, the migrations are simple and don't require any commands we haven't already encountered.

The companies Table

Create the model and migration for the companies table from the command line with:

```
$ ruby script/generate model Company
```

Edit db/migrate/002_create_companies.rb and insert this code:

```
class CreateCompanies < ActiveRecord::Migration
  def self.up
    create_table :companies do |t|
      t.column :name, :string, :null => false
      t.column :telephone, :string, :limit => 50
      t.column :fax, :string, :limit => 50
      t.column :website,  :string
      t.column :address_id, :integer
      t.column :created_at, :timestamp
      t.column :updated_at, :timestamp
    end
  end
  def self.down
    drop_table :companies
  end
end
```

The addresses Table

Create the model and migration for the addresses table from the command line with:

```
$ ruby script/generate model Address
```

Edit db/migrate/003_create_addresses.rb and insert this code:

```ruby
class CreateAddresses < ActiveRecord::Migration
  def self.up
    create_table :addresses do |t|
      t.column :street_1, :string, :null => false
      t.column :street_2, :string
      t.column :street_3, :string
      t.column :city, :string
      t.column :county, :string
      t.column :post_code, :string, :limit => 10, :null => false
      t.column :created_at, :timestamp
      t.column :updated_at, :timestamp
    end
  end

  def self.down
    drop_table :addresses
  end
end
```

Generating the Remaining Tables

Applying the migrations to the database is done via the command line with:

```
$ rake db:migrate
(in /home/demo/workspace/Intranet)
== CreateCompanies: migrating =======================================
-- create_table(:companies)
   -> 0.5015s
== CreateCompanies: migrated (0.5022s) ==============================

== CreateAddresses: migrating =======================================
-- create_table(:addresses)
   -> 0.2078s
== CreateAddresses: migrated (0.2089s) ==============================
```

Note that this creates both of the tables: Rails recognizes that our database is at version 1, meaning there are migrations for versions 2 and 3 to be applied.

You can use your MySQL client to check the generated tables. If you've made a mistake, you can roll back to a previous version of the database using:

```
$ rake db:migrate VERSION=1
```

(Replace "1" with the migration number you want to roll back to—see the section *Rolling Back to a Previous Version of the Database* for more details.)

With our database completed, we are now ready to look at fleshing out the basic models, adding validation and table-to-table relationships.

Models in Detail

ActiveRecord models are very powerful: they give you a great deal of control over how data is inserted into the database. As mentioned previously, they act as wrappers around your database tables: instead of writing a SQL statement to perform operations on a table, you create **instances** of ActiveRecord **model classes**, modify their properties, and then save them. ActiveRecord handles the SQL generation and execution in the background, so you don't have to write SQL by hand (though you can if you need to). You can also manage **associations** between tables using convenience methods on your models which removes much of the complexity it normally entails.

In this section, we will look at these aspects of models:

- Using **finders** to pull information out of tables.
- How Rails maps model **attributes** onto fields in database tables.
- Writing **validation** code for models.
- Defining **associations** between models.
- Using **unit tests** to ensure models and associations behave correctly.

 We'll only scratch the surface of ActiveRecord, as it would be impossible to cover all of its features in a short chapter. However, you will get an overview of what's available, and hints about where to find more information if you need it.

Creating New Records in a Table via Models

In this section, we'll be manipulating our models using the Rails **console** (command line with the Rails environment loaded). This helps enforce the separation between models and other components: by ignoring the graphical interface, we can concentrate on implementing business logic. This approach doesn't necessarily suit every type of application: for example, where work-flow is complicated and you aren't clear what the business rules are, exploring the interface using paper prototypes can help clarify what the application should do. As Rory and Jenny have a clear idea of what the *Intranet* application should do, a data-centric approach makes sense.

The first step is to start the console:

```
$ ruby script/console
Loading development environment.
>>
```

At the moment, we don't have any records in the database. We can use the console to add a few to the `people` table; at the same time, we can get an insight into how ActiveRecord operates.

If we're adding records to the `people` table, we need to create instances of the `Person` model class like this:

```
>> me = Person.new
=> #<Person:0xb7492134 @new_record=true, @attributes={"updated_at"=>nil,
"title"=>nil, "notes"=>nil, "gender"=>nil, "address_id"=>nil, "company_
id"=>nil, "date_of_birth"=>nil, "telephone"=>nil, "first_name"=>"",
"last_name"=>"", "created_at"=>nil, "keywords"=>nil, "mobile_phone"=>nil,
"email"=>""}>
```

What happened here? We created a new `Person` instance by calling the `new` method on the `Person` class. The console shows us the return value from each command we enter: in this case, the `new` method returns a `Person` instance, represented by `#<Person:...>`. The character string `0xb7492134` is just an internal identifier for the object, used by Ruby.

Note that this new instance has an **instance variable** called `@attributes`; this is simply a hash, where the keys are the names of the fields in the people table (`"gender"`, `"title"`, `"notes"` etc.); and the values of the keys are the current settings for those attributes (all `nil` at the moment). If we saved this model instance to the database now, we'd end up with a record full of empty fields. Instead, let us set some field values then save the record:

```
>> me.first_name = 'Elliot'
=> "Elliot"
>> me.last_name = 'Smith'
=> "Smith"
>> me.save
=> true
```

Here we are calling some of the instance methods ActiveRecord added to the `Person` class. Each attribute in the `@attributes` hash has a corresponding so-called "setter" method, which can be used to set the value of an attribute. The value you pass to the setter should match the database field type: strings for VARCHAR and TEXT fields, dates for DATE fields, integers for INT fields, etc.

At the end of the sequence of commands above, the `save` method is called to save the record to the database. (If you are curious, you can use your MySQL client to check that the record has been inserted.)

You may be thinking that you can see what cleverness ActiveRecord is up to by looking at the `Person` model class. Let's open it up in Eclipse. All the model files are stored in the `app/models` directory; the `Person` model is in the file called `person.rb` and looks like this:

```
class Person < ActiveRecord::Base
end
```

In fact, none of the setter methods on the class are visible in the source code: they are all being added by ActiveRecord behind the scenes. A set of methods for accessing attributes of a model instance ("getters") has also been added:

```
>> me.first_name
=> "Elliot"
>> me.last_name
=> "Smith"
```

The `update_attributes` method added by ActiveRecord enables multiple attributes to be updated simultaneously from a hash, where the keys are the names of the fields. The update is followed by a save to the database:

```
>> me.update_attributes(:email => "elliot@example.com", :title => "Dr.")
=> true
```

(This is used extensively in Rails to save values from submitted forms into the database.)

Other useful methods are the **find*** variants ("finders"), which warrant their own section (next).

Finders

ActiveRecord includes a range of methods for retrieving records from the database, known as **finder methods**. Each time you create a model class, these methods become available to that class; so each of *our* classes already has this capability.

Finders, like the attribute setters and getters of the previous sections, insulate the developer from writing SQL. They can be used to retrieve individual records, a whole set of records, or subsets of the records in a table. While working with ActiveRecord from the console, finders can be useful for retrieving records to work with.

We're going to use the console in the next few sections (start it with `ruby script/console` from inside your `RAILS_ROOT` directory). It is also useful if you have some records to experiment with: use the instructions in the previous section to insert a few.

Finding All of the Records in a Table

The simplest form of finder is the one which returns all of the records in a table:

```
>> results = Person.find :all
=> [#<Person:0xb7433d78 ...>, #<Person:0xb7433d3c ...>,
#<Person:0xb7433d00 ...>, #<Person:0xb7433cc4 ...>, #<Person:0xb7433c88
...>]
```

(Again, output is truncated for brevity.)

This finder returns an array of model instances; in this case, instances of our `Person` class. We can iterate through these with the standard array methods provided by Ruby, e.g.

```
>> results.each { |record| puts record.last_name }
Harker
Smith
Smith
Junket
Tribble
```

> The command line used above:
>
> `results.each { |record| puts record.first_name }`
>
> is a short-hand *block* syntax understood by Ruby. The `each` method effectively calls the block once for every element of the array, passing the element into the block as the `record` argument.
>
> We have already seen the longer block syntax in the section *Building a Model with Migrations*, where it was used to define a migration.

It is also possible to limit the number of records returned, e.g. to return the first 5 records (when the *people* table is ordered by *id*):

```
>> Person.find :all, :limit => 5
```

Or to get a subset of records starting at some offset:

```
>> Person.find :all, :limit => 5, :offset => 5
```

The above gets records 6-10 from the *people* table (ordered by the *id* field).

Virtual Attributes

ActiveRecord provides a default getter method for each attribute of a model class; these attributes get mapped onto fields in the database table. However, there are some situations where the default getters and setters are inadequate. For example, if you want to provide an alternative representation of a field or combine multiple real attributes into a single output attribute, you might need a custom getter.

In Rails, a pseudo-field derived from other real fields is referred to as a **virtual attribute**: while it is derived from and accessed in the same way as actual field values in the database table, a virtual attribute doesn't have a corresponding field of its own.

We'll write a `full_name` method, which will concatenate a person's title, first name, and last name into a formatted string. We also need to cope with situations where `title` has not been set, as it is not a required attribute:

```
class Person < ActiveRecord::Base
  # ... other methods ...
  def full_name
    out = (title.blank? ? '' : title + ' ')
    out + first_name + ' ' + last_name
  end
end
```

We'll make use of this in the next few sections when displaying records we retrieve.

Sorting Records

If we want to order the records, we can do this by passing an extra argument to the `find` method call:

```
>> results = Person.find :all, :order => 'last_name DESC'
...
>> results.each { |record| puts record.full_name }
Mrs. Jo Harker
Ms. Sarah Junket
Mr. Frank Smith
Dr. Elliot Smith
Mr. Jeff Tribble
```

Notice that the records are now ordered in descending order by last name (which is why Frank Smith comes before Elliot Smith); you can specify ASC to sort in ascending order (the default, if you specify neither ASC or DESC). You can pass any SQL fragment, which would ordinarily follow the ORDER BY keywords in a SQL statement, e.g.

```
>> results = Person.find :all, :order => 'last_name, first_name'
...
>> results.each { |record| puts record.full_name }
Mrs. Jo Harker
Ms. Sarah Junket
Dr. Elliot Smith
Mr. Frank Smith
Mr. Jeff Tribble
```

(Sorting by last name in ascending order, then by first name in ascending order where records have matching last names.)

Finding a Single Record

We can find a single record by ID:

```
>> Person.find 4
=> #<Person:0xb74a91d4 ...>
```

Note that this doesn't return an array, but a single instance of the Person model class.

What ActiveRecord does in the background is execute the following MySQL query:

```
SELECT * FROM people WHERE (people.id = 4) LIMIT 1;
```

In some cases, you won't want to use all of the fields in the table. You can improve the efficiency of your queries by just returning the fields you need using the :select option:

```
>> Person.find 4, :select => 'first_name'
=> #<Person:0xb74d8604 @attributes={"first_name"=>"Sarah"}>
```

In this example, the query is restricted to just returning the first_name field. Note that you will need to retrieve a person's ID if you want to be able to save the model instance back to the database. Also note the :select will work with find :all, too.

We can also retrieve an array of records with specific IDs:

```
>> Person.find [1,3]
=> [#<Person:0xb74a3d4c ...>, #<Person:0xb74a3d10 ...>]
```

Finding Records Matching Search Criteria

One method for finding records by criteria is by passing a :conditions option to find. For example, to find the first person with the last name "Junket":

```
>> Person.find :first, :conditions => "last_name = 'Junket'"
```

Or to find everyone with the surname "Smith":

```
>> Person.find :all, :conditions => "last_name = 'Smith'"
```

The :conditions option can also be passed an array, consisting of a SQL "template" as the first element, followed by the values to substitute into the template:

```
>> Person.find :all, :select => 'last_name, first_name',
:conditions => ["last_name = ?", 'Smith']
=> [#<Person:0xb74556ec ...>, #<Person:0xb74556b0...>]
```

Note what we've done here is passed an array to the :conditions find option, with a template and a substitution:

```
:conditions => ["last_name = ?", 'Smith']
```

The template should be a SQL fragment, suitable for placing after the WHERE clause in a SQL query. Any values to be substituted are represented by question marks (?) in the template. The :conditions array can be as complex as you want:

```
>> Person.find :all, :conditions => ["date_of_birth < ? AND last_name =
?", 20.years.ago, 'Smith']
=> [#<Person:0xb741da58...>]
```

This finds everyone born more than 20 years ago with the last name "Smith".

 By using the template plus substitutions format for conditions, we don't have to worry about correctly escaping strings in our SQL query, as ActiveRecord does it for us; we can also be assured that ActiveRecord will sanitize any values substituted into the SQL string, helping prevent SQL injection attacks.

It is also possible to use LIKE statements as :conditions to perform wild-card matches. However, note that these aren't as platform-portable as the above SQL statements. For example, to perform case-insensitive matches in PostgreSQL, you have to use the ILIKE keyword (rather than LIKE); while MySQL defaults to case-insensitive matching.

In the case of MySQL, we can do a wild-card match using `LIKE` with this syntax (to get everyone whose first name starts with "j" or "J"):

```
>> results = Person.find :all, :conditions => "first_name LIKE 'j%'"
...
>> results.each { |record| puts record.full_name }
Mr. Jeff Tribble
Mrs. Jo Harker
```

Finding Records Using Attribute-Based Finders

ActiveRecord provides one further set of conveniences for finding records: **dynamic attribute-based finders**. This mouthful means that you can make up finders based on field names in the table, on the fly. For example, to get all the people in the database with the first name "Elliot".

```
>> Person.find_by_first_name 'Elliot'
```

You can also specify multiple fields to filter on by joining the names of the fields with "and", e.g. to get everyone with the first name "Elliot" and last name "Smith":

```
>> Person.find_by_first_name_and_last_name 'Elliot', 'Smith'
```

By default, dynamic finders will return a single record; but they can also return an array by using `find_all_by`, instead of `find_by`:

```
Person.find_all_by_last_name "Smith"
```

Note that you can also pass standard finder options to dynamic finders, like `:select` and `:conditions`:

```
>> Person.find_by_first_name 'Elliot', :select => 'first_name'
>> Person.find_by_last_name 'Smith', :conditions => ['date_of_birth < ?',
20.years.ago], :select => 'first_name'
```

Finding Records by Raw SQL

One last resort for performing queries is to pass the raw SQL to ActiveRecord yourself. Instead of using the standard `find` method, you create the SQL "manually" (as you would if crafting a PHP application without an ORM layer). You then execute this string using the `find_by_sql` method:

```
>> Person.find_by_sql "SELECT first_name FROM people"
```

Note that `find_by_sql` returns an array of instances.

 In some situations, a call to `find_by_sql` is far faster than the standard `find` method. This is because ActiveRecord doesn't need to inspect the model classes to work out which fields are in the table and then generate the SQL. Instead, you are removing a chunk of processing time by doing the dirty work yourself. This approach is worth considering where your application has database bottlenecks or where it has many large tables.

Writing a Custom Finder

Don't forget that you can add your own finder-style methods to your class for extra convenience, too. In our *Intranet* application, we are very often going to want to get a list of everyone in the *people* table, sorted by name. We can write a wrapper round `find` to do this, inside the `Person` class:

```
class Person
  ...
  def self.find_all_ordered
    find :all, :order => 'last_name, first_name'
  end
end
```

Specifying a method name starting with the keyword `self` creates a new class-level method. We can call it like this:

```
>> results = Person.find_all_ordered
...
>> results.each { |record| puts record.full_name }
Mrs. Jo Harker
Ms. Sarah Junket
Dr. Elliot Smith
Mr. Frank Smith
Mr. Jeff Tribble
```

(This is the same output as when we used `find` in the section *Sorting Records*.)

Viewing the SQL

ActiveRecord does a lot of work in the background creating SQL statements for you. If you are curious about what ActiveRecord is doing, you can see the SQL statements in their raw form by reading the RAILS_ROOT/log/development.log file. For example, here's what Person.find :all gets translated into by Rails:

```
[4;36;1mPerson Load  (0.002825) [0m   [0;1mSELECT * FROM people [0m
```

The unusual characters are in the output ("[4;36;1m", "[0m" etc.), are colorization specifications, so that in editors which are capable of understanding ANSI colorization codes, you get different colors for different elements of the log. My preference is to turn off colorization by adding this line to the bottom of the config/environment.rb file:

```
ActiveRecord::Base.colorize_logging = false
```

This gives you far more sensible log output:

```
Person Load (0.000403)   SELECT * FROM people
```

The important part of this, besides the SQL statement, is the number between the brackets. This shows the length of time (in seconds) that the query took to execute.

Looking at the raw SQL queries can sometimes help identify problems with badly-formatted queries, or where large inefficient queries are being generated, which could be slimmed down using find_by_sql. We'll have more to say about the logs in the section on logging in chapter 6.

In the *production* environment, logging of SQL queries is turned off by default-you need to be in the *development* environment to see these messages.

Viewing Logs in Eclipse

Unfortunately, if you are looking at logs in Eclipse, you may find that the log file opens in an external editor. You can setup Eclipse to open them instead as follows:

1. Go to the **Window** menu and select **Preferences**.

2. In the **Preferences** dialog box, go to **General | Editors | File Associations**:

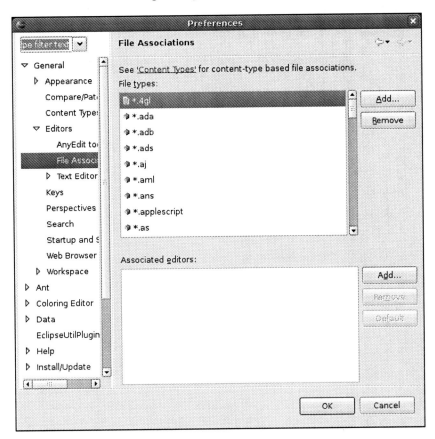

3. Click the **Add** button to add a new file association.

4. Enter *.log for the **File type** field:

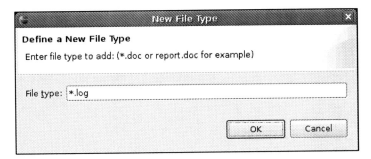

5. Click **OK**.

6. Click on **Add** (next to the **Associated editors** field) to setup an editor for this file type.

7. In the **Editor Selection** dialog, select the **SQL Text Editor** option:

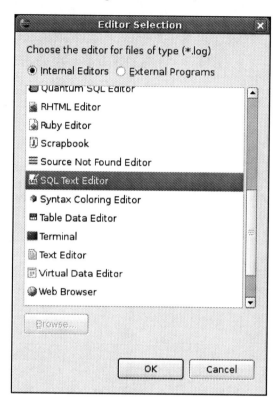

This editor does a decent job of highlighting SQL code, while leaving the rest of the logs readable. If you don't have the **SQL Text Editor**, choose **Text Editor** instead.

8. Click **OK**.

9. In the **Preferences** dialog, click **OK**.

The association should now be set up. Try opening a log file in Eclipse to check if it works.

Validation

The models we developed in the previous sections are working how we intended: we can insert new records into the database and retrieve them again. However, the current models do nothing to validate our input, making it possible to add new records where all of the fields contain empty strings. This is despite the fact that we specified that some fields in the database tables could not be set to null, as ActiveRecord automatically sets any unset string attributes to the empty string. MySQL treats an empty string differently from NULL; so a record with empty strings for the `first_name`, `last_name`, or `email` field is acceptable to MySQL when it is inserted. In the case of the *Intranet* application, this could mean many contact records without contact information.

Validation of data input is another aspect of ActiveRecord. In traditional web applications, validation can be cumbersome, to say the least. ActiveRecord provides a framework which makes validation virtually trivial. The validation framework handles validation in the model, independently of the front-end, so we can modify our models and test our validations using the console. We will also be using unit tests to verify our validation code wherever necessary (see the Testing section later in this chapter), rather than by manually testing through a front-end.

We'll take a look at validation in the context of the *Intranet* application, rather than in the abstract. We can set up most of the required validations using the `validates_*` methods in ActiveRecord, a whole family of methods for appending validation code to models. We will be using the most common and useful ones, demonstrating in detail how they can be applied to our `Person` model class.

We will also see how to add more complex custom validation to models, to capture situations not covered by the macro methods; then add validation to our other two models (`Company` and `Address`).

Validating People

Recall that in our data structure (see Chapter 2) we specified that each person added to the `people` table had to meet the following validation criteria:

- `first_name` and `last_name` should not be empty.

- `email` should be a valid email address and unique to this person.

- `gender` should be set to "M" or "F".

- `address_id` and `company_id` should reference records in the appropriate tables.

We can apply these validations by adding checks on the attributes of instances of the
`Person` model, as follows:

Checking for Empty Field Values

Use the `validates_presence_of` method for this. The validation code is added to
the class definition, inside the `app/models/*.rb` files. In the case of the `Person` class,
it goes in `app/models/person.rb`:

```
class Person < ActiveRecord::Base
  validates_presence_of :first_name,
   :message => "Please enter a first name"
  validates_presence_of :last_name,
   :message => "Please enter a last name"

  ...
end
```

`validates_presence_of` is actually a method call on the `Person` class, which adds
new instance methods to the class. The new instance methods are automatically
called when a record is created or updated. In this case, they check that the specified
attributes (`first_name` and `last_name`) contain non-blank values (i.e. not nil or the
empty string).

A symbol representing the name of the attribute (e.g. `:first_name`, `:last_name`)
is the first argument passed to the method. The second `:message` argument used in
the code above is optional; if you leave it off, ActiveRecord will use a default error
message. In the case of `validates_presence_of`, the default message is:

```
"<attribute> can't be blank"
```

You can restrict when validations are applied using an optional `:on` argument, e.g:

```
# validate when creating new records and updating existing records
# (this is the default)
validates_presence_of :first_name, :on => :save
# ONLY validate when creating new records
validates_presence_of :first_name, :on => :create
# ONLY validate when updating existing records
validates_presence_of :first_name, :on => :update
```

The `:on` option is available on all of the `validates_*` methods covered here.
However, in the *Intranet* application, we can just use the default behavior, and
validate on both creation of new records and updates to existing ones.

To test your validation code, use the console:

```
>> p = Person.new
=> #<Person:0xb7436850 ...>
>> p.save
=> false
>> p.errors
#<Person:0xb7436850 @new_record=true, @errors=#<ActiveRecord::
Errors:0xb74349d8 @errors={"first_name"=>["Please enter a first name"],
"last_name"=>["Please enter a last name"]} ...>
```

The `errors` method returns an object containing any current errors on the model. This method gets the content of the `@errors` instance variable, which contains the validation error messages, keyed by the name of the attribute. You can access errors for an individual attribute too:

```
>> p.errors['last_name']
=> "Please enter a last name"
>> p.errors['first_name']
=> "Please enter a first name"
```

The default error message strings are stored in a hash in ActiveRecord. These strings are used if you don't use a `:message` option when calling a validation message. The default error messages hash can be accessed using:
`ActiveRecord::Errors.default_error_messages`

You can set your own error messages by manipulating this hash. For example, to change the message for `validates_presence_of` errors (for example, from the default "can't be blank" to "must not be empty"), you can edit `config/environment.rb` and add this line:

`ActiveRecord::Errors.default_error_messages[:blank] = "must not be empty"`

Now any `validates_presence_of` failures will return an error message like "First name must not be empty".

Checking Against a Regular Expression

The `email` attribute should comply with the standard format for email addresses. We can specify this as a regular expression. I tend to try and find a suitable expression on the web for this purpose; here's one, which works for about 99% of the cases (from, `http://regular-expressions.info/email.html`):

```
/^[A-Z0-9._%-]+@[A-Z0-9.-]+\.[A-Z]{2,4}$/i
```

Note that it is possible that this regular expression will match some invalid email addresses, but it trades off completeness against simplicity.

We can apply this regular expression as a validation in the `Person` class using the `validates_format_of` method:

```ruby
class Person < ActiveRecord::Base
  EMAIL_REGEX = /^[A-Z0-9._%-]+@[A-Z0-9.-]+\.[A-Z]{2,4}$/i
  validates_format_of :email, :with => EMAIL_REGEX,
  :message => "Please supply a valid email address"
  ...
end
```

Here we've set up a constant `EMAIL_REGEX` inside the `Person` class; this is then passed as the `:with` option to the `validates_format_of` method.

We can test this from the console:

```
>> p = Person.new(:first_name => 'Elliot', :last_name => 'Smith')
=> #<Person:0xb742dbec ...>
>> p.email = 'elliot at example.com'
=> "elliot at example.com"
>> p.save
=> false
>> p.errors['email']
=> "Please supply a valid email address"
>> p.email = 'elliot@example.com'
=> "elliot@example.com"
>> p.save
=> true
```

Checking for Uniqueness

Another constraint we need is to restrict email addresses, so that we only have a single person associated with a given email address. ActiveRecord enables us to add multiple validations to a single field simply by calling multiple `validates_*` methods, one after another:

```ruby
class Person < ActiveRecord::Base
  EMAIL_REGEX = /^[A-Z0-9._%-]+@[A-Z0-9.-]+\.[A-Z]{2,4}$/i
  validates_format_of :email, :with => EMAIL_REGEX,
  :message => "Please supply a valid email address"
  validates_uniqueness_of :email, :message => "This email address
  already exists"
  ...
end
```

When you create a new record and `validates_uniqueness_of` is in place, ActiveRecord runs a query against the database. This checks whether any existing records have a field with a value equal to the attribute value in the new record. To demonstrate, let's add a new record using the console:

```
>> p = Person.new(:first_name => 'William', :last_name => 'Shakes', :
email => 'w.shakes@example.com')
=> #<Person:0xb790f4e0 ...>
>> p.save
=> true
```

That one was added OK. Now, try to add another record with the same email address:

```
>> p = Person.new(:first_name => 'Bill', :last_name => 'Shakes', :email
=> 'w.shakes@example.com')
=> #<Person:0xb790f4e0 ...>
>> p.save
=> false
```

The `save` method returns `false`, meaning that the save failed. You can see, "This email address already exists" error message if you examine `p.errors`. You can also see the SQL query that ActiveRecord ran to check for uniqueness by examining the `development.log` log file:

```
SELECT * FROM people WHERE (people.email = 'w.shakes@example.com')
LIMIT 1
```

Because this query returns a record, the validation fails and the record isn't saved. It's worth bearing in mind that this type of validation runs a query on the database *every* time it is called: consider carefully when to use it, and whether this extra overhead is warranted for your application. In the *Intranet* application, accuracy of data is very important to prevent duplicate contacts, so a check is vital. In the case of signing up for a newsletter, ensuring unique email addresses may be less crucial: perhaps it's not so important if someone receives two copies of a newsletter each month, as they can always get in touch to correct the error if annoyed. In that situation, the extra overhead of `validates_uniqueness_of` may not be desirable.

Checking for Inclusion in a Range of Values

The `gender` attribute should contain the value "M" or "F" ("male" or "female"). However, the *people* table merely constrains the gender attribute to being a one character string: it doesn't restrict that string to one of the two allowed values. We are going to enforce the constraint using validation.

The first step is to setup constant GENDERS, which stores the valid values for the gender attribute:

```
class Person < ActiveRecord::Base
  GENDERS = {'M' => 'male', 'F' => 'female'}
  . . .
end
```

We could have used a separate genders table to store this data, but decided not to (see the tip box below for the reason). The next step is to add some validation, which checks whether the gender attribute is set to one of the keys in the GENDERS hash:

```
class Person < ActiveRecord::Base
  GENDERS = {'M' => 'male', 'F' => 'female'}
  validates_inclusion_of :gender, :in => GENDERS.keys,
  :message => "Please select 'M' or 'F' for gender"

  . . .
end
```

The validates_inclusion_of method creates a validation which compares an attribute value against some enumerable object like an array. The enumerable object is passed using the :in option. In this case, we are using the keys of the GENDERS array as the enumerable object (referenced by GENDERS.keys). The validation is case-sensitive: so the values 'm' and 'f' will not be accepted. In the application, it is likely that we'd use radio buttons or a drop-down box to select gender in a form, in which case this validation might seem redundant. However, the rule ensures that, if our forms were maliciously manipulated to return an invalid or empty value for gender, we could catch errors before they got to the database.

Why use a hash to store genders, rather than a table? This is a decision made for pragmatic reasons (to cut down on the number of database tables), but strictly speaking it goes against relational database principles: really, we should have a genders table, which stores all valid genders, and should reference the appropriate gender_id in the people table. For now, the hash solution is adequate: as we only use gender information in a single table, we are effectively folding the hypothetical genders table into the people table (the only place it is used). If we needed to use gender elsewhere, a separate table would be the proper approach.

Test the validation using the console:

```
>> p = Person.new
=> #<Person:0xb74ecafc ...>
>> p.gender = 'X'
=> "X"
>> p.save
=> false
>> p.errors
=> #<ActiveRecord::Errors:0xb74e83bc @errors={"gender"=>["Please select
'M' or 'F' for the genre"], ...} ...>
>> p.gender = 'M'
=> "M"
>> p.save
=> true
```

Validating Related Records

Validation of the related company and address for a person depends on associations with other tables. This type of validation is covered in detail in the sections *Validating a Person's Address* and *Validating a Person's Company* (after the associations, themselves have been set up).

Summary

Here is the complete validation code for the `Person` model:

```
class Person < ActiveRecord::Base
  EMAIL_REGEX = /^[A-Z0-9._%-]+@[A-Z0-9.-]+\.[A-Z]{2,4}$/i
  validates_format_of :email, :with => EMAIL_REGEX,
  :message => "Please supply a valid email address"

  validates_uniqueness_of :email,
  :message => "This email address already exists"

  validates_presence_of :first_name,
  :message => "Please enter a first name"

  validates_presence_of :last_name,
  :message => "Please enter a last name"

  GENDERS = {'M' => 'male', 'F' => 'female'}
  validates_inclusion_of :gender, :in => GENDERS.keys,
  :message => "Please select 'M' or 'F' for the genre"

  ...
end
```

Validating Companies

The validation code for the `Company` model in `app/models/company.rb` is very simple, as we only need to ensure a company has a name:

```
class Company < ActiveRecord::Base
  validates_presence_of :name,
    :message => "Please enter a company name"
end
```

Validating Addresses

The validation code for the `Address` model in `app/models/address.rb` is as follows:

```
class Address < ActiveRecord::Base
  validates_presence_of :street_1,
    :message => "Please enter an initial line for the address"
  POSTCODE_REGEX = /^[A-Z][A-Z]?[0-9][A-Z0-9]? ?[0-9]
  [ABDEFGHJLNPQRSTUWXYZ]{2}$/i
  validates_format_of :post_code, :with => POSTCODE_REGEX,
    :message => "Please enter a valid post code"
  def validate_on_create
    if Address.find_by_street_1_and_post_code(street_1, post_code)
      errors.add_to_base('Street address and post code already exist
      in the database')
    end
  end
end
```

The UK postcode regular expression is from Wikipedia (http://en.wikipedia.org/wiki/UK_postcodes). It will allow some invalid postcodes through; but like the regular expression for email addresses (see section, *Checking Against a Regular Expression*), it is simple to follow and will catch 95% of cases.

The first line of the address (`street_1`) is validated, as an initial address line and post code are required to uniquely identify a UK address.

The final validation (highlighted) is the most interesting, as it demonstrates how to perform a custom validation not available using the default Rails methods. This is done by defining a `validate_on_create` method, which is run to validate any records when they are created.

The `validate_on_create` method can check attributes on the instance using whichever criteria you like. For example, you could validate a host name against a DNS look-up service or check a country code against a web service (neither of which is possible with the macros). ActiveRecord runs any custom `validate_on_create` method in tandem with validations defined using the `validates_*` macros.

In this case, the `street_1` and `post_code` attributes on the new instance are used to look up a record in the addresses table: if an address with matching `street_1` and `post_code` already exists, validation fails, and a generic error message is added to the model instance (`add_to_base` enables adding an error message to the whole instance, rather than a particular field).

> An alternative approach to ensuring the uniqueness of the combination of `street_1` and `post_code` would be to add a unique index to the database table, based on these two columns. Then, if an INSERT was performed with matching field values, it would fail due to the index constraint. However, you would then need to write some custom error catching code to trap this error and present it meaningfully through the model. The approach here is simpler and just makes use of existing features of ActiveRecord.

There is `validate_on_update` method, to be applied only on updates to records; and also a `validate` method that you can define to perform validation on *both* record creation and updates.

Other Types of Validation

There are several more esoteric `validates_*_of` methods, which are summarised below (along with those with already seen), with examples of how you can use them.

- `validates_uniqueness_of`, `validates_presence_of`, and `validates_format_of` are covered above.

- `validates_acceptance_of`
  Used where a user must tick a box to agree to the terms and conditions (or similar). There doesn't have to be an attribute corresponding to the tick box in the model.

- `validates_confirmation_of`
  Compares an attribute with a submitted form field to ensure they contain the same value.

- `validates_exclusion_of`
  Compares an attribute value against an enumerable object and only returns true if the attribute value is not in that object (the inverse of `validates_inclusion_of`).

- `validates_length_of`
  Ensures that an attribute's value is not too long or too short. You can set a minimum length, a maximum length, or a range the length should sit within.

- `validates_numericality_of`
  Ensures that an attribute is a number. Can be constrained to be an integer, or allow both integers and floating point numbers.

- `validates_associated`
  In the section on *Associations Between Models*, we'll see how to use this method.

Another method worth mentioning is `validates_each`, which enables you to create a custom validation for one or more attributes by running them through a block. It is used as the basis for Rails' built-in validation methods. See the documentation of `ActiveRecord::Validations::ClassMethods` for more details of how to use it (and for more details about the methods listed above).

Testing

Testing web applications is a laborious process. Often, it consists of developers sitting in front of web browsers and "pretending" to use the system, clicking around and filling forms with garbage. There are several draw-backs to this approach:

- **Incompleteness-**
  It is difficult to follow every possible path through the application. Testing of some actions may be neglected or missed entirely if they only occur under unusual circumstances.

- **Inconsistency-**
  The first time the application is tested, one set of paths through the application will be used; when forms are completed and submitted, some fields will be left empty, others filled. On subsequent tests, different paths may be followed and different form fields completed; and different again the next time; and so on. This makes it difficult to compare different test sessions, as there is no consistency in how the application is used during different sessions.

- **Unrepeatability-**
  Because the testing process is essentially random, when bugs are encountered it is often difficult to reconstruct the actions which led to the bug occurring.

It is possible to ameliorate some of these problems by writing a test script, which human testers follow, to ensure that the same parts of the application are tested the same way in different sessions. But writing these scripts is time-consuming and tedious.

An alternative approach is to use **automated testing**. In environments where setting up the test harness is a cumbersome task, automated testing can in itself be time-consuming. For example, PHP has several unit testing frameworks, but they are rarely used as they are a pain (a small pain, but still a pain) to install and configure, before you even start learning how to write the tests.

By contrast, Rails makes testing easy and seductive. Each time you use the generators to create new components for your application, Rails adds test stubs for your code, depending on the type of component. The types of tests provided by Rails breaks down into:

- **Unit tests-**
  These tests the models in the application. You can use them to check that your validation code works as expected, and to test associations between models. We'll look at these in this chapter.

- **Functional tests-**
  These test actions on controllers. Rails provides some convenient classes for emulating an HTTP client as it interacts with your application: so you can do things like fill in a form and submit it, and check that Rails correctly adds new records to the database. Functional tests are less about testing the database and more about testing that correct data is being assigned to instance variables, routing is working correctly, the response code is correct (success/redirect), the session/cookies are being updated properly, the correct template is being rendered, etc.. This makes them less important than unit testing, but still very useful for testing large, complex applications.

- **Integration tests-**
  These enable testing of workflows across controllers. For example, if you had a login form protecting the list of contacts, you could test that the list is correctly protected; then test that a user is able to login to access the list.

For most applications, thorough unit testing goes a long way towards improving the stability of the code: it becomes easy to trace where changes are being made to the model code, and where assumptions are coming undone (known in the testing vernacular as **regressions**—behavior which previously worked, but which is broken by a code modification). If models do change, unit tests provide a good prompt as to which controllers and views also need to change as a consequence. Unit testing is a pragmatic solution, which a company can easily invest in; while functional and integration testing are useful, they add yet more time to the development cycle.

Remember, also, that there is a separate **testing** environment baked into each Rails application (see the section, *Configuring the Rails Environments*): you can run tests without affecting either the development or production databases. The test stub generators remove the pain of installing and configuring the test harness; and the separate environment removes the havoc that automated testing can wreak on a real database. These two factors mean that testing in Rails is a pleasure.

For the purposes of the *Intranet* application, at least for now, we are going to rely on unit testing. We'll return to functional and integration testing in later chapters.

Setting Up for Testing

In our application, the testing framework has been automatically applied during our work with the generators. To take advantage of it, we just need to setup a test database. Follow the instructions in the section *Creating a Database and System Account* to add a new database; the process is summarized below:

```
mysql> CREATE DATABASE intranet_test;

Query OK, 1 row affected (0.18 sec)

mysql> GRANT ALL PRIVILEGES ON intranet_test.* TO intranet@localhost
IDENTIFIED BY 'police73';

Query OK, 0 rows affected (0.25 sec)

mysql> FLUSH PRIVILEGES;

Query OK, 0 rows affected (0.00 sec)
```

We've used the same database user (`intranet`) for the `intranet_test` database as we used for the `intranet` database: if you prefer, you can use a separate dedicated testing user.

We also need to edit `config/database.yml` to configure the `test` database:

```
test:
  adapter: mysql
  database: intranet_test
  username: intranet
  password: police73
  socket: /var/run/mysqld/mysqld.sock
```

Now, we are ready to run the tests from the command line with `rake`:

```
$ rake test:units
(in /home/rory/workspace/Intranet)
/usr/bin/ruby1.8 -Ilib:test "/usr/lib/ruby/gems/1.8/gems/rake-0.7.1/lib/
```

```
rake/rake_test_loader.rb" "test/unit/person_test.rb" "test/unit/company_
test.rb" "test/unit/address_test.rb"

Loaded suite /usr/lib/ruby/gems/1.8/gems/rake-0.7.1/lib/rake/rake_test_
loader

Started

...

Finished in 0.861688 seconds.

3 tests, 3 assertions, 0 failures, 0 errors
```

So far, so good. Running the command `rake test:units` initiates a Rake task, which does the following:

1. Removes any existing tables and data from the `test` database (which is why it should be a separate database from `development` or `production`).

2. Clones the structure of the current `development` database into the `test` database. None of the data is copied into the `test` database, just the table structures: any test data you want to pre-populate the `test` database with is added using **fixtures** (next section).

3. Loads all of the `*.rb` files in `RAILS_ROOT/test/unit`. These files contain test classes (aka **test cases**), which inherit from the `Test::Unit::TestCase` class (from Ruby's built-in unit testing library). In our case, there are three files, corresponding to our three models:

    ○   `test/unit/address_test.rb`

    ○   `test/unit/company_test.rb`

    ○   `test/unit/person_test.rb`

    The set of test cases is collectively known as a **test suite**.

4. Any methods prefixed with `test_` inside the test cases are run. In addition, if a `setup` method is defined for a test case, this method is run *before* each of the `test_` methods; if a `teardown` method is defined, it is run *after* each of the `test_` methods completes.

    Each `test_` method contains **assertions** about the expected behavior of the models in the application. If the expectations are met, all assertions in the test return `true` and the test passes; if any expectation fails (i.e. any assertion returns `false`), the test fails. Failures are reported as they occur; if runtime exceptions occur during the tests, they are also reported and cause the test in which they occur to fail.

5. When all the tests complete, a summary of the results is shown:
   - ° **tests:** the number of `test_` methods run
   - ° **assertions:** the number of assertions made during the tests
   - ° **failures:** the number of tests which failed
   - ° **errors:** exceptions which occurred during testing

In the next section, we'll see how a test case works, and write our own.

Anatomy of a Test Case

The default test case for the Person model (in `test/unit/person_test.rb`) is defined as:

```
require File.dirname(__FILE__) + '/../test_helper'
class PersonTest < Test::Unit::TestCase
  fixtures :people

  # Replace this with your real tests.
  def test_truth
    assert true
  end
end
```

The first line loads the `test_helper.rb` code from another file inside the `test` directory. This file governs the general behavior of tests; we'll return to it in the next section.

The `fixtures` method loads some test data into the testing database, using database records defined in YAML files (see the section, *Setting Up a Database Connection* for more information about YAML). We'll come onto fixtures shortly.

The only default test method is `test_truth`. This calls the `assert` method with the argument `true`, which always returns `true` (it always passes). We need to replace this dummy method with our own tests.

What Should be Tested?

The next question when applying unit tests to a model is "What should we test?". My answer to that is: test *all validations, associations, and utility methods*. This might seem excessive, as ActiveRecord already has a test suite, which checks that the validation macros work correctly. However, what we are testing is that instances of our models adhere to the behavior we expect them to have; not whether the validation code performs validation (which we know it does).

Thorough testing like this is particularly important where several people are working on a single code base. As an example, imagine that Rory writes some validation code, which says a person must have a first name. In another part of the application, he makes the assumption that any people he displays will have first names (as he's decided they aren't valid otherwise), and writes some view code, displaying people and their first names.

Meanwhile, Jenny decides that an empty first name is OK: as long as someone has a last name, their first name is unimportant. She removes Rory's validation code for first names.

The next time Rory runs his view code, he gets a regression: any people he tries to display who don't have a first name causes an error to be raised. Rory is perplexed and spends the afternoon working out what's going on.

In this situation, the tests for the validation rules on `Person` would be broken by Jenny's change to the code. The next time the test suite runs, the test failures will help Rory see what has changed. This makes it much easier to keep the behavior of the application stable, as it forces Jenny to rewrite any tests for the `Person` model if she wants to change the validation code. It also highlights to Jenny where her change will have an impact on other parts of the application: she can just see which tests fail and fix the code to make them pass again.

Now we have all agreed that testing is a good thing, the next step is to put in place some **fixtures**: data we can mangle during testing to see whether our expectations about a model hold up.

Fixtures

When you create a model, a blank fixtures file is also created (as well as the test stub discussed previously). The fixtures file is a way of creating dummy records so that each time you run your tests, you have a consistent data set to work from. Rails automatically loads fixtures when running test cases, converting them into records in the test database.

The fixtures file for a model is added to the `test/fixtures` directory; the name of the fixtures file is the database table name + `".yml"` (so we have `addresses.yml`, `companies.yml`, and `person.yml`). Each fixtures file is written in YAML: the top level keys are easy-to-remember names for the individual records; indented under each key are the field names and values for each record.

By default, a test case just loads the fixtures for the model under test. If you want to load other fixtures for other models, you can just append extra arguments to the `fixtures` method call (the first line inside the test class definition):

```
fixtures :people, :companies
```

This can be useful when testing associations (see *Associations Between Models*).

Following our own guidelines, we want to test the `find_all_ordered` method. To do this, we need at least three records in the `person.yml` fixture file, so we can check whether they are ordered by last name, and whether two people with the same last name are additionally ordered by first name. During the tests, we will reset attributes on these test records and try to save them back to the test database to exercise other parts of the validation code:

```
ginger:
  id: 1
  title: 'Mrs.'
  first_name: 'Ginger'
  last_name: 'Bloggs'
  email: 'ginger@example.com'
  gender: 'F'
fred:
  id: 2
  first_name: 'Fred'
  last_name: 'Bloggs'
  email: 'fred@example.com'
  gender: 'M'
albert:
  id: 3
  first_name: 'Albert'
  last_name: 'Always'
  email: 'albert@example.com'
  gender: 'M'
```

Notice that the records are put into the YAML file in non-name order, to make sure the sorting is being done by the `find_all_ordered` method, and isn't just due to the ordering of the fixtures file. Also notice that all of the records are valid, having an email address, first name, last name, and gender. However, it is not necessary to setup the attributes which aren't validated and which we're not testing (like `telephone`, `mobile_phone`, etc.).

Transactional and Instantiated Fixtures

Each time Rails runs a test method, it does so inside a database transaction: any changes made during the course of running the test method are undone when the test completes (using a SQL ROLLBACK command). In other words, the *fixtures are transactional*, effectively being "replenished" after each test.

With MyISAM tables, we have to be careful: transactions are not supported and have no effect when running our tests. The consequence is that any changes we make during a test (e.g. deleting a record from a table) impact on later tests. Data you were expecting to be available may have disappeared, or may not have the attributes you expected. This can cause chaos: your tests become dependent on the order in which they are applied and what happened in tests previous to the current one.

The fix is simple: turn off transactional fixtures during testing if you are using MyISAM tables. Edit this line in `test/test_helper.rb`:

```
self.use_transactional_fixtures = true
```

And change it to:

```
self.use_transactional_fixtures = false
```

 If you are using a database or table type which supports transactions, leave this setting as `true`: it makes running the test suite faster and more efficient.

The other change you can make to the `test/test_helper.rb` file is to turn on **instantiated fixtures**. All this means is that Rails will convert any fixtures that you define into instance variables on the test case. This makes it easier to reference records added from your fixtures from inside your test cases.

Change the line:

```
self.use_instantiated_fixtures = false
```

to:

```
self.use_instantiated_fixtures = true
```

This does add a slight overhead, so you may want to leave it set to `false` if you have a lot of test cases or fixtures.

Tests for the Person Model

We are now ready to write some tests for the `Person` model. We have the following expectations about its behavior:

- A person should have a valid email address.
- No two people can have the same email address.
- A person without a first name is invalid.

- A person without a last name is invalid.

- A person's gender must be set to 'M' or 'F'.

- The `full_name` method should format a person's title, first name, and last name into a correctly-formatted string. We also need to check that the output is correct where a person doesn't have a title.

- The `find_all_ordered` method should correctly sort people. The array returned should sort people by last name and then by first name in ascending order.

We can add test methods to check each of these expectations.

A person should have a valid email address

We need to test whether a record can be saved with an invalid email address. So, we will reset the email address for one of the fixture records and try to save it; we expect it to fail (return `false`):

```
def test_reject_invalid_email_addresses
  @fred.email = 'fred @ hello.com'
  assert !@fred.save
  @fred.email = 'fred bloggs@hello.com'
  assert !@fred.save
end
```

Some points to note:

- You can reference fixtures with the name of the record, prefixed with "@". This returns a model instance you can manipulate. If you have turned off instantiated fixtures (see the previous section), you need to reference `people(:fred)` to get the model instance instead.

- We want the save to fail; so our assertion states: "We're expecting the `save` to return `false`. So, taking the logical inverse (not) of the value returned by `save`, we're expecting to get `true`."

- You might want to add other invalid email addresses that you are likely to encounter, to make sure that the regular expression rejects them all.

No two People can have the Same email address

This one is simple:

```
def test_email_must_be_unique
  @fred.email = @albert.email
  assert !@fred.save
end
```

Here, we just set Fred's email to the same value as Albert's, then try to save Fred's record. We expect this to fail.

A person without a first name is invalid

```
def test_must_have_first_name
  @fred.first_name = ''
  assert !@fred.save
end
```

Here, we just set Fred's last name to the empty string and try to save his record. We expect it to fail.

A person without a last name is invalid

```
def test_must_have_last_name
  @fred.last_name = ''
  assert !@fred.save
end
```

Very similar to the test for :first_name (see above).

A person's gender must be set to 'M' or 'F'

```
def test_reject_invalid_genders
  @fred.gender = 'P'
  assert !@fred.save
end
```

Here, we just set Fred's gender to something other than "M" or "F" and try to save his record. We expect this to fail.

The full_name method should produce a correctly-formatted string

We need to test cases where a person has a title, and cases where they don't:

```
def test_full_name_correctly_formatted
  assert_equal 'Mrs. Ginger Bloggs', @ginger.full_name
  assert_equal 'Fred Bloggs', @fred.full_name
end
```

The find_all_ordered method should correctly sort people

This one is slightly more complicated, as we need to test that:

- All people are returned by the method.
- The records are in the ascending order of last_name.
- Where the last_name fields of two records are the same, they should be in ascending first_name order.

Here's the code:

```
def test_find_all_ordered
  people_in_order = Person.find_all_ordered
  assert_equal 3, people_in_order.size
  assert people_in_order[0].last_name <= people_in_order[1].last_name
  assert people_in_order[1].last_name <= people_in_order[2].last_name
  # fred should come before ginger,
  # even though they both have the same surname
  assert_equal 'Fred', people_in_order[1].first_name
  assert_equal 'Ginger', people_in_order[2].first_name
  assert people_in_order[1].first_name <= people_in_order[2]
    .first_name
end
```

Things to note:

- We use a new type of assertion, `assert_equal(expected, actual)`, to compare an expected value with an actual value.

- We use `<=` to compare fields in pairs of records returned by the `find_all_ordered` method.

- Because we know which fixtures are loaded, we can use expectations about which record is where to do further testing, like how the people are ordered by `first_name` when their `last_name` field values are the same. In our fixtures, we know that Fred Bloggs should come before Ginger Bloggs in the array, and can explicitly test this.

Test for positives as well as negatives

One thing which can catch you out is that *fixtures don't have to be valid*: for example, when first writing the fixtures for `Person`, I missed out gender attributes. My tests worked fine when I was checking for saves failing; but when I tried to check whether a save was successful, the tests failed, due to the lack of a valid `gender` attribute (not for the reason I thought they should fail).

I suggest including a test which checks whether one of your fixtures will save to the database. That way you can be sure that you *are* testing with what you *think* you are testing with, i.e. valid fixtures which will save to the database. For example:

```
def test_sanity
  assert @fred.save
end
```

Other Types of Assertion

Several other types of assertion are possible; they are listed below, along with those we've already seen:

- `assert(expected)`
  Passes if `expected` is `true`.

- `assert_dom_equal(expected, actual)`
  Passes if the two HTML strings `expected` and `actual` are equivalent. Its inverse, `assert_dom_not_equal`, is also available.

- `assert_tag(conditions)`
  Passes if the response body meets the criteria specified in the `conditions` hash. For example, this assertion checks that the response body contains a `<title>` HTML element with text `"Intranet"`:

  `assert_tag :tag => 'title', :child => /^Intranet$/`

  The inverse, `assert_no_tag`, is also available. Both of these assertions make most sense in the context of functional testing: we'll see an example of how to use them in the chapter where functional and integration testing is covered.

- `assert_instance_of(klass, object)`
  Passes if `object` is an instance of the class `klass`.

- `assert_kind_of(klass, object)`
  Passes if `object` has the class `klass`, or if `klass` is a superclass of `object`'s class, or if `klass` is one of the modules included in `object`'s class.

- `assert_equal(expected, actual)`
  Passes if `expected` and `actual` are equal (tested using the `==` operator).

- `assert_not_equal(expected, actual)`
  Passes if `expected` and `actual` are not equal.

- `assert_nil(object)`
  Passes if `object` is nil; `assert_not_nil` is also available.

- `assert_raise(ExceptionClass) { ... }`
  Passes if an exception of the specified `ExceptionClass` is raised by the following block.

- `assert_nothing_raised {...}`
  Passes if the supplied block does not raise an exception.

- `assert_match(regular_expression, string)`
  Passes if `string` matches `regular_expression`; its inverse, `assert_no_match`, is also available.

- `assert_recognizes(expected_options, path)`
  Passes if path, when passed through routing, produces the expected_options hash as output. For example, the following assertion passes if routing matches the path 'companies' to the `companies#index` controller/action pair:

  ```
  assert_recognizes({:controller => 'companies', :action =>
  'index'}, 'companies')
  ```

  This can be used to unit test your routing.

- `assert_generates(expected_path, options)`
  This is like the inverse of `assert_recognizes`: it passes if `options`, when passed to routing, produces `expected_path` as output. For example, we could check that the `companies#index` controller/action pair is assigned the route 'companies':

  ```
  assert_generates('companies', {:controller => 'companies', :
  action => 'index'})
  ```

- `assert_routing(path, options)`
  This combines `assert_generates(path, options)` and `assert_recognizes(options, path)` into a single assertion, checking that routing works in both directions (for generation of paths from options, and recognition of options from paths).

- `assert_redirected_to(options)`
  Passes if the controller action just called redirected to the same place as specified by the redirection `options`. We'll see this in use in the section on functional testing in Chapter 5.

- `assert_response(expected_code)`
  Passes if the response code was of the type expected_code. We'll see this used in a functional test in Chapter 5.

- `assert_template(expected_template)`
  Passes if the response was rendered using the template expected_template. This is used in functional tests (see the section on functional tests in Chapter 5).

- `assert_valid(object)`
  Passes if the ActiveRecord instance `object` validates.

These can be used inside `test_` methods in a similar way to how we've seen `assert` and `assert_equal` being used earlier.

Becoming Driven by Testing

While some of the tests we wrote might feel like overkill, they provide a high degree of peace of mind. I always feel happier when I know my code can be run through a suite of automated tests to highlight any assumptions I've made, which may have been broken.

Another advantage is that the tests become essential for bug fixing as coding progresses. If you come across a bug, you can write a test to replicate the conditions which produce the bug. At this point, the test will fail, as you haven't fixed the bug yet. Then, you can modify the code which causes the bug until the test passes. Before you know it, you are doing **test-driven development (TDD)**.

We haven't approached the *Intranet* application from a TDD perspective, as TDD is still alien to many developers, and requires a paradigm-shift in how development is approached. However, I would encourage you to at least retro-fit tests to your application, so you get a taste of the benefits; and to code a test to encapsulate each bug you encounter. Over time, you may find that it becomes natural to write tests first then write the code to make them pass. Rails makes this as painless as possible.

We've only covered unit tests for the `Person` model here. Tests for the other models are available in the code repository for the book, and follow a similar pattern. Hopefully, the guidelines given for writing the `Person` model tests can be extended to other models you create.

Associations between Models

In Chapter 2, we used the Outlook address export as the initial basis for designing the *Intranet* application's database structure. Rather than have a single table, which replicated Outlook's export format directly, we decided to use three tables to prevent duplication of data: `addresses`, `companies`, and `people`. We then created associations between tables by putting "pseudo" foreign keys into appropriate tables. The resulting associations are:

1. An address belongs to zero or more people, and each person has one or no address (we might not have home addresses for every person in the database).

2. An address belongs to zero or one company, and each company has one address (a company address is mandatory).

3. A person belongs to one company (required), and each company can have zero or more associated people.

The advantage of this is that if a company has multiple employees, we only record the company details once in the `companies` table; we then link `people` to the company using the `company_id` foreign key field in the `people` table. Similarly, address data is common to both people and companies: by separating it out into a single table, we can search addresses by referencing the single `addresses` table, rather than having to search across both the `people` and `companies` tables. We can also associate multiple people with a single address (for example, a married couple will have a joint address).

Despite our data structure, ActiveRecord remains unaware of the associations between tables. However, it only needs a small nudge to recognize them. The addition of a few simple lines of code to the model classes will enable ActiveRecord to manage the relationships for us, so we can reference a person's company from a `Person` instance, a company address from a `Company` instance, and so on. In the next three sections, we'll see how each relationship in the database can be transformed into an association between models.

Parent to children (one-to-many): addresses to people

The `addresses` and `people` tables have a **one-to-many** relationship in the database. In other words, a record in the `addresses` table may be related to zero or more records in the `people` table. The table on the "many" side of the relationship contains a foreign key to the table on the "one" side of the relationship. Ignoring fields irrelevant to the relationship, this can be represented in a standard database diagram as:

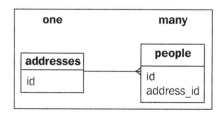

In our Rails application, this kind of database relationship is represented in ActiveRecord as an association between the `Person` and `Address` models. The association is marked in each of the participating models.

In the `Person` model:

```
class Person < ActiveRecord::Base
  belongs_to :address
  ...
end
```

In the `Address` model:

```
class Address < ActiveRecord::Base
  has_many :people
  ...
end
```

We can generalize the translation from a one-to-many relationship in the database to model associations, so we could use it with any pair of related tables:

- Where you have a **one-to-many relationship** in the database between the table `parents` (on the "one" side of the relationship) and the table `children` (on the "many" side, containing the foreign key):
    - In the `Parent` model class, insert `has_many :children`
    - In the `Child` model class, insert `belongs_to :parent`
- Which modifies instances of the classes as follows:
    - `Parent` instances get a `children` method (which returns an array of `Child` instances); and a `children=` method (which accepts an array of `Child` instances as an argument and sets the children collection).

       The parent also gets other methods, which enable new objects to be added to the collection of children, such as `children << child`, which appends a new instance `child` to the collection; `children.build(attributes={})`, which constructs a new `Child` instance using the `attributes` hash and links it to the parent (without saving); and `children.create(attributes={})`, which builds a `Child` instance from `attributes` and also saves it.

       As the collection `children` is an array, all the standard array methods, such as `empty?` and `size`, work as expected.

       Finally, it is possible to interrogate the collection using `find` to retrieve the subset of children matching specific criteria. For example, you could get an `Address` instance:

       `addr = Address.find 1`

       Then use `find` on its `people` collection to get an array of all the women living at that address:

       `women = addr.people.find(:all, :conditions => {:gender => 'F'})`

    - `Child` instances get a `parent` method (which returns a `Parent` instance); and a `parent=` method (which accepts a single `Parent` instance as an argument).

Before we can see the effect of this, we need to create an `Address`:

```
>> addr = Address.new(:street_1 => '44 Monty Avenue', :city =>
'Molltoxeter', :post_code => 'MX12 1YH')  # create an address

>> addr.save

=> true
```

We can now assign this address to a person (assuming, you have at least one person in the database):

```
>> pers = Person.find :first  # find a person

>> pers.address = addr  # assign an address to the person

>> pers.save

=> true
```

This is all you need to associate the new address with the person. Once associated, you can retrieve a person's address using the `address` method:

```
>> pers = Person.find :first  # find a person

=> #<Person:0xb74a4228 ...>

>> pers.address  # retrieve the address for the person

=> #<Address:0xb74a2504 @attributes={"city"=>"Molltoxeter", "updated_
at"=>"2006-11-03 14:33:20", "county"=>nil, "street_1"=>"44 Monty Avenue",
"street_2"=>nil, "post_code"=>"MX12 1YH", "street_3"=>nil, "id"=>"5",
"created_at"=>"2006-11-03 14:33:20"}>
```

By using the `belongs_to` method in the `Person` class, we have appended new `address` (a getter) and `address=` (a setter) methods to instances of that class:

- When `address` is called, ActiveRecord retrieves a record from the `Address` table where the `address.id` field equals the value in the person's `address_id` attribute.

- When `address=` is called with an `Address` instance as an argument, the `id` of that `Address` instance is set as the `address_id` attribute for the person.

If you have multiple people associated with address, you can also query in the other direction, from an address to an array of associated people:

```
>> a = Address.find :first  # find an address

>> a.people  # find the people associated with the address

=> [#<Person:0xb744a5c8 ...>, #<Person:0xb744a58c ...>]
```

One point worth stating about associations is that they don't have to be symmetrical: if you never intend to find the people associated with an address (for example), you don't have to add has_many :people to the Address class. The belongs_to :address association in the Person class will still work without it.

Validating a Person's Address

Now that the relationship between the people and addresses table has been established, we are in a position to validate associations between their respective models (Person and Address). In Chapter 2, the validation rules we specified stated that a person can optionally have a home address. In cases where a person does have a home address, when we validate a person, we also need to validate that address. This is useful in situations where we are creating a new person and address simultaneously: it ensures that before we save the person into the database, any address assigned to them references a valid address.

Rails provides a convenient validates_associated method for this purpose, which we can add to the Person model:

```
class Person < ActiveRecord::Base
  belongs_to :company
  belongs_to :address
  validates_associated :address
  ...
end
```

Note that this method only performs validation where an address has been assigned: where the address for a person is blank (nil), validation of the address is skipped. Validation succeeds where an address assigned to a person in turn passes all of its own validation rules (i.e. the validations on the Address class). In situations where the associated record is *required* (e.g. a company must have an address), you need to use validates_presence_of to check for the associated record, as well as validates_associated. See section *Validating a Company's Address* for an example of how to do this.

Parent to child (one-to-one): addresses to companies

These two tables have a **parent-to-child** relationship in the database; this is like a one-to-many relationship, except there is at most one record at the "many" side of the relationship. In other words, a record in the addresses table is a parent of zero or one record in the companies table. The "child" in the relationship is the table containing the foreign key:

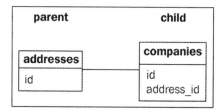

This might seem a slightly odd way of describing this relationship, but it is perfectly legitimate in ActiveRecord terms: "parent-child" doesn't necessarily denote a dependency in this context.

In the Company class, we add belongs_to:

```
class Company < ActiveRecord::Base
  belongs_to :address
  . . .
end
```

In the Address class, we add has_one:

```
class Address < ActiveRecord::Base
  has_one :company
  . . .
end
```

Again, we can generalize this translation:

- Where you have a **parent-to-child relationship** in the database between the table parents (on the "parent" side of the relationship) and the table children (on the "child" side, containing the foreign key):
  - In the Parent model class, insert has_one :child
  - In the Child model class, insert belongs_to :parent

- This modifies instances of the classes as follows:
  - ○ `Parent` instances get a `child` method (which returns a `Child` instance); and a `child=` method (which accepts a `Child` instance as an argument). They also get `build_child(attributes={})` and `create_child(attributes={})` methods. The former constructs a `Child` instance and links it to the parent, but doesn't save it; the latter builds the `Child` instance, links it to the parent, and saves it too.
  - ○ `Child` instances get a `parent` method (which returns a `Parent` instance); and a `parent=` method (which accepts a single `Parent` instance as an argument)

Testing the association from the console follows a similar pattern to testing the one-to-many relationship of the previous section:

```
>> comp = Company.find :first # find a company
=> #<Company:0xb7432888 ...>
>> addr = Address.find :first  # find an address
=> #<Address:0xb7430150 ...>
>> comp.address = addr  # assign the address to the company
=> #<Address:0xb7430150 ...>
>> comp.save  # save the company
=> true
>> comp.address  # retrieve the address for a company
=> #<Address:0xb7430150 ...>
>> addr.company  # retrieve the company associated with an address
=> #<Company:0xb7427f00 ...>
```

Validating a Company's Address

One other requirement of the data structure designed in Chapter 2 is that a company must have a valid address: this is vital for the contacts database to have any value.

How can we check that the address associated with a company is valid? We need to ensure that:

1. An associated address has been assigned to the company.
2. The associated address is itself valid.

We can capture these requirements using `validates_presence_of` and `validates_associated` in tandem:

```ruby
class Company < ActiveRecord::Base
  has_many :people
  belongs_to :address

  validates_presence_of :name,
  :message => "Please enter a company name"

  validates_presence_of :address,
  :message => 'Address must be supplied'
  validates_associated :address,
  :message => 'Address is invalid'

end
```

`validates_presence_of` ensures that an address has been assigned to the company; `validates_associated` ensures that the address (if assigned) is itself valid.

 If you create an association between two tables which don't support foreign keys (like MyISAM tables), the only way to enforce the association is to add some validation code to the models. Without this validation, ActiveRecord will happily accept nil values in foreign key fields.

Parent to children (one-to-many): companies to people

This relationship is very similar to the `addresses` to `people` relationship:

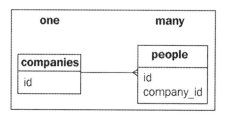

It can be marked in the `Company` model class with:

```ruby
class Company < ActiveRecord::Base
  has_many :people
  ...
end
```

And in the `Person` class with:

```
class Person < ActiveRecord::Base
  belongs_to :company
  # ... other methods ...
end
```

Validating a Person's Company

The code for validating the company for a person is similar to that for validating their address. A person doesn't necessarily have to be associated with a company at all; so we can dispense with `validates_presence_of`, and just use `validates_associated`:

```
class Person < ActiveRecord::Base
  # ... other methods ...
  validates_associated :company
end
```

Many-to-many relationships

Our application doesn't (yet) contain any **many-to-many relationships** in the database structure. But it's easy to think of situations where we might want to have this kind of relationship. For example, Ken might decide he wants to be able to categorise companies: each company will have zero or more categories, and each category will have zero or more associated companies. This would require a many-to-many relationship.

The typical way of implementing a many-to-many relationship in a database is by adding a **link table** between the two related tables:

- The link table stores pairs of IDs:
  - One ID from the table on the "left" of the relationship (the "sinisters" table).
  - One ID from the "right-hand" table (the "dexters" table).
- Each of the related tables has a one-to-many relationship with the link table.

 "Sinister" and "dexter" are terms from heraldry, denoting placement of an object on the left of a heraldic symbol or on the right, respectively.

In the case of categories and companies, we might end up with:

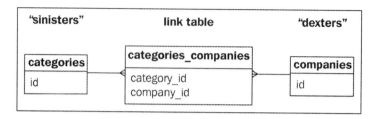

ActiveRecord makes it convenient to manage the associations between the models for these tables: use the method has_and_belongs_to_many in each model:

```
class Categories < ActiveRecord::Base
  has_and_belongs_to_many :companies
  ...
end

class Companies < ActiveRecord::Base
  has_and_belongs_to_many :categories
  ...
end
```

We can generalize this to the following guidelines:

- Where you have a **many-to-many relationship** in the database between the table sinisters and the table dexters:
  - In the Sinister model class, insert
    has_and_belongs_to_many :dexters
  - In the Dexter model class, insert
    has_and_belongs_to_many :sinisters

- Create a link table called dexters_sinisters with two fields:
  - dexter_id
  - sinister_id

  The name of the link table should be composed of the names of the two tables you are linking, arranged in alphabetical order, with an underscore in between.

- This modifies instances of the classes as follows:
  - Sinister instances get a dexters method (which returns an array of Dexter instances); and a dexters= method (which accepts an array of Dexter instances as an argument).

○　Dexter instances get a sinisters method (which returns an array of Sinister instances); and a sinisters= method (which accepts an array of Sinister instances as an argument).

Dependencies

In our database structure, we specified that when an address is deleted, we should remove its associated company. This makes sense, given that we don't want any companies to have invalid addresses; without the dependency, we could delete an address, but still have references to it in the company_id field of the companies table.

To specify the dependency, pass an optional :dependent => :destroy option to the has_one method call in the parent class:

```
class Address < ActiveRecord::Base
  has_one :company, :dependent => :destroy
    ...
end
```

The effect of this is to delete a company when its associated "parent" address is deleted. If you are going to use this method for dependency tracking, you need to be clear about the consequences, and ensure that project stakeholders are in agreement: do they really want cascading deletion of companies if an address is removed?

Also note that you can specify other :dependent options with the has_one method:

- has_one :company, :dependent => :nullify
  Sets the foreign key in the related company record to null, rather than destroying it.

- has_one :company, :dependent => :delete
  Deletes the associated company without calling its destroy method.

Similarly, you can use a :dependent option with the has_many method, as used in the Company class, e.g.

- has_many :people, :dependent => :destroy
  Destroys all dependent records in the people table when a company is destroyed.

- has_many :people, :dependent => :nullify
  Sets the company_id field to null for dependent records in the people table when the company is destroyed.

- has_many :people, :dependent => :delete_all
  Removes all dependent records in the people table when a company is destroyed, but without calling the destroy method.

Note that you can't set a :dependent option when using
has_and_belongs_to_many.

Testing Associations

It's often useful to test validation of associations, as well as validation of attributes.
For example, in our model, we have a custom validation which checks whether the
address_id attribute references a real Address in the database. We can write a unit
test for the Company model which checks this validation code, as follows.

First, create a fixture for a valid address in test/fixtures/addresses.yml:

```
acme_hq:
  id: 1
  street_1: '14 Blockfield'
  street_2: 'Minsterton'
  city: 'Jupiterton'
  post_code: 'BX1 4FG'
```

Next, create a fixture for a company in test/fixtures/companies.yml:

```
acme:
  id: 1
  name: 'Acme'
  address_id: 1
```

Note how this references the valid address_id (= 1) for the fixture we created above.

Load the addresses fixtures into the unit test for Company in
test/unit/company_test.rb:

```
class CompanyTest < Test::Unit::TestCase
  fixtures :companies, :addresses
  ...
end
```

Finally, write a test method to check that the validation code for the association
behaves as expected:

```
class CompanyTest < Test::Unit::TestCase
  fixtures :companies, :addresses
  def test_must_have_real_address
    # Should fail with invalid address
    @acme.address = nil
    assert !@acme.save
    # Should save when assigned a valid address
    @acme.address = @acme_hq
    assert @acme.save
  end
end
```

Putting the Project into Context

Throughout this chapter, we have been building our application up, based on the data structure developed in Chapter 2. We have put in place the whole of the model layer for the application, including the necessary validation code and associations between models. We have also assured ourselves that the model is stable, by building some tests to confirm its behavior.

But there are a couple of areas we have neglected so far:

1. How can this work be shared with other members of the team (via the Subversion repository)?
2. How can we get a list of Outlook contacts into the database?

The remainder of this chapter covers these topics.

Storing a Project in Subversion

We've done quite a bit of coding in this chapter, but so far we're the only developers who can see it. It's high time we committed what we've written to the Subversion repository.

If you're using Eclipse, you may have been wondering what the question marks on the file and directory icons mean:

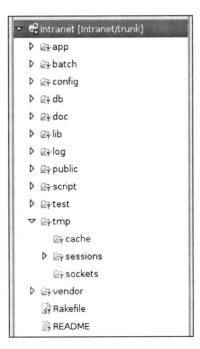

The question marks highlight the directories and files which the Subversion repository doesn't know about yet. These are the files we need to commit.

Before we leap in, it's worth taking some time to decide whether we need all of the highlighted files. Some of the files in the application are temporary, and don't need to be included. The next section describes how to exclude these files from the repository.

Ignoring Temporary Files

As well as the source code, our application directory contains several temporary files in the following directories:

- **db:** If you dump your database structure, it is stored in a file called `schema.rb` inside this directory. As this file can be reconstructed dynamically, it is a good idea to exclude it from the repository.

- **log:** Contains log data (in `*.log` files) for individual Rails environments. When you run your applications using Mongrel (see Chapter 2), the log file for Mongrel is also stored here.

- **tmp/cache:** If you use view caching (see section on view caching) to improve your application's performance, cache fragments will be stored here.

- **tmp/sessions:** If you followed the brief introduction to the scaffold in the section: *The Scaffold*, and accessed your application via a web browser, there may be several session files stored in this directory, prefixed with `ruby_sess`. These files store session data for connected clients, and can occasionally be orphaned when sessions end (e.g. the user closes their browser). By the way, provided no clients are connected, you can just delete these files.

- **tmp/sockets:** In some configurations (mainly, if running Rails applications under FastCGI), socket files will be stored here.

- **tmp/pids:** When running Rails under Mongrel, the process ID (PID) files identifying the server processes will be stored here.

Ideally, we want to exclude all temporary files from the Subversion repository: they are only applicable to the machine which created them. Any missing files will be created as soon as the application runs on a different machine, so there is no harm in excluding them. Other bonuses are that checking out an application is faster (no big log files); and that potentially sensitive information (e.g. debugging information in `development.log`) is not included when the application is distributed.

Subversion provides a facility for setting filename patterns which should be **ignored** (i.e. not committed to the repository and only stored in the working copy). This is done by setting a Subversion property called `svn:ignore` on each directory which contains temporary files. This property is a newline-separated list of filename patterns; any files with matching names are ignored and excluded from commits.

Files can be added to `svn:ignore` using the `svn` command line tool (have a look at `svn help propedit`); however, Eclipse provides a simple wrapper around this functionality, so we'll use that instead:

1. Right-click on the directory containing the files we want to ignore (see the list above): `tmp/sessions`, for example.

2. Select **Team | Set Property...**

3. In the **Set an svn property** dialog box, select **svn:ignore** from the **Property name** drop-down box. Ensure the **Enter a text property** radio button is ticked, and enter `ruby_sess.*` in the text area (a pattern which matches the temporary Ruby session files we want to ignore—you can use an asterisk character as a wild-card). The completed dialog box should look like this:

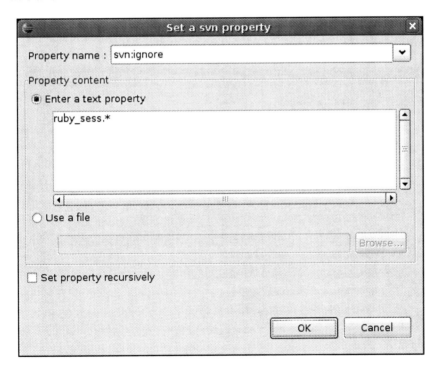

4. Click **OK**.

The svn:ignore property is now set on the tmp/sessions directory. If at any time you want to edit or delete properties, right-click on the directory again and select **Team | Show Properties** from the context menu.

Following the same steps, set the following svn:ignore properties on the other locations:

- db: set to schema.rb.

- log: set to * (ignore everything in this directory).

- tmp/cache: set to *.

- tmp/sessions: set to *.

- tmp/sockets: set to *.

- tmp/pids: set to *.

Committing Code to the Repository

Finally, commit the code to repository, follow these steps.

1. Right click on the project name (*Intranet*, in our case).

2. Select **Team | Commit** from the context menu. You should see this dialog box:

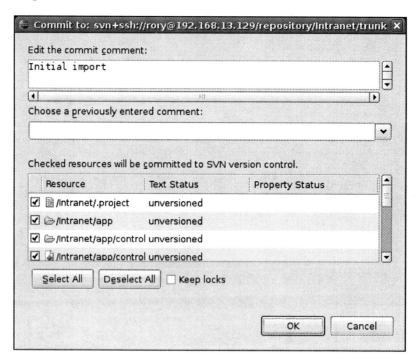

Enter a suitable comment in the **Edit the commit comment** text area; click on the **Select All** button to select all resources for commit to the repository.

3. Click **OK**. Eclipse will whirr away, committing the code to the repository. Once it is finished, you should see this in the resource view:

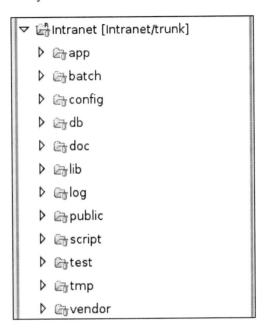

Note that the yellow "barrels" on the files and directories indicate that they have been successfully added to the repository, and that they are in sync with it.

Each time you modify anything inside the project, Eclipse highlights the changed file with a white asterisk on a black background; it will also highlight any directories which contain a modified file, however deep the file is in the directory structure, with the same icon. You can right-click on the project or on the changed file(s) and select **Team | Commit** to commit the changes to the repository.

If you create new files, you will need to add them in to version control: simply right-click on the file and select **Team | Add to Version Control**.

Try to use helpful comments each time you commit changes to the repository. Ideally, you should outline the *reasoning* behind the change, rather than explain the mechanics of what has changed. The repository can be queried to discover which parts of the code have changed; but it can't be queried for why the change occurred. For example, a comment like the fillowing:

"Added national insurance numbers for people."

This is more useful than:

"Added ni attribute to Person."

Processing Data

The original impetus behind the *Intranet* application was to make Mary's address book available to everyone working at Acme. So far, we have deconstructed Mary's Outlook address book export file, built a database from it, and developed a set of Rails models to wrap that database. The next step is to get the data, which was exported from Outlook, and process it with a **script** to insert records into the Intranet database. Rather than doing this manually, we are going to use the power of Ruby, coupled with ActiveRecord, to do the import for us.

Exporting the Data from Outlook

Microsoft Outlook provides an export facility for contact data (**File | Import and Export**). The Acme team exports to a spreadsheet initially, as this makes it easier to do the initial data analysis. We won't dwell on the export process, as it is self-explanatory and fairly trivial: the Outlook documentation provides some good guidance on how to do this.

From the spreadsheet, they produce a tab-separated flat-file database, `contacts.tsv`. Here's a fragment of the file:

```
Title  First Name  Last Name  Company             Job Title     Business Street 1        Business Street 2      Busir
Mr.    Alex    Sprech  Mock Plumbers    Director       12 Pretend Row             Madeupton      Suffix  LX1 2TT
Ms.    Angela  Gurns   Madeup Company Ltd.    Proprietor                                        34 Bark Avenu
Dr.    Frank   Monk    Monk Parts Ltd. IT Director     The Low Cottage High Street  Mockton       Wessex  EX1 3RT  The M
Mr.    Geoff   Spec    Spectacular Suppliers  CIO     The Villa       Sham Avenue       Toringham            BX1 5
Mrs.   Sarah   Walker  Western Antiques       Proprietor     84 Paris Road   The Mombles    Lithfield      Toringham
```

The first line of the file contains the field names; each subsequent line represents a single contact from Outlook, with tabs between the field values.

One issue which is immediately apparent is that some of the fields in the Outlook export file have new line characters in them. This is a problem, as the new line character is also used to delineate individual records (one record per line). The first fix is a manual one, therefore: removing any new line characters within field values. The result is this (record 3 for Frank Monk is the only one affected):

```
Title    First Name    Last Name        Company        Job Title      Business Street 1      Business Street 2      Busir
Mr.      Alex     Sprech   Mock Plumbers    Director         12 Pretend Row                Madeupton        Suffix  LX1 2TT
Ms.      Angela   Gurns    Madeup Company Ltd.     Proprietor                                              34 Bark Aven
Dr.      Frank    Monk     Monk Parts Ltd. IT Director      The Low Cottage
High Street      Mockton                  Wessex   EX1 3RT The Manor        18 Frankley Way      Spiriton        Washtershire
Mr.      Geoff    Spec     Spectacular Suppliers    CIO      The Villa        Sham Avenue      Toringham        BX1 5
Mrs.     Sarah    Walker   Western Antiques         Proprietor       84 Paris Road    The Mombles      Lithfield       Toringham
```

> This might be impractical for thousands of records: in such cases, the alternative would be to do more parsing of the raw text files to clear out anomalies. For example, the first pass might count tab characters, and combine multiple lines with too-few tabs into a single line with the correct number of tabs.

The next step is mapping the columns in the text file onto tables and fields in the database.

Mapping a Text File to Database Tables

The script will have to break up each row of the text file into multiple instances of our models: a `Person` instance, a `Company` instance, an `Address` instance for the person's home address and an `Address` instance for the person's work address. To do this, the columns in the text file must be mapped onto the models in the *Intranet* application and attributes of those models. The table below describes how the Acme team decides to do this mapping. As two addresses are constructed for each line in the text file, the company `Address` instance is marked as *Address(c)*, and the personal `Address` instance as *Address(p)*.

Field exported from Outlook	Maps to model/attribute	Notes
Title	Person/title	-
First Name	Person/first_name	Required.
Last Name	Person/last_name	Required.
Company	Company/name	-
Job Title	Person/job_title	-
Business Street 1	Address(c)/street_1	-
Business Street 2	Address(c)/street_2	-
Business Street 3	Address(c)/street_3	-
Business City	Address(c)/city	-

Field exported from Outlook	Maps to model/attribute	Notes
Business State	Address(c)/county	-
Business Postal Code	Address(c)/post_code	-
Home Street	Address(p)/street_1	-
Home Street 2	Address(p)/street_2	-
Home Street 3	Address(p)/street_3	-
Home City	Address(p)/city	-
Home State	Address(p)/county	-
Home Postal Code	Address(p)/post_code	-
Business Fax	Company/fax	-
Business Phone	Company/telephone	If a value is provided for this field and for *Company Main Phone*, this field is ignored
Company Main Phone	Company/telephone	If a value is provided for this field and for Business Phone, this field is used
Home Phone	Person/telephone	-
Mobile Phone	Person/mobile_phone	-
Birthday	Person/date_of_birth	DD/MM/YY
E-mail Address	Person/email	Required.
Gender	Person/gender	"male" or "female"; if not set, "male" is assumed
Keywords	Person/keywords	-
Notes	Person/notes	-
Web Page	Company/website	-

Any other fields in the text file are ignored.

Another aspect of adding lines from the text file is doing it in the correct order. The associations we defined earlier in this chapter (see the section Associations Between Models) indicate that we should add records to the database in this order:

1. Personal address

2. Company address

3. Company (referencing the company address just added as the value for the `address_id` field)

4. Person (referencing the company just added as the value for the `company_id` field, and the personal address just added as the value for the `address_id` field)

We also need to consider the validation rules we defined earlier (see the section Validation). These may prevent some of the data in the Outlook export file from being added to the database: for example, if a person has no email address, his record is invalid according to our validation rules, which requires `first_name`, `last_name`, and `email` to contain values. The approach taken by Acme to deal with this is as follows:

1. Write the script so that it highlights errors as they occur, e.g. print the line of the import file where the error occurs and show the validation errors thrown.

2. Run the script with the initial text file.

3. Fix problems with the text file as they are highlighted during the import. For example, if an address cannot be saved because of a missing post code, determine the post code for that address; if a person cannot be saved because their email address is missing, ring them up and find out the their email address.

4. Roll the database back to a blank slate.

5. Re-run the script.

6. Re-iterate steps 2 to 5 until the script returns no unexpected or unwanted errors.

This approach wouldn't work in situations where the import is to be run periodically with no human intervention. In situations like this, the only approach may be to relax the validation rules to allow broken data into the system. In the case of Acme, where they are planning to do a one-off import, they can afford to be picky, and make sure the data is clean before it is inserted into the database.

Coding the Script

Once Acme has cleaned their data as far as possible, and decided a process for further purifying the data as they go, they are ready to start coding. Acme stores the script in `db/import` inside their Rails application; they call it `import_from_outlook.rb`. Rather than go through the whole script line-by-line, we'll have a look at a pseudo-code overview of the script over the next two pages. The full code for the script is available from the book's code repository.

```
# Script for importing Outlook address data into Intranet.
# Where data is retrieved from columns in the import file, the mapping
# described in the section Mapping a Text File to Database Tables is
used
# to work out, which column it goes into in the database
# Each time a save fails, show an error message and the line number
# in the file where the error occurred.
# Run this script through script/runner
```

open contacts.tsv file (tab-separated contacts file exported from
Outlook)
read in the first line (which contains the column headings)
split the first line around the tab character "\t" into array raw_
field_names
create a hash which maps the field name onto its index position in the
array; this makes it easier to reference fields within the subsequent
lines by field name, rather than position
for each remaining line:
  split around tab character into an array of values

  # parse out company address
  get company street_1 and post_code
  if there is an existing address with the same street_1 and post_code:
    use that for the company address
  else:
    parse out the remaining address fields to create a new address
    save new address
    use it for the company address
  end

  # parse out personal address
  get personal street_1 and post_code
  if there is an existing address with the same street_1 and post_code:
    use that for the personal address
  else:
    parse out the remaining address fields to create a new address
    save new address
    use it as the personal address
  end

  # company
  get the company name field
  if there is an existing company with that name:
    use that company as the person's company
  else:
    parse out the remaining company fields to fill out the company
    details associate the company with the company address
    extracted earlier
    save new company
  end

  # person
  parse out the person fields to create a new person (using the
mapping)
  associate with personal address
  associate with company
  save new person
end # no more lines in file

One of the most important tips in this script is how to load the Rails environment to make the database available without having to run the application in a server setting. Rails makes this simple: you just need to run the `script/runner` script that is included with your application, passing it the location of the script file, e.g.

```
$ ruby script/runner db/import/import_from_outlook.rb
```

Once the script is ready, the Acme developers tests it repeatedly against the data exported from Mary's Outlook address book, until they are happy it is as error free as possible. This is made possible by their migrations, which enable them to start each test run from a blank slate by running the following commands from the command line (inside `RAILS_ROOT`):

```
$ rake db:migrate VERSION=0
$ rake db:migrate
$ ruby script/runner db/import/import_from_outlook.rb
...
```

Here is a tangible example of the benefits of migrations: the Acme developers can repeat the cycle of destroying the database, rebuilding it, then inserting the data as many times as they need to, until they have ironed out any problems with the import file.

Summary

In this chapter, we have covered a lot of ground. We have gone from an idea and an expectant Rails installation to a full-fledged data model, populated from an external data source, with full validation and unit test suite. We have also written a script to get the data into the application, and shared the code development across the team.

We also had a tantalizing glimpse of how Rails exposes this data to end users through a browser interface when we applied the scaffold. In the next chapter, we will exploit the full power of Rails to go beyond the scaffold, building the logic for the application controllers, and fleshing out the user interface.

5

Building the User Interface

In the last chapter, we worked on implementing a solid model layer for the application. While the console and unit tests are a fine way for developers to access the models, they are not a suitable interface for the intended users of the system (Acme administrative staff). This chapter describes how to build a web interface onto the models we have developed, including:

- A walk-through of creating a controller from scratch
- How to use **views**, **layouts**, and **helpers**
- Using **pagination**
- Linking views together to create **drill-downs**
- Adding **style-sheets**
- Writing **custom helpers** and **partials**
- Writing complex controller actions to **update multiple models simultaneously**
- Fleshing out the application functionality

By the end of the chapter, we will have a basic, fully-functional web-based CRM application.

Controllers and Views: A Recap

The model layer of the last chapter is the first part of the Model-View-Controller jigsaw. Implementing a user interface on top of the model layer means building the two remaining MVC components (see the section *Model-View-Controller Architecture* at the start of Chapter 4):

1. **Controllers**, which handle the control flow and interact with the model layer
2. **Views**, which present data to the user and enable them to interact with the controllers

How do you decide which controllers and views do you need to build? Rails helps us with our decision making by suggesting a convention: one controller for each model. The controller for the model handles all of the operations on it; typically the **CRUD** operations, i.e.

- Creating a new instance
- Retrieving all the instances of the model
- Updating an instance
- Deleting an instance

Making a controller for each model seems a sensible place to start. In the rest of the chapter, we will build up the following controllers, corresponding to the models we built in the previous chapter:

Controller class	File containing controller definition (in `app/controllers`)
PeopleController	`people_controller.rb`
CompaniesController	`companies_controller.rb`
AddressesController	`addresses_controller.rb`

Notice how we are applying the conventions mentioned in Chapter 4 (*Rails and MVC*): the controller name is the name of the model, pluralized, with "Controller" appended. The file name is the lowercase version of the controller class name, with underscores separating discrete words.

There is nothing to stop you having a single controller, which manages all of your tables. However, this would make the class definition too complex. By sticking to the conventions, we get a neat segregation of the actions and views specific to a particular model.

We'll be looking at the workflow for building a simple controller, explaining where to put the code that defines the controller actions and where to put the associated views. Along the way, we'll see how to organize the layout for your application and customize the look and feel with a stylesheet.

Creating a Simple Controller and Its Views

Remember in the last chapter that we created a simple controller and view for the `people` table using the scaffold? The scaffold is a powerful tool for getting started with Rails: it creates some boilerplate code for the controller and all its view components with a single command. However, as a learning tool it is not too useful. Initially, the controller can be baffling and take some time to understand; in addition, it produces terrible HTML, which has to be manually fixed. So, instead of sticking with the scaffold for the `Person` model, we will build a controller and views for that model from scratch.

The first thing we need to do is clean up the files created by the scaffold, so we can start from a clean slate. We can use a script to remove the controller and associated tests (while leaving the model intact):

```
$ script/destroy controller people
```

However, this doesn't remove the views. These reside in `app/views/people`, so remove the files inside this directory (e.g. in Eclipse, highlight them and press the **Delete** key).

There are a few other places where we have some residue from the scaffold, which should be removed:

1. `app/views/layouts/people.rhtml`
2. `public/stylesheets/scaffold.css`

Now, we are ready to create the controller. Although it might seem crazy, we are actually going to use a generator to replace some of the files we just deleted. However, this will give us nice clean class definitions that we can modify at our leisure:

```
$ script/generate controller people
      exists  app/controllers/
      exists  app/helpers/
      exists  app/views/people
      exists  test/functional/
      create  app/controllers/people_controller.rb
      create  test/functional/people_controller_test.rb
      create  app/helpers/people_helper.rb
```

The most important file for us is `app/controllers/people_controller.rb`. We could have manually created this file for ourselves; the generator just makes it easy and means we don't have to remember the syntax for declaring the controller class.

Open the file using Eclipse and edit it to look like this:

```
class PeopleController < ApplicationController
  def index
    render :text => 'Hello world'
  end
end
```

Next, start the server:

$ script/server

Browse to `http://localhost:3000/people`. You should see:

Not much to look at yet, but it demonstrates how easy it is to create a controller to serve content. Let's look at the class definition step by step:

```
class PeopleController < ApplicationController
  ...
end
```

The first line declares a new class called `PeopleController`. The less-than symbol (`<`) denotes inheritance in Ruby. In this case, our class is inheriting from an `ApplicationController` class. If you look carefully in the `app/controllers` directory, you should see a file called `application.rb`. This is the one that contains the `ApplicationController` class definition that our controller inherits from:

```
class ApplicationController < ActionController::Base
  session :session_key => '_Intranet_session_id'
end
```

This class, in turn, inherits from the `Base` class inside the `ActionController` module, one of the core Rails libraries. The `ApplicationController` class sits between our controllers and the core Rails libraries. This makes it simple for us to add functionality to all of our controllers: any methods we define inside the `ApplicationController` class become available to any of our inheriting controllers, which turns out to be very useful.

> The `session` method call in the `ApplicationController` class definition sets the key used for session cookies belonging to this application. See Chapter 8 for more details.

The next part of the class definition adds an action method called `index` to the controller:

```
. . .
   def index
      render :text => 'Hello world '
   end
. . .
```

All this method does is write some text into the response, using the built-in `render` method (available to all controller classes). The `render` method is the primary means of writing content to the response. It accepts a variety of arguments, as we'll see shortly; for now, we are using a `:text` option to send a string to be rendered. This bypasses the Rails templating system entirely, sending raw text to the response.

When we visited the URL `http://localhost:3000/people`, how did Rails know to call the `index` method? In Chapter 4 (*Rails and MVC*), we saw how the default routing in Rails breaks up the path in the URL into a *controller name* and an *action* to call on that controller. The controller name here is "people", so the `PeopleController` was invoked; as there is no action specified, Rails routes the request to the default action, `index`.

That's all there is to it. However, writing an application this way doesn't get us much further than PHP or similar languages. To render a whole HTML page, we would have to put the template in-line inside the method definition, which would be terrible. Fortunately, Rails has a view framework, which makes it easy to separate HTML templates from the controller actions, and tie the two together with conventions. In the next section, we'll use this to write a view, which displays a list of people in our database.

Views and Layouts

Before writing a view, we need to understand how Rails composes views into a full HTML page. The default language for writing Rails views is called ERb (Embedded Ruby). It's "embedded" because, the Ruby code is inserted among standard HTML tags; the code generates dynamic content inside the HTML page, based on the data retrieved from the model layer. You might also see the template language referred to as RHTML (Ruby HTML), as it is a particular dialect of ERb focused on web pages. Here's an ERb template, which will produce the same output as our existing index method, but nicely wrapped in valid XHTML:

```
<?xml version="1.0" encoding="UTF-8"?>
<!DOCTYPE html PUBLIC "-//W3C//DTD XHTML 1.0 Strict//EN" "http://www.
w3.org/TR/xhtml1/DTD/xhtml1-strict.dtd">
<html xmlns="http://www.w3.org/1999/xhtml" lang="en_GB" xml:lang="en_
GB">
<head>
<title>Intranet</title>
<meta http-equiv="Content-Type" content="text/html;charset=utf-8" />
</head>
<body>
<p><%= 'Hello world' %></p>
</body>
</html>
```

The non-HTML part of this page (the embedded Ruby bit) is the highlighted `<p><%= 'Hello world' %></p>` line. When Rails reads a template file like this one, it scans for any sections surrounded by the `<%` and `%>` tags. The Ruby code between the tags is then run; in this case, the code is `= 'Hello world'`. This prints a string into the response, replacing the tags and the code (the `=` character is a shortcut to print a string). The resulting HTML rendered to the response for this line is:

```
<p>Hello world</p>
```

The `<% %>` tags are used to inject dynamic elements into a page (like `<?php ... ?>` in PHP, or `<% ... %>` in ASP). As well as printing strings into the output, the tags may also wrap any valid piece of Ruby code: we'll see more of this later.

Adding a View to the Application

Associating a view with a controller action is achieved by placing the RHTML for the view into a file with the right name, in the right location inside the app directory.

The formula for the location of a view is:

```
<TEMPLATE_ROOT>/<controller>/<action>.rhtml
```

Here, `<TEMPLATE_ROOT>` is the root directory for views, with the default being `RAILS_ROOT/app/views`; `<controller>` is the name of the controller this view is associated with, and `<action>` is the action, which renders this view to the user. In our case, using the default `TEMPLATE_ROOT`, the file for the `people` controller and `index` action is called:

```
RAILS_ROOT/app/views/people/index.rhtml
```

Create a file with this name and add the RHTML code from the previous section to it.

> To modify the `TEMPLATE_ROOT` for your application, you can add a line to the configuration file for the appropriate environment (i.e. `production.rb` or `development.rb` inside the `config` directory) or for all environments (by editing `environment.rb`). For example, this will set the `TEMPLATE_ROOT` to a directory `my_views` inside the `RAILS_ROOT` directory:
>
> ```
> config.action_controller.template_root = File.
> join(RAILS_ROOT, 'my_views')
> ```

For a view to be rendered by an action, the action must either explicitly or implicitly call the `render` method. To make our `index` action explicitly render our new RHTML template, the index method inside the `PeopleController` could look like this:

```
def index
  render :action => 'index'
end
```

This is the same `render` method used in the previous version of the code, but with the argument `:action => 'index'` (instead of `:text => 'Hello world'`). This argument is specifying that `render` should use the template associated with the current controller's `index` action (i.e. `index.rhtml`). However, because this is such a common pattern, Rails allows us to simply omit the `render` line altogether:

```
def index
end
```

To test the template, start the server with `script/server` and browse to `http://localhost:3000/people`. You should see practically the same page in your browser as before, but now rendered from the template rather than using inline text output directly from the controller.

You can use Eclipse to generate the first XHTML page for a new Rails project (**File | New | Other**, then select **PHP > HTML file**). This means you don't have to remember the DOCTYPE syntax for the XHTML file, or the elements commonly inside the `<head>` element.

You can use Firefox's **Web Developer Toolbar** (`http://chrispederick.com/work/webdeveloper/`) to ensure that your first template page is a valid XHTML; then periodically test other pages to make sure you are not breaking things as you add more complex markup.

If you don't already use XHTML for your web applications, there are good reasons to start doing so. XHTML enforces a clean separation between the meaning of a page (marked up using HTML tags) and how the page is presented (which is encapsulated in a separate CSS file); see `http://www.w3.org/TR/xhtml1/` for more details.

Displaying Model Instances in a View

How do we get data from our database into a view? To make this more concrete, let's look at displaying a list of people using our `index` action, rendering the records through the `index.rhtml` template.

The first step is to get the data from the database via the `Person` model in the `PeopleController`, by adding some code to the `index` method:

```
class PeopleController < ApplicationController
  def index
    @people = Person.find_all_ordered
  end
end
```

This method now makes use of the `find_all_ordered` method on the `Person` model class (see the section *Writing a Custom Finder* in Chapter 4), which returns all the records from the `people` table, ordered by last name, then by first name. The return value from the class method call is stored in an instance variable `@people` (the '@' marks it as an instance variable). Any instance variables set inside an action like this are available to the next-rendered view template (`index.rhtml`, in our case). In this case, the instance variable is set from the model; however, we can set any instance variable we like using whatever method we want, and it will be automatically available to the template.

As the finder in this case returns an array of model instances, we can loop over them using ERb (put this code inside the `<body>` tag):

```
<h1>People list</h1>
<table>
<tr>
<th>Name</th>
</tr>
<% @people.each do |person| -%>
<tr><td><%= person.last_name + ', ' + person.first_name %></td></tr>
<% end -%>
</table>
```

Here, we are using a block (highlighted) to iterate over the @people array, and creating an HTML table row for each person. Used in this way, the block acts like a foreach in PHP: it enables processing each element of the array in turn, assigning one to a temporary variable (here called person) on each iteration. (Note that the person variable doesn't need to be an instance variable, as it is only used within the scope of the block.)

The -%> at the end of the first line is a new piece of syntax we haven't used before (notice the extra minus sign). This removes any newline characters from the end of a line of ERb code when that line of code is run. Where a template contains lines of ERb that don't produce any output, the - ensures that each such line produces no newline characters in the source. Without the -, ERb that produces no HTML will still add a newline character to the HTML source.

Inside the block, we have access to all of the standard methods on the model instances; here, the methods correspond to the field names in the people table. In this case, we are just showing each person's last and first names.

Test the new view at http://localhost:3000/people (you don't need to restart the server if it is already running, as the views will be refreshed automatically):

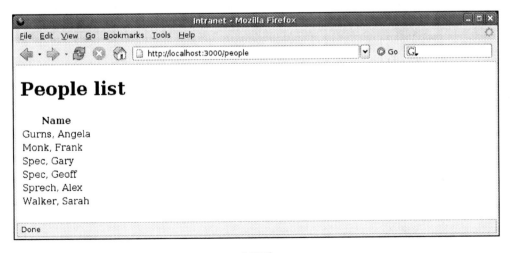

This view is very basic, and can get very long as the database fills up. The solution to this is to add some pagination to the results so that we can display just a few records at a time.

Pagination

Pagination in other languages can be a real pain. But Rails provides a variety of wrapper classes that make pagination simple.

We are going to add a paginator to the `index` action for our application. The first step is to replace our current method definition with one that uses the paginator classes:

```
def index
  @paginator, @people = paginate :person, :per_page => 2,
  :order => 'last_name, first_name'
end
```

The method we're calling here is `paginate`, available to all controllers. This takes a symbol representing the model class we want to paginate over (`:person`) as its first argument. Rails converts this into a reference to the correct class (`Person`), and calls that class's `find` method. The rest of the arguments specify conditions for the `find`:

1. `:per_page` defines the number of records to return on each page (we're using 2 here, as we don't have many records, but want to be able to check that pagination is working).

2. `:order` sorts the records (see the section *Sorting Records* in Chapter 4).

The method returns an array with two elements: an instance of the `ActionController::Pagination::Paginator` class (which we'll return to momentarily), and an array of model instances. We map the elements of the returned array onto two instance variables, `@paginator` and `@people` respectively.

Our `index.rhtml` view already uses the model instances to create the list of person names, so we can test the new index action at `http://localhost:3000/people`. You should see the first two records from the database displayed. Now, try accessing `http://localhost:3000/people?page=2`; you should see the next two records. Rails is automatically parsing the page parameter from the request URL and retrieving the appropriate records for the page (in the case of MySQL, by using a `LIMIT` clause in the query). We're currently supplying the page parameter manually, but what we really want is an automated set of "pager links" at the base of the page, where each link points to an individual page of results.

We could manually code the pager links in HTML, but fortunately Rails provides some useful HTML-generation methods we can use instead, called **helpers**.

Helpers

A Rails helper is a Ruby method used within ERb, which generates some HTML or JavaScript output. These methods can be called from any view template and are available automatically to all templates. It is also possible to create your own helpers, either for use with any controller or on a per-controller basis (see the section *Custom Helpers* later in this chapter).

The helper we're interested in here is `pagination_links`, which will create a series of page links. The helper can be invoked in the `app/views/people/index.rhtml` view template with:

```
<p><%= pagination_links(@paginator) %></p>
```

Place this at the bottom of the page, just before the `</body>` tag. Browse to `http://localhost:3000/people` and you should see:

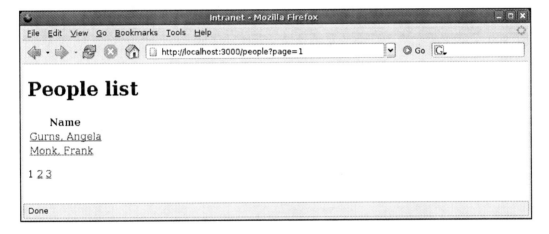

Note the links to the results pages at the base of the page. The `pagination_links` helper can also be supplied with other options to customize its behavior:

```
# show links to the 3 pages before and the 3 pages
# after the current page (default is 2 either side);
# any pages not linked to are represented by '...'
pagination_links(@paginator, :window_size => 3)

# include a link to the current page (default is false)
pagination_links(@paginator, :link_to_current_page => true)

# add some extra querystring parameters to each link URL
pagination_links(@paginator, :params => { :day => 'today' })
```

It's also relatively simple to interrogate the paginator to find the current page number and the total number of pages, making it possible to do **Previous** and **Next** links:

```
<p>
<% page_num = @paginator.current.number -%>
<% last_page_num = @paginator.last.number -%>
<%= link_to('Previous', :page => page_num - 1) + " " unless 1 ==
page_num -%>
<%= pagination_links(@paginator) %>
<%= link_to('Next', :page => page_num + 1) unless last_page_num ==
page_num -%>
</p>
```

The highlighted sections of the code demonstrate how to query the paginator to find the current page and its number (`@paginator.current.number`), and how to work out the last page number (`@paginator.last.number`—there is also `@paginator.first` for the first page). Next, two links are added using the `link_to` helper, which creates an HTML `<a>` element (more on this helper in the next section). However, here the helper is called conditionally by appending an `unless` clause. This compares the current page number (`page_num`) with 1 to decide whether to display the **Previous** link; and with the total number of pages (`last_page_num`) to decide whether to generate the **Next** link.

Linking to Another View

The people list view doesn't tell us much about a person (just their name). The next logical view for us to build is a detailed view for a single person; this will be accessible from the list view by a hyperlink on a person's name, creating a so-called **drill-down**.

The first step is to put a link onto each name when it is displayed. There is another Rails helper (see the previous section), which can help here, called `link_to`. This will turn any string into an HTML link (`<a>`) element, enabling you to either specify an absolute URL or a URL for a controller, and/or action inside the application. Edit the `app/views/people/index.rhtml` template and change the code that lists people so it looks like this:

```
<% @people.each do |person| -%>
<tr><td>
<%= link_to person.full_name, :action => 'show', :id => person.id %>
</td></tr>
<% end -%>
```

Recall that we defined the `full_name` method in Chapter 4 (see the section *Virtual Attributes*), to show a person's title, first name, and last name. Visit `http://localhost:3000/people` and you should see a list of links, rather than plain text names. If you view the HTML source, there is a line like this for each person:

```
<a href="/people/show/3">Mr. Frank Monk</a>
```

This is what `link_to` produces. Dissecting the code above, line by line, explains what's going on:

1. First, we call the `link_to` method, passing three arguments:

    o   The text for the link (`person.full_name`).

    o   The action the link should point to, used to construct the `href` attribute for the `<a>` element. Note that we don't have to specify the controller: unless we specify to the contrary, Rails assumes the current controller (`people`) as the destination.

    o   An `id` to add into the URL. This is a special argument, which tells Rails to set the ID part of the URL, in this case from the person's ID.

2. The destination for the link is built from the controller, the action, and the ID parts. These are joined together according to the routing configuration (see Chapter 7 *Improving the User Experience* for more information on routing).

3. The `link_to` method returns an HTML `<a>` element with the generated `href` attribute and link text. This is printed to the output using the standard `<%= ... %>` syntax.

`link_to` can also take optional arguments to insert extra attributes into the `<a>` element. For example, we can append arbitrary parameters to the URL produced by passing them as extra options:

```
<%= link_to 'Bill', :action => 'show', :id => person.id,
:random => 'true' %>
```

which produces the following:

```
<a href="/people/show/1?random=true">Bill</a>
```

(We used this approach in the previous section to add a `page` parameter to the query string.)

As another example, if we wanted to set the HTML `class` and `title` attributes, we could do the following:

```
<%= link_to full_name, { :action => 'show', :id => person.id },
{ :title => "Show details", :class => "person_link" } %>
```

{Why all the extra braces}?

In the first version of the `link_to` method call, we passed a few arguments without needing to use any braces; in the second version, we separated the arguments into two groups, each delimited by braces: the first set for building the `href` attribute of the `<a>` element, and the second specifying extra HTML attributes. This is because, if you pass a range of arguments to a Ruby method using `key => value` syntax, but without braces, Ruby will gather all of those: `key => value` pairs into a hash. In the case of `link_to`, if we leave the braces off, all of the arguments after the first are gathered into a hash of URL options. This isn't what we want—only some of them are used to generate the URL, and the rest are to add attributes to the HTML elements.

The method signature for `link_to` actually has four parameters:

```
link_to(link_text, url_options, html_options, more_
options)
```

By adding the braces when we call the method with multiple `key =>` `value` pairs as arguments, we are explicitly dividing those pairs into two separate hashes, one for `url_options` and the second for `html_options`. (`more_options` is yet another hash, which is passed through to the main URL-generation function on the controller, which we don't need to worry about.) This *is* what we want.

Many Rails methods have similar signatures and will try to do smart things with hashes. Sometimes they fail, and you get odd error messages. If in doubt, you can always put braces around the arguments passed to a method to explicitly group them.

Once we have the link, we need to hook it up to the controller. Note that our links point to an action called `show` in the `PeopleController` class, so we add this next:

```
def show
  @person = Person.find(params[:id])
end
```

We are again using the `find` method of the `Person` class within this action. But rather than retrieving all the people in the database, we are using the `id` parameter from the request to determine the ID of the person to retrieve. The `params` method, available to every controller, returns a hash containing all the GET and POST parameters from the request. In this case, `params` contains an `:id` key, which holds the ID passed in the request; the value of the `:id` key, in turn, is derived from the request URL, using routing to decompose the URL into its component parts (the inverse of how routing composes URLs from component parts, e.g. when used internally by `link_to`).

The final step is to add a view to show the person's details. This goes in `app/views/people/show.rhtml` (so that it is automatically associated with the `show` action):

```
<!DOCTYPE html PUBLIC "-//W3C//DTD XHTML 1.0 Strict//EN" "http://www.
w3.org/TR/xhtml1/DTD/xhtml1-strict.dtd">
<html xmlns="http://www.w3.org/1999/xhtml" lang="en_GB" xml:lang="en_
GB">
<head>
<title>Intranet</title>
<meta http-equiv="Content-Type" content="text/html;charset=utf-8" />
</head>
<body>
<h1><%= @person.full_name %></h1>
<p><strong>Job title:</strong> <%= @person.job_title %></p>
<p><strong>Email address:</strong> <%= mail_to @person.email %></p>
<p><strong>Telephone:</strong> <%= @person.telephone %></p>
<p><strong>Mobile phone:</strong> <%= @person.mobile_phone %></p>
<p><strong>Date of birth:</strong> <%= @person.date_of_birth %></p>
<p><strong>Gender:</strong> <%= @person.gender %></p>
<p><strong>Keywords:</strong> <%= @person.keywords %></p>
<p><strong>Notes:</strong><br/><%= @person.notes %></p>
</body>
</html>
```

The important part of the code is highlighted, which displays the fields from the retrieved `Person` instance. In all cases, except for `email`, the attribute is displayed as it is; in the case of the email attribute, another built-in helper called `mail_to` is used to convert the email address into a "mail to" link.

However, the eagle-eyed among you will have noticed that we have a big chunk of repeated HTML in the `show.rhtml` view template (the header for the HTML file, above the `<body>` tag, and from `</body>` down), which is the same as the HTML in the `index.rhtml` view template. In the next section, we'll see how to fix this so the "wrapper" HTML only occurs in one place. You may also have noticed that we have blanks in the display where attributes have not been set: we will fix this later in the chapter (see the section *Custom Helpers*), where we'll look at writing some custom helpers to manage this, displaying a "not defined" message instead.

Adding a Layout

Rails provides a way of abstracting out the "wrapper" portions of an RHTML page (the bits above and below the content of a view) into a separate **layout template** (**layout** for short). A layout typically contains the boiler-plate HTML, which occurs on every page: for example, the DOCTYPE declaration, <head> element, links to stylesheets or JavaScripts common across the application, etc. In most cases, it makes sense to use one layout for the whole application (which makes the views for every controller look the same); however, Rails does provide the facility to set a different layout for each controller, or for a group of controllers, covered briefly below.

All layouts are stored in the app/views/layouts directory. Within this directory, convention is used to associate a layout with one or more controllers, or with the application as a whole. To associate a layout with every controller in an application, it should be named application.rhtml; to associate a layout with a particular controller, it should be named after the controller: for example, a layout specific to PeopleController would be called people.rhtml. Rails will use the most-specific layout available when rendering an individual view template.

For the *Intranet* application, copy one of the existing view templates from app/views/people (index.rhtml will do) to app/views/layouts. Rename the file to application.rhtml and modify its content to the following:

```
<!DOCTYPE html PUBLIC "-//W3C//DTD XHTML 1.0 Strict//EN" "http://www.
w3.org/TR/xhtml1/DTD/xhtml1-strict.dtd">
<html xmlns="http://www.w3.org/1999/xhtml" lang="en_GB" xml:lang="en_
GB">
<head>
<title>Intranet</title>
<meta http-equiv="Content-Type" content="text/html;charset=utf-8" />
</head>
<body>
<%= yield %>
</body>
</html>
```

The highlighted section of the above code outputs the content generated by the view template for the action; this is then wrapped inside the layout template to produce the final page rendering.

In the view templates, instead of outputting the whole of the wrapper HTML (DOCTYPE, <head>, etc.), now, we just need to generate the HTML that goes inside the <body> element. The code for app/views/people/show.rhtml looks like this as a result:

```
<h1><%= @person.full_name %></h1>
<p><strong>Job title:</strong> <%= @person.job_title %></p>
<p><strong>Email address:</strong> <%= mail_to @person.email %></p>
<p><strong>Telephone:</strong> <%= @person.telephone %></p>
<p><strong>Mobile phone:</strong> <%= @person.mobile_phone %></p>
<p><strong>Date of birth:</strong> <%= @person.date_of_birth %></p>
<p><strong>Gender:</strong> <%= @person.gender %></p>
<p><strong>Keywords:</strong> <%= @person.keywords %></p>
<p><strong>Notes:</strong><br/><%= @person.notes %></p>
```

We also need to edit app/views/people/index.rhtml, removing everything from (and including) <body> up, and everything from (and including) </body> down, leaving just the content specific to that view. If you now visit http://localhost:3000/people, the page should remain unchanged, even though, behind the scenes, it is being rendered via a layout.

Using an application.rhtml layout is fine for cases where you want every controller to have the same layout; and we have already seen that per-controller layouts are also possible by naming the layout after the controller. However, it is also possible to bend the conventions further. You can force a layout for a controller using the layout method inside the controller class definition, e.g.

```
class PeopleController < ApplicationController
  layout 'pretty'
  ...
end
```

This would force the PeopleController to use the layout in app/views/layouts/pretty.rhtml. Using this technique makes it possible to arbitrarily associate controllers with layouts, entirely overriding the conventions.

Page Titles in Layouts

Having a single layout for the whole application makes it significantly simpler to write views, as we don't have to worry about duplicating HTML in multiple places. However, our current setup doesn't support different titles for each page, as the content of the <title> element is set once in the layout. This makes the browser history completely meaningless, and removes a potential navigation element.

Rails comes to the rescue once more. Any instance variables initialized in a controller action are available to the layout, as well as to the view. So we can set a title for each action and then output this inside the `<title>` element in the layout.

First, for each action in `PeopleController`, set a variable called `@page_title`:

```
def index
  @paginator, @people = paginate :person, :per_page => 2,
  :select => 'id, last_name, first_name',
  :order => 'last_name, first_name'
  @page_title = "People (page #{@paginator.current.number})"
end

def show
  @person = Person.find params[:id]
  @page_title = "Profile for " + @person.full_name
end
```

The `@page_title` variable can contain information about the context of the action — in our case, the number of the results page we are on for the `index` action, and the person's full name for the `show` action. We can now make use of this variable in the `app/views/layouts/application.rhtml` layout, inside the `<title>` element:

```
<title><%= @page_title || 'Intranet' %></title>
```

The `||` syntax means that the content of the `@page_title` variable is used for the page title if it has been set; if it is `nil`, the string `'Intranet'` is used as a default instead. We can also access this variable inside view templates, to make the page `<title>` element have the same content as the page `<title>` element. For example, in `app/views/people/show.rhtml` we can do the following:

```
<h1><%= @page_title %></h1>
<p><strong>Job title:</strong> <%= @person.job_title %></p>
...
```

Adding a Stylesheet

Styling the simple views created in the previous sections can be done through a standard CSS stylesheet. For example, we could put borders and padding on tables, and change the font in the following manner:

```
{
  font-family: verdana, arial, helvetica, sans-serif;
}
table, tr, td, th {
  border: solid #777 thin;
  padding: 5px;
```

```
    border-collapse: collapse;
    text-align: left;
    vertical-align: top;
}
```

The Rails convention is to put stylesheet files into the `public/stylesheets`
directory. The name of the stylesheet isn't too important, and you can use `core.css`,
`base.css`, or similar; for *Intranet*, we'll use `base.css`.

If you place your stylesheets in `public/stylesheets`, you can use the
`stylesheet_link_tag` helper to pull your stylesheets into a page. In our case, as
we want the stylesheet to be used for every page, and every page uses the same
layout (`app/views/layouts/application.rhtml`), it makes sense to call the helper
from that layout:

```
<head>
<title><%= @page_title || 'Intranet' %></title>
<meta http-equiv="Content-Type" content="text/html;charset=utf-8" />
<%= stylesheet_link_tag 'base' %>
</head>
```

which produces the following:

```
<link href="/stylesheets/base.css?1165272734" media="screen"
rel="Stylesheet" type="text/css" />
```

You may be wondering why a seemingly random number has been
appended to the generated URL (in this case, `1165272734`). This number
is called the **Rails asset ID**, and represents the last time the referenced file
was modified. Browsers cache assets they fetch, using the URL (including
the querystring) as the key for the cached asset. As Rails includes the
file modification time in the URL for an asset (stylesheets, JavaScripts,
images), the browser cache is forced to store different versions of the asset
under different keys. This ensures that the browser always fetches new
versions of assets when the asset file has been modified.

Note that this only happens in the development environment; in
production, the URLs just reference the asset, without a querystring,
so they are cached just once by the browser, using its standard
caching settings.

The `stylesheet_link_tag` takes one or more stylesheet file names, minus the `.css` suffix, and with no path information (providing the stylesheet is in `public/stylesheets`). If your stylesheets are in unconventional locations, you can pass a path to the stylesheet, e.g.

```
# link to '/styles/core.css'
stylesheet_link_tag '/styles/core'
# link to '/stylesheets/mystyles/fancy.css'
# (relative paths are append to '/stylesheets')
stylesheet_link_tag 'mystyles/fancy'
```

You can also pass an `options` hash to set attributes on the `<link>` element produced, e.g.

```
stylesheet_link_tag 'print', :media => 'print'
```

Adding a Controller for Companies

The previous sections went into some detail about the concepts of controllers and views, and how they fit together. In this section, we will fast-track the creation of another controller and a view (for companies), both to get a feel for the flow of creating a controller, and to summarize what we've just covered.

Create the CompaniesController

First, generate the controller for the `Company` model from the command line:

```
$ script/generate controller companies
```

Now, add the `index` action (which will display a list of companies) to `app/controllers/companies_controller.rb`:

```
class CompaniesController < ApplicationController
  def index
    @paginator, @companies = paginate :company, :per_page => 10,
    :order => 'name'
    @page_title = "List of Companies"
  end
end
```

Create the Index View

Add the view for the index action (in app/views/companies/index.rhtml):

```
<h1><%= @page_title %></h1>
<table>
<tr>
<th>Name</th>
<th>Phone</th>
<th>Fax</th>
<th>Website</th>
</tr>
<% for company in @companies -%>
<tr>
<td><%= company.name %></td>
<td><%= company.telephone %></td>
<td><%= company.fax %></td>
<td><%= link_to(company.website, company.website) %></td>
</tr>
<% end -%>
</table>
<p>
<% page_num = @paginator.current.number -%>
<% last_page_num = @paginator.last.number -%>
<%= link_to('Previous', :page => page_num - 1) + " " unless 1 ==
page_num -%>
<%= pagination_links(@paginator) %>
<%= link_to('Next', :page => page_num + 1) unless last_page_num ==
page_num -%>
</p>
```

Note that the pagination code here is identical to the code in the people index template. We will investigate a way to avoid this repetition later in the chapter (see the section *Rendering Pagination Links with a Partial*).

Because this view contains almost all the information relating to a company (barring the company address, which we'll return to later in the section *Showing Associated Records*), a view to show a single company is redundant, as it will contain no more information than the index view. For now, then, we can leave this action out. There is an important point here: if you don't need an action, don't add it to the controller. This is also an advantage of custom-building your actions and views, as opposed to using the scaffold to generate them for you.

Test It!

That's all the work we need to do to view the list of companies. Fire up the server and browse to: http://localhost:3000/companies. You should see the following page:

You may notice that there are gaps in some of the cells in the table, if a company doesn't have a particular attribute specified (e.g. missing fax or telephone number). We will deal with this situation later (see the section *Default Messages for Empty Fields* later in this chapter).

Summary

This section demonstrated the whole process of writing controllers and their views, showing how to build the CompaniesController to display data from the Company model. With a firm grounding in the concepts underlying controllers, views, layouts, and helpers, we are well prepared for building more complex actions and views, including those for managing data input and validation.

Advanced View Techniques

In this section, we will look at a few utility features and techniques for extending views.

Custom Helpers

As discussed earlier, a helper is a method that encapsulates logic that might otherwise clutter a view template. Rails includes a multitude of built-in helpers, some of which we've already encountered (`link_to`, `mail_to`, `stylesheet_link_tag`), and others we'll meet shortly (see the section *C*UD (Create, Update, Delete)* later in this chapter). However, it is sometimes useful to create custom helpers, to centralize the view logic in an application. Examples of cases where we might want to do this are given below:

- Displaying an image wrapped inside a link tag, perhaps with `class` attributes on both the `<img>` and `<a>` elements

- Showing error messages with consistent styling across the whole application

- Formatting date objects into a more readable format

- Showing consistent text for empty fields (e.g. "not specified") when displaying a model instance

- Displaying a login link to users who haven't logged in yet, or showing a username if they are logged in

In all of these cases, the logic could be put directly in the template; but too much clutter makes templates hard to follow and repetitive. Helpers provide a means to keep templates clean and simple while not restricting the flexibility of views.

There is one more consideration when writing helpers: Rails provides two locations where you can put them:

1. *Controller-specific*
   In a file specific to the controller, in `app/helpers/<controller>_helper.rb`, where `<controller>` is the name of the controller. For example, helpers specific to `PeopleController` would go in `app/helpers/people_helper.rb`; these might include methods to format a person's name or email address.

2. *Application-level*
   In a file shared by all controllers, in `app/helpers/application_helper.rb`. This might include generic date formatting or error message helpers.

Rails will automatically load the controller-specific helpers when a controller is invoked, and the application-level helpers for every controller invocation. We will look at an example of both types of helpers in the next two sections, each of which will take some logic out of our views.

Virtual attributes and helpers (a recap)

In Chapter 4, we saw how to write virtual attributes which derive from real fields in the table but have no corresponding field of their own. Virtual attributes should be used where the output will be used in multiple contexts; helpers should be used to manipulate data to view-specific output. That distinction should be kept in mind here: the helpers we're writing produce output we're only going to use in HTML views.

Default Messages for Empty Fields

When displaying individual records, the current `show.rhtml` template shows an ugly blank where a field has no set value. Instead, it may be better to show a default message where a record has a blank field, e.g. "not specified". We will potentially need this functionality in multiple views, so it makes sense to add the helper to `app/helpers/application_helper.rb`:

```ruby
module ApplicationHelper
  # Display a default message for empty fields.
  #
  # +field_value+ is the value to process.
  def d(field_value=nil)
    if field_value.blank?
      return content_tag('em', 'not specified')
    else
      return field_value
    end
  end
end
```

The d method (helper) defined here is passed a field value, which is interrogated by the Rails convenience method `blank?`; `blank?` returns `true` if the value is empty or nil. If no argument is passed, the value `nil` is assigned to `field_value` by default (the parameter `field_value=nil` in the method signature specifies the default). If the field value is blank, the helper supplies a default empty field message inside an `<em>` element, via the `content_tag` helper: this takes a string representing an HTML tag as the first argument, and the content to put inside the tag as its second argument; optionally, you can pass extra `:attribute => value` pairs to add to the HTML element.

This method can be called wherever a field could be blank. For example, we can rewrite `app/views/people/show.rhtml` using it (highlighted lines below):

```
<h1><%= @page_title %></h1>
<p><strong>Job title:</strong> <%=d @person.job_title %></p>
<p><strong>Email address:</strong> <%= mail_to @person.email %></p>
<p><strong>Telephone:</strong> <%=d @person.telephone %></p>
<p><strong>Mobile phone:</strong> <%=d @person.mobile_phone %></p>
<p><strong>Date of birth:</strong> <%=d @person.date_of_birth %></p>
<p><strong>Gender:</strong> <%= @person.gender %></p>
<p><strong>Keywords:</strong> <%=d @person.keywords %></p>
<p><strong>Notes:</strong><br/><%=d @person.notes %></p>
```

However, for fields that are never empty (because we made sure they had a value when performing validation), we don't need to use the `d` function.

Date Formatting

The display for a person's date of birth defaults to the international standard date notation (YYYY-MM-DD, e.g. "1968-01-08"). However, this is alien to most people: it would make more sense to show a "humanized" version of the date instead (e.g. "8th January 1968"). We could first add a generic date formatting method to the `application_helper.rb` file to do this:

```
module ApplicationHelper
  ...
  # Display date in human-readable format, e.g. "8th January 1968".
  #
  # Returns +nil+ if +date_to_format+ is blank.
  def human_date(date_to_format)
    if date_to_format.blank?
      out = nil
    else
      # Get the day part of the date with
      # the "ordinal suffix" (th, rd, nd) appended
      day = date_to_format.day.ordinalize

      # strftime accepts a formatting string, which specifies
      # which parts of the date to include in the output string
      out = date_to_format.strftime("#{day} %B %Y")
    end
    out
  end
end
```

The `strftime` method used in the `human_date` method is very useful for formatting `Date` and `DateTime` objects. It accepts a format string, much like PHP's `strftime` function, containing placeholders for elements of the date and/or time, marked with a preceding "%" character. Here are the placeholders you can use with the Ruby version of `strftime`; the examples, all use 6th December 2006 at 9:30 a.m. as the date being formatted:

Placeholder...	Is replaced by...	Example
%A	Full day name	Wednesday
%a	Short day name	Wed
%w	Day of the week (0...6, with Sunday being 0)	3
%d	Day of month, zero-padded	06
%e	Day of month, with a leading space if less than 10	6
%j	Day of the year (001...366)	340
%U	Week number (00...53); the first Sunday of the year is treated as the first day of the first week	49
%W	Week number (00...53), the first Monday of the year is treated as the first day of the first week	49
%B	Full month name	December
%b	Short month name	Dec
%m	Month number, zero-padded	12
%H	Hour of day, zero-padded	09
%Y	Four-digit representation of the year	2006
%y	Two-digit representation of the year	06
%I (capital i)	Hour of the day, 12-hour clock (01...12)	09
%M	Minute of hour, zero-padded	30
%S	Seconds of minute, zero-padded	00
%T	Time (same as "%H:%M:%S")	09:30:00
%c	The preferred date and time representation	Wed Dec 6 09:30:00 2006
%x	Preferred date representation without time	12/06/06
%X	Preferred time representation without date	09:30:00
%p	The meridiem in uppercase (AM or PM)	AM
%P	The meridiem in lowercase (am or pm)	am
%%	Literal percentage symbol (%)	%
%F	ISO date representation (same as "%Y-%m-%d")	2006-12-06

"Zero-padded" means that a single leading zero is added to the representation of the time part if its value is less than 10.

Here are a few more examples of format strings for `strftime`, using some of these placeholders:

- Standard UK date format: `"%d/%m/%Y"` –
  Example output: "06/12/2006"
- Standard UK date format with short year: `"%d/%m/%y"` –
  Example output: "06/12/06"
- Standard UK date format with time: `"%d/%m/%Y %T"` –
  Example output: "06/12/2006 09:30:00"

We can now modify `app/views/people/show.rhtml` to use our new `human_date` method:

```
<p><strong>Date of birth:</strong>
<%=d human_date(@person.date_of_birth) %></p>
```

Showing Associated Records

The views we've created so far show one or more records from a single table. However, more often than not, tables in the database are related to each other. We need to be able to pull records out of the related tables and show them alongside each other.

In the *Intranet* application, the `show.rhtml` template for the `PeopleController` shows a person's details, as stored in the `people` table. As well as these details, we also need to show a person's home address. The address is stored in a separate table, `addresses`; the `address_id` field in the `people` table acts as a foreign key, referencing a record in this table (see Chapter 4 *Working with Rails*).

We can access a person's address inside the `show.rhtml` template through the `@person` instance, using its `address` method:

```
<% address = @person.address -%>
```

The `address` method is automatically available on instances of the `Person` class, as the `Person` class declares a `belongs_to` relationship with the `Address` model (see the section *Associations between Models*, in Chapter 4).

We can then append some more ERb code to `show.rhtml` to display attributes from the address (but only if the person has an address — the conditional parts are highlighted):

```
<p><strong>Address:</strong><br/>
<% address = @person.address -%>
<% if address -%>
<%= address.street_1 %><br/>
<%= address.street_2 + tag('br') unless address.street_2.blank? -%>
<%= address.street_3 + tag('br') unless address.street_3.blank? -%>
<%= address.city + tag('br') unless address.city.blank? -%>
<%= address.county + tag('br') unless address.county.blank? -%>
<%= address.post_code %>
<% else -%>
<%= d %>
<% end -%>
</p>
```

This code fragment demonstrates how to conditionally execute a block of code inside an RHTML template, using `if...else...end`. It also calls the `d` helper defined earlier, to display an error message if the person doesn't have a home address set.

Refining Using a Helper

There are several repeated lines in the template, which show parts of the address (plus a `<br />` element), but only if they have a value, e.g:

```
<%= address.street_2 + tag('br') unless address.street_2.blank? -%>
```

This is a good case where an application-level helper can reduce the repetition in a template:

```
module ApplicationHelper
  ...
  # Display +field_value+ followed by a <br> element,
  # but only if +field_value+ is set; otherwise return nil.
  def field_with_break(field_value)
    unless field_value.blank?
      return field_value + tag('br')
    else
      return nil
    end
  end
end
```

We can now reduce the address part of the template to:

```
<p><strong>Address:</strong><br/>
<% address = @person.address -%>
<% if address -%>
<%= address.street_1 %><br/>
<%= field_with_break address.street_2 -%>
<%= field_with_break address.street_3 -%>
<%= field_with_break address.county -%>
<%= field_with_break address.city -%>
<%= address.post_code %>
<% else -%>
<%=d nil %>
<% end -%>
</p>
```

Showing an Address with a Partial

The show.rhtml template is specific to a person: it shows their details, including their home address. However, companies can also have addresses: so we will need to include some code to render a company's address in app/views/companies/index. rhtml (we've avoided this so far).

One option would be to add a block of address-rendering code to app/views/ addresses/index.rhtml, to show the address for each company; this would be similar to the code we already have in app/views/people/show.rhtml. But this would mean repeating ourselves, as we would have identical blocks of code in multiple locations.

In addition to adding repetition, we are already breaking Rails conventions by rendering addresses from inside views for PeopleController. Typically, the templates for a model are stored in a folder specific to the corresponding controller; but here, the RHTML code for rendering an Address is tied into the template for the Person model. But, at the same time, we don't want to show an address in its own full-page template: we only want to show it in conjunction with a person or company. So adding a full template for displaying an address inside a layout is unnecessary.

Rails provides a solution for this situation: **partial templates** (or **partials** for short). A partial is used to generate a page fragment (typically RHTML), which can be used inside other templates. They can be called from inside other RHTML files, or even rendered directly from inside a controller (in lieu of a full-page template), to produce a "fragment" of output.

By convention, Rails partials are included in the views directory for the controller. In our case, a partial for addresses goes in app/views/addresses. To distinguish partials from full-page templates, an underscore is prepended to the name of the partial: for example, the partial to show an address would intuitively be called _show.rhtml. Our partial should therefore go in the file app/views/addresses/_show.rhtml; the content can be cut and pasted from the show.rhtml file for people (app/views/people/show.rhtml), and looks like this:

```
<% if address -%>
<%= address.street_1 %><br/>
<%= field_with_break address.street_2 -%>
<%= field_with_break address.street_3 -%>
<%= field_with_break address.city -%>
<%= field_with_break address.county -%>
<%= address.post_code %>
<% else -%>
<%= d %>
<% end -%>
```

The main difference between the original we copied and this code is that references to the @person variable have been removed. Instead, a local variable called address is referenced. Provided this variable is passed to the partial when it is called from a controller or view, the partial can be used inside any other template.

Another difference is that paragraph tags have been removed from the partial. This means the output can be used either inside paragraphs (e.g. when showing a person) or inside table cells (e.g. in the companies list).

To render the partial inside another template, call it using the render method, e.g. in app/views/people/show.rhtml:

```
...
<p><strong>Notes:</strong><br/><%=d @person.notes %></p>
<p><strong>Address:</strong></p>
<p><%= render :partial => 'addresses/show',
:locals => {:address => @person.address} %></p>
```

Two things to note here are:

- The render method takes an option :partial, which specifies the path to the partial, relative to the views directory. Note that the underscore at the front of the partial name and the ".rhtml" suffix are excluded.

- The :locals option can send a hash of :name => value pairs to the partial. You can think of these as arguments being passed to a method: each pair is converted into a variable (here, address) set to the value passed in (here, the address instance associated with the person, @person.address). These variables then become available within the partial.

We can also reuse this partial inside `app/views/companies/index.rhtml`:

```
<% for company in @companies -%>
<tr>
<td>
<%= link_to company.name, { :action => 'show', :id => company.id },
{ :title => "Show details for this company" } %>
</td>
<td><%= company.telephone %></td>
<td><%= company.fax %></td>
<td><%= link_to(company.website, company.website) %></td>
<td><%= render :partial => 'addresses/show',
:locals => {:address => company.address} %></td>
</tr>
<% end -%>
```

Rendering Pagination Links with a Partial

The two `index.rhtml` templates we have written so far (one for people, the other for companies) have a repeated section of pagination code at the bottom. Rather than having this code in two places, it is better to put it in one file and pull this into the individual templates: a partial (see previous section) is an obvious solution.

However, the pagination code is not associated with any particular model; so where should it go? There is yet another Rails convention, which suggests that partials with no obvious "home" go into a directory called `app/views/shared`. Create this directory and add a file to it called `_paginator.rhtml`, which will contain the paginator code. The content of this file can be modified from the code at the bottom of `app/views/people/index.rhtml`:

```
<p><% page_num = paginator.current.number -%>
<% last_page_num = paginator.last.number -%>
<%= link_to('Previous', :page => page_num - 1) + " " unless 1 ==
page_num -%>
<%= pagination_links(paginator) %>
<%= link_to('Next', :page => page_num + 1) unless last_page_num ==
page_num -%></p>
```

The main change is replacing `@paginator` with `paginator` (minus the '@'). Instead of using an instance variable, we will instead pass the required variable in using the `:locals` option to `render`.

Call the new partial from `app/views/people/index.rhtml` and `app/views/companies/index.rhtml`, replacing the existing paginator code:

```
<%= render :partial => 'shared/paginator',
  :locals => { :paginator => @paginator } %>
```

Partial or helper?

Everything we've done with partials so far could also have been achieved with helpers: both enable the generation of chunks of content to insert inside templates, encapsulating logic, and repeated mark-up. So when should you use a partial and when a helper?

A good guideline is to look at the amount and complexity of markup (HTML or XML), you intend to generate. If you are primarily creating markup with little logic, *use a partial*: this is a much more natural way of laying out HTML or XML fragments. If you are doing a lot of logic in the partial, *use a helper*: too much logic looks ugly and awkward inside a partial, and is difficult to read when surrounded by HTML code.

Adding a Menu

Now that we have two controllers, navigating between them is becoming a pain: each time we want to get to a controller, we have to type the right path into the address bar in the browser. We need a menu.

There are several options to consider when deciding where to locate a menu:

- When using a single layout for our whole application (as we are), the layout template (`app/views/layouts/application.rhtml`) is the logical location for the menu. The menu can just be added as a standard RHTML fragment.

- When using different layouts for different controllers (see the earlier section, *Adding a Layout*), each layout might have its own menu, too. In this case, each menu could be coded into the appropriate layout, possibly using a helper to ensure consistency of styling.

- A variant of the above is where there are different layouts for different controllers, but with a single menu common to all of them. In this case, the menu could be stored in a partial, and pulled into the appropriate place in each layout.

To keep things simple, we'll put our menu into `app/views/layouts/application.rhtml`. We always have the option to extract it into a partial or helper later, if we want to. This is the revised `<body>` element, including the menu links:

```
...
<body>
<div id="menu">
  <p>Menu</p>
  <ul>
    <li><%= link_to 'Companies', :controller => 'companies' %></li>
    <li><%= link_to 'People', :controller => 'people' %></li>
  </ul>
</div>
<div id="content">
  <%= yield %>
</div>
</body>
...
```

The page is separated into two separate `<div>` elements, one for the menu and one for the page content. The menu itself is an unordered list; each list element uses the `link_to` helper to generate a link to the specified controller; as no action is specified, the `index` action is assumed in both cases.

Without some extra styling, the menu will be at the top of the page and will be displayed as a bulleted list. This can be fixed with some simple CSS to position the two `<div>` elements adjacent to each other, style the colours, and turn off bullet points on the menu list items (in `public/stylesheets/base.css`):

```
#menu {
  float: left;
  width: 15%;
  background-color: #FFF280;
  padding: 1% 1% 0 1%;
}
#menu > ul > li {
  list-style-type: none;
  margin-left: -2.5em;
}
#content {
  float: right;
  margin-left: 2%;
  margin-right: 2%;
  width: 79%;
}
```

The result makes our application look more like the real thing:

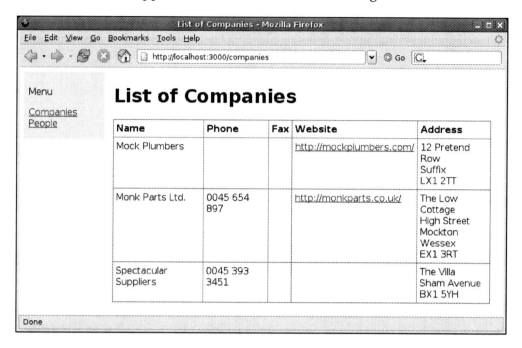

While this goes some way to making navigation easier, we still have the issue that if we go to the root of the web server, we get the Rails welcome page. We will fix this later by setting a specific controller and action as the default for the application, using routes (see Chapter 7 *Improving the User Experience*). When we go to the root of the application, we will then get the default controller/action, instead of the welcome page.

C*UD (Create, Update, Delete)

The previous sections of this chapter described how to do the **Retrieve** part of CRUD: pulling records from the database and formatting them as HTML. In this section, we will look at the other parts of CRUD: creating records, updating them, and deleting them.

We'll start with adding people, as this is the most likely way new data would make its way into the database: someone rings up Acme, and the member of staff adds their details to the database, such as name, email address, and phone number. They would probably want to attach a company record to the person at the same time, too.

Creating a Person

As with retrieve operations, we need two elements to implement person creation:

1. *Controller actions* to manage displaying the form for creating a record, as well as performing operations on the model to add the record to the database.

2. A *view* to display the interface, which enables the user to input the data for the new record.

Tackling the controller first, we can add a new action to app/controllers/people_controller.rb, which displays the form; and a create action, which manages adding the data to the database:

```
class PeopleController < ApplicationController
  # ... other actions ...

  # Only accept post requests to the new action;
  # redirect to index otherwise
  verify :method => :post, :only => :create,
  :redirect_to => {:action => :index}

  # Display a form to add a person, or attempt to save
  # if data posted in the request.
  def new
    @page_title = 'Add a new person'
    @person = Person.new
  end

  # Save submitted data to the database
  def create
    @person = Person.new(params[:person])
    if @person.save
      redirect_to :action => 'index'
    else
      @page_title = 'Add a new person'
      render :action => 'create'
    end
  end
end
```

The verify method ensures that the create method only accepts POST (and not GET requests). Any non-POST requests get automatically redirected to the index action. This prevents malicious users sending GET requests to create new people in the database.

When the `create` action runs, an instance variable, `@person`, is created and populated with parameters from the request; specifically, those associated with `:person`. As in PHP, Rails parses POST parameters into a hash of name-value pairs, accessible via the `params` method. So a POST body like this:

```
day=today&name=ell
```

is parsed into the hash:

```
{ :day => 'today', :name => 'ell' }
```

Additionally, Rails understands the specially formatted fields in HTML forms with names of the form `object[field]`. POST parameters with a name formatted like this create a sub-hash within the main `params` hash. The key into the sub-hash is derived from the first part of the field name (`object`). In our case, a POST request like the following:

```
day=today&name=ell&person%5Bfirst_name%5D=bill&person%5Blast_
name%5D=brum
```

is parsed into the hash:

```
{ :day => 'today', :name => 'ell', :person => { :first_name => 'bill',
:last_name => 'brum' } }
```

> If you're wondering about the `%5B` and `%5D` parts of the POST parameters, these are the URL-encoded representations of the [and] characters respectively. An `<input>` element like this:
>
> ```
> <input type="text" name="person[first_name]"
> value="Bill" />
> ```
>
> ends up sending a URL-encoded POST parameter like this:
>
> ```
> person%5Bfirst_name%5D=bill
> ```

Within the controller, we can then retrieve just the POST parameters relating to the person by accessing the `:person` key inside `params`, which would give us `{ :first_name => 'bill', :last_name => 'brum' }`.

Once `@person` has been instantiated, the action tries to save the input, which will return true or false. In cases where the save is successful, the `redirect_to` helper is used to send the client back to the index page (which lists all the people in the database).

Where the save fails, the default `app/views/people/new.rhtml` template is rendered. (Recall that if `render` is not explicitly called, the default is to call `render :action => <action_name>`, where `<action_name>` is the name of the action being executed.)

We'll create the form template next, used to insert the details for the person. To keep things simple, we'll start with a basic version of the form, which only displays the *required* fields for a person (`first_name`, `last_name`, `email`, `gender`):

```
<% form_for :person, @person, :url => {:action => 'create'} do |f| %>
<p><strong><label for="person_first_name">First name</label>:</
strong><br />
<%= f.text_field :first_name %></p>
<p><strong><label for="person_last_name">Last name</label>:</
strong><br />
<%= f.text_field :last_name %>
</p>
<p><strong><label for="person_email">Email address</label>:</
strong><br />
<%= f.text_field :email %></p>
<p><strong><label for="person_gender">Gender</label>:</strong>
<%= f.select :gender, Person::GENDERS.keys %></p>
<p><%= submit_tag 'Save' %></p>
<% end %>
```

This template does the following:

1. Uses the `form_for` method to create a form object for the `Person` model, using the `@person` instance to populate the fields of the form. As we are creating a new object, `@person` initially has blank fields. However, each time we POST to the `create` action, a new `@person` is created and populated with values from the request. So, if we are trying to save the new person and have validation errors, the object will contain the values we just set for each field. This means Rails can re-display the form and re-fill the fields with the values we first entered, and show this alongside the validation error messages.

2. Creates the individual form fields using more **Rails form helpers**. Note that each helper is called as a method on the object returned by `form_for` (f), e.g.

    ```
    f.text_field :first_name
    ```

    The `text_field` helper creates a standard HTML `<input>` element, generating the name of the element from the name of the model and setting its value by calling the `first_name` method on the model instance (`@person` here). The resulting HTML is:

    ```
    <input id="person_first_name" name="person[first_name]" size="30"
    type="text" value="" />
    ```

    Note that the `id` attribute is set to the name of the model, followed by an underscore, then the name of the attribute. The `for` attributes on the `<label>` elements are formatted in the same way.

You can specify extra HTML options by passing them to `text_field`, e.g.

```
f.text_field :first_name, :size => 20, :class => 'myfield'
```

The other form helper used in the form is `select`:

```
f.select :gender, Person::GENDERS.keys
```

`select` creates a `<select>` element, with options derived from a collection. In this case, we pass in the keys from the `Person::GENDERS` hash (i.e. `['M', 'F']`), which yields:

```
<select id="person_gender" name="person[gender]">

<option value="M">M</option>

<option value="F">F</option>

</select>
```

You can pass a hash of `name => value` pairs as the collection argument; but the `select` helper uses the `name` part of each pair to create the `<option>` `value` attribute, and uses the `value` part of each pair to create the `<option>` text. Passing the whole `Person::GENDERS` hash:

```
f.select :gender, Person::GENDERS
```

therefore, gives the wrong output (the full gender name is used for the `value` attributes on the `<option>` elements):

```
<select id="person_gender" name="person[gender]">

<option value="male">M</option>

<option value="female">F</option>

</select>
```

Here is a case for making `Gender` a model in its own right: this would give us the flexibility to format the genders so that they are suitable for creating a drop-down. As it is, we will stick with the simple solution for now, using the short form of the gender for both the option values and text.

To test the new form, browse to `http://localhost:3000/people/new`. Try adding one or two people and check that they appear in the people index. Don't worry about displaying validation errors for the moment: we'll come to that shortly.

Refining with a Helper

Notice all the repeated HTML code in the `create.rhtml` template (highlighted below)?

```
<p><strong><label for="person_first_name">First name</label>:</strong><br
/>
<%= f.text_field :first_name %></p>
<p><strong><label for="person_last_name">Last name</label>:</
strong><br />
<%= f.text_field :last_name %>
</p>
```

Time to add a custom helper! (Note that there is a minimal amount of HTML code to create here, so a helper is fine, rather than a partial.) We can make this an application-level helper, as we're likely to need it in other forms. We can also take the opportunity to use the helper to mark required fields with an asterisk:

```
module ApplicationHelper
  # ... other helpers ...
  # Format a label element for a form field.
  #
  # +options+ can include:
  #
  # [:required] If +true+, an asterisk is added to the label.
  # [:field_name] If true, the for attribute on the label
  #               is set from +model+ + +field_name+;
  #               otherwise, for attribute is set from
  #               +model+ + lowercased and underscored +label_text+.
  #
  # Example call:
  #    label(:person, 'Email')
  #
  # Example output:
  #    <strong><label for="person_email">Email</label>:</strong>
  def label(model, label_text, options={})
    # Use the field_name option if supplied
    field_name = options[:field_name]
    field_name ||= label_text.gsub(' ', '_')
    # The value for the for attribute.
    label_for = (model.to_s + '_' + field_name).downcase
    # The <label> tag
    label_tag = content_tag('label', label_text, :for => label_for)
    # Add an asterisk if :required option specified.
    label_tag += '*' if options[:required]
```

```
      # Finish off the label.
      label_tag += ':'
      # Wrap the <label> tag in a <strong> tag.
      content_tag('strong', label_tag)
   end
end
```

This is now ready for use in the form template, e.g.:

```
<p><%= label :person, 'First name', :required => true %><br />
<%= f.text_field :first_name %></p>
<p><%= label :person, 'Last name', :required => true %><br />
<%= f.text_field :last_name %></p>
```

Validation Errors

One of the beauties of the Model-View-Controller architecture is that the validation code we added to our models in Chapter 4 *Working with Rails* is still quietly doing its work in the background. If you attempt to add a person and leave one of the required fields blank, calling @person.save will return false, as the validation fails. Although, difficult to spot, Rails will also modify the view, wrapping any form element for which validation failed in a <div> element, e.g.:

```
<div class="fieldWithErrors"><input id="person_first_name"
name="person[first_name]" size="30" type="text" value="" /></div>
```

By styling this <div> with some CSS (in public/stylesheets/base.css), we can highlight the fields with errors, putting a red border around them, e.g.

```
.fieldWithErrors {
  border: 0.2em solid red;
  display: table;
}
```

Try saving an invalid person record now: any fields with errors are surrounded by a red border. Note that this works best in Firefox; in Internet Explorer, the red border spans the width of the whole page, rather than hugging the input element as it does in Firefox.

While automatic addition of a `<div>` is a cute trick, it does mean that the layout for forms built with the form helpers is somewhat limited: `<div>` elements appearing in the middle of your HTML can throw your format into unexpected shapes. This is why it's safest to put the label on one line and the input element after a linebreak (`<br />`) within the same paragraph. If you want more control over layout and want to avoid these automatic `<div>` elements, you can create input elements using the lower-level `*_tag` helpers, e.g. for a text field:

```
<%= text_field_tag 'person[email]', @person.email %>
```

(Note that there is no need to reference the form being built, `f`, as there is with the `text_field` helper.) If you take this approach, Rails will not wrap the field with a `<div>` if it throws a validation error; which means, you will have to manually highlight fields with errors too, perhaps with a custom helper.

The model validation rules defined in the previous chapter also set error messages when validation fails; we saw how to use these from the command line. We can get all the error messages for a model using another helper, `error_messages_for`:

```
<%= error_messages_for :person %>
```

This will display a block with a red frame, with errors shown as bullet points. Alternatively, we can get at the error messages (if any) for individual fields using the `error_message_on` method. For example, to place the error message for the `first_name` text field under the text input element:

```
<p><%= label :person, 'First name', :required => true %><br />
<%= f.text_field :first_name %>
<%= error_message_on :person, :first_name %></p>
```

Where an error message occurs, this helper adds a `<div>` to the view, with text set to the error message for the field, e.g. if validation of `first_name` fails this code will render:

```
<p><strong><label for="person_first_name">First name</label>*:</
strong><br />
<div class="fieldWithErrors"><input id="person_first_name"
name="person[first_name]" size="30" type="text" value="" /></div>
<div class="formError">Please enter a first name</div></p>
```

This `<div>` can easily be styled with CSS in `public/stylesheets/base.css`, e.g. to put error messages in slightly smaller, red text:

```
.formError {
  color: red;
  font-size: 0.9em;
}
```

We'll add the remaining error messages later, in the section *Finishing Touches*.

The Flash

Giving the user feedback about problems with their input is vital; but equally important is giving some feedback about actions that completed successfully. Currently, the user gets no feedback about whether their actions added a new person; they have to scan the list of people to see their new record.

What's needed is a short informational message indicating that the action was successful; this message needs to be carried from the action that adds the record to the view that is displayed next. However, we are currently using a redirect when the save is successful, back to the `index` view. The action we redirect to by default doesn't know anything about the previous action, due to the stateless nature of HTTP requests and responses.

The solution in other languages is to place the message into the client **session**, to maintain the client's state between the two requests. Indeed, Rails provides session classes, which provide the same functionality. However, for this particular use case (storing a short piece of data across two requests, which can be immediately discarded when it's been used), Rails provides a further convenience within sessions called **the flash**. Values stored in the flash have exactly the property that we need: they are set up in response to one request, and then available to the response of the next request (from the same client). After the second request, they are cleared out automatically. This means we can put a message into the flash in the `create` action, then display it in the `index` action, if the two occur in sequence. Rails manages clearing out the message once it's been displayed.

Adding a message to the flash in the `create` action is simple (highlighted below):

```ruby
class PeopleController < ApplicationController
  # ... more actions ...
  def create
    @person = Person.new(params[:person])
    if request.post? and @person.save
      flash[:notice] = 'Person added successfully'
      redirect_to :action => 'index'
    else
      @page_title = 'Add a new person'
      render :action => 'new'
    end
  end
end
```

The flash is a hash, associated with a client session. To set a value in this hash, you use the `flash` method to return the hash; then specify the key you want to set (`:notice` here) and its value (`"Person added successfully"`).

The next step is to display this in the view. We don't need to do anything in the controller to get at the content of the flash, as it is accessible by default from every view template. We can put items from the flash wherever we want them, in any template (associated with a layout, action, or partial). In the *Intranet* application, we could need flash notices in any view, so the logical location for it is in the layout template for the whole application (`app/views/layouts/application.rhtml`):

```
<div id="content">
<% if flash[:notice] -%>
<p class="notice"><%= flash[:notice] %></p>
<% end -%>
<%= yield %>
</div>
```

The `if...end` ensures that a paragraph tag is only added if the flash has been set; the `<p>` tag itself is styled with `class="notice"`, which we can define in the CSS file to show flash messages in green (`public/stylesheets/base.css`):

```
.notice {
   color: green;
}
```

Try adding a new person: you should get your confirmation message displayed at the top of the page in green.

 The flash isn't restricted to containing just text: any Ruby object can be placed inside it. If you need to retain an object between actions (for whatever reason), it can also be used as a temporary store for that.

Finishing Touches

Putting all of the above together gives us the following template for `app/views/people/new.rhtml`:

```
<h1><%= @page_title %></h1>
<p>Required fields are marked with &quot;*&quot;.</p>
<% form_for :person, @person, :url => {:action => 'create'} do |f| %>
<p><%= label :person, 'Title' %> <%= f.text_field :title, :size => 8
%></p>
<p><%= label :person, 'First name', :required => true %><br />
```

```
<%= f.text_field :first_name %>
<%= error_message_on :person, :first_name %></p>
<p><%= label :person, 'Last name', :required => true %><br />
<%= f.text_field :last_name %>
<%= error_message_on :person, :last_name %></p>
<p><%= label :person, 'Job title' %>
<%= f.text_field :job_title %></p>
<p><%= label :person, 'Telephone' %> <%= f.text_field :telephone, :
size => 16 %>
<%= label :person, 'Mobile', :field_name => 'mobile_phone' %>
<%= f.text_field :mobile_phone, :size => 16 %></p>
<p><%= label :person, 'Email address', :field_name => 'email', :
required => true %><br />
<%= f.text_field :email %>
<%= error_message_on :person, :email %></p>
<p><%= label :person, 'Gender', :required => true %>
<%= f.select :gender, Person::GENDERS.keys %>
<%= error_message_on :person, :gender %></p>
<p><%= label :person, 'Date of birth' %>
<span id="person_date_of_birth">
<% this_year = Time.now.year -%>
<%= f.date_select :date_of_birth, :order => [:year, :month, :day], :
include_blank => true, :end_year => (this_year - 100),
:start_year => this_year %>
</span></p>
<p><%= label :person, 'Keywords' %> <%= f.text_field :keywords %></p>
<p><%= label :person, 'Notes' %><br />
<%= f.text_area :notes %></p>
<p><%= submit_tag 'Save' %> | <%= link_to 'Cancel', :action => 'index'
%></p>
<% end %>
```

Note that we've added all the required labels (marked with an asterisk where the field is required) and validation error notifications.

We've also used a couple of new helpers here (highlighted):

- `date_select` creates a series of drop-downs (`<select>` elements) for selecting the separate elements of a date and time. The `:order` option specifies how to arrange the drop-downs; `:start_year` and `:end_year` specify the range of years to show. If `:start_year` is less than `:end_year`, the year `<option>` elements are sorted in descending order.

The resulting `<select>` elements have specially formatted names, which Rails will re-compose into a single date-time string when the form is submitted. This string is used to set the date for the person's date of birth when the model is saved back to the database.

- `text_area` creates an HTML `<textarea>` element.

A final finishing touch is to add a menu item linked to the `create` action (in `app/views/layouts/application.rhtml`):

```
. . .
<li><%= link_to 'People', :controller => 'people' %>
<ul>
<li><%= link_to 'Add a person', :controller => 'people',
:action => 'new' %></li>
</ul>
</li>
. . .
```

Updating a Person

Once records are in the contact database, we may still need to go back periodically and alter them. Fortunately, we can reuse a lot of the code and techniques from the previous `new` and `create` actions to accomplish this.

Firstly, we need `edit` and `update` actions to manage displaying the form and inserting the record:

```
class PeopleController < ApplicationController
  # .. other actions ...
  # Add update to the list of actions, which only
  # accept post requests
  verify :method => :post, :only => [:create, :update],
  :redirect_to => {:action => :index}
  def edit
    @person = Person.find(params[:id])
    @page_title = 'Editing ' + @person.full_name
  end
  def update
    @person = Person.find(params[:id])
    if @person.update_attributes(params[:person])
      flash[:notice] = 'Person updated successfully'
      redirect_to :action => 'index'
    else
```

```
        @page_title = 'Editing ' + @person.full_name
        render :action => 'edit'
      end
    end
  end
```

The `edit` action fetches a person's record from the database using a finder (the person's ID is passed in as part of the URL, in much the same way as it is for the `show` action in the `PeopleController`, and available from `params`) and creates `@page_title` from the person's name; then it renders the form for editing the person's details. The `update` action attempts to update the person's record using the request parameters (but only if the request is a POST, as set by the `verify` method). The `update_attributes` method updates all of the model instance's attributes, and then attempts to save the instance to the database, returning true (save successful) or false (save failed, normally due to validation errors).

Next, we need a template to display a form when someone edits an existing person's record. This will be virtually the same as the form for adding a person; plus, the `text_field` and other form helpers we used for the `create` form will automatically populate the form with the details in the retrieved `Person` instance (`@person`). However, the form will need to submit to a different URL (`/people/update/X`, where X is the person's ID, rather than to `/people/create`). The obvious answer to this is to put the form into a partial, called `_form.rhtml`; then turn the `new.rhtml` and `edit.rhtml` templates into wrappers around it, e.g. `new.rhtml` looks like this:

```
<% form_for :person, @person,
:url => {:action => 'create'} do |f| %>
<%= render :partial => 'form', :locals => {:f => f} %>
<% end %>
```

`_form.rhtml` contains all of the code taken out of this template, plus the title at the top of the page and the instruction about required fields—see the source code repository for the complete listing. One other point to note is that we now have to pass the `f` argument into the partial as a local, otherwise, the partial has no access to it.

The `edit.rhtml` template looks like this:

```
<% form_for :person, @person,
:url => {:action => 'update', :id => @person.id} do |f| %>
<%= render :partial => 'form', :locals => {:f => f} %>
<% end %>
```

Rather amazingly, that's it. The last step is to add links to `app/views/people/index.rhtml` view, which points to the update form for each person's record (the changed parts of the template are highlighted below):

```
<table>
<tr>
<th>Name</th>
<th>Actions</th>
</tr>
<% for person in @people -%>
<% full_name = person.last_name + ', ' + person.first_name -%>
<tr>
<td>
<%= link_to full_name, { :action => 'show', :id => person.id },
{ :title => "Show details", :class => "person_link" } %>
</td>
<td>
<%= link_to 'Edit', :action => 'edit', :id => person.id %>
</td>
</tr>
<% end -%>
</table>
```

Try clicking through few of the edit links from the index page to ensure that you can see the form populated correctly. Also, check that the validation still works correctly.

Opportunities for Refactoring

Rails provides a lot of helpers for common tasks, so you don't have to keep reinventing the wheel when writing views. However, your own application is likely to have chunks of code that occur in multiple places. Always keep an eye out for opportunities for refactoring this type of code, and make use of the framework to remove duplication: in Rails parlance, this is known colloquially as **DRY-ing out** your code (where DRY stands for "Don't Repeat Yourself"). In this section, we'll see a few places where we can DRY out our *Intranet* application.

Using Filters

Filters are a useful tool in Rails. They enable you to run some method before, after, or even around an action (like servlet filters in Java). This makes them ideal for implementing functionality like authentication and authorization (you can prevent an action being run, if a person is not logged in), and logging (e.g. you could log the parameters passed to one or more of the actions in a controller).

However, they are also useful for more mundane tasks, like setting the stage for an action by creating instance variables before it runs. This means we can take repeated code out of actions and put it into a controller method, then use a filter to run that method before each action wherever that code is needed.

In the `PeopleController` we have three actions, which each run the same piece of code (highlighted):

```ruby
def show
  @person = Person.find(params[:id])
  . . .
end

. . .
def edit
  @person = Person.find(params[:id])
  . . .
end

. . .
def update
  @person = Person.find(params[:id])
  . . .
end
```

The first step in turning this into a before filter is to add a private method to the bottom of the `PeopleController` class definition, which does the preparation for the action:

```ruby
private
def get_person
  @person = Person.find(params[:id])
end
```

This method is scoped as `private` so that it is not publicly available; without this keyword, the default is for the method to be public, which would actually expose it as a controller action. In addition, the method is placed at the bottom of the class because the `private` keyword will apply to any method definitions following it (unless those methods are explicitly marked as `public` or `protected`). This keeps the action method definitions public, while protecting methods like this one, which are only intended for internal use by the controller.

Next, strip out the lines from the `show`, `edit`, and `update` actions (the ones highlighted above), which this method replaces.

Finally, add a `before_filter` definition to the `PeopleController` class definition:

```
class PeopleController < ApplicationController
  before_filter :get_person, :only => [:show, :update, :edit]

  # ... other methods ...
end
```

Here, the `:only` option specifies that actions in front of we want the filter to run. An `:except` option is also available, so we can rewrite the above as:

```
class PeopleController < ApplicationController
  before_filter :get_person, :except => [:index, :new, :create]

  # ... other methods ...
end
```

If neither an `:only` nor `:except` option is used, the filter runs before all controller actions.

If you call `before_filter` multiple times when defining a controller, each of the applicable filters will be applied before an action is run.

The sister `after_filter` method enables you to call some method after action invocations. For example, the following `after_filter` globally replaces the word "People" in the output from a template with the word "Fools":

```
class PeopleController < ApplicationController
  after_filter :replace_with_fools
  # ... other methods ...

  private
  def replace_with_fools
    response.body.gsub!(/People/, 'Fools')
  end
end
```

Not very useful, but mildly amusing. The important point is that the response body is accessible via the `response.body` method call; the filter can either change the response body in place (as it is done here by `gsub!`), or modify and then reset it using `response.body=`. You can also set response headers or otherwise modify the response with an `after_filter`, perhaps based on properties of the output from a template. More practical uses of an `after_filter` might be to write a hard copy of a generated response to a debug log, or to email an administrator if certain phrases occur in generated content.

Creating Application-Level Controller Methods

When we perform the `create` and `update` actions, adding a new record or modifying an existing one respectively, both actions set a message in the flash and redirect back to the `index` action, e.g. from `create`:

```
def create
  @person = Person.new(params[:person])
  if request.post? and @person.save
    flash[:notice] = 'Person added successfully'
    redirect_to :action => 'index'
  else
    @page_title = "Add a new person"
    render :action => 'new'
  end
end
```

There is an opportunity here to slim down our code. But rather than create a method on the controller itself, we'll create it on the `ApplicationController` (in app/controller/application.rb), so we can use this functionality in any controller:

```
class ApplicationController < ActionController::Base
  session :session_key => '_Intranet_session_id'
  # Set +message+ under the :notice key in the flash,
  # then redirect to the index action.
  private
  def redirect_to_index(message=nil)
    flash[:notice] = message
    redirect_to :action => 'index'
  end
end
```

Then rewrite the `create` action to use it:

```
def create
  @person = Person.new(params[:person])
  if request.post? and @person.save
    redirect_to_index 'Person added successfully'
  else
    @page_title = "Add a new person"
    render :action => 'new'
  end
end
```

And modify the `update` action too:

```
def update
  if @person.update_attributes(params[:person])
    redirect_to_index 'Person updated successfully'
  else
    @page_title = "Editing " + @person.full_name
    render :action => 'edit'
  end
end
```

We can use the `redirect_to_index` method in any controller, inside any action where we want to set the flash and redirect back to the controller's index. Small adjustments like this can radically improve the readability and coherence of your code.

Deleting a Person

Adding a delete action is pretty trivial: the scaffold does it in a few lines of code. However, in the scaffold, the code for doing the deletion (the `destroy` action) is *ugly*, for two reasons:

1. Confirmation of the action is performed through JavaScript (when you click on a **Destroy** link). If a user has JavaScript disabled, they don't get a chance to confirm the deletion, and it goes ahead, recklessly.

2. Early versions of the scaffold put the `destroy` action behind a link (not behind a form). This works OK, but doesn't account for accelerator software (like the Google Web Accelerator). Accelerator software works with the browser to pre-fetch possible future pages by following links on the current page; then, when one of the possible pages is visited, it loads more quickly, as it is already cached locally. Unfortunately, some Rails applications, when used with accelerator software, ended up having their database emptied: the accelerator fetched all the **Destroy** links, disregarding the JavaScript confirmation prompts, and destroying all the records in the database!

   The solution in newer versions of the scaffold is to use a weird JavaScript hack, which, when a **Destroy** link is clicked, turns the link into a form with `method="post"` and submits it; then puts a filter on the `destroy` action so it only accepts POST requests. This is bad. While it solves the accelerator problem, it completely breaks the links for browsers without JavaScript support (e.g. screen readers, Lynx).

A simple and more accessible approach is to place a confirm step between the user clicking on the **Destroy** link and the `destroy` action being executed. The confirm step displays a form with method set to "post" and a big **Confirm** button: the record only gets deleted if the user clicks on the button. This prevents the accelerator problem, gets around ugly scaffold-style hacks, and makes **Destroy** links usable in browsers without JavaScript.

And it's very simple to implement in Rails. First, add `delete` and `confirm` actions to `PeopleController`:

```ruby
class PeopleController < ApplicationController
  before_filter :get_person, :only => [:show, :edit, :update, :
confirm, :delete]

  verify :method => :post, :only => [:create, :update, :delete],
    :redirect_to => {:action => :index}

  # ... other methods ...

  def confirm
    @page_title = "Do you really want to delete \
    #{@person.full_name}?"
  end

  def delete
    if 'yes' == params[:confirm]
      @person.destroy
      redirect_to_index 'Person deleted successfully'
    end
  end

  # ... private methods ...
end
```

Note that the `confirm` and `delete` actions are added to the before filter's `:only` option, so that the `@person` variable is populated with the record to be deleted (see the earlier section *Using Filters*). The `delete` action will only perform the deletion in response to a POST request (set using the `verify` method), which must contain a parameter `'confirm'` with the value `'yes'`.

Next, create a view to display the confirmation form (in `app/views/people/confirm.rhtml`), which is shown when the `confirm` action is first called:

```erb
<h1><%= @page_title %></h1>
<% form_tag :action => 'delete', :id => @person.id do %>
  <%= hidden_field_tag 'confirm', 'yes' %>
  <p><%= submit_tag 'Yes' %> |
  <%= link_to 'Cancel', request.referer %></p>
<% end %>
```

We've used the simple `form_tag` helper here, which generates a plain HTML form from URL parameters. Clicking the **Confirm** button submits a `'confirm=yes'` parameter via a POST request to the right action and ID. That's why the `hidden_field_tag` helper is used to add this form element:

```
<input type="hidden" name="confirm" value="yes" />
```

The other new feature we haven't seen before is use of `request.referer` to set the URL of the **Cancel** button. The `referer` method returns the URL of the page the user was on before visiting this one, so it's a useful way to send a user back to where they came from, canceling the current action.

Finally, add another link into the people index view for each person (`app/views/people/index.rhtml`) to delete a person's record:

```
<td>
<%= link_to 'Edit', :action => 'update', :id => person.id %> |
<%= link_to 'Delete', :action => 'confirm', :id => person.id %>
</td>
```

Is deletion a good idea?

One other consideration is whether to allow deletions at all. Deleting a record may destroy valuable historical data about interactions with a customer you are perhaps no longer dealing with, or who has gone out of business.

It might be better to instead disable a person's record, but keep a copy of it in the database, and then filter out inactive records from the person list unless the user specifically requests to see them. A simple implementation may be to add a Boolean `active` column to the `Person` model, which could be used to filter the people `index` view. We aren't going to go down this route with *Intranet*, for the sake of simplicity.

Adding Edit and Delete Links to a Person's Profile

This is a trivial change, but it makes a big difference to usability. Add two links to the `show.rhtml` template for a person: one to edit the person, and one to delete their record:

```
<p><%= link_to 'Edit', :action => 'edit', :id => @person.id %> |
<%= link_to 'Delete', :action => 'confirm', :id => @person.id %></p>
```

Now, you can skip around the application to your heart's content.

Editing Multiple Models Simultaneously

So far, we have dealt with the simple case where a controller manages create, update, and delete operations for a single instance of the Person model at a time. However, this is only part of the story.

Each person also optionally has an associated address, stored in the addresses table. We separated addresses from people, as companies also have addresses: it is good practice to store all instances of a certain type of data in a single table. In the case of *Intranet*, this makes searching for an address far easier, as we only have to search over a single table in the database. On the other hand, it makes managing addresses tougher, as we potentially have two controllers (PeopleController and CompaniesController) that can create and modify Address instances.

While this use case is not rare, it is difficult to find good examples of implementations in the wild. Hopefully, we will address (excuse the pun) this deficiency in the next section. We'll implement a single form, which will enable a user to both add a new person to the database and optionally, at the same time, add a new address.

Adding a New Address for a Person

To insert an address at the same time as we insert or edit a person's record, we need to add some new address fields at the bottom of app/views/people/_form. rhtml. The user can use these fields to enter the address at the same time as they enter a person's details. As we're going to need these address fields when creating companies too, we'll put them into a partial, app/views/address/_form.rhtml, so we can reuse them more easily:

```
<% if address.errors[:base] -%>
<p><%= error_message_on :address, :base %></p>
<% end -%>
<p><%= label :address, 'Street 1', :required => true %><br />
<%= text_field :address, :street_1 %>
<%= error_message_on :address, :street_1 %></p>
<p><%= label :address, 'Street 2' %><br />
<%= text_field :address, :street_2 %></p>
<p><%= label :address, 'Street 3' %><br />
<%= text_field :address, :street_3 %></p>
<p><%= label :address, 'City' %><br />
<%= text_field :address, :city %></p>
<p><%= label :address, 'County' %><br />
<%= text_field :address, :county %></p>
<p><%= label :address, 'Post code', :required => true %><br />
<%= text_field :address, :post_code %>
<%= error_message_on :address, :post_code %></p>
```

A few points to note about this form:

- We are not referencing an `@address` instance variable when creating the form fields here, but use `address` instead. We'll pass this `address` argument in as a local variable (through the `:locals` option) when we render the partial.

- We are not going to create a new form to contain the address, but simply place the fields relating to the address inside a surrounding form. In the current case, this will put the address fields inside the person form. This means we can submit data for the person and the address simultaneously.

- We are using the `text_field` helpers and specifying `:address` as the first argument to each method call. This will yield a set of form elements with names in the format `address[<field_name>]`, where `<field_name>` is the name of a field in the `addresses` table.

- The `label` helper we developed earlier in this chapter is used throughout.

- The highlighted parts of the code are where validation messages will be shown. Note that the top error message references `:base`, which is not a field associated with an `Address` instance. In fact, this refers back to a generic error message we set if there is a validation error on the whole instance; namely, if `street_1` and `post_code` reference an existing address (see the section *Validating Addresses* in Chapter 4). This message is shown at the top of the form, as it applies to the whole address, and not just to a single field.

Next, we pull this form into the main form for adding a new person (`app/views/people/_form.rhtml`):

```
. . .
<p><%= label :person, 'Notes' %><br />
<%= f.text_area :notes %></p>
<div id="address">
<h2>Enter address details (optional)</h2>
<%= render :partial => 'addresses/form',
:locals => {:address => @address} %>
</div>
<p><%= submit_tag 'Save' %></p>
```

The new lines are highlighted. These just render the new partial inside a `<div>` element, passing a local `:address` variable to the `app/views/addresses/_form.rhtml` partial. At the moment, `:address` references an instance variable, `@address`, which we haven't set yet. Let's do that in the controller (`app/controllers/people_controller.rb`). While we're doing this, let's add some code to save a person's address and assign it to the person, too:

```
class PeopleController < ApplicationController
  # ... other actions ...
  def new
```

```
      @page_title = "Add a new person"
      @person = Person.new
      @address = Address.new
   end
   def create
      @person = Person.new(params[:person])
      @person.build_address(params[:address])
      if @person.save
         redirect_to_index 'Person added successfully'
      else
         @page_title = "Add a new person"
         @address = @person.address
         render :action => 'new'
      end
   end
end
```

We're just creating a new `Address` instance here, and building it from the `:address` part of the request parameters (which gathers all the form fields whose names begin with "address" into a hash), using the `build_address` method automatically added by the association (see the section *Associations between Models* in Chapter 4). As we're creating a new `Person`, Rails will save the address to the database when we save the person associated with it.

This works perfectly well if both the person and address validate first time. However, we get problems if we want to add a person without an address. Our code won't let us do this, as it always tries to save the address, which sometimes we don't want to fill in (e.g. if we don't have someone's home address).

To fix this, we'll add a class method to the model, `from_street_1_and_post_code`, which will give us an address, depending on whether the user has supplied the `street_1` and `post_code` parameters; in cases where they haven't supplied a `street_1` or `post_code`, it returns `nil`. The method utilizes the Rails `find_or_initialize_by_*` method to either retrieve an existing address or initialize a new one (without saving it). This method is similar to the `find_by_*` methods discussed in Chapter 4 (in the section *Finding Records Using Attribute-Based Finders*), and can be passed multiple fields to initialize a record. There are also `find_or_create_by_*` methods available to models, which will additionally save records they create. `from_street_1_and_post_code` also updates the attributes of the retrieved or initialized object from a hash of parameters passed to the method:

```
class Address < ActiveRecord::Base
   # ... other methods ...
   # Look up or initialize an address from params
```

```
# if street_1 or post_code supplied;
# otherwise return nil; NB does not save the address.
#
# +params+ is a hash of name/value pairs used to set
# the attributes of the Address instance.
def self.from_street_1_and_post_code(params)
  params ||= {}
  street_1 = params[:street_1]
  post_code = params[:post_code]
  if street_1.blank? and post_code.blank?
    address = nil
  else
    address = find_or_initialize_by_street_1_and_post_code(street_1,
post_code)
    address.attributes = params
  end

  address
end
end
```

We then modify the `create` action to use this new model method:

```
class PeopleController < ApplicationController
  # ... other actions ...
  def create
    @person = Person.new(params[:person])
    @person.address = Address.from_street_1_and_post_code(params[
        :address])

    @address = @person.address || Address.new
    if @person.save
      redirect_to_index 'Person added successfully'
    else
      @page_title = "Add a new person"
      render :action => 'new'
    end
  end
end
```

If no `street_1` or `post_code` parameters are in the request, `Address.from_street_1_and_post_code` returns `nil`, and the person's address is set to `nil`; however, we still need a valid `Address` instance for use in the view. So, in the second highlighted block, we set the `@address` instance variable to the person's address; or, if it is `nil`, to a new `Address`.

When @person.save is called, the validity of the new person record is checked. Recall from Chapter 4 that a person's address is only valid if it is nil or a valid Address instance. If the person is valid and their address is valid or nil, both will be saved; otherwise, neither is.

Try adding some new people to the application, with valid person and address details, with valid person details only, with valid address details only, and with invalid person and address details. You should only see validation error messages on the address if either street_1 or post_code is set; otherwise, the person should be added without an address (providing the person fields validate).

Using Functional Testing for Complex Actions

The actions defined in the previous section are sufficiently complex to feel nervous about. We need to be sure that the controller responds correctly to different combinations of request parameters: street_1 set, but post_code not; valid address, but invalid person; and so on. In Chapter 4, we saw how unit testing can be used to codify expectations about how models should validate. **Functional testing** can be used in a similar way for controllers, to store expectations about how they should work and ensure that those expectations aren't broken by changes to the code.

Functional tests effectively interact with the application in the same way that a client browser does, making requests to controller actions and receiving responses; the testing occurs on the responses, where we can check that the correct response codes were received, the response body contained the correct HTML, validation is managed correctly, the client was redirected correctly, and so on.

Each time you generate a controller, Rails adds a functional test skeleton for it to the test/functional directory, with the name <controller name>_controller_test. rb. To write functional tests for the PeopleController class, for example, we need to modify test/functional/people_controller_test.rb. Open this file and delete the test_truth method (which is just a stub to demonstrate the format of testing methods).

We want to test expectations about how the `PeopleController`'s `create` action should respond to different request parameters, as outlined in the table below:

Person parameters	Address parameters	Expectation	Test method to create
Invalid	Any	Person not created; address not created; form displayed again	test_create_bad_person
Valid	No street_1 and no post_code	Person created with nil address; redirected to index	test_create_person_nil_address
Valid	post_code, but no street_1	Person not created; validation errors returned for the address; form displayed again	test_create_bad_street_1
Valid	street_1, but no post_code	Person not created; validation errors returned for the address; form displayed again	test_create_bad_post_code
Valid	Valid (street_1 and post_code both supplied)	Person and address both created successfully; redirected to index	test_create_person_address

Note that we're mapping each expectation to be tested onto a separate test method. For functional testing, as for unit testing, the test methods are named `test_*`, a special name which Ruby's testing framework uses to identify methods to include in the test suite. Aside from the requirement to be prefixed with `test_`, you can give your methods any name you wish: here, the method name includes the name of the action being tested (`create`) and `bad` to denote cases where we're testing against invalid request data.

Here's how we code the first test, `test_create_bad_person`. Add the test inside the `PeopleControllerTest` class definition in `test/functional/people_controller_test.rb`:

```
# Test the create action with bad request parameters
def test_create_bad_person
  # Send a post request to the create action with no parameters
  post :create
  # The response should be rendered using the people/new template
  assert_template 'people/new'
  # The response should contain a div with class 'formError'
  assert_select 'div[class=formError]'
end
```

Some points to note:

- The `post` method used sends a POST request to the specified action on this controller. There is also a `get` method to send a GET request. Both can be supplied with a parameters hash (see later in this section).

- `assert_template` can check whether an action renders a particular template, specified relative to the views directory. Here we make sure that the `PeopleController`'s `new` template (which shows the form for adding a new person) is rendered.

- `assert_select` is a very powerful method for checking the content of the response body. It can be supplied with very fine-grained **selectors** (similar to CSS or XPath selectors), which attempt to find a matching element in the response body.

 Other `assert_*` methods can also be used inside functional tests: see the section *Other Types of Assertion* in Chapter 4 for a full list of methods available.

To run the functional tests, call the following from the command line:

```
$ rake test:functionals
...
Started
..
Finished in 0.103625 seconds.

2 tests, 3 assertions, 0 failures, 0 errors
```

Any failed tests or errors are reported, along with the details of the test where they occurred. Note that we've run two tests here, as the `CompaniesController` also has a stub for its functional tests.

Next is `test_create_person_nil_address`, to test that a POST request with valid person parameters, but no address parameters, correctly creates a person with a `nil` address:

```
def test_create_person_nil_address
  # Clear out the people table
  Person.delete_all
  # Post new person details with blank address
  post :create, :person => {
    :first_name => 'Bob',
    :last_name => 'Parks',
```

```
      :email => 'bob@acme.biz',
      :gender => 'M'
  }
  # Check there is one person in the database
  person = Person.find(:first)
  assert_equal 'bob@acme.biz', person.email

  # Check their address is nil
  assert_equal nil, person.address

  # Check we get redirected to the index after creation
  assert_redirected_to :action => :index
end
```

Here we're sending some data in the POST body by passing a hash of parameters to the `post` method. Note that you have to mirror the structure of the request as it would arrive from the form, meaning that you have to nest all of the `person` parameters inside a nested hash, keyed by `:person`. Also note that we can use `assert_redirected_to` to specify a route we expect the controller to redirect to; the parameters passed to this mirror those used with `link_to` and `url_for`. In this case, if a person's record is successfully created, we expect to be redirected back to the `index` action on this controller.

Similarly, to test requests where partial (invalid) address parameters are supplied, we do:

```
def test_create_bad_street_1
  # Post valid person details, but with empty value for street_1
  post :create,
    :person => {
      :first_name => 'Bob',
      :last_name => 'Parks',
      :email => 'bob@acme.biz',
      :gender => 'M'
    },
    :address => {
      :post_code => 'B15 1AU'
    }
  # Check the new form is shown again
  assert_template 'people/new'
  # Check we get validation errors for street_1 input element
  assert_select 'div[class=fieldWithErrors]' do
    assert_select 'input[id=address_street_1]'
  end
end
```

Note that this follows a similar format to the previous test, but that we are also passing an :address key in with the post parameters, specifying an invalid address (missing a street_1 attribute). We then use assert_select to test for the presence of a <div> element with class attribute equal to fieldWithErrors; and nest a further assert_select inside it, to check that the error <div> is wrapping the <input> element with id attribute set to address_street_1. This tests that the form is displayed again, with an error message next to the street_1 form field.

> assert_select statements can be nested arbitrarily deep in tests, and selectors can be far more complex than shown here: see the Rails documentation for the HTML::Selector class for details of the full syntax.

test_create_bad_post_code is similar to the previous test, and is not listed here: see the source code for the complete listing.

Our final test, test_create_person_address, checks that if valid person and address data are supplied, both a person and an address are created and correctly associated:

```
def test_create_person_address
  # Clear out the people and addresses tables
  Person.delete_all
  Address.delete_all
  # Send post with valid person and address
  post :create,
    :person => {
      :first_name => 'Bob',
      :last_name => 'Parks',
      :email => 'bob@acme.biz',
      :gender => 'M'
    },
    :address => {
      :street_1 => '11 Harley Street',
      :post_code => 'B15 1AU'
    }

  # Check person created
  person = Person.find(:first)
  assert_equal 'bob@acme.biz', person.email
  # Check address created
  address = Address.find(:first)
  assert_equal 'B15 1AU', address.post_code
```

```
      # Check person's address is the created address
      assert_equal person.address_id, address.id
      # Check redirected to index
      assert_redirected_to :action => :index
   end
```

This test uses many of the same methods as previous tests. The main things we're testing here are that the person and address are created, and that the `address_id` attribute for the person is set to the `id` of the newly-created address (highlighted).

This section has been a whirlwind tour of the potential of functional testing, and we've only skated over the surface of its possibilities. As you can see, it can be time-consuming to test every possible combination of request parameters; however, where you are writing mission-critical software, or software where the controller logic is complex, functional testing is a vital technique for ensuring consistency and stability in your application.

Updating a Person and Their Address

Luckily for us (thanks to Rails), the code for editing an existing person and their address is virtually identical to the code for creating a person. The chief difference is that the `edit` and `update` actions retrieve an existing person and their address (if available):

```
class PeopleController < ApplicationController
  before_filter :get_person, :only => [:show, :update,
    :edit, :confirm, :delete]
  verify :method => :post, :only => [:create, :update,
    :delete], :redirect_to => {:action => :index}
  # ... other methods ...
  def edit
    @page_title = 'Editing ' + @person.full_name
    @address = @person.address || Address.new
  end
  def update
    @person.address = Address.from_street_1_and_post_code(params[:
address])
    @address = @person.address || Address.new
    if @person.update_attributes(params[:person])
      redirect_to_index 'Person updated successfully'
    else
      @page_title = 'Editing ' + @person.full_name
      render :action => 'edit'
    end
  end
end
```

The only minor issue with this code is that an edit to someone's address will actually add a new address to the database, rather than update the old one. The old one will remain until manually removed from the system. However, it does mean that if someone enters an address that already exists in the database, that address is used instead of creating a new one. There is also the potential for creation of duplicate or near-duplicate addresses, if there are slight differences between how `street_1` and `post_code` are typed.

Finally, we need an `app/views/people/edit.rhtml` template to present a form for editing a person, which pulls in the existing `_form.rhtml` partial we created earlier:

```
<% form_for :person, @person,
:url => {:action => 'update', :id => @person.id} do |f| %>
<%= render :partial => 'form', :locals => {:f => f} %>
<% end %>
```

Summary

The functionality put in place throughout this section gives users all the tools they need to edit people and their addresses. However, this doesn't complete the functionality required in the *Intranet* application: the next section covers how to build the remaining pieces.

Fleshing Out Companies and Addresses

The *Intranet* application is missing some functionality before it will be really useful. It still needs to:

- Provide `create`, `update`, and `delete` actions for companies (we already have an `index` view for companies, which we can continue to use).

- Enable users to associate a person's company (from the person `update` and `create` views).

- Delete addresses if they are no longer attached to a person or company.

In this section, we will briefly see how to implement this functionality. The techniques should be familiar from the previous sections, but extra detail is given for any new techniques.

Managing Companies

The remaining actions we need for companies are `delete`, `new`, `create`, `edit`, and `update`. Action methods go into `app/controllers/companies_controller.rb`; views go into `app/views/companies`.

Stubbing Out the Navigation

We want the `index` view to link to the `edit` and `delete` actions for each company. Add a new **Action** column to `app/views/companies/index.rhtml`, and add two links for each company row:

```
<td>
<%= link_to 'Edit', :action => 'update', :id => company.id %> |
<%= link_to 'Delete', :action => 'delete', :id => company.id %>
</td>
```

At the moment, these links don't lead anywhere; but having them available makes it easier to find your way around while building up the remaining functionality.

A Shared View to Confirm Deletions

It turns out that the view and action for confirming company deletion are virtually identical to those for confirming deletion of a person. Here is another refactoring opportunity.

First, move `app/views/people/confirm.rhtml` to `app/views/shared/confirm.rhtml`. This makes the view for confirming a deletion into a shared template, easily usable by any controller. We need to make this view generic, so it will work with any object (currently, it references `@person`). Modify it like this (`@object` replaces `@person` in the highlighted line):

```
<h1><%= @page_title %></h1>
<% form_for :action => 'delete', :id => @object.id do %>
<%= hidden_field_tag 'confirm', 'yes' %>
<p><%= submit_tag 'Yes' %> |
<%= link_to 'Cancel', request.referer %> </p>
<% end %>
```

Next, modify the `confirm` and `delete` actions in `app/controllers/people_controller.rb`, extracting the code that is common to those actions for any controller into separate private methods (`confirm_delete` and `do_delete`):

```
def confirm
  prompt = "Do you really want to delete #{@person.full_name}?"
  confirm_delete(@person, prompt)
```

```
    end
    def delete
      do_delete(@person)
    end
    private
    def confirm_delete(object, prompt)
      @object = object
      @page_title = prompt
      render :template => 'shared/confirm'
    end
    private
    def do_delete(object)
      if 'yes' == params[:confirm]
        object.destroy
        object_name = object.class.name.humanize
        redirect_to_index object_name + ' deleted successfully'
      end
    end
  end
```

Now the `confirm_delete` method manages confirmation of the deletion of any generic object, and the `confirm` action in `PeopleController` just invokes this method, passing in the `@person` instance variable and `@person.full_name` as a prompt. The prompt is displayed in the confirmation screen, which is constructed by rendering the `shared/confirm.rhtml` template. (The `:template` option will render any template, including ones for controllers other than the one currently being invoked.)

The `delete` action calls the `do_delete` method, which in turn calls the object's `destroy` method; a bit of class reflection is used to create the message for the flash (`#{object.class.name.humanize}` yields a human-readable version of the class name of the object).

Move the `confirm_delete` and `do_delete` methods into the `ApplicationController` class so they are available to every controller.

Finally, add `delete` and `confirm` actions to `CompaniesController` too, referencing the generic `confirm_delete` and `do_delete` methods:

```
  class CompaniesController < ApplicationController
    # ... other methods ...
    def confirm
      @company = Company.find(params[:id])
      prompt = "Do you really want to delete #{@company.name}?"
      confirm_delete(@company, prompt)
```

```
  end
  def delete
    @company = Company.find(params[:id])
    do_delete(@company)
  end
end
```

The final thing to do is add some delete links to the `app/views/companies/index.rhtml` template:

```
<%= link_to('Delete', :action => 'confirm', :id => company.id) %>
```

The beauty of this refactoring is that it makes it trivial to add `delete` and `confirm` actions to any controller from this point on. The `confirm` action should pass the object we're trying to delete plus some prompt to the `confirm_delete` method; the `delete` action should call `do_delete` with the object to delete; and Rails will do the rest.

Attaching a Person to a Company

A likely scenario would be for a person to change company: someone at Acme would then search for a person's record to modify their company association. Adding this functionality to the person edit form is actually very simple, as we are simply setting the `company_id` for a record in the `people` table. As this is a simple attribute, we merely need to add a drop-down box of companies to the form for editing a person. First, we need to get the list of companies to populate the drop-down by adding another `before_filter` for the `PeopleController`'s `edit`, `new`, `update`, and `create` actions (any action that is expected to render the form):

```
class PeopleController < ApplicationController
  before_filter :get_companies, :only => [:edit, :new, :update,
    :create]
  # ... other methods ...
  private
  def get_companies
    @companies = Company.find(:all, :order => 'name')
  end
end
```

Then add the drop-down box to the `app/views/people/_form.rhtml` partial, before the address entry part of the form:

```
<h2>Company (optional)</h2>
<p><%= f.collection_select(:company_id, @companies, :id, :name,
:include_blank => true)
%></p>
```

The `collection_select` helper creates a `<select>` element around the output from `options_from_collection_for_select`. As a company is optional for a person, the `:include_blank` option is set to true so that a blank option is displayed at the top of the drop-down. Rails will now manage this attribute as it manages the other simple attributes for a person (like `first_name`, `last_name`, etc.).

We can also amend the `show` view for a person (in `app/views/people/show.rhtml`) to display the name of the company they work for:

```
<p><strong>Company:</strong>
<%= (@person.company ? @person.company.name : d) %></p>
```

Creating and Updating Companies

The basic actions for creating or updating a company (without its address) are similar to the initial actions created earlier in this chapter, and fairly trivial. We'll skip those and go straight to the more complex case: creating or updating a company *and* an address from a single form.

Unlike a person, where the address is optional, a company must *always* be assigned an address. The validation code on the `Company` model we wrote in Chapter 4 ensures that an address must be supplied, and that the address is itself valid. So providing we assign an address and check the validity of the company, Rails will cascade validation to the associated address. If the company validates, it means the address is valid too, and we can save both safely.

Below is the code for the `new`, `create`, `edit`, and `update` actions. It again uses the `Address.from_street_1_and_post_code` method we defined in the section *Adding a New Address for a Person*, to either find an existing address to assign to a company or create a new one from the supplied `:address` parameters:

```
class CompaniesController < ApplicationController
  def new
    @page_title = 'Add a new company'
    @company = Company.new
    @address = Address.new
  end

  def create
    @company = Company.new(params[:company])
    @company.address = Address.from_street_1_and_post_code(params[
        :address])
    # @company.address might be nil,
    # so set a sensible default if it is
    @address = @company.address || Address.new
    if @company.save
```

```
      redirect_to_index 'Company added successfully'
    else
      @page_title = 'Add a new company'
      render :action => :new
    end
  end

  def edit
    @company = Company.find(params[:id])
    @page_title = 'Editing ' + @company.name
    @address = @company.address
  end

  def update
    @company = Company.find(params[:id])
    @company.address = Address.from_street_1_and_post_code(params[
          :address])
    @address = @company.address || Address.new

    if @company.update_attributes(params[:company])
      redirect_to_index 'Person updated successfully'
    else
      @page_title = 'Editing ' + @company.name
      render :action => 'edit'
    end
  end
end
```

ActiveRecord handles validation of the address associated with the company, so we can be certain that `@company.save` only succeeds when both the company and its address are valid.

Here is the form partial, which goes with these actions (`app/views/companies/_form.rhtml`):

```
<h1><%= @page_title %></h1>
<p>Required fields are marked with &quot;*&quot;.</p>
<% if @company.errors[:address] -%>
<p><%= error_message_on :company, :address %></p>
<% end -%>
<p><%= label :company, 'Company name', :field_name => 'name',
:required => true %><br />
<%= f.text_field :name %>
<%= error_message_on :company, :name %></p>
<p><%= label :company, 'Telephone' %><br />
<%= f.text_field :telephone %></p>
<p><%= label :company, 'Fax' %><br />
```

```
<%= f.text_field :fax %></p>
<p><%= label :company, 'Website' %><br />
<%= f.text_field :website %></p>

<h2>Address*</h2>
<div id="address">
<h3>Enter address details</h3>
<%= render :partial => 'addresses/form', :locals => {:address =>
@address} %>
</div>
<p><%= submit_tag 'Save' %>  | <%= link_to 'Cancel', :action =>
'index' %></p>
```

Note that any validation errors to do with the company's `address` are at the top of the form (highlighted). If the address fails to validate, the error message will appear here.

We will also need a template for the `new` action (`app/views/companies/new.rhtml`):

```
<% form_for :company, @company,
:url => {:action => 'create'} do |f| %>
<%= render :partial => 'form', :locals => {:f => f} %>
<% end %>
```

and one for the `edit` action (`app/views/companies/edit.rhtml`):

```
<% form_for :company, @company,
:url => {:action => 'update', :id => @company.id} do |f| %>
<%= render :partial => 'form', :locals => {:f => f} %>
<% end %>
```

Finally, add a link to the menu (in `app/views/layouts/application.rhtml`) to create a new company:

```
<%= link_to 'Add a company', :controller => 'companies', :action =>
'new' %>
```

That completes the functionality for adding and updating companies. Again, you may want to ensure that this works as expected by adding some functional tests for this controller: an example is given in the code repository for the book.

Managing Addresses

Earlier we saw that addresses don't really have a life of their own: they are always associated with a company or a person, and don't need to be treated as entities in their own right. So, it seems a wasted effort to spend too long writing administration pages for them (and time is running out for Rory and co.).

However, it is clear that addresses may become orphans if there are no longer companies or people associated with them. At the moment, there is no way to tidy up if a company is deleted and its address orphaned.

There are several ways to approach this issue. Here are a few suggestions:

1. **Create a scaffold for the Address model.** This will quickly supply CRUD operations for the model, but won't make it simple to identify orphaned addresses without some modification (e.g. displaying entities associated with each address).

2. **Run a scheduled task to clear up the database.** Using cron or similar, scan the database every evening for addresses that no longer have associated companies or people and delete them.

3. **Cascade deletions to addresses.** Each time a person or company is deleted, check and delete any addresses that have become orphans as a consequence.

The last of these is the most interesting and tidiest: rather than managing addresses through their own administration screens and having to manually identify orphans, we can have them deleted automatically *when they become orphans*.

 This approach is not suitable if you want to maintain addresses regardless of whether they are associated with any other entities in the database.

Adding a Callback to Company Deletions

To manage addresses that no longer have an associated company or person, we an add a **callback handler** for the `Person` and `Company` model classes. Each time an instance of either is deleted, we check whether any associated address is orphaned as a result, and, if it is, delete it too.

A callback enables you to trigger events in response to actions on records in the database, such as a new record being added, a record being updated, or a record being deleted. There are about a dozen callback points available (see the documentation for `ActiveRecord::Callbacks`), but the one we're interested in is `after_destroy`, which enables you to specify an action to trigger after a record is destroyed. In this case, it will enable us to clear out orphaned addresses after a company or person is destroyed.

First off, create a callback handler in one of the two models — Company is as good as any. This is defined by creating a new method called `after_destroy` in the Company class definition:

```
class Company < ActiveRecord::Base
  # ... validation methods etc. ...

  def after_destroy
    unless address_id.blank?
      address = Address.find address_id
      if address.people.empty? and address.company.nil?
        address.destroy
      end
    end
  end
end
```

Note that, despite the callback being triggered after the Company instance has been destroyed, it still has access to the attributes the model instance had *before* the record was destroyed. This means we can reference the company's `address_id` and use it to look up its associated address. The callback handler checks whether the potentially-orphaned address still has either an associated company, or one or more associated people, by querying the database. If the address is not associated with any other records, it can be safely deleted.

Rather than copying this callback handler into the Person class definition, it would be better to keep things DRY and have the handler in a single location. But where should we put it? In the case of controllers, we have the `ApplicationController` class we can use for any methods we want to make available to all controllers. However, we don't have a similar "superclass" for our models, so there is no obvious location to put the callback to make it accessible to both Person and Company.

Instead, we can use an **observer** as the location for the callback handler. Observers are special classes that wait for and then respond to lifecycle events on ActiveRecord classes, such as addition of new records, updates to records, or deletion of records. You specify which events trigger the observer by creating methods named after the type of event, such as the `after_destroy` method we just saw.

Either an observer can be assigned to a single model (in which case, you just need to create a class named after the model, e.g. a `PersonObserver` observer would observe events occurring on the Person model); or, you can create an observer with an arbitrary class name and instruct it to watch for events across multiple models using the `observe` method. We'll take the latter approach and write one observer that manages addresses in response to events occurring on the Person or Company model.

Locate the observer in `app/models/address_owner_observer.rb` and cut and paste the `after_destroy` callback method from the `Company` class into it. The other slight modification required is that the callback should accept an object to be manipulated (here called `record`): this will represent the just-deleted person or company. You also need to declare the class, inheriting from the `ActiveRecord::Observer` class:

```
class AddressOwnerObserver < ActiveRecord::Observer
  observe Person, Company

  def after_destroy(record)
    unless record.address_id.blank?
      address = Address.find address_id
      if address.people.empty? and address.company.nil?
        address.destroy
      end
    end
  end
end
```

We need to add the new check on the `address_id` (highlighted), as an address is optional for people, but not for companies.

The final step is to "switch on" the observer by adding it to the application's configuration inside `config/environment.rb`. Note that there is already a commented-out line inside the configuration that sets the value for `config.active_record.observers`. Uncomment this line and set the value to the name of your observer, e.g. (highlighted)

```
Rails::Initializer.run do |config|
  # ... other settings ...

  # Activate observers that should always be running
  config.active_record.observers = :address_owner_observer

  # ... yet more settings ...
end
```

The observer now works as a callback handler for both model classes. The easiest way to see it in effect is to use the console:

```
$ script/console
Loading development environment.
>> a = Address.new(:street_1 => '78 Blink Street',
:post_code => 'B14 2QQ')
=> #<Address:0xb75c7b0c ...}>
>> a.save          # Save the address to the database
```

```
=> true
>> c = Company.new(:name => 'Charming Pottery')
=> #<Company:0xb759ba84 ...}>
>> c.address = a            # Associate the address with the company
=> #<Address:0xb75c7b0c ...>
>> c.save        # Save the company to the database
=> true
>> c.address_id       # ID of the address associated with the company
=> 16
>> c.destroy       # The callback is triggered by this method call
=> #<Company:0xb759ba84 ...>
>> Address.find 16      # Try to retrieve the address from the database
ActiveRecord::RecordNotFound: Couldn't find Address with ID=16

...
```

As you can see, the callback handler deleted the new address we just created, in response to deletion of the company it was attached to.

Unit Testing for Callbacks

Unit tests are a good way to encapsulate the kind of callback checks we performed manually with the console (above), making sure that they behave as expected. For example, to test the this callback, the unit test could:

1. Create an address
2. Create a person
3. Create a company
4. Assign the address to the person
5. Assign the address to the company
6. Delete the company
7. Verify that the address still exists in the database

Conversely, you could write a test to verify that an orphaned address *is* correctly deleted. For example:

```
# Test that the after_destroy call-back for Company
# correctly triggers deletion of an orphaned address.
def test_deletes_orphaned_address
  @acme.destroy
  assert_raise(ActiveRecord::RecordNotFound) { Address.find 1 }
end
```

See the source code repository (`test/unit/company_test.rb`) for example unit tests, which perform more callback testing.

A Very Quick Interface for Addresses

While we are managing addresses via their associated companies and people, it is sometimes useful to get an overview of all the addresses in the system. But, because we're doing most of the management in other pages, it seems a waste of effort to build a whole interface. One of the beauties of Rails is that we can very quickly add a management interface for a model, which we can flesh out later or just leave it as it is. We saw the **scaffold generator** in the last chapter, which adds all the files to implement a CRUD interface for a model. However, there is an even simpler way to implement a scaffold for a model (in our case, the `Address` model).

First, create a controller for the model:

```
$ script/generate controller addresses
```

Next, edit the controller (`app/controllers/addresses.rb`):

```
class AddressesController < ApplicationController
  scaffold :address
end
```

The `scaffold` method builds all the actions for the controller invisibly: simply pass it the name of the model to scaffold for. It also generates the required views without creating any files in your application. If you create any actions with the standard scaffold names (e.g. `create`, `new`, `edit`, `update`) inside the controller, your method will override the default scaffold ones. Using the `scaffold` command inside your controller class definition can be a good first step to getting a controller up and running: any actions you haven't yet defined for your controller are provided by the scaffold defaults.

Next, start the server (if it's not already running) and browse to `http://localhost:3000/addresses`. You should see a list of addresses in the system. That's all you need to do to get a quick interface for addresses up and running; you could even add it to the menu system (though, remember that we set up companies as dependent on addresses: if you delete an address, any associated company is also destroyed).

Summary

Throughout this chapter, we've grown a user interface over the solid model we built in Chapter 4. Rather than using simple scaffold-style controllers and views, we've dug deep into the patterns and techniques you will need to implement complex functionality in real-world applications.

Even with this level of coverage, there is still an embarrassment of riches to be discovered in Rails: we have only scratched the surface of what's possible. However, you can hopefully see how the template system, helpers, filters, and observers provide an excellent foundation for creating minimal, powerful code, and get an idea of how models, views, and controllers fit together.

In the next chapter, armed with a fully-functional *Intranet* application, we will see how to deploy to a production server, ready for the assault of real users.

6

Into Production

Running a Rails application in the production environment is a crucial part of any project. It represents the successful completion of a working application and delivery of that application to its customer base. It is rarely the final stage. All applications we have worked on have needed modifying from their initial production incarnation.

So, what is needed to get a Rails application into the production environment?

- A working Rails application.
- A production server environment.
- A system for transferring development Rails code to the production environment.

This chapter will describe how to create a Rails production environment. In particular, the decisions we need to make to successfully get a small business application up and running. Error handling in the production environment is a little different to that of the development environment and therefore some coverage of error handling is presented. We will also describe some systems that will make it easier to backup and restore your application.

An Application Ready for Production

In many Rails tutorials and guides there is a common theme: don't worry about the production environment, it is something you can sort out later. I strongly believe this is a mistake.

Do not wait until your application is built before you create and test the production environment!

If you cannot get your application working in the production environment, any time you spent creating that application has been wasted.

Our application may be the most beautifully crafted piece of coding ever created, but if we cannot present it to our users, we might as well have created a chocolate teapot.

Therefore, it is important, before we spend time developing our application, that we create and test our production environment. This is particularly important with Rails because at the time of writing, creating a good production environment can be the most problematic part of Rails development. The good news is that solutions to most of the common problems are being developed and are coming on line all the time. In particular, the creation of Mongrel (a Ruby web server that will be discussed later in the chapter) has greatly simplified the process and removed the worst headaches.

Rory comes to similar conclusions. He does not want to spend all week creating his application just to find that it only works on his computer. The whole point of the task Ken has set for him is to make the contact data available to everyone in the company. Even if others can browse his computer, he does not want his system to slow down to provide everyone else with a new service. However, he also spots a conundrum: "I need an application to test the production environment, but I want to do the test before I create an application." The solution is to create a simple test application that can be passed to the production system and tested there. Scaffold makes it very easy to create a basic working application. So, Rory creates and develops a test application:

1. Rory first creates a test application in an empty folder.

    ```
    $ rails TestApp
    ```

2. Scaffold needs an existing SQL table to create the correct application code, to match the table structure. Moving into the application folder, Rory creates a test model first, so he can use migration to create the initial database table.

    ```
    $ ruby script/generate model TestThing
    ```

3. He then modifies `001_create_test_things.rb` by removing the comments. He thereby creates the migration code shown below. As this is a very basic test, only one database field is required.

    ```
    class CreateTestThings < ActiveRecord::Migration
      def self.up
        create_table :test_things do |t|
          t.column :name, :string
        end
      end
      def self.down
        drop_table :test_things
      end
    end
    ```

4. Rory is using MySQL and decides to use the default Test schema for all the environments of this test application. He modifies `database.yml` to suit. The resulting `database.yml` is shown below. Notice that all environments use the same database schema and therefore have the same content.

```
development:
   adapter: mysql
   database: Test
   username: root
   password: password
   host: localhost

test:
   adapter: mysql
   database: Test
   username: root
   password: password
   host: localhost

production:
   adapter: mysql
   database: Test
   username: root
   password: password
   host: localhost
```

5. Rory then creates the new table using Rake.

```
$ rake migrate
```

6. Finally, he can create the scaffold, which he tests with the help of WEBrick or Mongrel. The application is available at: `"http://localhost:3000/test_things/list"`

```
$ ruby script/generate scaffold TestThing
$ ruby script/server
```

Rory, now, has a working Rails application that he can test in his production environment. It has only the minimum of functionality, but it is all that is needed to demonstrate the viability of the production environment.

The Application Server

At this point, it is worth reviewing the specification of a server platform that will host a production Rails environment. For small business applications, it is initially practical to run the Rails application, a web server, and database, all on the same computer. There are a number of steps that can be taken to improve performance as use of the application increases. However, for most purposes, when putting your first application into production, the single server solution is a good starting point.

Memory

As mentioned in Chapter 3: *Laying the Foundations*, the main consideration for a Rails server is plenty of RAM. Rails and databases are memory intensive. Each Rails instance typically uses 25 to 35Mb of RAM. While this may not be a lot for a dedicated server, it can be significant on a shared server. For example, Rory only has a single server that also acts as a file and print server, web server, and the company email server. This arrangement is typical of many small businesses. On a shared server, the additional memory used for each Rails instance, and the database behind the application can easily take the used memory beyond the size of the physical memory. At this point, the operating system will more aggressively use the hard disk as memory cache and the performance of the server will plummet as a result.

[I would consider 1Gb RAM a minimum for a Rails production server, and would recommend at least 2Gb of RAM.]

Central Processor Unit–CPU

A modern computer with a single CPU will deliver Rails-generated web pages in a timely fashion over a local area network. Differences of CPU speed of one or two steps are unlikely to make a significant impact on performance. When specifying a server, use the budget that may have been used to upgrade the processor a couple of steps to upgrade the memory instead.

However, a Rails application can hog a CPU occasionally. For example, in Rory's application, the process of importing data from a CSV file is likely to take a few seconds during which Ruby will push the CPU to maximum usage and therefore negatively impact the other applications also running on the server. In this situation, multiple processors can allow other processes to carry on while Ruby loads one of the CPUs. Therefore, while not necessary, having a server with multiple CPUs is advantageous. Of the two, having a server with two moderate performance CPUs is preferable to having a server with a single very fast processor. In these days, of multi-core processors, having a dual core processor provides similar benefits to having two separate CPUs.

Hard Disks

Rails applications are relatively small as they mainly comprise simple text files. For example, an intranet application that provides multiple functions and services to a small business can typically comprise 1400 files spread over 700 folders and yet take up less than 10Mb of disk space. Of course, the data stored in the database takes up much more disk space, but for many small applications MySQL takes up less than 1Gb of the disk space, including the data files. In these days, when it is getting difficult to buy a hard disk with a capacity of less than 100Gb, disk space used by a Rails application is rarely an issue.

However, access speed to the disks can be an area where performance can be improved especially in boosting the performance of the database. The simplest and best way to increase disk access speeds is to use an array of disks instead of a single hard disk. A RAID 1 system (pair of mirrored disks) will provide enhanced read speeds (as well as improved fault tolerance), though slower write speeds, when compared to a single disk. RAID 5 systems (at least three disks) provide faster read and write speeds, with performance improving as more disks are added to the array. That is, a seven disk array will be faster than an array of three identical disks on the same controller.

The increase in performance and additional fault tolerance (both RAID 1 and 5 systems are designed to handle the loss of one of the disks in the array), make RAID 1 or 5 an attractive option for any business server, including those hosting a Rails production environment.

Network Interface Card–NIC

Rails applications are designed to work over the Internet, where bandwidth is typically two orders of magnitude less than that available on a business' local area network (LAN). For example, currently most users would consider 10Mb/s a fast Internet connection, but a small business can easily buy a small 1Gb/s LAN switch for less than $40. So, a Rails application will not be throttled by a standard 100Mb/s dedicated network connection. However, the key word is dedicated. In a shared server environment, there may be another service that is hogging the network connection. For example, a user may be downloading a large file from the server. A faster network connection will lessen the impact of providing multiple services simultaneously, to multiple users over a single interface. Therefore, if you have a

100Mb/s network, providing a 1Gb/s connection from your server into the core of the network it is likely to improve the service performance. This will require a 1Gb/s NIC in your server and a 1Gb/s port in your core LAN switch.

Don't Forget Backup

If our application becomes as popular as I am sure we all hope they will, our users will start to rely on them. One consequence of this is that if there is a failure, there must be a way to recover the system quickly and with the least loss of data. Therefore, regular backup is essential. Two databases in particular need to be backed up: your main database, and your Subversion repository. Traditionally, tape systems have been used for backup, but recently network attached storage (NAS), often in the form of dedicated disk arrays, have become a popular alternative. An in-depth discussion on the pros and cons of the different backup solutions is beyond the scope of this book. Suffice to say that the key point is that we invest in a reliable backup system, and use that system to regularly backup our user's data and our Rails code.

Your First Production Server

In summary, your first production server should have:

- Plenty of RAM as a must.
- Multiple CPUs, hard disk RAID, and fast network connections are desirable.
- Include a system to back up your Subversion repository and main database.

Setting up the Server

Once you have your server platform, the next task is to create a Rails environment.

Installing Ruby and Rails

The process for installing Ruby and Rails on a server is exactly the same as the installation on a development system described in Chapter 3: *Laying the Foundations*. So for example, installation on a Windows 2003 server would involve the following steps:

- Install Ruby using the one-click installer.
- Use gems to install Rails:

```
gem install rails --include-dependencies
```

It is as straightforward as that!

Copying the Files to the Server

As a Rails application comprises a collection of text files, creating an application on a production server can be as simple as copying the application folder on a development system to the production server. There is no compiling to be done, nor registering the application with the system. As long as Ruby and Rails is installed and running correctly, just copying the application files to another location creates a copy of that application in the new location.

The copying can be done by sharing the target folder and copying over the files, transfer via FTP, or even zipping up the folder and emailing it. The options are as plentiful as there are different ways of copying files from one computer to another.

However, there is a straightforward way to transfer the application files to the server without relying on a development computer having a current production version of the application ready. That is, to transfer the files directly from the Subversion repository. This allows you to easily control which version of the application is passed to the server and provides a simple mechanism to update the production server as development continues. To achieve this, Subversion (or at least a SVN client such as TortoiseSVN) must be installed on the server (see installation details in Chapter 3: *Laying the Foundations*). As the server is also the obvious place to host the Subversion repository, there is a good chance it is already installed on the server.

Using Subversion to Transfer the Application to the Production Environment

The command to create a new copy of an application from a Subversion repository is:

```
$ svn checkout <source location> <destination>
```

A -r switch can be used to specify the revision of the application to be checked out.

```
$ svn checkout svn+ssh://rory@192.168.13.129/repository/Intranet -r
100 intranet
```

This command running at the server will checkout a copy of Rory's application to a folder called "intranet". The revision 100 has been checked out.

On an intranet, where the server and network are controlled by the application owner, using checkout to create the production system is useful, in that we then have svn tools on the server that allow us to easily compare the production version of the application with the latest development version. If we were hosting the application on an externally hosted server (for example, our ISP's server on the Internet), providing easy links back into our SVN repository is not such a useful thing to do and would present a security risk. Therefore, if the application is being hosted externally, use "`svn export`" to create a non-version-controlled copy of the application.

Therefore, if this command is followed by:

```
$ cd intranet
$ ruby script/server
```

...an instance of WEBrick or Mongrel will start on the server and the application will become available at `http://server_name:3000/` where `server_name` is the network name of the server. However, this does assume the production database is available and the application is configured to use it (see below).

Once the application has been checked out on the server, it can be kept up-to date using:

```
$ svn update
```

...to update the server to the latest version, or:

```
$ svn update -r 101
```

...to update the server version of the application, to the repository version 101.

Update can also be used to roll back to a previous version. Therefore,

```
$ svn update -r 100
```

...will revert the application back to version 100, replacing files with earlier versions where changed, deleting files added as part of revision 101, and adding files deleted in revision 101.

Excluding Files from the Repository

Populating the production environment from the repository does raise an issue: there are files in the application that are specific to the current instance. For example, the log files. One thing we do not want to do is transfer a copy of the development log to the production server, especially as this file can get very big, very quickly.

When I first started using Rails, I could not work out why my server lost a gigabyte of hard disk space when I updated the production version of my application. I had created an infinite loop on a development platform at one point during development. What I had not noticed was that this had resulted in a huge log file. As the log files were then included in the repository, checking out a copy of the repository resulted in me copying development.log to the server, and therefore a significant loss of disk space. When I tracked down the problem, I quickly worked out how to remove log files from the repository!

Fortunately, files such as log and temporary files are created on the fly by Rails if they do not exist. Therefore, if they are excluded from the repository, they will be automatically created in any checked out copy when the application is started.

Excluding files was discussed in Chapter 4: *Working with Rails* and a method was described using Eclipse. However, if we find ourselves needing to remove these files at the server, we can remove them directly using svn. The following svn commands (run in the application root) will remove log and temporary files from the repository:

```
$ svn remove log/*
$ svn propset svn:ignore "*.log" log/
$ svn update log/
$ svn remove tmp/*
$ svn propset svn:ignore "*" tmp/
$ svn update tmp/
$ svn commit -m "remove log and tmp files and ignore them in future"
```

The Production Database

Installation of MySQL is described in Chapter 3: *Laying the Foundations*. The process of installing the database on a server is the same as installing it on a development system so it is not repeated here.

In the section above, which describes transferring of the files to the production server, it was stated that the application could be started if the production database was available and the application was configured to use it. It is time to discuss the implications of that statement.

There are two places where the production database is likely to be hosted: on the Rails server itself, or on a dedicated database server accessible over the network. Having the database on the same server as the Rails application is the simplest solution and the one outlined for Rory's application. It means a simpler configuration and less hardware to provide. However, it also means that the server's processing power has to be shared with the Rails application and the database engine, together with any other applications running on the server.

Moving the database to a dedicated server provides better performance as operation of the database engine is not impeded by other process and the full speed and processing power of a server can be dedicated to the database. These benefits usually outweigh the disadvantage of placing a network connection between the application and the database. That is, the major work in database entry and retrieval is not the passing of the initial and resultant data back and forth, but rather the processes required to search through the database and safely insert or retrieve that data within all the other data held in the database. As an analogy, for a magician performing a card trick, handing out cards is the easy part of the process. The difficult bit is shuffling and manipulating the pack to make sure the correct cards are handed out, and returning cards to the pack in a manner that they can easily be retrieved later, at the end of the trick.

For the initial stage of small application development, hosting the database on the same server as the Rails application provides acceptable performance, and this arrangement is described here. Moving the database to a separate server is a common way of improving performance as the use of an application grows. This will be discussed in Chapter 9: *Advanced Deployment* (which describes a number of strategies used when scaling up an application and improving performance).

Separating Development and Production Databases

I recommend not to use the same database for production and development systems. Rails already separates database schema into development, test, and production. However, it is still fairly easy to accidentally run a development system in production mode and thereby expose live data to an incomplete system. Also, it can be useful to run an application in production mode while developing an application, but we will want to do so in a safe environment away from the production server.

To clarify this point: A Rails application runs slightly differently in the production mode to how it runs in the development mode. When developing an application, you may want to run the application in the production mode to check for problems that are specific to the production mode (for example, issues with caching). If you are not to expose production data to a development system, a development system needs its own "production" environment, and therefore its own production database area.

Also, occasionally problems can manifest on a production system that were not evident on development systems. We then need to determine if there is something specific to the server that is causing the problem. To do that, it is useful to run Rails on the server in a configuration that is as close as possible to that used in development work, and therefore we would want to run the production server in development mode. Also, in trouble-shooting problems specific to the server environment, it can be useful to run unit and function tests. Therefore, the production server needs to be able to run its own test environment.

The easiest way to achieve this is to run databases locally on each development system. With an open source database such as MySQL, this is easy to achieve as MySQL can easily be installed on many systems. For a commercial database, such as Oracle, you may well want to use an alternative strategy, such as having a central development database server or instance.

However, this poses a problem. If different databases are used during development and in production, how will the application know, which database to use and how to access it when it is moved from one environment to another? There are two solutions to this problem, both of which involve the configuration of the database configuration file "database.yml":

Localhost database–single database.yml

The host name "localhost" is a generic name used across most operating systems, to describe the local computer. It is usually tied to the TCP/IP loopback address of 127.0.0.1. Therefore, if you make a connection to localhost, you are not making a connection to a specific system, but rather the local system. If you configure database.yml to use the database on localhost, the application will look for an instance of the database running on the local computer. When the application is running on a development computer, the application will use the database on that development computer. When running on the production server, it will look for a database on that server. Therefore, the same database.yml can be used in production and development. This is how the database.yml used in Rory's TestApp is configured and is evident from this excerpt:

```
production:
 adapter: mysql
 database: Test
 username: root
 password: password
 host: localhost
```

Not having to have different configuration files for each environment greatly simplifies configuration and this is the technique I would recommend to use initially. However, there are some disadvantages, like the following:

- The same user name and passwords are used in both development and production server systems, which means your production database is only as secure as your development systems.

- If you host the database on a separate server, it will no longer be accessible via localhost and therefore it will be more difficult to create a single `database.yml` that will work in both the development and production environments. Therefore, although we may start by using the localhost solution, as we scale up our application, we will probably need to move to a different system.

Separate Development and Production database.yml files

An alternative approach is to create different `database.yml` files; one for *development*, and another for *production*. The main problem then is making sure the production version is not overwritten by the development version when updating the application. Therefore, an essential step is to exclude `database.yml` from the Subversion repository:

```
$ svn remove config/database.yml
$ svn propset svn:ignore "database.yml" config/
$ svn update config/
$ svn commit -m "Removing database.yml and ignoring it in future"
```

That means, we will have to maintain versions of this file elsewhere. It is also a good idea to provide an example copy for the developers. The advantage is greater flexibility. The disadvantages are as follows:

- The possibility that in spite of our steps to avoid it, a development version of `database.yml` could replace the production version, or vice versa.

- It becomes difficult to test the `database.yml` outside of the production environment. If you make a typographical error in the production version, the error will only become apparent in production. Conversely, tests of the development `database.yml` are of limited relevance to the production application. It is fortunate that `database.yml` is a fairly simple file. If we use this method, it is a good idea to keep this configuration file simple.

Ruby heresy – I hate YAML

Ruby enthusiasts seem to always prefer YAML over other configuration file formats such as XML. Personally, YAML leaves me cold. My biggest problem with it is that white space characters have specific meaning for YAML. That means that substituting a space with a tab in a YAML file such as database.yml can break your application. Worse errors in Rails resulting from tab substitution gives very little indication of the root cause of the problem. As text editors can automatically replace pairs of spaces with tabs, the problem can easily catch out the unwary. **Always be very careful when editing YAML files, that you do not replace a space or series of spaces with a tab.**

There are other techniques, such as dynamically generating elements of database.yml based on environmental variables, but the two methods described above are the simplest and probably the best starting points.

Using Migration in Production

The default rake migrate command creates development mode database tables. On the server, we need to create production mode database tables. Therefore, we need to alter the migration command to suit.

```
rake environment RAILS_ENV=production db:migrate
```

The Rails Database User

In the example of a test application given at the start of this chapter, the root account was used in the database set up. While this can be a convenient and expedient thing to do, it is not the best practice (as has already been discussed in Chapter 4: *Working with Rails*).

The alternative to using the master account is to create a dedicated account for the application. This account should then be restricted to being able to access and alter only those parts of the database that stores the application data. Using the same Rails database user name and password for development and production makes using a shared localhost database.yml simpler, and is the technique used in our *Intranet* application.

However, there is no reason why you cannot use a different sa or root password on the production server to that on development servers, and this is a good idea, especially if development systems are taken off-site.

The Web Server

Prior to the middle of 2006, setting up the web server to host the application on a production server was hard work, involving a lot of manual configuration, trial, and error. And then came, Mongrel! Mongrel is a fast HTTP library and server for Ruby. Installing it is straightforward and using this utility has greatly simplified publishing Rails applications. In fact, Mongrel is now the default Rails web server, and once installed will replace WEBrick as the local web server started via script/server.

Mongrel

Installing Mongrel on a server (or other Rails system) is carried out via gem:

```
$ gem install mongrel --include-dependencies
```

Once installed, we can start a mongrel instance by opening a console or command prompt in the root directory of our application and entering the following command:

```
$ mongrel_rails start -d
```

This will start a mongrel instance serving the Rails application on port 3000. To view the application's default page, browse to this URL:

```
http://localhost:3000/
```

There are a number of options that we can use to modify the configuration of Mongrel. We can list all the options by using the -h switch:

```
$ mongrel_rails start -h
```

For example, to run a Mongrel instance on the default HTTP port 80 and in production mode, start mongrel like this:

```
$  mongrel_rails start -d --port 80 --environment production
```

...or more concisely:

```
$  mongrel_rails start -d -p 80 -e production
```

Mongrel Service on Windows

If using a Windows server, we can install a service based instance of Mongrel by using a gem called mongrel_service. This gem is installed with this command:

```
c:\> gem install mongrel_service --include-dependencies
```

Once installed, we can create a new Mongrel service using the command
`mongrel_rails`. For example:

```
c:\> mongrel_rails service::install -N myapp \ -c c:\my\path\
to\myapp -p 4000 -e production
```

This will install a service called "myapp", and will serve the application whose root can be found at the path "`c:\my\path\to\myapp`". The application will be available at port 4000 and will be run in production mode.

In this example, the service name is simply "myapp". I would recommend that you make the name a little more descriptive on your production server. Windows runs a lot of services and we will want to easily locate the Mongrel service in amongst them. The name specified by the -N switch is just a label, so we are not confined to simply having the application name. Quotes can also be used to enter a multiple word string as the name. Therefore, in the service creation command, we could replace:

```
-N myapp
```

...with something like:

```
-N "Rails app myapp on port 4000"
```

The service can be managed via the Services GUI (accessed via Administrators Tools in Control Panel).

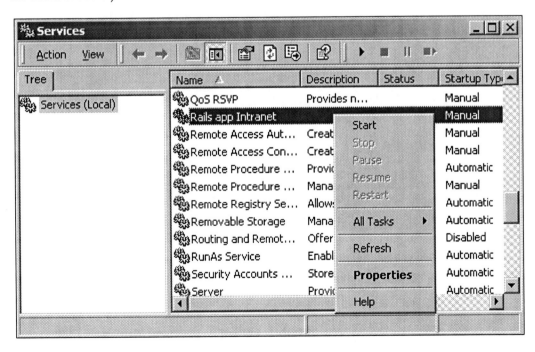

The previous screenshot shows Mongrel services highlighted in the Services GUI. The menu shown can be accessed by right-clicking on the service. The service can be started and stopped via this menu, or buttons on the toolbar.

Selecting "Properties" from the menu opens the service properties GUI. If on this screen we change the "Startup type" from Manual to Automatic, the service will be started as Windows starts.

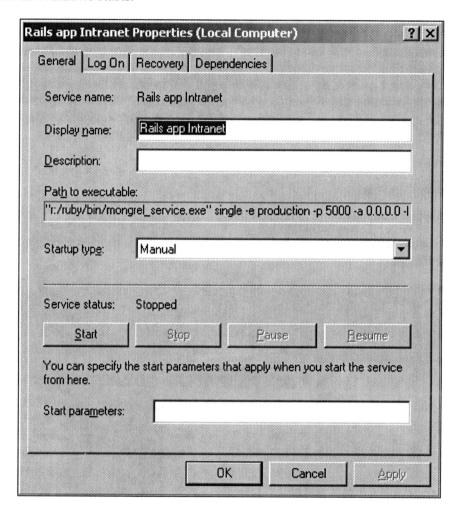

A Mongrel service can be removed from the command prompt using the service:remove option. For example:

```
c:\> mongrel_rails service:remove -N "Rails app Intranet"
```

The service is initially disabled and is only completely removed on system reboot.

Limitations of Mongrel

Although, Mongrel has greatly simplified the delivery of Rails applications, it is not without its own limitations. The main three are:

- Mongrel only serves Ruby applications (including, but not exclusively, Rails applications) and static HTML documents. If we also want to host another non-Ruby application (such as a PHP Wiki for example), we will need to run the other application on another web server, either independently or behind a proxy shared by our Rails application.

- Only one action can be carried out at a time on a single Mongrel instance. Therefore, if two actions are requested at the same time, Mongrel will only start processing the second action when it has completed processing the first. So, in an instance where two users request a new page at the same time, the users whose request arrives at the server second, will experience a delay while the first user's request is processed.

- Mongrel's performance is good enough for many small applications on its own, but it is not as fast as some other web servers. If we find the performance of our application is not as good as required we may have to use Mongrel in combination with another web server to improve performance. However, this is not the only option to boost performance. We should also consider reviewing our application and removing bottlenecks, and consider using strategies such as caching. Performance improvements gained via these actions may well be significantly better than those gained by changing the web server system.

In spite of these limitations, for many small applications, a simple Mongrel instance will provide an adequate web service. It is certainly a good starting point.

Mongrel behind Apache

The limitations of Mongrel can be mitigated by hosting Mongrel behind Apache. Apache is the most widely used web server on the Internet. It is a very flexible and a versatile web server that can run on many operating systems including Windows XP and 2003 server, Mac OS, and all flavors of Linux. The application can be downloaded from `http://www.apache.org`, a website that also contains a great deal of documentation on the use of Apache.

Hosting Mongrel behind Apache means, using Apache as the main web interface for the user, and then using Apache's proxying capabilities to pass those requests to Mongrel that require dynamic processing by the Rails application. The advantages of this arrangement are:

- Apache can host other dynamic web applications such as PHP, and static web sites. This means that you are not limited to a single web development or hosting environment. Of course, on discovering the wonders of Ruby on Rails, you may well not want to develop dynamic websites using other languages and frameworks. However, you may have existing applications that you wish to continue supporting. Also, there are a lot of web applications available that you may want to take advantage of. As much as you may enjoy developing Rails applications, there is no point reinventing the wheel every time. It is likely that for some applications, the simplest and most expedient option will be to bring in a pre-existing application rather than build a solution from scratch. Therefore, it makes sense to use a system that will not greatly limit your options.

- Apache can provide a way for an application to be delivered via a cluster of Mongrel instances. That is, you can use Apache's traffic management and load balancing capabilities to spread the load across multiple instances of Mongrel. So, if two users send requests for dynamic content, Apache will direct the first request to one Mongrel instance, and the second to a different Mongrel instance. Mongrel clustering will be described in more detail in Chapter 9: *Advanced Deployment*.

- Apache is faster than Mongrel at delivering static content (for example, image files and style sheets). You can configure Apache to bypass Mongrel to deliver these files directly. A description of how to do this is given later in the chapter in the discussion "Configuring Apache to Act as a Proxy for a Rails Application".

Setting up Apache to support other dynamic web application systems is beyond the scope of this book. Also, to start with, we will probably not need to cluster multiple Mongrel instances, or have to squeeze out that extra bit of performance that bypassing Mongrel for static content will provide.

Therefore, at this stage of application development, it is enough to say that hosting your Mongrel instance behind Apache is a good idea. I will describe here how to configure Apache to work with a single instance of Mongrel. Information on how to use Apache to improve performance and scale up your application will be presented in Chapter 9: *Advanced Deployment*.

Installing Apache

To take advantage of the simplest and most straightforward techniques for using Apache with Mongrel, it is strongly recommended that version 2.2 of Apache or later is used. The proxy modules available with earlier versions of Apache were not as easy to configure and set up to proxy Mongrel.

For detailed instructions on installing Apache, look at the documentation at `http://www.apache.org`. The basics are presented here and should give you enough information for a basic installation.

Apache on Linux and Mac OS X

The following instructions describe how to install Apache on a Linux system. Note that *VERSION_NO* must be replaced by the version number of the application that you are installing.

Download a copy of the application:

```
$ lynx http://httpd.apache.org/download.cgi
```

Extract the source code into a new folder and move to that folder:

```
$ gzip -d httpd-VERSION_NO.tar.gz
$ tar xvf httpd-VERSION_NO.tar
$ cd httpd-VERSION_NO
```

You must then configure the code prior to compiling it.

```
$ ./configure --prefix=APPLICATION_ROOT
```

Replace *APPLICATION_ROOT* with the location where you want Apache to be installed. If the prefix option is left out, Apache is installed at `/usr/local/apache2`.

Then compile and install Apache.

```
$ make
$ make install
```

Some systems may require you to use sudo to install the application. So, for example, you may need to use this alternative command to install.

```
$ sudo make install
```

The configuration of Apache is controlled by the file `httpd.conf`, which is located in the *conf* folder in the root of Apache's application folders (that is at the location you specified with *APPLICATION_ROOT* or `/usr/local/apache2`). You should check through the contents of this file at this stage and update them to suit your system.

You can then test the application by making sure it starts.

```
$ APPLICATION_ROOT/bin/apachectl -k start
```

Then browse to `http:/localhost`, and you will see a message, which will confirm that Apache is running.

The same process can be used to install Apache on a Mac running OS X. That is, download the source code and unpack it into a suitable location. Then use this:

```
./configure
make
sudo make install
```

...to install Apache in the default application location.

Apache on Windows

You can download the Apache source files and compile them yourself on a Windows system. However, most Windows users will find it easier to install Apache with a binary installer that uses Windows Installer to simplify the process. Installation is simply a case of downloading the binary installer (a *.msi file), double clicking on it to run the installer, and then following the wizard through. Make sure that when prompted you select the option "for All Users, on Port 80, as a Service" rather than "only for the Current User, on Port 8080, when started Manually".

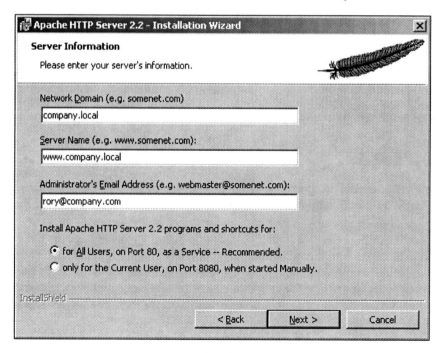

Using a Windows Server as a Production host is a viable option

When I started writing this chapter, I thought one of the statements I would be writing at this point would be "Windows is not a sensible platform to act as a production host for Rails". In preparing for this chapter, I read up on a number of methods people had used to achieve Mongrel clusters on Windows systems. They were all complicated and very much in the early stages of development. As clustering is the easiest way to scale-up an application, using a platform where this option was not available is extremely restrictive and therefore would not be a sensible approach, in my opinion. However, two things have changed. The latest version of Apache (2.2.3) now supports a greatly improved and simplified proxy module, and Mongrel has been developed to use `mod_proxy_balancer`, which is a component of the Apache proxy. These changes mean that Apache is now much easier to use with Mongrel, and this simple configuration is available on Windows as well as Linux, Mac, and other UNIX based systems. This allows you to choose the operating system that best suits your situation. I would recommend you use the one you are most familiar with. If you are a Windows user, do not feel this will restrict your ability to take advantage of the best Ruby on Rails has to offer.

This will install Apache into the folder:

```
C:\Program Files\Apache Software Foundation\Apache2.2
```

It will also install a service called Apache2, which can be started, stopped, and set to automatically start on boot from the Services GUI in the same way as described above for a Mongrel service.

Domain Name System (DNS)

Running a local DNS server provides the greatest flexibility in controlling access within our network. This will allow us to configure the names of the systems on our network and provide clear Internet style URLs.

It is common for a company to run a private network using private IP addresses (for example: 192.168.x.x or 10.x.x.x), which are separated from the Internet by a Network Address Translation (NAT) system. In such an environment it is commonly thought good practice to use a local root domain name space for our private network. So our private domain will end ".local" rather than ".com" or similar. So, instead of `companyname.com`, we would use `companyname.local` within our network. The advantages of this arrangement are that it separates the name space we use on the Internet from that used internally, and it also makes it more difficult for someone to access an internal system from the Internet, thereby helping us control access to our application.

If we use public IP addresses within our organization, we may control the name space ourselves or the DNS may be hosted by our Internet Service Provider (ISP). In this case, we may well use our Internet name space internally. However, that should not prevent us from being able to control the DNS and add new host names as required.

Adding our own host names (A records) to our DNS allows us to do the following:

- Create a host name of www and bind it to the IP address of our server. That will allow us to use `http://www.companyname.local` to access our application rather than `http://servername.companyname.local`. That is mainly a cosmetic change, though it is surprising the number of users who are confused by a web address that does not start www.

- Create a host name that is specific for the application. If we create an A record that maps our application name to the IP address of our server, we will be able to use a URL of `http://applicationname.companyname.local`. When using Apache, we can use this application-specific URL to help route traffic to the correct destination.

Configuring Apache to Act as a Proxy for a Rails Application

To act as a proxy for Rails, Apache requires the following modules: `proxy_module` and `proxy_http_module`. These two modules rely on `mod_proxy.so` and `mod_proxy_http.so` respectively and we will require both to be present in the modules folder of our Apache application.

As stated in Chapter 3: *Laying the Foundations*, `mod_proxy` is available with the default install of Apache 2 on some Linux distributions, but not enabled. To enable it, run this command as root:

```
$ a2enmod proxy
```

and then:

```
$ /etc/init.d/apache2 force-reload
```

We will then need to modify the `httpd.conf` file (in Apache's conf folder) to configure Apache to proxy Mongrel. Always make a copy of `httpd.conf` before you start editing it, in case you need to go back to the previous configuration.

First, uncomment the two `LoadModule` statements for `proxy_module` and `proxy_http_module` by removing the # marks at the start of the relevant lines.

```
LoadModule proxy_module modules/mod_proxy.so
#LoadModule proxy_ajp_module modules/mod_proxy_ajp.so
```

```
#LoadModule proxy_balancer_module modules/mod_proxy_balancer.so
#LoadModule proxy_connect_module modules/mod_proxy_connect.so
LoadModule proxy_http_module modules/mod_proxy_http.so
#LoadModule proxy_ftp_module modules/mod_proxy_ftp.so
```

Then add a new section:

```
<VirtualHost www.companyname.local:80>
   ServerName www.companyname.local
   ServerAlias  www.companyname.local

   ProxyPass / http://www.companyname.local:4000/
   ProxyPassReverse / http://www.companyname.local:4000
   ProxyPreserveHost on

</VirtualHost>
```

Replace `www.companyname.local` with the full DNS name for your server. This configuration assumes that the Mongrel instance will be using port 4000.

We can also add the following lines between the `ServerAlias` statement and the first `ProxyPass` statement:

```
ProxyPass /images !
ProxyPass /stylesheets !
```

This will cause Apache not to pass requests for files in the images and stylesheet folders Mongrel. The effect of this is for static image and style sheet files to be served via Apache, rather than Mongrel. As Apache is quicker at handling static files, this provides a performance boost. If Apache's document root is set as the public folder in the Rails application, this will work as it is. However, it is more likely that we will have to tell Apache where these files are, by using an Alias entered immediately after the two new Proxy Pass lines:

```
Alias /images /path/to/public/images
Alias /stylesheets /path/to/public/stylesheets
```

Apache will need to be restarted for the change to take affect. Failure to start indicates that Apache was unable to work with the new configuration. This may be a syntax error or absence of a required file (`mod_proxy.so`, for example). If this happens, check the file `/logs/error.log` that should contain the information needed to identify the source of the problem.

Rory's Production Installation

Rory is now ready to install the components required to provide a production environment for his Rails application. He installs: Ruby; the Rails, and Mongrel gems; a SVN client, MySQL, and Apache on his server. He then follows these steps to install and run his test application.

1. From a development PC he adds the test application to a Subversion repository called `test_app`. His local domain is `company.local`, and he has unimaginatively called his server "server".

    ```
    svn import -m "Rails test application"
                        http://server.company.local/svn/test_app
    ```

2. He then moves to his server. As it is on his network he is easily able to access it directly. He then uses the SVN client to download the application to his server using "svn checkout".

3. Rory then uses migration to create the MySQL database tables (he does not have to create a scheme, as a test scheme already exists. As he is using root access for this test, he also does not have to create a user account at this point).

    ```
    $ rake db:migrate
    ```

4. From the application folder, he runs "ruby script/server" to start an instance of Mongrel. He browses to `http://server.company.local:3000/` and checks that the application is working at this point. Once he has made this check, he stops this Mongrel instance.

5. Again from the application folder, he starts up a Mongrel instance to serve his application.

    ```
    $  mongrel_rails start -d -p 4000 -e production
    ```

6. He browses to `http://server.company.local:4000/` and checks that the application is working at this point too.

7. He moves to the Apache application folder and first makes a copy of `conf/httpd.conf`. He edits `httpd.conf` and restarts the Apache server. He then uses a browser to test the application.

Using Two Host Names to Simplify Routing

Rory already has web pages and applications running on his server. If he were simply to route all traffic to Mongrel, these other resources would cease to be available. He therefore decides to provide two name spaces for Apache to use, one for Rails and one for the existing pages. He therefore updates his DNS server by adding a new A host record of "intranet" mapped to the IP address of his server.

He already has an A host record of "www" mapped to his server, and he intends keeping this for his existing systems.

He then updates his `httpd.conf` as follows:

- He removes the comments from the two `LoadModule` statements for `proxy_module` and `proxy_http_module` as described above.

- He comments out the default name of the server and adds two virtual hosts. One for www, and the other for *Intranet*.

- He also adds a line defining the IP address of his server (in this example, 10.0.0.1) as a `NameVirtualHost`. This tells Apache that virtual hosts are being used for the service at this address. Without this line, the system will see the virtual hosts as clashing and revert to the first one it finds.

```
# ServerName www.company.local:80

NameVirtualHost 10.0.0.1

<VirtualHost www.company.local:80>
  ServerName www.company.local
  DocumentRoot "C:/Program Files/Apache Software Foundation/
               Apache2.2/htdocs"
</VirtualHost>

<VirtualHost intranet.company.local:80>
  ServerName intranet.company.local
  ServerAlias intranet.company.local

  ProxyPass / http://intranet.company.local:4000/
  ProxyPassReverse / http://intranet.company.local:4000
  ProxyPreserveHost on
</VirtualHost>
```

He then stops and restarts his Apache server. He tests the system by first browsing to `http://www.company.local` where he finds he is able to access his existing web pages. He browses to `http://intranet.company.local`, and using this URL, he is able to access his test application.

Once Rory is satisfied that his test application is working, and therefore his production environment also works, he stops the Mongrel instance and deletes the test application folder, thereby removing the test application from his system. He then restores the `httpd.conf` and restarts Apache.

Rory Puts his Intranet Application into Production

As development of his application progresses, Rory gets to the point where he wants to load the application onto the production server, so that a wider user base can access it. He is fairly sure that the application is ready for more public viewing and he has tested it thoroughly in development mode. To get the *Intranet* application onto the server and running in production mode, Rory follows the steps he used to get the test application into production mode. That is with one exception: instead of checking out the test application from the Subversion repository, he checks out the *Intranet* application.

Errors in Production

One of the features of production mode is that error messages are suppressed or greatly simplified at the browser. As some errors only manifest at the server, it is important that you are able to identify the cause of errors, so as to fix them. The best resource for doing this is the `production.log`, which is located in the log folder of your application.

Providing an in-depth description of all error types and resultant logs is beyond the scope of this book. Therefore, instead, I have decided to use a couple of examples of problems I have found recently in a live application. These examples show the production log and describe the symptoms, cause, and fix for each problem. They demonstrate the type of log entry that a problem can generate, and how I was able to use that information to correct the problem.

Slow List Rendering due to Placement of Additional Data Processing in Loop

This example shows how adding additional processing within the loop building lines in a list view table, negatively impacted the performance of the application. It also shows how this problem was highlighted by information within the production log.

Symptom

The code for rendering a list of job codes had been simplified to make it easier to maintain. However, on putting into production, the list page became very slow. I investigated the production log and found this:

```
Processing JobcodeController#list (for 192.168.0.234 at 2006-12-19
11:42:59) [GET]
  Session ID: 34901004e225fb2b8c43d3933b021049
  Parameters: {"action"=>"list", "controller"=>"jobcode"}
Rendering  within layouts/jobcode
Rendering jobcode/list
Completed in 8.42200 (0 reqs/sec) | Rendering: 0.24800 (2%) | DB:
8.14200 (96%) | 200 OK [http://miggins.bromyard.local/jobcode]
```

The key information from the log was that the list action was taking almost eight and half seconds to complete, and that 96% of this time was taken up accessing the database (last line).

Cause

I had created a new class method and instance method to identify whether an item was live — that is its timestamp matched the current timestamp. The code for these methods was in the Jobcode model method:

```
#When new job codes are added to the database or updated they are
  given a timestamp
#The current timestamp is the most recent one used.
def Jobcode.current_timestamp
  last_timestamp = Jobcode.find(:first, :order => 'timestamp desc').
  timestamp
end

#Job numbers are only live if they have been updated
#or added during the last update
def is_live?
    self.timestamp == Jobcode.current_timestamp
end
```

I then used the is_live? method, to highlight the inactive job codes with an alternative style in the list view table:

```
<% @jobcodes.each do |code| -%>
  <% if code.is_live?
      class_name = "no_alert"
    else
      class_name = "alert"
    end -%>
  <tr class=<%= class_name %>>
```

This meant that when listing each job code, the current_timestamp method was run. So, each line resulted in a query to the database. It was all these calls to the database that was taking up most of the eight and a half seconds.

Fix

I added "@lastest_timestamp = Jobcode.current_timestamp" to the controller's list method as the latest timestamp only needed to be ascertained once. I then tested against @latest_timestamp on each line:

```
<% @jobcodes.each do |code| -%>
  <% if code.timestamp == @lastest_timestamp
      class_name = "no_alert"
    else
      class_name = "alert"
    end -%>
  <tr class=<%= class_name %>>
```

This meant that each test was made against a single variable held in memory rather than a new call to the database. The result was a significant performance improvement:

```
Processing JobcodeController#list (for 192.168.0.234 at 2006-12-19
11:52:34) [GET]
  Session ID: 34901004e225fb2b8c43d3933b021049
  Parameters: {"action"=>"list", "controller"=>"jobcode"}
Rendering  within layouts/jobcode
Rendering jobcode/list
Completed in 0.29600 (3 reqs/sec) | Rendering: 0.11000 (37%) | DB:
0.15400 (52%) | 200 OK [http://miggins.bromyard.local/jobcode]
```

This example demonstrates how page completion statistics in the production log can be used to identify bottlenecks in the application. Removing such bottlenecks can be one of the best performance boosts you can make to an application.

The main cause of this problem was poor coding, rather than an inherent Rails problem. However, a key reason for presenting it here is that it demonstrates the impact of poor coding decisions vary depending on where the code is put. It is very easy to put poorly-thought-through-functionality within a loop, and as a result, for the impact of poor coding decisions to be greatly amplified.

In particular, list views by their nature are places where additional processing on each loop through the data can greatly slow down the page load. For this reason it is usually a best practice to get the data as close as possible to the final output within the controller method. Ideally, looping through the data in the view should only involve placement of data within the page and not additional processing of the data.

Application Error Following the Transferring of New Code to Production

This is an example of an error seen at the server, but not on the development system. The problem occurred due to a simple oversight, but such oversights can be difficult to track down. Fortunately, the information need to track down the problem was present within the production log.

Symptom

This problem manifested in production, so the only error message at the browser was "Application Error". Returning to the development system and following exactly the same steps produced no error. However, the production log showed a long error message, within which was a key piece of information.

```
Processing JobcodeController#list (for 192.168.0.234 at 2005-12-19 11:36:47) [GET]
  Session ID: 34901004e225b2b8c43d3930b021049
  Parameters: {"action"=>"list", "controller"=>"jobcode"}
Rendering within layouts/jobcode
Rendering jobcode/list
ActionView::TemplateError (No rhtml, rxml, rjs or delegate template found for jobcode/_list_table) on line #17 of app/views/jobcode/list.rhtml:
15:     <% end %>
16:     </li>
17: <%= render :partial => 'list_table' %>
18:
19: <% @
20:    <div c
   c:/ruby/lib/
   c:/ruby/lib/

┌──────────────────────────────────────────────────────────────────────────┐
│ The line that held the key information about the error                     │
│ ActionView::TemplateError (No rhtml, rxml, rjs or delegate template found for jobcode/_list_table) │
│ on line #17 of app/views/jobcode/list.rhtml:                               │
└──────────────────────────────────────────────────────────────────────────┘

   c:/ruby/lib/ruby/gems/1.8/gems/actionpack-1.12.5/lib/action_view/base.rb:266:in 'render'
   c:/ruby/lib/ruby/gems/1.8/gems/actionpack-1.12.5/lib/action_view/partials.rb:59:in 'render_partial'
   c:/ruby/lib/ruby/gems/1.8/gems/actionpack-1.12.5/lib/action_controller/benchmarking.rb:33:in 'benchmark'
   c:/ruby/lib/ruby/gems/1.8/gems/actionpack-1.12.5/lib/action_view/partials.rb:58:in 'render_partial'
   c:/ruby/lib/ruby/gems/1.8/gems/actionpack-1.12.5/lib/action_view/base.rb:278:in 'render'
   #{RAILS_ROOT}/app/views/jobcode/list.rhtml:17:in '_run_rhtml_jobcode_list'
   c:/ruby/lib/ruby/gems/1.8/gems/actionpack-1.12.5/lib/action_view/base.rb:316:in 'compile_and_render_template'
   c:/ruby/lib/ruby/gems/1.8/gems/actionpack-1.12.5/lib/action_view/base.rb:292:in 'render_template'
   c:/ruby/lib/ruby/gems/1.8/gems/actionpack-1.12.5/lib/action_view/base.rb:251:in 'render_file'
   c:/ruby/lib/ruby/gems/1.8/gems/actionpack-1.12.5/lib/action_controller/base.rb:726:in 'render_file'
   c:/ruby/lib/ruby/gems/1.8/gems/actionpack-1.12.5/lib/action_controller/base.rb:548:in 'render_with_no_layout'
   c:/ruby/lib/ruby/gems/1.8/gems/actionpack-1.12.5/lib/action_controller/layout.rb:245:in 'render_without_benchmark'
   c:/ruby/lib/ruby/gems/1.8/gems/actionpack-1.12.5/lib/action_controller/base.rb:53:in 'render'
   c:/ruby/lib/ruby/1.8/benchmark.rb:293:in 'measure'
   c:/ruby/lib/ruby/gems/1.8/gems/actionpack-1.12.5/lib/action_controller/benchmarking.rb:53:in 'render'
   c:/ruby/lib/ruby/gems/1.8/gems/actionpack-1.12.5/lib/action_controller/base.rb:942:in 'perform_action_without_filters'
   c:/ruby/lib/ruby/gems/1.8/gems/actionpack-1.12.5/lib/action_controller/filters.rb:368:in 'perform_action_without_benchmark'
   c:/ruby/lib/ruby/gems/1.8/gems/actionpack-1.12.5/lib/action_controller/benchmarking.rb:69:in 'perform_action_without_rescue'
   c:/ruby/lib/ruby/1.8/benchmark.rb:293:in 'measure'
   c:/ruby/lib/ruby/gems/1.8/gems/actionpack-1.12.5/lib/action_controller/benchmarking.rb:69:in 'perform_action_without_rescue'
   c:/ruby/lib/ruby/gems/1.8/gems/actionpack-1.12.5/lib/action_controller/rescue.rb:82:in 'perform_action'
   c:/ruby/lib/ruby/gems/1.8/gems/actionpack-1.12.5/lib/action_controller/base.rb:408:in 'process_without_filters'
   c:/ruby/lib/ruby/gems/1.8/gems/actionpack-1.12.5/lib/action_controller/filters.rb:377:in 'process_without_session_management_support'
   c:/ruby/lib/ruby/gems/1.8/gems/actionpack-1.12.5/lib/action_controller/session_management.rb:117:in 'process'
   c:/ruby/lib/ruby/gems/1.8/gems/rails-1.1.6/lib/dispatcher.rb:38:in 'dispatch'
   c:/ruby/lib/ruby/gems/1.8/gems/mongrel-0.3.13.3-mswin32/lib/mongrel/rails.rb:73:in 'process'
   c:/ruby/lib/ruby/gems/1.8/gems/mongrel-0.3.13.3-mswin32/lib/mongrel.rb:551:in 'process_client'
   c:/ruby/lib/ruby/gems/1.8/gems/mongrel-0.3.13.3-mswin32/lib/mongrel.rb:550:in 'process_client'
   c:/ruby/lib/ruby/gems/1.8/gems/mongrel-0.3.13.3-mswin32/lib/mongrel.rb:636:in 'run'
   c:/ruby/lib/ruby/gems/1.8/gems/mongrel-0.3.13.3-mswin32/lib/mongrel.rb:636:in 'run'
   c:/ruby/lib/ruby/gems/1.8/gems/mongrel-0.3.13.3-mswin32/lib/mongrel.rb:625:in 'run'
   c:/ruby/lib/ruby/gems/1.8/gems/mongrel-0.3.13.3-mswin32/lib/mongrel.rb:966:in 'run'
   c:/ruby/lib/ruby/gems/1.8/gems/mongrel-0.3.13.3-mswin32/lib/mongrel.rb:965:in 'run'
   c:/ruby/lib/ruby/gems/1.8/gems/mongrel_service-0.1/bin/mongrel_service.rb:84:in 'service_main'
   c:/ruby/lib/ruby/gems/1.8/gems/mongrel_service-0.1/bin/mongrel_service:153
   c:/ruby/bin/mongrel_service:18
```

Cause

The key entry in the log that led me to the cause of the problem was this line:

```
ActionView::TemplateError (No rhtml, rxml, rjs or delegate template
found for jobcode/_list_table) on line #17 of app/views/jobcode/list.
rhtml:
```

One of the modifications I had made recently was to extract the list code from one view and create a partial based on that code. I then used the partial in two different views. However, I forgot to add the new partial file to the Subversion repository. When I updated the production code, the file was omitted because it was not in the repository.

Solution

I added the partial file to the repository and ran `svn` update again on the server. This uploaded the file to the production system.

This problem demonstrates that it is possible to have errors in the production systems that are not in the development system. Therefore, you need to be able to test and bug track in the production environment. A second point is that errors can result in long entries into the log. In my experience, the most useful information is in the first few lines of the log entry (that is, near the top of the log). Do not be overwhelmed by long log entries. Start from the top and work down through each line. You will often find the root cause in the first few lines.

Back Up Rails

An important aspect of delivering an application to end users, that is easily over-looked, is back up. If our application is to be used regularly, users need to be assured that should disaster strike, we will be able to restore the application. More importantly we can restore their data that they have stored within the application. Therefore, backup is an important part of any production environment.

In this section, I will briefly outline a couple of systems that we can use to more easily back up a Rails application.

Backing Up the Code Repository

One strategy that could be used to back up our application code is simply to back up the files in the application folder. There are two issues with this. It is difficult to backup files that are in use, and therefore unless we shutdown our application during backup, it is likely that not all of the files will be backed up. Second, backing up the application folder only backs up the most recent version of an application. Previous versions would be lost unless we keep an extensive set of back ups.

There is a simple solution to both problems and that is to back up the Subversion repository. This contains not only the current version of the application, but also the earlier versions and newer development versions. Subversion has a facility to export its contents to a file. This file can be easily restored to a new instance of Subversion.

To create an export file from the repository use `svnadmin`'s dump option:

```
$ svnadmin dump path_to_repository > dump_filename
```

For example, on a Windows system we could use the following command to create a dump file.

```
$ svnadmin dump c:\repository > dumpfile.dump
```

We can use a `svnadmin` dump to export only parts of the repository. We can also make incremental backups (the default is a full backup. An incremental backup will contain only the files that have changed since the last full backup). The following shows the syntax for an incremental backup of revisions 100 to 104 of a repository.

```
$ svnadmin dump –incremental –revision 100:104  path_to_repository >
dump_filename
```

To recover the Subversion repository, you would use the `svnadmin` load option after first recreating a blank repository. The syntax of the commands would be:

```
$ svnadmin create repository_name
$ svnadmin load repository_name < dump_filename
```

To create a scheduled automatic backup, we could run the `svnadmin` dump command within a batch file and then use a cron or scheduled task to run the batch file at an appropriate time. This would create a simple file that can be easily incorporated into our standard backup routine.

However, we could also use Ruby to run a backup dump. The example below shows the contents of a file called `BackupSVN.rb` and will backup a repository at `"c:\repository"` on a Windows system.

```
filename = "svn_output#{Time.new.strftime('%Hh%Mm%Ss%a%d%b%Y')}.dump"
repository_location = 'c:\repository'
exec "svnadmin dump #{repository_location} > #{filename}"
```

Running the program will create a dump file. The `Time.new.strftime('%Hh%Mm%S s%a%d%b%Y')` element causes the filename to include a simple time stamp. As with a batch file, such a batch process could be scheduled with cron or a scheduled task.

Back Up the Database

A number of ways for backing up a MySQL database are documented at `http://dev.mysql.com/doc/refman/5.1/en/backup.html`.

On a Windows system the easiest method is via MySQL Administrator. This is an administration utility that can be downloaded from `http://www.mysql.com`. This application provides recovery and scheduled backup facilities and is cross platform. The backups generate files that can be easily incorporated into a standard backup to tape or network storage.

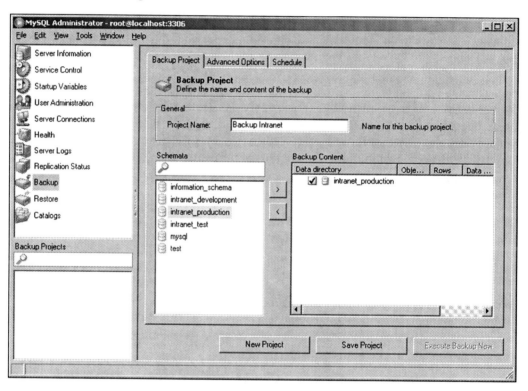

However, it is possible to use a Ruby script to generate MySQL backups too.

For example, we could use MySQL's `mysqldump` utility, which acts in a very similar way to `svnadmin`'s dump option. In its default mode, `mysqldump` not only outputs the data, but also the SQL code needed to recreate the tables and then insert the data into the new tables. The dump, therefore, automatically saves the data with the code required to recreate the table structures as they were at the time. Restoring the dump data will not require us to run a migration, and therefore we do not need to track the migration version with each data dump.

Like `svnadmin`, `mysqldump` is accessible from the command line and can get a full listing of the options available by entering:

```
$ mysqldump --help
```

The command to create a dump file of all tables in the database is:

```
$ mysqldump --all-databases -u root -p > dump.sql
```

The `-p` switch will force the system to prompt for the root password. In a script we will need to replace the `-p` switch with the `--password` switch. This longer switch allows us to specify a password. So, if the root password was PASSWORD, we could add the following line to our Ruby backup script to generate a backup dump file for the MySQL database.

```
filename = "mysql_output#{Time.new.strftime('%Hh%Mm%Ss%a%d%b%Y')}.sql"
exec "mysqldump --all-databases -u root --password=PASSWORD >
#{filename}"
```

On a Windows system, you may need to provide a path to the MySQL bin folder, but once that is done, the script works as it is given above.

Combining Your Backup Scripts

Unfortunately, `exec` terminates the Ruby instance. Therefore, an `exec` call has to be the last line of a backup script. We cannot simply paste the MySql backup script onto the end of the Subversion backup script to combine the two into one script, as only the first exec call will trigger. However, there is another way to execute shell commands within Ruby, and that is to use `popen`. Below is an example of Ruby code that will execute both backup commands:

```
def run(command)
  IO.popen(command, 'r+') do |io|
    io.close_write
    output = io.readlines
    for line in output
      puts line
    end
```

```
      end
  end
  filename = "svn_output#{Time.new.strftime('%Hh%Mm%Ss%a%d%b%Y')}.dump"
  repository_location = 'c:\repository'
  run("svnadmin dump #{repository_location} > #{filename}")
  filename = "mysql_output#{Time.new.strftime('%Hh%Mm%Ss%a%d%b%Y')}.sql"
  run("mysqldump --all-databases -u root --password=PASSWORD >
  #{filename}")
```

The run method defined in the first half of that code can be used to execute other shell commands. Therefore, you can add additional maintenance tasks to this script as required.

The "for line in output" loop, prints out the lines returned by the shell command. As the outputs of the two backup processes are piped to files, the combined backup code will return nothing to the console. If you were to add this to the end of the code:

```
  run('ping 127.0.0.1')
```

...the output of the ping command would be output to the console after the two backup processes had completed.

Summary

The application is now running in the production mode.

In this chapter, we have described how to create and maintain a production environment. We have also described how to pass code into this environment, and backup and restore both the code and the data that the application generates.

At this stage, we have used simple solutions to get the application into production and have not described in any detail some of the more advanced systems that can be used to automate production roll-out (for example, by using Capistrano) and scaling up the application (for example, by clustering). These systems will be discussed in Chapter 9: *Advanced Deployment*.

Rory's application is now available to a wider audience. Naively, he thinks that means he is close to completing his task. However, when more users start investigating the application, their reactions and actions are not quite what he expected. He soon realizes that getting the application into production mode is not the end of the story.

7

Improving the User Experience

It would be nice to say that at this point, the application was finished. The design brief has been satisfied, and the main user has looked over the production instance and expressed her satisfaction. Rory has taken a simple list of contacts and converted it into an application that is available throughout the organization; not just to view, but also for others to add and modify contact information. He has taken steps to ensure that the system is reliable, performs reasonably well, and has even gone to the trouble of developing a backup regime. Anyone would think the project was finished. That is anyone who has not put a new application in front of a group of users.

In this chapter, we will concentrate on the tools we can use to improve the user experience. These include providing links into the application, providing search tools, enhancements in the user interface, and providing help to the users.

It is the end of the week and time for Rory to present the new application to Ken. Rory is asked to demonstrate the new application to Ken on his PC. At first, the demonstration goes well, especially when Ken realizes how easy it is to access with no need to install a new application on his system.

Easy Access to the Application

Then Ken raises the first issue. "How am I going to get back to that web page?". Rory's first thought is to add a bookmark, but when he opens Ken's bookmarks his eyes are assaulted by a cascade of disorganized bookmarks. He should have realized that they would not be well managed when he saw Ken's desktop was packed full of shortcuts to applications and documents.

In general, users hate having to remember the URL to an application. So, if you want users to use your application regularly, you need to give them an easy way in.

Use Routes to Simplify the Entry Point URL

The URL Rory used to access the application during the demonstration was:

```
http://intranet.company.local/people/list
```

In fact, he missed a trick here. Because there is an index action in the people controller, and as discussed in Chapter 5, Rails will use that action to return content to the browser if no action is specified in the URL. So, Rory could have used:

```
http://intranet.company.local/people
```

However, he could have simplified the URL further still, by modifying the application's routes. These are modified via /config/routes.rb. Rory could add the following to simplify the entry URL further still:

```
map.connect '', :controller => "people"
```

This would simplify the entry URL to a pathless default action of:

```
http://intranet.company.local
```

However, before this works, Rory must first, either rename or delete the file /public/index.html, as Rails will always try to return this page if no path to a controller is specified in the URL. Only after it has failed to find an index.html document, will it look in routes.rb for an alternative.

The map.connect entry has to be inserted between:

```
ActionController::Routing::Routes.draw do |map|
```

...and the final

```
end
```

The simplest syntax to use with the route is:

```
map.connect 'url_path', :controller => 'controller_name', :action =>
'action_name'
```

Where url_path is the part of the URL that is to be entered after the basic web server address, so that Rory could add a path:

```
map.connect 'sales_contacts', :controller => 'people', :action =>
'list'
```

This would allow him to use this URL to access the list of people:

```
http://intranet.company.local/sales_contacts
```

Build a Fast, Clear Home Page

There is a problem with making the pathless default action point at a particular part of your application: it does not scale well. It is fine when the application is simple and has a single main role. In this situation, having a single path into the application works fine. However, as applications grow, more functions will be added and a single entry looses its usefulness.

The solution is to create a home page, which contains links to different parts of our application. As we develop our intranet we can add links on our homepage, to each new function or application.

Get the home page right and users will use it as their default home page. To achieve that we will need three things:

- Provide links to external resources that the users use regularly.
- A simple, clear design that is easy to navigate.
- The fastest possible page load.

The home page needs a clear layout with a number of well chosen links. It also needs to appear as soon as the browser opens. If users start to detect that a home page is delaying their access to web resources, they will stop using it. Users will put up with a short delay while going to a specific part of an application, but they will not tolerate a delay that occurs every time they open their browser.

The easiest way to ensure that the page loads as quickly as possible is to make it a static HTML page. Any dynamic content will increase the time the page takes to load. A user's home page is the one place, in my opinion, where the speed of static content outweighs the easy maintenance and flexibility of dynamic content. We can use CSS to control the layout of the page, and thereby simplify the HTML code and make it easier to maintain.

If we already have an intranet or are hosting our Rails application behind an Apache server, we can host the page within our existing static content. Another option is to host it within our Rails application, and there is already a place provided for it. We can name the home page `index.html` and put it into our Rails application's public folder, replacing the existing file of that name. We then put the CSS file for this page in the `/public/stylesheets` folder and update the path in our `index.html` to suit. Remove any entries in `routes.rb` of the type:

```
map.connect '', :controller => "controller_name"
```

Then, if we type the basic path to our server into our browser, we'll be taken to our new home page. For Rory this means that he accesses a home page by entering `http://intranet.company.local` in his browser.

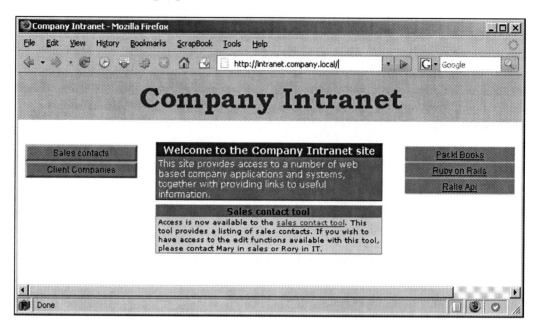

Users Need to be Able to Find Items Easily

One feature of the application that Ken highlights quickly is the time it takes to search through the lists of companies and people in the application. He asks Rory to build in a search function.

Use the Index View as the Core of the Search View

When Rory starts to write a new search view, he soon realizes that he is repeating the same code that he has in his index view; that is a list of records. The difference is that in the index view all records are being shown, whereas in the search view, a subset of all the records is being shown. If he renders the index view, but passes it the result of the search call, the coding will be greatly simplified.

If the index view is rendered when processing the search action, the index view needs to contain the search form; that is the form where the users submit their search criteria. This is often a good thing, rather than being a problem. That is, users are presented with a search option each time they access an index view. They can start querying and sampling the index list without having to move to a separate view. However, to achieve this, the search form needs to be small and simple.

It is a good idea to provide immediate user access to a quick and simple search tool. Often, this is the only search option required. However, if more advanced options are required, we can always add a second advanced search action.

If you would prefer not to have a search box in your list view, an alternative approach would be to extract from the list view, the code that displays the list of contacts, and put that code into a partial. You could then use the same partial for both the search and list views.

Search–The First Attempt

Rory's first attempt at a search function is not satisfactory and inherently insecure. However, it makes a good starting point for describing how to add search functionality. it also demonstrate some problems that can occur.

To create a search function, Rory initially adds a search form by altering the start of `views/companies/index.rhtml` to:

```
<h1><%= @page_title %></h1>
<p><%= form_tag({:controller => 'companies',
                 :action => 'search'},
                {:method => :get}) %>
<label for="term">Find company with name:</label>
<%= text_field_tag "term" -%>
<%= submit_tag 'Go' %>
</form></p><br />
```

He then adds the following method to the companies' controller:

```
def search
  name = params[:term]
  @paginator, @companies = paginate :company,
          :per_page => 10,
          :order => 'name',
          :conditions => "name = '#{name}'"
  @page_title = "List of companies called #{name}"
  render :action => 'index'
end
```

He uses `@page_title` to create a page title that is specific to the search. This is useful when navigating back and forth through the browser history, as each search will have a different title and therefore will be more easily identified.

When Rory enters a company name into the search textbox and clicks on the **Go** button, the entry for that company is listed and he can navigate to the show or edit view from there. However, as he starts trying a few options he discovers a problem. He enters a company name that includes an apostrophe and an error is generated. When he investigates this further he finds there is something missing from his current code.

Do Not Trust User Input

The problem with Rory's code is that it relies on the user entering a correctly formatted search term, and not entering potentially damaging code. Consider these two examples:

- The user enters a name such as "O'Connell and Son". The SQL WHERE clause generated from this entry will be "WHERE name = 'O'Connell and Son' ". This will cause a SQL error, as the apostrophe in the company name will pair with the first apostrophe within the conditions statement. The WHERE clause in the SQL statement will effectively become "WHERE name = 'O' ". The second part "Connell and Son' " will appear to the database parser as an additional code statement and as it does not match any valid SQL statement, an error is generated.

- The user injects SQL into their query. For example, they could enter a term "Bob'; Delete from users; Select * from companies where name = 'Bob" which would result in a where clause: "WHERE name = 'Bob'; Delete from users; Select * from companies where name = 'Bob' ".

- This would parse as three SQL commands:
    - The ActiveRecord generated SQL query ending with
      `name = 'Bob'`
    - `Delete from users`
    - `SELECT * FROM companies WHERE name = 'Bob'`

- The ActiveRecord SQL query and the final SELECT statement will do no harm, but the DELETE statement will delete all records from the table users.

There is a convention that SQL code is written with all reserved words in *upper* case, and *lower* case is used for program specific identifiers. However, as the example of SQL injection demonstrates, code that does not conform to this convention will still be processed and executed. The convention is useful as most developers find that it makes SQL code easier to read. Therefore I would recommend that you use that convention, but you do not have to.

Fortunately there is a Rails construct that will deal with both issues. Rails will run a number of processes on an entry including removing any potentially harmful code, if we pass :conditions an array formatted as follows:

- **Element 1**: The string containing the text you want inserted into the SQL WHERE statement, with any variables replaced with a question mark. So "name = #{name}" becomes "name = ?".

- **Element 2**: The variable you wish to substitute into Element 1 at the question mark location.

Therefore, to use this technique in Rory's code, he would change the conditions statement. So the controller code became:

```
def search
  name = params[:term]
  @paginator, @companies = paginate :company,
            :per_page => 10,
            :order => 'name',
            :conditions => ["name = ?", name]
  @page_title = "List of companies called #{name}"
  render :action => 'index'
end
```

Besides dealing with errors in a user's input, this technique also handles different data types. For example, rather than having to reformat dates into the default SQL format (YYYY-MM-DD) before using them in a query, Rails will do that for us. So to restrict the returned records to only those created on a given date, we would use:

```
:conditions => ["created_on = ?", date]
```

We can also have a number of variables within each statement. In this case, Element 2 will either need to be replaced with a list of the substitutes, or with an array containing the variables that need to be substituted into the first element. Either way, the set of substitutes must be in the order they are to be substituted into the first element. For example, if we wanted to only return companies created in the last ten days, whose names were "Bloggins", we could use either:

```
:conditions => ["name = ? and created_at > ?", name, 10.days.ago]
```

...or create an array:

```
condition_elements = [name, 10.days.ago]
```

...and use that in the :conditions statement:

```
:conditions => ["name = ? and created_at > ?", condition_elements]
```

Handle Nothing

There are two conditions that need to be handled. There are no companies in the database, and/or no companies are returned by the current search.

Between the end of the search form and the start of the table displaying the list of companies, Rory can add a conditional statement. If there is no data returned from the query, the statement will return a message to the user instead of an empty table.

```
<% unless @companies.empty? -%>
<h2> No companies match your criteria </h2>
<% else -%>
```

...and to the end of the code, add an end to close the if statement as follows:

```
<% end -%>
```

He could also add code to differentiate between there being nothing to show because a search has failed, or because there is no data in the database.

Users Need to be Able to Search Without Knowing Exactly What They Are Looking for

With Rory's code as it is, the user needs to know the name of the company they are searching for to get a successful result to their search. For example, if a company name was "Biggum", and a user searched for "Bigum" the company would not be located with this search. As it will be common for users not to know the exact name or spelling of a company name, we need to provide them with another way to search. There are two approaches to dealing with this problem:

- Provide a search tool that is less specific. That is, a tool that will let a user search for part of the company name and return a list of all matches.

- Provide a list of matching results, as the search criteria is entered, from which the user can select the correct match.

The second approach is a more complicated process. In the first, all that is required is a small change to the way the database is queried. Whereas in the second approach, a system has to be put in place to continually monitor a user's input and update a list showing matching companies as new characters are added to the search string. However, in Rails, the second approach is actually simpler to create, because a number of helpers have been created that automate the process. The automated process relies on AJAX which deserves a section on its own. So rather than introducing it here, I will initially describe the first approach, and then use the second approach as an introduction to using AJAX with Rails.

A Less Specific Search

SQL provides a way of constructing a conditional WHERE statement so that instead of looking for an exact match, the system returns any rows where the field being queried simply contains the string being searched for. This only works with character string fields, but can be a very useful technique to use with text searches.

When we use a `Class.find` method in Rails, ActiveRecord builds a SQL statement from our code input, and uses that to query the database. As we have already seen, ActiveRecord uses the contents of the conditions element to construct the WHERE clause of the SQL query. So when searching for companies called "Biggum" Rory's code:

```
:conditions => ["name = ?", name]
```

...would be translated to:

```
WHERE name = 'Biggum'
```

The WHERE clause has the format:

```
WHERE field_name = search_string
```

The alternative approach replaces the equals operator (=) with the operator LIKE. If LIKE is used on its own, it simply replaces the equals operator when comparing string character fields. However, when combined with the % operator, it becomes more flexible as the % becomes a wild-card entry. So:

- LIKE 'be' — matches field entries that consist only of the character string 'be'
- LIKE 'be%' — matches field entries that start with the character string 'be'
- LIKE '%be' — matches field entries that end with the character string 'be'
- LIKE '%be%' — matches field entries that contain the character string 'be'

So if Rory changes his code to use the format:

```
WHERE field_name LIKE '%search_string%',
```

...users entering new search stings will only need to know that the company name contains a certain sequence of characters. It then becomes a fairly simple task for most users to find a sequence of characters that will return a search result that contains the company name they are looking for.

To achieve this, Rory could simply replace the conditions entry with:

```
:conditions => "name LIKE '%#{name}%'"
```

However, as discussed above, by so doing Rory would expose his application to problems caused by users' incorrectly formatted entries. Instead a better approach is to use:

```
:conditions => ["name LIKE ?", "%#{name}%"]
```

Note that the % operators have to be added to the right-hand-side of the statement, otherwise ActiveRecord will insert a set of apostrophes inside the % operators.

As we may want to use LIKE in many places within our application, the best DRY practice is to add a method to prepare text for use in a LIKE statement. Rory adds the following to application.rb:

```
protected
# Adds apostrophe to text for SQL LIKE statement.
# prep_for_like('search')              > '%search%'
# prep_for_like('search', 'start')     > 'search%'
# prep_for_like('search', 'match')     > 'search'
def prep_for_like(text, placement='contain')
  case placement
    when 'match'
      text
    when 'start'
      "#{text}%"
    when 'end'
      "%#{text}"
    else
      "%#{text}%"
  end
end
```

Rory could then update the conditions statement to:

```
:conditions => ["name LIKE ?", prep_for_like(name)]
```

Case Insensitive Searches

With MySQL, the WHERE statements are case insensitive in the default configuration. That is the statement `WHERE field = 'HELLO'` will find all of these variations: Hello; HELLO; hello; or even heLLo. However, many databases are case sensitive. Even with MySQL, an administrator can turn off case insensitivity.

If you find your database is case sensitive, you will need to adjust your search code so that users do not have to match the case that a string is stored in within the database. The easiest way to do this is to force both the query string and the text being compared, into the same case— either upper or lower. In fact, it is a good practice to use this technique for all search queries in case your application is moved to a database that is case sensitive.

In SQL the function `LCASE` converts a string to lower case. Therefore, the following variation of the conditions statement forces SQL to do a case insensitive comparison.

```
:conditions => ["LCASE(name) like LCASE(?)", prep_for_like(name)]
```

Adding AJAX to the Mix

Like many web acronyms, such as PHP and SOAP, the technology represented by the letters AJAX no longer match exactly the words being represented. In particular, AJAX need not be Asynchronous, nor involve XML. The technology has moved on, but the original acronym remains. So rather than spending time describing the processes in detail, let's describe what AJAX can bring to our application:

- Direct client side access to the browser's rendering engine. That is, the page being presented to a user can change and be modified by the user's direct interaction with the browser.

- Data transfer between the server and browser without page reload. Page elements can be updated without having to reload the whole page.

- Client side processing. Much of the processing being carried out by AJAX elements is carried out by the user's browser, and therefore the processor within the user's computer rather than server processors. So AJAX can be used to spread the processor load.

Most of this processing is created through the use of JavaScript, a scripting language that has become the *de facto* universal browser scripting language. JavaScript has been around since 1995 and none of the "new" AJAX processes and methods are in themselves ground breaking. Even the key background data transfer API typically used by AJAX (that is XMLHttpRequest) had been used in many applications before the term AJAX was coined.

What AJAX has brought to web development is the packaging of these processes and methods into easy-to-use cross browser compliant libraries. These AJAX libraries have made it much easier to add JavaScript functionality into a web application. They provide structured access and syntax for functions and classes that have been tested and proven on the main web browsers such as Internet Explorer, Mozilla, Opera, Konqueror and Safari. This cross browser, functionality is important as each browser can treat JavaScript differently. For example, Microsoft's Internet Explorer uses a variation of JavaScript called JScript. AJAX libraries are coded to handle the variable behavior of the different browsers. This invaluable functionality makes it far easier to write one set of code that will work correctly in all these browsers.

 Do not confuse JavaScript with Java. They are two separate programming languages and should be treated quite separately. Code from one is not interchangeable with code from the other.

Rails uses two AJAX libraries:

- Thomas Fuchs' `script.aculo.us` (`http://script.aculo.us`)
- Sam Stephenson's Prototype (`http://prototype.conio.net/`)

These are located in the `public/javascripts` folder within a Rails application.

However, not only are these libraries made available within the default Rails installation, but also a number of Ruby Helpers have been created to simplify still further the incorporation of AJAX into a Rails application. It is possible to add many effects purely with Ruby objects and methods. However, some knowledge of JavaScript is helpful when tweaking an application to work exactly as wanted.

So without further ado, let us start using AJAX to provide an alternative search tool, and in doing so, start demonstrating what AJAX can do and how easily it can be added into our applications.

Make the AJAX Libraries Available to our Rails Application

Before our Rails application can use AJAX functions and classes, we must first make the libraries available to the pages generated by the application. In HTML we would do this by adding code, such as the following, to the head section of the page:

```
<script src="/javascripts/prototype.js type="text/javascript">
```

This would make the Prototype library available to the HTML page. We would have to add a second statement to make the `script.aculo.us library` available and additional lines for any other libraries.

In Rails, a helper method is used to make AJAX available to our application pages. The method is `javascript_include_tag`. The addition of an identifier `'prototype'` as shown in the following code generates the HTML code:

```
<%= javascript_include_tag 'prototype' %>
```

There is also a default action that will load all the AJAX libraries in the `javascripts` folder:

```
<%= javascript_include_tag :defaults %>
```

As well as loading the Prototype and `script.aculo.us` libraries, this statement will also load `application.js`. This file is empty (except for a comment) when created, and is the place to add any custom JavaScript classes and functions that we may wish to add to our application.

The ideal place to insert `javascript_include_tag`, is into layouts. Then all views that are presented within these layouts will get access to the AJAX libraries. For Rory, this means inserting a line between `<head>` and `</head>` in `views/layouts/application.html`.

Enhancing Search with Auto-complete

The auto-complete AJAX helpers create a system that monitors an input text box and provides the user with a drop-down list of results that match the user's input as they type. The user can then select from the list the item they are searching for. Note that for version 2.0 of Rails, auto-complete will not be included with the default Rails installation. However, it will still be available as a separate plug-in.

For Rory's application, we will create an auto-complete function for the company name search system. To do this he makes the following modifications:

- In the Controller, `companies_controller`, he adds the following on its own line, before any of the method definitions:

  ```
  auto_complete_for :company, :name
  ```

- Then in the view `companies/index.rhtml` he replaces the text box in the search form with the following:

  ```
  <%= text_field_with_auto_complete :company, :name %>
  ```

- Now when Rory navigates to the company/index view in his browser the auto-completion function appears.

List of companies

Find company with name: pl

Go

Name	Phone	Fax	Website	Address
Mock Plumbers			http://mockplumbers.com/	12 Pretend Row Madeupton

Mock Plumbers
Spectacular Suppliers

In the figure above, the letter **p** was typed and a list of the three company names appeared in a drop-down list below the text box. On entering an **l**, the list reduced by one (the company with a name that did not contain "pl"). Once selected with a mouse click, the chosen complete company name is automatically entered into the text box.

There is one more modification for Rory to make to `companies_controller`. At the moment the search method is waiting for a "term" to be returned in the HTML header. However,

```
text_field_with_auto_complete :company, :name
```

...will return the data in a field entitled `company[name]`. If Rory were to look at the new URL for the search view, he can see that `?company%5Bname%5D=` plus the search string is appended to the companies/search URL on submission of the form. `%5B` and `%5D` are hexadecimal representation of the HTML characters `[` and `]` respectively. To access the data in the HTML header field `company[name]`, Rails uses the following construct— `params[:company][:name]`. Therefore, the search controller method needs to be updated to use this construct instead of `params[:term]`. At the same time Rory can rearrange the start of the method so that the params statement is only required once. This will make it easier to modify this element as required. Rory also uses an `if` statement to catch instances where no name data is passed to the search method.

Rory's modified search method is shown below. The code first gathers the name passed from the auto_complete form, checks that data has been passed and is not an empty string, and then passes the name to a paginated company find method. The method uses the index view to display the resulting subset of companies that match the search criteria and a search specific page title is created by including the searched for string in `@page_title`.

```
def search
    name = params[:company][:name]
    if name and name.length > 0
```

```
      @paginator, @companies = paginate :company,
             :per_page => 10,
             :order => 'name',
             :conditions => ["UCASE(name) like UCASE(?)",
                                   prep_for_like(name)]
      @page_title = "List of companies with names that
                  contain '#{name}'"
      render :action => 'index'
   else
      redirect_to :action => 'index'
   end
end
```

So in three lines of code and a small modification to the search method, auto-complete has been implemented. It is so simple to implement that I think it is worth commenting on just how complex the underlying tasks are that Rory has just enabled.

- An observer has been implemented that watches the text box and triggers an action when a user makes an entry of a single character into the text box.

- The text entered into the text box is then retrieved.

- An XMLHttpRequest is used to send the retrieved text to the server where it is used to generate a query of the database.

- The results of that query are then returned to the browser via XMLHttpRequest.

- The query results are used to build a drop-down list.

- The drop-down list is displayed. That drop-down has the following features:
    ○ It is displayed within a box above the existing page content, immediately below the text box.
    ○ Styling is used to highlight the currently selected item.
    ○ Each entry is made active so that selecting it triggers the next event, and passes a reference to that next event from which the item selected can be determined.

- The selected entry is then inserted into the text box.

In fact just the following two lines enable all of that functionality. The controller code:

```
auto_complete_for :company, :name
```

...and the view code:

```
<%= text_field_with_auto_complete :company, :name %>
```

Cross referencing auto-complete

Most tutorials for Rail's auto-complete feature use the standard arrangement where the auto-complete entries are created from the field being queried. However, we do not have to generate the auto-complete drop-down list from the field we are ultimately populating or querying with the entry into the text box.

Consider this example. We have a table, listing the names of children and another table, listing the names of adults. We want to offer the users a search box for them to use to search through the surnames of adults, for surnames that match those in the table of children. The basic solution would be to raise the auto-complete on :adult and :surname. Then as the user started to enter text into the search box, they would be prompted with a list of existing adult surnames. However, the list would contain surnames that did not match names in the child surname list, but only appeared in the adult list.

An alternative approach would be to raise the auto-complete on `:child` and `:surname`, and then use the resulting `params[:child][:surname]` to build a query of the adults table. Both `auto_complete_for :child, :surname` and the handling of `params[:child][:surname]` would appear in the adult controller. That way, users will be prompted to select surnames that actually match the existing child surnames.

Some of the most useful instances of auto-complete that I have implemented, have used this technique.

Auto-complete—Wow!, but...

My first reaction on implementing auto-complete was "Wow!". Most people who I demonstrated it to were similarly impressed. In the next few days I went through the application I was working on and added auto-complete to various text boxes; after all, it was only a few lines of code and did not take long to add.

Over the following weeks I became more familiar with auto-complete and as I did, I found myself slowly removing the auto-complete occurrences. I now use it sparingly in a few key instances. There were certain issues I had with using the Rails Auto-complete helper. They are as follows:

- When errors occur, they are both obvious to the user and difficult to debug. When auto-complete fails, the usual result is that page styling gets altered when typing starts in the text input box. Typically the text size for the page decreases and the selection list fails to appear. (You can replicate this effect by commenting out the `auto_complete_for` statement in the controller).

- Often error messages are generated neither at the browser nor at the server.

- Errors occur after a user enters input at the browser. Most page source viewers pull a fresh copy of the page from the server. That is, a fresh copy showing the page before the user input.

- Therefore they do not show how the page is altered as the user makes their input. This makes it difficult to determine the cause of the problem. A dedicated JavaScript debugging utility must be used to visualize the problem.

- Auto-complete makes it difficult to alter if something goes wrong. There are no obvious configuration settings to tweak. We have no choice but to delve into the underlying helpers and methods.

- Auto-complete can slow down user input. In a simple text box search form, if we want to search for entries containing the word "plumber", we simply: select the input box, type the word; and press the *Enter* key. If we do that with auto-complete enabled, we will not search for "plumber". With auto-complete, as we type "plumber" a list appears of matching entries in the database, with the first one selected in yellow. Entering carriage return via the keyboard selects the highlighted entry and inputs that into the form. It does not enter the string we have typed.

It is now clear to me that much of the reason I had problems with auto-complete was that I was adding it because it was a cool feature. I was not adding it because its features addressed a specific problem or requirement of the application. If not used appropriately, auto-complete simply adds complications and its own set of issues to the application.

Use of AJAX—the Lessons Learned from Auto-Complete

I have spent some time here describing and then picking apart a single Rails AJAX helper method. I did not do this because I think auto-complete is a particularly bad method. In fact, I believe that when used appropriately, auto-complete is a very useful addition to the developer's tool box. The reason I chose to highlight some of the problems with auto-complete is that it is easy to implement and test auto-complete for yourself. It is also easy to replicate the problems I have described above. Most importantly, a more general set of lessons can be derived from the lessons learned from using auto-complete.

- The use of AJAX is seductive, in that it can be easy to implement, looks so good and currently is associated with a lot of kudos in web circles.

- When we add an AJAX function, we will add both benefits and burdens. For example, AJAX is more difficult to debug than standard Rails applications.

- If the "out-of-the-box" functionality does not quite match what we want, it can be difficult to make small changes to the functionality of an AJAX helper method.

- AJAX can provide functionality that would be difficult to achieve in another way.

Use AJAX because it addresses a problem that would be difficult to deal with another way.

Used appropriately, AJAX is an excellent addition to the functionality available to us as small business application developers. Use it where it is not needed and you will simply make your application more difficult to maintain.

Before I go on to describe some more AJAX techniques, there is one last point to make. If you return to Chapter 1: *Introduction* and look at the reasons put forward for using Ruby on Rails to build small business applications, you will find one of the benefits of this system was stated as:

> ... *reliance on simple defined open standards means that the work of the user's web browser is kept to a minimum, with most of the complicated work being carried out at the web server.*

AJAX reverses this approach. It adds processing and complication to the browser side of the application. It puts more reliance on users' browsers behaving as we expect them to. It increases the likelihood that a user's choice of browser and/or browser plug-ins could affect the functionality of our application. The more we use AJAX, the more we move away from the paradigm of concentrating the complication at the server where it is easiest to control. Using AJAX will always cause a trade off away from simple maintenance and toward a rich user interface. That should not stop us making the decision to accept such a trade off when appropriate, but should mean that we make it as a conscious decision following an assessment of the pros and cons.

Having highlighted some of the issues with using AJAX, I will now describe a couple of AJAX functions that I have found particularly useful.

Show and Hide Company Address Using link_to_remote

One aspect of the application that Ken points out to Rory is that the listing of companies is very long and takes a lot of scrolling up and down to navigate. Ken asks why each company has to take up so much space within the index view. When Rory examines the layout of the list of companies, he realizes that the company addresses greatly increase the vertical height of each company entry. If he removes the addresses from the listing, there will be more companies shown in any view of the company index view.

Rory discusses with Mary whether he could remove addresses from the company index view. Mary is not keen. She states that it is sometimes useful to compare company addresses while investigating the relationship between companies or while planning a series of visits. However, she does agree that most of the time, the addresses are not needed. "What would be great," she says "would be if you choose an option to simply view an address and then hide it again." Rory thinks that the AJAX helper `link_to_remote` might provide him with just the tool to do this.

The AJAX helper `link_to_remote`, provides a modified HTML anchor on a page. The anchor is different from a standard HTML anchor in that instead of providing a link to another web page, the `link_to_remote` anchor provides a link to a JavaScript function. That function modifies an element on the current page. Therefore, the `link_to_remote` feature needs to do three main tasks:

1. Provide a link on the page and a set of rules for what to do when that link is activated.
2. Identify an element to be modified on the page.
3. Find the correct content to display within the identified page element when activated.

A Simple link_to_remote

`link_to_remote` is used within a view. The syntax is:

```
link_to_remote(name, options = {}, html_options = {})
```

...where `name` is the anchor text to be displayed at this point. Details of the options available can be found at:

```
http://api.rubyonrails.com/classes/ActionView/Helpers/
PrototypeHelper.html
```

Here, I will describe a basic set of options, and later on when discussing Rory's requirement I will describe some more advanced options.

One of the simplest usages of `link_to_remote` is like this:

```
<%= link_to_remote "Say Hello",
            :update => "output_place",
            :url => {:action => 'say_hello'} -%>
```

This code does three things, stated as follows:

1. It displays the string `"Say Hello"` at this point in the page and places that text within an HTML anchor.

2. It defines `"output_place"` as the name of the element on the page that will be modified when the anchor is activated.

3. The entry `:url`, specifies that the action `'say_hello'` will provide the content used to modify `"output_place"`.

At the moment, clicking on the created anchor link does nothing because neither `output_place` nor the action `say_hello` have been created.

A DOM Object to Update

XHTML and HTML pages have a hierarchical structure defined by the **Document Object Model (DOM)**. Each page element is defined as an object and placed within the structure defined by the DOM. An early definition of this model as it related to HTML can be found here:

`http://www.w3.org/TR/1998/REC-DOM-Level-1-19981001/introduction.html`

More up-to-date definitions can be found via a web search for `dom definition`.

Therefore each element within an XHTML document can be related to every other element within the document by their relative positions within the DOM. So consider this part of an XHTML page:

```
<div id="fruit_list">
    <ul>
            <li>Apples</li>
            <li>Pears</li>
            <li>Oranges</li>
    </ul>
</div>
```

Its DOM representation would be as shown below.

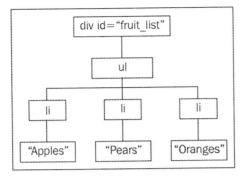

From this you can see that:

- The ul element is lower within the hierarchy than the div element.
- The ul element is a child or descendant object of the div parent.
- The ul element has three li descendant elements.
- The three li elements are at the same level and are called sibling elements.
- The text within an li tags is a decedent element of that li element.

We can navigate up, down and across this structure using JavaScript.

 I will use some JavaScript here as it makes it easier to explain what the AJAX helper method is doing. While knowledge of JavaScript is helpful when using AJAX, the Rails AJAX helpers make it possible to carry out many sophisticated JavaScript driven operations without entering any JavaScript code. The AJAX libraries themselves simplify the JavaScript coding, and Rails is able to manipulate those library functions and objects via Ruby code. Therefore, do not worry at this point if you do not have any knowledge of JavaScript.

However, first we must get to a starting point. All XHTML and HTML documents have a root ancestor element called "document" and we could start from this point and navigate down to the div containing the fruit list within the DOM. However, there is an easier way in which JavaScript allows us to navigate directly to a named element. In the example above there is one named object, the div element. Its name fruit_list is defined by the id attribute. The following JavaScript code creates four objects by first accessing the named div and then navigating from that point down through the DOM to access elements at each level below:

```
<script language="JavaScript" type="text/javascript">
  var fruit_list_div = document.getElementById("fruit_list");
```

```
    var the_ul = fruit_list_div.getElementsByTagName("ul")[0];
    var li_elements = the_ul.getElementsByTagName("li");
    var second_li_text = li_elements[1].innerHTML;
    alert(second_li_text);
</script>
```

The output of this script is an alert box containing the word "Pears". That is the text contained within the second `li` element.

The Prototype library contains a set of functions that make navigating the DOM a little simpler. The JavaScript below does the same as the script above, but uses Prototype functions to simplify the script:

```
<script language="JavaScript" type="text/javascript">
  var fruit_list_div = $("fruit_list");
  var the_ul = fruit_list_div.down("ul");
  var li_elements = the_ul.immediateDescendants();
  var second_li_text = li_elements[1].innerHTML;
  alert(second_li_text);
</script>
```

The key functions to point out are:

- `$("fruit_list")` – returns the DOM element with the ID `fruit_list`. In our example, that is the `div` element.

- `element.down("ul")` – returns the first child `ul` below the current element. There is also an "up" function that allows us to navigate to parent nodes.

- `element.immediateDescendants()` – returns an array of all the elements immediately below the current element.

A full description of the Prototype API can be found here:
`http://www.prototypejs.org/api`

This example demonstrates that it is easy to access an element within the DOM using `$(element_id)`, if we uniquely identify the element with an ID. It is also fairly straightforward to navigate and collect elements near the named element.

If we return to our `link_to_remote` example, we need to identify an element as "`output_place`" that will be modified when the link is activated. The simplest solution is to add a `div` element at the place in the document where we want any new content to appear:

```
<div id="output_place"></div>
```

This can be anywhere within the page displayed when the view is rendered. We can then grab this element with $("output_place"). In fact, the link_to_remote helper even puts the ID within $(), so all the helper needs is the entry:

```
:update => "output_place"
```

Create a say_hello Action

Lastly we need to create the code that will generate content to be placed within the output_place div when the link is activated. So in the controller we add the following code to create a new action called say_hello.

```
def say_hello
  render :text => "Well hello there!"
end
```

If we now navigate to the view containing the link_to_remote, and click on the link **Say Hello**, Rails will render the text **Well hello there!** within the output_place div.

Increasing the Functionality of link_to_remote

One of the best things about link_to_remote, is the number of simple-to-use advanced options. These allow us to extend and control the operation of link_to_remote very easily. A full listing of the options is available at http://api.rubyonrails.com. Rather than detail each option, I will use them here to show how Rory can achieve his objective of being able to hide and show the address entries.

Show and Hide

When Rory starts thinking about what he requires he draws up the following list:

- An initial arrangement with the elements displayed as desired when the page is first loaded.
- A show action displaying the extra content the user will see when selecting the show link.
- A hide action that will remove the extra content created with the show action.
- A link that indicates the current state, and that can be used to switch between, show and hide states.

However, the simplest AJAX actions are to add and remove whole elements. Also, it is easier to replace a link than alter it. Therefore, the way the AJAX tools work lend themselves to a different arrangement.

- In many cases the arrangement of the initial elements and the final arrangement after the hide action, will be the same. So rather than having one action that creates the initial state, and then another that reproduces that effect, a simpler arrangement is to use a partial. Insert the partial on page load, and then reinsert it when returning to the previous state.

- If the hide element has no content, it is in effect "hide all content". We can replace the partial with a rendering of an empty element.

- Have a partial that contains the extra content. In effect the show/hide action is then switching between the partial currently being shown and its alternative.

- Have two link scripts. Hide the inactive one and make the current one visible, That is, display the hide link when the extra content is shown, and display the show link when the extra content is hidden.

Alternating link_to_remote Elements

To work through how to create the required show/hide effect, it is simplest to start with alternating links. Coming up is some view code that achieves a very simple show and hide effect with link_to_remote links.

```
<p>
  <span  id="show_alternative_link">
    <%= link_to_remote "Show Alternative Partial",
         :update => "output_place",
         :url => {:action => 'show_alternative_stuff'},
         :success => "$('show_alternative_link').hide()",
         :complete => "$('show_initial_link').show()" %>
  </span>
  <span style="display: none;" id="show_initial_link">
    <%= link_to_remote "Show Initial Partial",
         :update => "output_place",
         :url => { :action => 'show_initial_stuff' },
         :success => "$('show_initial_link').hide()",
         :complete => "$('show_alternative_link').show()" %>
  </span>
</p>
<div id="output_place"><%= render :partial => 'initial_stuff' -%></
div>
```

- The two links are placed together within a single pair of p tags.

- Each link is uniquely identified by an enveloping named span.

- The span containing the link that will hide the content is initially hidden using a style attribute within the span tag: `style="display: none;"`

- Both links update the same div element: `output_place`.

- The show link displays content as prescribed by the `show_alternative_stuff` action, and the hide link displays content as prescribed by the `show_initial_stuff` action.

- Both links use the `:success` option. This allows us to specify an additional AJAX or JavaScript command to trigger if the `link_to_remote` process is successful. Both links use this option to hide themselves. The link will remain in place if the `link_to_remote` fails, allowing the user to try again.

- Both links use the `:complete` option to show the alternative link. The complete option triggers an AJAX or JavaScript command when the `link_to_remote` action is completed.

Alternative Actions

Before we can use this code, the `show_initial_stuff` and `show_alternative_stuff` actions will need to be configured in the controller:

```
#Renders a partial called some_stuff
def show_alternative_stuff
  render :partial => "alternative_stuff"
end
def show_initial_stuff
  render :partial => "initial_stuff"
end
```

The `show_stuff` action renders a partial. That is the partial passed to the browser to display within the target `"output_place"` div. The `show_initial_stuff` action renders the same partial that was initially displayed within the `output_place` div.

So lastly we need to create two partials and place them within the controller's view folder. For this example, the content of the `_initial_stuff.rhtml` file is:

```
<h2>This is the initial partial</h2>
<p>This is the original text to be displayed.</p>
```

The content of the `_alternative_stuff.rhtml` file is:

```
<h2 style="color:green;">This is the replacement partial</h2>
<p style="color:red;">This is some alternative text to be displayed.</p>
```

Now when we click on the link "Show Alternative Partial" the contents of `_alternative_stuff.rhtml` replaces the initial text in the `output_place` div. Then clicking on the "Show Initial Partial" link returns the contents of "`output_place`" div to its initial state.

Debugging JavaScript

As I stated earlier, JavaScript can be difficult to debug. One very useful tool to help debug our AJAX actions is Firebug (`http://getfirebug.com/`). Firebug is a Firefox plugin. The figure below shows the response information from activating the **Show Initial Partial** link

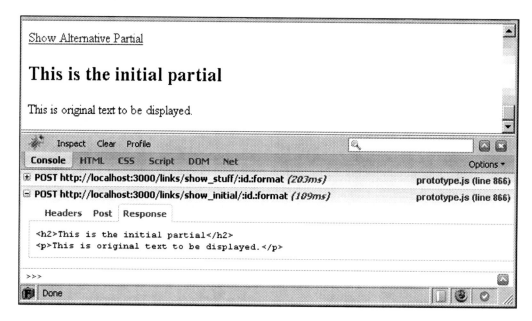

Such information is often essential when tracking down AJAX related problems.

Show/Hide within the Company Index List

Fortunately, the company address in Rory's index view is already being rendered as a partial. So instead of creating a new partial, all Rory has to do is alter the place where the partial is rendered. That is, instead of it being loaded as the page is built, it will be rendered as a response to a `link_to_remote` action.

The table cell is currently created with the following code in the view `app/views/companies/index.rhtml`:

```
<td><%= render :partial => 'addresses/show', :locals => {:address =>
company.address} %></td>
```

Rory needs to replace this content with two `link_to_remote` entries and an output `div`. He also needs to move the render code to a new action within the controller.

He starts by adding new actions to the controller `app/controller/companies_controller.rb`:

```
def show_address
   @address = Address.find(params[:id])
   render :partial => 'addresses/show', :locals => {:address => @address}
end

def hide_address
   render :text => " "
end
```

For the `show_address` action, he moves the render statement from the view to the controller's action code. Then adds a method to identify the address and pass it to the partial. The render code is altered to use `@address` for the local address.

The `hide_address` simply renders a blank entry.

The content of the company list table cell is then updated from:

```
<td><%= render :partial => 'addresses/show', :locals => {:address =>
company.address} %></td>
```

...to:

```
<td><%
    show_link = "show_address_#{company.id}"
    hide_link = "hide_address_#{company.id}"
    output_place = "address_#{company.id}"
  %>
  <span id="<%= show_link -%>">
    <%= link_to_remote "Show",
          :update => output_place,
          :url => {:action => 'show_address', :id =>
    company.address_id},
          :before => "$('#{output_place}').update('Loading ...')",
          :success => "$('#{show_link}').hide()",
          :complete => "$('#{hide_link}').show()"
    %>
  </span>
  <span id="<%= hide_link -%>" style="display: none;">
    <%= link_to_remote "Hide",
          :update => output_place,
          :url => {:action => 'hide_address'},
```

```
                  :success => "$('#{hide_link}').hide()",
                  :complete => "$('#{show_link}').show()"
        %>
    </span>
    <div id="<%= output_place -%>"></div>
</td>
```

A few things to note:

- For each company, there is now a set of hide and show links, and an output `div`. If Rory used the same names throughout the list, the system would be unable to determine which links to show and hide, and which output `div` to put the address content. Therefore, Rory has to uniquely identify each link and output `div`. He does this by appending the company ID to each tag ID. So for the first company, the ID of the `show_address` span tag becomes `show_address_1`.

- As having to append the company ID to a number of elements in many places is repetitive and prone to error, Rory adds a small section to the start of the new code, where the IDs of the current show link, hide link and output `div` are defined.

- Rory uses the `:url` option to add a parameter to the `show` link that will pass the `addressid` to the controller action. This ensures that selecting each `show` link will result in the correct address being shown.

- As the address takes a little time to load, Rory adds a `:before` option to the `show` link. This alters the content of the output `div` as the `link_to_remote` action starts, and **Loading...** is displayed. This text is overwritten when the output `div` is updated with the address, and therefore the loading message disappears on completion.

Using AJAX to Edit a Field in Line

There is an AJAX helper method `in_place_edit_for` which is combined with a second method `in_place_editor_field` to create a simple way to edit a field in place. To demonstrate, try the following.

- Add this to `app/controllers/people_controller.rb` (below the before_filter lines):

  ```
  in_place_edit_for :person, :notes
  ```

- Then change `app/views/people/show.rhtml` so that the line:

  ```
  <p><strong>Notes:</strong><br/><%=d @person.notes %></p>
  ```

...becomes:

```
<p><strong>Notes:</strong><br/><%=d in_place_editor_field
        :person, :notes %></p>
```

- Then browse to a person and select the show option. If you now hold your mouse cursor over a notes value, it will go yellow (you may have to go into an edit view to create some notes before this option becomes available – see note below on limitations). Clicking on the value opens a simple form in which you can alter the note and save it.

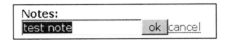

While this method is very easy to implement, it is not very flexible and is difficult to extend. Some of the limitations are stated as follows:

- The form simply contains a text input field, so we have to use a different technique to update entries from selection lists or use Rails date selection tools.

- The technique relies on there being an entry to update. If nothing is entered there is no value to click on; so no way to view the form. Therefore, we cannot add information via this technique; only update existing entries.

- It is difficult to validate any entries submitted via the in_place_editor.

- The in_place_editor is aimed at the show view. However, in line editing is most useful when it can be done from a list view and the tool is not so easy to use within a list.

In my opinion, it is easier to go to an edit view and make changes, rather than go to a view, and then reveal and submit each in_place_editor form. Using a standard edit view uses fewer clicks than using an in_place_editor enabled show view.

So rather than using the in_place_editor, return the people controller and show view to their previous state and I will demonstrate how Rory can achieve similar results via link_to_remote, and another AJAX helper method, form_remote_tag.

Render an AJAX Form via link_to_remote

Mary comes to Rory with a new request. She is finding that telephone numbers are used more than anything else in the application and she wants a quick and easy way to enter and update them. Preferably she would like to change them without leaving the index view. Rory decides to extend what he has learned using link_to_remote to satisfy Mary's request.

The first step is to create a `link_to_remote` in the telephone cell of the company list. As it needs to appear with any existing data, he makes it very small, simply a plus sign. So in `app/views/companies/index.rhtml` he replaces:

```
<td><%= company.telephone %></td>
```

...with:

```
<td><%
    tele_output = "telephone_#{company.id}"
   -%>
  <%= link_to_remote "+",
          :update => tele_output,
          :url => {:action => 'show_update_telephone', :id =>
                  company.id } -%>
    <span id="<%= tele_output -%>"><%= company.telephone -%></span>
  </td>
```

This is a simple `link_to_remote`.

Rory then updates `app/controller/companies_controller.rb` by adding two new methods:

```
def show_update_telephone
  @company = Company.find(params[:id])
  render :partial => 'update_telephone', :locals => {
                            :company => @company}
end
def update_telephone
  @company = Company.find(params[:id])
  @company.telephone = params[:telephone]
  @company.save
    render :text => @company.telephone
end
```

The action `show_update_telephone` is used by the `link_to_remote`. It causes a partial `_update_telephone.rhtm` to be rendered and passes a company object to the partial. The partial contains an AJAX form and the method `update_telephone` handles the data returned by that form. Here is the content of `app/views/companies/_update_telephone.rhtm`:

```
<% tel_output = "telephone_#{company.id}"
   tel_form = "telephone_form_#{company.id}" %>
<div id=<%= tel_form %>>
  <%= form_remote_tag(:update => tel_output,
                    :url => { :action => :update_telephone },
```

```
                        :complete => "$('#{tel_form}').remove()" ) %>
        <%= text_field_tag :telephone, company.telephone %>
        <%= hidden_field_tag :id, company.id %>
        <%= submit_tag "Update" %>
    <%= end_form_tag %>
  </div>
  <div id="<%= tel_output %>"></div>
```

As with the previous `link_to_remote` tags, the company ID is appended to tag names so that each telephone entry within the list is uniquely identified.

The main new element is the `form_remote_tag`. This is quite like a standard `form_tag`, except that, it uses an AJAX `XMLHttpRequest` to submit the data. Therefore any data input into the form is passed to the server without refreshing the whole page. Most of the options used by `link_to_remote` are available to `form_remote_tag`, and Rory uses the `:complete` option to remove the form once a new entry has been submitted.

The rest of the form is generated using standard form elements. It is this that gives this technique such advantage over the `in_place_editor`. Any form element available to us in a standard form can be used in the form partial. While this form is used to update a single field, it would be easy to add additional fields and options (such as replacing a whole list row with an input form) become possible with only fairly small changes to the basic technique.

A Little script.aculo.us: Drag and Drop

The AJAX functionality described so far has concentrated on tools provided by the Prototype library. Before leaving AJAX, an example is given here of some `script.aculo.us` functionality that could be added to Rory's application. Drag and drop is used to allow a user to grab an address and put it aside while searching through the addresses on a page.

Make an Element Draggable

Prototype tools mainly allow users to access data from outside and then use it within, the user interface. The `script.aculo.us` tools concentrate on allowing a user to manipulate the interface itself. One of the simplest functions to make available to the user, is the ability to drag one element on a web page to another location on the same page. That is, to make the element draggable.

The behavior of a draggable object is defined within the AJAX class Draggable. To make an element draggable we need to create a new instance of an object of the JavaScript class Draggable, and associate that new object with the element. This can be done by adding the following code to a view:

```
<%= javascript_tag "new Draggable('element_id')" -%>
```

Where `element_id` is the id of the element to be dragged. Rails provides a helper method to simplify this still further:

```
<%= draggable_element :element_id -%>
```

> Always place the code that associates a DOM element with a Draggable object below the HTML that defines the DOM element on the page.

Unlike objects in Rails, JavaScript can be sensitive to where an object is created and used. If the code that associates an element with a Draggable object, is put before the code that defines the element within the DOM, the code will not work as we desire it to. JavaScript will not look ahead in the HTML code for an element that matches the `element_id`. It will only look back through the DOM elements that have already been defined. It will, therefore, fail to find the element and then associate the Draggable object with a null. This will not raise an error — it just will not make the element draggable when it is placed on the page.

Therefore, this will not work as desired:

```
<%= draggable_element :element_id -%>
<div id="element_id">stuff to be dragged</div>
```

Whereas this will work:

```
<div id="element_id">stuff to be dragged</div>
<%= draggable_element :element_id -%>
```

We wish to make the addresses in the company list draggable. These addresses are displayed in a div element whose name is defined by `output_place`. We, therefore, already have an ID for the element to be dragged. Adding a `draggable_element` statement below the `output_place` div and using the `output_place` variable to define the element will make addresses draggable:

```
<div id="<%= output_place -%>"></div>
<%= draggable_element output_place -%>
```

Once the draggable functionality is implemented, it becomes possible to show any address and then drag it to another part of the company list page, where it will stay when released. It is worth playing with this behavior as it has some unexpected results. Drag an address to another part of the page and then click on the "hide" link for this address. The address disappears as expected. However, if we then click on the "show" link, the address does not appear in its normal position, but back in the place where we dragged it. This is because not only the content of the div was moved by dragging, but also the div itself. Therefore, when the link_to_remote call behind the "show" link is triggered, it inserts the address into the div at its new position. The :revert option causes a dragged element to return to its original position when dropped. In this instance, :revert provides a more predictable behavior.

There is also the issue of whether a user would know that an element is draggable. Unless we provide clues as to the draggability of an element, there is no clue for a user that an element can be dragged; the element will look just like the static elements around it. CSS is the obvious way to overcome this. We can define a "draggable" DOM class and use that to define style elements in the page's style sheet to alter the appearance.

The modification to the output_place element shown below incorporates both a :revert option and Draggable class definition.

```
<div class="draggable" id="<%= output_place -%>"></div>
<%= draggable_element output_place,
:revert => true -%>
```

To display visual clues to the user, we also add a definition of .draggable to base.css:

```
.draggable {
    cursor : move;
}
.draggable:hover{
    background : yellow;
}
```

This causes the pointer (cursor) appearance to change as the mouse pointer moves over the draggable element. It also turns the background color of a draggable element to yellow while the mouse is over that element.

A Place to Drop the Element

Dragging elements around a page may have some use, but draggability becomes much more useful if we can use the fact that an element has been dragged somewhere to drive another event. This is particularly the case if we can pass information from the dragged element to the triggered event.

The simplest way to achieve this is to use another set of AJAX objects called droppables. These are DOM elements that can receive dragged elements. Using Rails, an element can be defined as droppable like this:

```
<div id="drop_place_id">drop it here</div>
<%= drop_receiving_element :drop_place_id %>
```

To demonstrate how to use droppables, let us create a new area at the bottom of the company list page, which includes:

- An area where droppable elements can be dropped (address_drop)
- An element where new output can be created (address_drop_output)
- And the code that defines address_drop as a droppable and an action that results from an element being drop.

```
<div id="address_drop">
<h2>Address drop</h2>
<p><span id="address_drop_output">Drop an address here.</span></p>
</div>
<%= drop_receiving_element :address_drop,
        :update => "address_drop_output",
        :url => {:action => 'show_address'},
        :before => "$('address_drop_output').update('Loading ...')" -%>
```

Note that the drop_receiving_element method allows the same options that we have used before with link_to_remote:

- :update defines the DOM element that will be modified when the event is triggered.
- :url defines the controller method that will handle the action.
- :before allows us to give the users an indication that something is changing.

We now have somewhere to drop our addresses. However, to use the dropping process to determine a particular event we need to pass information from the dropped element to the controller. Fortunately, the method drop_receiving_element provides a mechanism to do this: the dropped element's ID is passed to the controller and can be accessed at the controller via params[:id].

In Rory's application, it should then be fairly easy to use the element id with the companies_controller's show_address method to output the dropped address. However, the design of the show_address method and the link_to_remote code that use it means that there is a small complication. The Rails object ID used to create each address droppable's ID is a Company object, whereas show_address uses Address object IDs. There are two ways to handle this—detect the type of ID being passed to the method and alter the way the method handles the ID to suit; or change the `link_to_remote` code so that it also uses the company ID. The first provides better performance (because we do not always first have to find a company before we can look up an address) the second is more scalable (because more of the code is reused, that is we are not using a different set of code for each option). There is a third option which is to use an address ID to identify the droppables, but there is a possibility that this would not create unique IDs on the page as two companies could share the same address. I will use the second option as it demonstrates the important components and how they can be used together.

First we will modify the `link_to_remote` to use the company ID, pass the same parameter name to the controller as the default `drop_receiving_element` (that is, `:id`), pass the same information (`output_place`) and alter the names of the elements so that they are a little more meaningful.

```
<%
   show_link = "show_address_for_company_#{company.id}"
   hide_link = "hide_address_for_company_#{company.id}"
   output_place = "address_for_company_#{company.id}"
%>
<span id="<%= show_link -%>">
   <%= link_to_remote "Show",
       :update => output_place,
       :url => {:action => 'show_address', :id => output_place},
       :before => "$('#{output_place}').update('Loading ...')",
       :success => "$('#{show_link}').hide()",
       :complete => "$('#{hide_link}').show()"
   %>
</span>
```

We then need to modify the `companies_controller show_address` method to handle the fact that the ID being passed to it will now be a Company ID and will have the prefix `"address_for_company_"` to deal with:

```
def show_address
   @address = Company.find(params[:id].delete(
              "address_for_company_")).address
   render :partial => 'addresses/show', :locals => {
                                        :address => @address}
end
```

With these changes implemented, the user is now able to choose an address and drag it to the area with the heading "Address drop". When they do this, the address will appear below the heading.

This example shows how some of the techniques used with `link_to_remote` can also be used with drag and drop elements to provide additional functionality. In particular, it demonstrates how drag and drop can be used to trigger events, and provide information to the process controlling the event that will allow it to alter its behavior (depending on the identity of the element dropped).

Further AJAX

I have only touched the surface of AJAX here. I hope I have demonstrated some simple techniques that achieve some effects that are particularly useful in small business application development. The AJAX helper methods I have demonstrated here are easy to use and very flexible.

However, there is a wealth of AJAX objects and functions available both through Ruby and directly via JavaScript. Some of the most exiting developments for Rails developers are coming via RJS (Ruby-generate JavaScript) which can be used to combine JavaScript functions to achieve complex tasks without the developer writing any JavaScript – all coding being in Ruby. If you wish to pursue AJAX on Rails further, a good start is an Internet search on "RJS Rails". There are also a number of dedicated books on the subject starting to appear.

Help!

One simple truth of software is that users are not developers. However, most discussion on documentation for Rails applications revolves around the developer and ignores the needs of the user. There is a system to automatically generate documentation that can greatly help a developer. I will discuss this system here, but I will also discuss help for users. The two are not the same and the latter is often neglected when discussing application development.

RDoc–Documentation for the Developer

The system for automatically generating system documentation is called RDoc. This is part of Ruby gems and therefore installed when we install Rails. RDoc extracts the definitions of classes, methods and attributes from a Rails application and presents them within a structured collection of HTML documents. Perhaps the most widely used example is `http://api.rubyonrails.com`, which is itself created with RDoc.

To create a similar set of documents within the application doc folder, run this command at the application root:

```
rake doc:app
```

A doc/app folder is then created with a fresh set of RDoc documents within it. Access the documentation via doc/app/index.html.

The default format of the documents is the same as that used by the Ruby core documentation as the following screenshot shows.

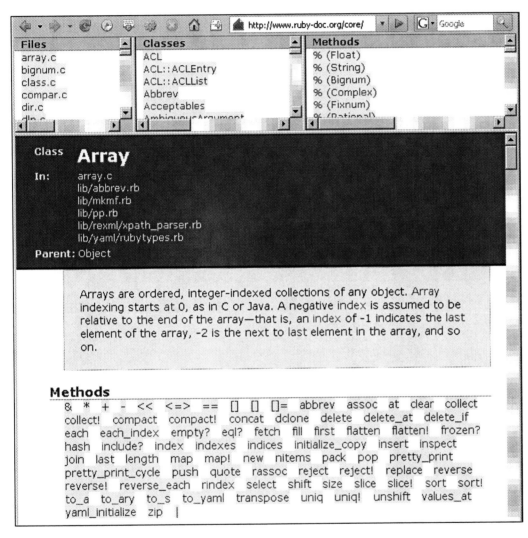

The upper three panes allow a user to browse and select particular source **Files** (left pane), **Classes** (center pane) and **Methods** (right pane).

RDoc pulls out each method from its `def` declaration. It populates the output with any comments we add immediately before the method. For example, this method:

```
#This comment will be displayed in the rdoc
def rdoc_help_example
  render :text => "Help!"
end
```

...will create this entry within the RDoc documentation, as shown below:

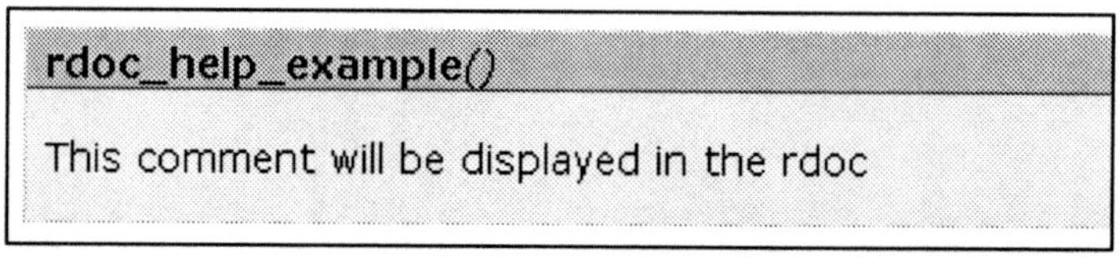

rdoc_help_example()

This comment will be displayed in the rdoc

Clicking on the method name opens a new window, as shown below, containing the method's source code:

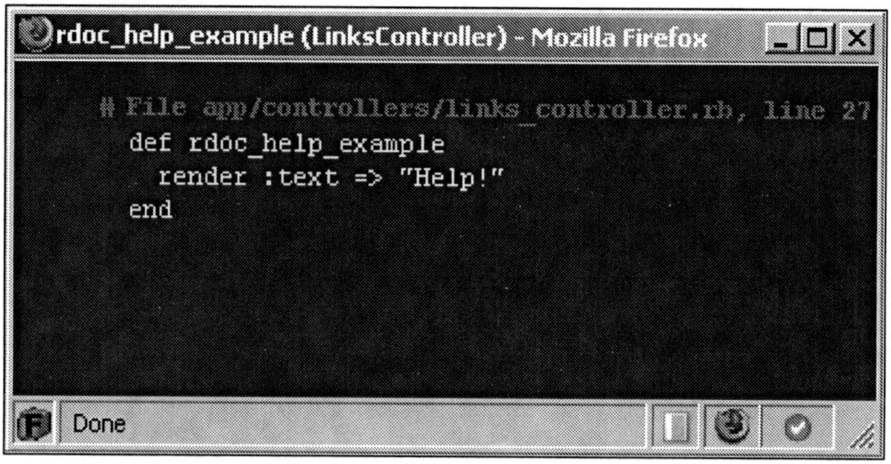

```
rdoc_help_example (LinksController) - Mozilla Firefox

# File app/controllers/links_controller.rb, line 27
def rdoc_help_example
  render :text => "Help!"
end

Done
```

This system makes it very easy to document our application for our own records and to help colleagues and others who develop or debug our application at a later date.

Help for the User

RDoc is a good tool for developers, but users need something different. They will not want to know how all the underlying components work, nor need to be able to see source code. What they need to know is what to click on or select to achieve the task at hand. RDoc does not provide that. What is needed is a different system for end-user help.

The solution I use and recommend is a wiki. We can use an off-the-shelf wiki application such as DokuWiki (`http://wiki.splitbrain.org/wiki:dokuwiki`), or build one ourselves in Rails.

The one prerequisite is that an individual wiki page should be directly accessed via a URL. This means that some wikis, are not suited to application help documentation. (For example, TiddlyWiki is an excellent personal wiki that I used a lot to keep notes when I started Rails development. However, it relies on client side JavaScript links to access individual wiki entries, and the URL remains constant as simply that of the TidlyWiki document. Therefore it is not suitable for a Rails help system.)

A wiki provides the following advantages:

- Built-in tools to help us create attractive documents with text formatting and image insertion.
- The writing tools are available within the browser. We do not need another application to write entries.
- Built-in search tools to assist users to find the help entry they need.
- User control to allow a team of people to help you maintain and develop the help system.

The most important advantage is the last one. In my opinion, the best help systems are those that actively encourage user input. With a wiki, we can allow our users to correct, update and improve on our help entries. Users are the best people to know what they need with a help system, so why not provide them with the tool for them to update as they require.

Instiki Wiki Help

Rory decides to use Instiki, a wiki based on Rails, for his user help system. Rory installs Instiki by downloading the files from the project's rubyforge page (`http://rubyforge.org/projects/instiki/`) and unziping them to their own directory. He then uses Mongrel to host a new instance of the Instiki application.

Instiki is built using Rails and therefore can be hosted in the same way as Rory's Intranet application. On Linux, the application can be started simply by running "instiki". To host the system via Mongrel on a Windows system, we would have to carry out a couple of tweaks.

- Add the path to the application's `lib/native/win32` folder to your system path. Instiki uses a SQLite database, and the Windows drivers are held in this folder.

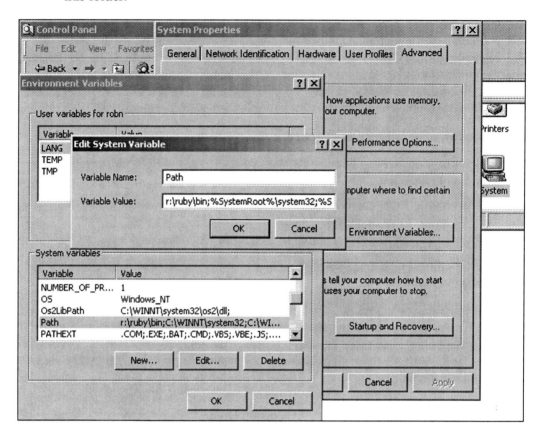

- Then add a new Mongrel service instance:

```
mongrel_rails service::install -N instiki \ -c <path to instiki>
-p 2500 -e production
```

As Instiki is a Rails application, we can modify it in the same way as any other Rails application. For example, in version 0.11.0, if we create new content via a Firefox browser, the main text area is too large and becomes displaced down the page. An examination of the code shows that the text area is defined in line 17 of `app/views/wiki/new.rhtml`:

```
<textarea name="content" id="content" style="width: 450px; height:
500px">
```

A similar text area in `app/views/wiki/edit.rhtml` which is displayed correctly in Firefox is defined via:

```
<textarea name="content" id="content" style="width: 70%; height:
500px">
```

By changing the width configuration to 70% in `new.rhtml`, the form is displayed correctly in Firefox. We could even extract the form code as a partial and then use the same code in both views as both forms have a lot of similarity. The advantage of using a Rails wiki is that we can easily develop it to suit our needs.

Rory decides to provide a new virtual server at `wiki.company.local` in the same way that he created `intranet.company.local` (see Chapter 6: *Into Production*) and adds a virtual host to his Apache configuration. To do this, he creates a new DNS A Host called "wiki" using his server's IP address, and adds the code below to `httpd.conf`:

```
</VirtualHost>
<VirtualHost wiki.company.local:80>
    ServerName wiki.company.local
    ServerAlias wiki.company.local
    ProxyPass / http://wiki.company.local:2500/
    ProxyPassReverse / http://wiki.company.local:2500
    ProxyPreserveHost on
</VirtualHost>
```

On first entry, he sets up the Instiki application to use a base path of "help".

1. Name and address for your first web

The name of the web is included in the title on all pages. The address is the base path that all pages within the web live beneath. Ex: the address "rails" gives URLs like */rails/show/HomePage*. The address can only consist of letters and digits.

Name: Help   Address: help

2. Password for creating and changing webs

Administrative access allows you to make new webs and change existing ones.

Everyone with this password will be able to do this, so pick it carefully!

Password: ••••••••   Verify: ••••••••

Setup

Rory then creates a helper method to create links to the wiki, so that he has one place to update the URL for the wiki, should he need to move it. Therefore in `app/helpers/application_helper.rb`, he adds:

```
#Generates a link to the wiki page holding relevant help
information.
def help_link(wiki_entry_name=nil)
  wiki_url = "http://wiki.robhome.local/help/show"
  if wiki_entry_name
    wiki_url += "/#{wiki_entry_name}"
    link_text = "Help for #{wiki_entry_name.underscore.humanize}"
  else
    wiki_url += "/HomePage"
    link_text = "Help"
  end
  link_to link_text, wiki_url, {:target => '_blank'}
end
```

For his first wiki he creates a new entry called CompanyList and in this he writes a guide as to the use of the company listing in the application index view. He then goes to `app/views/companies/index.rhtml` and adds a new `help_link` to the bottom of the page:

```
<%= help_link 'CompanyList' %>
```

The Best User Help Systems

If you look at a help page you have written, and find that it can be summed up as a list of features available in the application, I would be safe to bet that you have not written the best help system you could. How many help systems have you used where the entry for "the X feature button" reads "this button activates the X feature". Yet most systems I have used have plenty of entries just like that.

So how do we avoid just listing the features? The best way I have found is not to treat the help system as the place to describe all the features available. Instead, use the help system to describe the processes a user goes through to carry out the tasks they achieve via the application.

For example, look at two help system entries for using the facility to edit telephone numbers within the company list created earlier in this chapter:

1. The plus sign at the start of a telephone number allows you to edit that number.

2. To edit a telephone number, click on the plus sign at the start of telephone number. The number will then appear in an input box in which you can edit the number. Change the number to the correct entry and then click on the Update button. The new number will then be saved to the server. You must be logged on to access this feature.

The first entry simply tells the user what the plus sign is. The second tells the user how to use the feature, when accessed via the plus sign. The first describes the feature, the second the process to go through to achieve the task of changing a telephone number. The second entry is better in that it tells a user how to use the feature, and in doing so, it also describes what the feature does.

When writing user help information, I recommend the following:

- Look at each user interface and list the tasks that users are likely to carry out using that interface.

- For each task, note down the steps a user will need to go through to use that user interface to achieve the task. Use this list as the core of the help document.

- If there are a number of similar tasks, describe the simplest first, and then describe how to alter the steps to achieve the different similar tasks.

- When you have finished, go back over the user interface and make sure that all the features have been used somewhere within the tasks steps, If you find a feature that is not described with a task step, then simply describe what that feature does. Even then think of an example of how a user may use that feature, and describe that if you can. (However, if you are unable to think of an example task for the feature, I would question why that feature is included within the interface. A better option may be to remove the feature!)

Keep Talking to Users

Rory's application is now in production and he has been responding to user issues and feedback. In my experience this period can be the most fruitful in the development process. This is the time when very small adjustments could have large impacts on the usefulness of the application. It is often only when users start to use an application that they really appreciate how it can make their job easier. It is then that they start making comments like: "It would be great if I could see this information in that screen".

An example: I built a stock control system for a purchasing team. The system allowed users to track the purchasing and selling of equipment, and replaced a shared Excel spreadsheet. The users liked the system, but it was a month into using it when one of them said: "It would be great if we had an easy way of viewing a list of all the ordered kit that we are expecting to arrive this week". An hour later, there was a link on the main screen that took the users to just such a listing. In fact, there were three links – one to show last week's expected deliveries, one to the the present week's, and another to next week's. Those three links became three of the most used links in the application. In one step I had made it much easier for users to see what they should be expecting to come in through the door. I thought I had already provided tools to give all the views a user would use, but I had missed the combination of stock on order and delivery in the current week. The users never before had such a simple way of viewing this information, and had also not imagined it was possible, and therefore had not asked for it when the system was specified.

This is one example, but it has been a common one for me. The key point is that the best way to improve the user experience is for you to keep an open communication with the users. Keep listening to your users. They are the source of your most productive modifications.

Summary

In this chapter, we have described how to improve the users' experience by simplifying entry to the application, adding search facilities, and providing a help system.

We have also introduced AJAX, initially looking at a basic set of helper methods (`auto_complete`) that easily provide some advanced enhancements to form fields.

We have then looked at some of the problems that these basic techniques highlight. We went on to show how a particular, more advanced helper function (`link_to_remote`) can be used to update and expand the information on a page without reloading the page. This method is very flexible and some variations are shown, including using `link_to_remote`, to load a form that can then be submitted again without reloading the page. Some drag and drop functionality is also described. These AJAX examples give a feel of what can be achieved using these systems and how they can be used within Rails.

Lastly, we described help systems and the importance of using different help systems to support users and other developers. The two groups require different information and therefore require help in different ways.

8

Extending the Application

In this chapter, we're going to see how to extend the *Intranet* application, using mock (but hopefully realistic) feedback from users as a basis for the extensions. The feedback covers both desired enhancements to existing features, and new feature requests. Doing this will demonstrate more breadth of the features provided by the Rails, and how to logically add new components to an application.

The feedback received from the users included:

- Adding people **search facilities**
- **Handling errors** properly
- Using **sessions and cookies** for user authentication
- Doing simple **task tracking**
- Adding **file uploads**

We're also going to look at integrating the work of other programmers into a project. The primary means for doing this is through **plugins**, so we'll see how to discover and install them for your own applications.

Dealing with User Feedback

Users at Acme have been putting the *Intranet* system through its paces for a few weeks. They are generally happy with how it works, and Ken (the Managing Director) is pleased with its progress. But comments from users indicate that a few niggling issues have arisen during the pilot phase. Rory and Jenny have put aside some time to deal with these issues, as well as time to add new features to the system. They arranged the feedback from users in order of priority and ended up with the following list of points to address:

- **"It's too hard to find people. When I'm on the phone with someone, I need a quick way to locate their record."**
  Rory and Jenny knew that simple listing of people would be insufficient in day-to-day work. As the system fills up with contacts, it takes longer and longer to page through the listing to find someone. They decide to extend the system to enable searching for a person by name, part of a name, keywords, or notes associated with them.

- **"Sometimes I bookmark pages, and then when I come back to them everything's broken."**
  Rory and Jenny have done little to capture possible errors in the application. For example, if someone tries to access the record of a company that has been deleted, they get a nasty default Rails `ActiveRecord::RecordNotFound` error message. They decide to tidy up the system, so it handles common errors more elegantly.

- **"I need to record the tasks I carry out, so I can see the history of what I've done with a client."**
  This request was made by quite a few members of staff, so Rory and Jenny decide that it should be given some priority. They opt for a simple task tracking utility, which will allow activities to be attached to a person's record. Each task will also be associated with an individual user of the system, so future enhancements could include tracking who's carried out which activities. They decide not to attempt a full-fledged calendar, as this would require too much work.

- **"I quite often send documents to people, but can't store them on the Intranet."**
  A file upload facility would enable members of the staff to attach documents (e.g. quotes, presentations) to tasks.

Having decided on a plan of work, they tackle each feature request in turn. We'll be working alongside them as they make these changes to the system.

Adding a Search Facility

The first step in extending the system is to enable searching for people. This requires changes to a few parts of the system:

- A new **action,** which performs the search against the `Person` model, retrieving an array of `Person` instances from the database. As the search only uses the `Person` model, the logical place to locate the action is in the controller, which manages the other actions for that model: `PeopleController`. We'll call the action `search`.

- A **view template** to display the results of the search. We already have a view template that can render an array of Person instances: app/views/people/ index.rhtml. Therefore, we can just reuse that template, with some minor modifications such as a different page title.

- A **form** where a user can type a search term and perform the search. We can add this to the layout for the application (app/layouts/application. rhtml) to make it available from any page.

Once this functionality is in place, we'll be able to search the people table with a URL like this:

```
http://localhost:3000/people/search?term=James
```

We first need a search action on the PeopleController (in app/controllers/ people_controller.rb). This is fairly similar to the index action: it retrieves a set of records from the database using a paginator and displays them. As noted above, we can also use the same view template (index.rhtml) to output the HTML, but we'll have to explicitly call it inside the action (highlighted below) as the action name doesn't match the template name. Here's the action in full:

```
def search
  @paginator, @people = paginate :person, :per_page => 10,
    :select => 'id, last_name, first_name',
    :order => 'last_name, first_name'
  @page_title = "Search results (page #{@paginator.current.number})"
  render :action => 'index'
end
```

Test this at http://localhost:3000/people/search?term=Jeff (put anything you like at the end of the URL — it's not being used yet). You should see something very similar to the index page for PeopleController, but with a different title (**Search results...**). This proves that the route, action, and template are all working together.

Next, we need to use the term parameter passed in the URL to narrow the results. In Chapter 4 (*Finding Records Matching Search Criteria*), we saw how to use a :conditions option to restrict the results returned by find. We can also use a :conditions option with the paginate method to restrict by our search term (highlighted):

```
def search
  # Get the search term from the querystring and put
  # percentage signs round it so it can be used with a LIKE query
  term = "%#{params[:term]}%"
  @paginator, @people = paginate :person, :per_page => 10,
    :select => 'id, last_name, first_name',
```

```
    :order => 'last_name, first_name',
    :conditions => ['last_name LIKE :term or first_name LIKE :term \
    OR notes LIKE :term OR keywords LIKE :term', {:term => term}]
    @page_title = "Search results (page #{@paginator.current.number})"
    render :action => 'index'
  end
```

The :conditions option here uses an alternative syntax available for SQL templates: instead of a question mark in the query (as used in Chapter 4, *Finding Records Matching Search Criteria*), you can use **named placeholders**, prefixed with a colon character. Then, you can use a hash as the second element of the array (here, {:term => term}) to specify the values to insert into the placeholders. Here we're using a single value, which gets inserted into four places in the query. This is a neat shortcut, particularly when you need to put the same value into multiple places in the query.

Now, try doing a search for someone in your database. For example, if you have a person called "Jeff" in your database, try doing:

http://localhost:3010/people/search?term=jeff

As we used LIKE in the query, the search is case-insensitive (at least, when using MySQL). Hopefully, the page should only show people matching your query, e.g.:

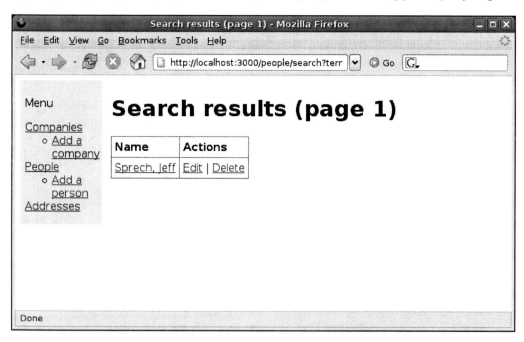

The last step is to add a search form. To keep things simple, we'll add it to the layout directly (`app/views/layouts/application.rhtml`), at the bottom of the menu:

```
<li><%= link_to 'Addresses', :controller => 'addresses' %></li>
</ul>

<p>Search people</p>
<% form_tag({:controller => 'people', :action => 'search'}, {:method
=> :get}) do -%>
<p><input type="text" name="term" size="8" value=""/><br/>
<%= submit_tag 'Go' %></p>
<% end -%>
</div>
```

As we haven't got a model instance we are working with here, `form_for` (which we used in Chapter 5, e.g. in the section *Creating a Person*) isn't really applicable. The simpler `form_tag` helper generates an HTML `<form>` element, which doesn't need to reference a model. It's also possible to pass both URL options (the first argument) and HTML options (the second argument) to the helper, to customize its behavior: in this case, we set the method to GET, to pass the `term` variable in the querystring.

Handling Errors

By default, Rails doesn't handle various errors that normal people make when using web applications. When URLs are being cut and pasted from email clients, they can often lose characters; when people bookmark pages inside an application, the bookmarks may be rendered invalid by someone else making changes to the system (e.g. deleting records). These and other user "errors" can make Rails produce unfortunate error messages, which could baffle normal users, even with the application running in the production environment. For example, here's what happens if you try to display a person whose record doesn't exist (in the production environment):

It turns out there are five common classes of error to catch:

1. **Missing records**, as in the example above.

2. **Unknown actions**. For example, if you visit `http://localhost:3000/people/foo`, you will get an **Unknown action: No action responded to foo** error message. This is because Rails can't map the `foo` part of the URL onto a valid action in the `PeopleController` class.

3. **Routing errors**. These occur if Rails can't map the URL onto a valid controller. For example, visiting `http://localhost:3000/bar`, you will get a **Routing Error: no route found to match "/bar" with {:method=>:get}** error message. This is because none of the routes specified in the routing configuration can map the URL to a valid controller and action.

4. **General application errors**. These can occur for any number of reasons: missing Ruby libraries, broken code, infinite loops which overflow the stack, etc. However, in most cases, Rails will still be running and capable of rendering an intelligible error report.

5. **Rails falling over**. Occasionally, Rails itself will break and your application will become completely unavailable. This tends to happen if Rails is running on FastCGI (which is still often the case if you run applications on shared hosting), and far, far less when Rails is running on Mongrel. As these errors break Rails itself, they are caught by the web server running the application.

Each of these errors is relatively easy to catch and handle.

Catching Missing Record Errors

Missing record exceptions (of the class `ActiveRecord::RecordNotFound`) occur where a model's `find` method is called with an ID that doesn't match a record in the database. One approach to catching this type of error would be to put error catching code directly into `PeopleController`. For example, we could modify the `get_person` method to redirect to the index if the `Person.find` method call raises an exception:

```
private
def get_person
  @person = Person.find(params[:id])
rescue
  redirect_to_index 'Person could not be found'
end
```

This utilizes the `rescue` construct available in Ruby (similar to the `try...catch` or `try...except` of other languages) to capture any errors raised by `Person.find`. It then reuses the `redirect_to_index` method if such an error occurs (see *Creating Application-Level Controller Methods* in Chapter 5) to set a message and show the index page of the current controller.

The above approach can be useful where you want very fine-grained control over exceptions. However, there are several situations in the *Intranet* application where this type of exception can occur, and fine-grained exception handling is not really necessary: a more generic approach would be more suitable. Rails provides a controller-level hook called `rescue_action_in_public` that we can exploit to manage errors in a more generic fashion. Add the following method definition to `app/controllers/application.rb` (inside the `class` definition):

```
protected
def rescue_action_in_public(exception)
  if exception.is_a?(ActiveRecord::RecordNotFound)
    @message = "Record not found"
  end
end
```

The `rescue_action_in_public` method accepts exceptions thrown by actions, enabling you to change the response depending on the kind of exception raised (`is_a?` is used here to check the class of the exception). In this case, we are just setting up an instance variable `@message` with a user-friendly error message. However, if you navigate to a non-existent record *you'll still get a stack trace of the error, even in the production environment*. This is because we are working on *localhost*: Rails knows that we are working on the same machine where the server is running, and thus is assuming we're *really* developing and not in production.

To fix this assumption, add another method definition to `app/controllers/application.rb`:

```
protected
def local_request?
  false
end
```

The `local_request?` method is called each time a controller action is triggered. By default, it returns `true` if the client IP address is 127.0.0.1; by making it return `false` in all situations, no requests are treated as local by virtue of their IP address.

Now, in the production environment, you should see an "Application error" page instead of a stack trace for missing record errors. In the development environment, you will still get a stack trace for these errors: Rails still treats every request as local when the application is running in that environment. This behavior is governed by the production environment settings in `config/environments/development.rb`, namely:

```
config.action_controller.consider_all_requests_local = true
```

If you want to run your application in the development environment (with automatic reloading of changes to classes and templates), but still test your error catching code, set this value to `false` to get the non-local error messages.

> Rails also provides a generic `rescue_action` method, which works in almost the same way as `rescue_action_in_public` (it takes an exception as an argument, and you can respond to different classes of exception inside its body). The only difference is that `rescue_action` doesn't care whether requests are local or not: it will *always* perform the error trapping you define inside it. I'd only recommend using this if you never want to display stack traces in the browser, and just want to work directly with the log files.

To display a custom page with an error message, create a new page in `app/views/shared/exception.rhtml`:

```
<h1>An exception occurred</h1>
<p class="exception"><%= @message %></p>
```

Note that it renders the `@message` instance variable, set by `rescue_action_in_public`, inside a paragraph.

Next, add a new style to `public/stylesheets/base.css` to style the error message in the template:

```
.exception {
  color: red;
}
```

Then render that template from the `rescue_action_in_public` method:

```
protected
def rescue_action_in_public(exception)
  if exception.is_a?(ActiveRecord::RecordNotFound)
    @message = "Record not found"
  end
  render :template => 'shared/exception'
end
```

Now, when you generate a missing record error by entering a bogus person ID, you should see a styled error page when running in production or when `consider_all_requests_local` is set to `false`:

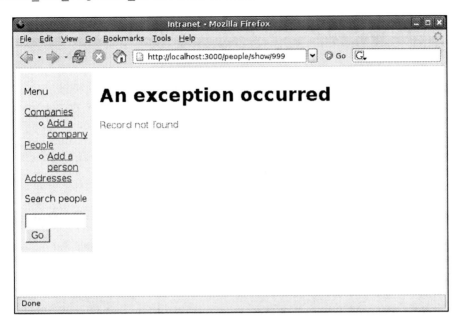

Rails' default behavior is to render a plain HTML page when errors occur, located in the public directory: `404.html` for routing errors and `500.html` for general errors. While this works OK, it doesn't show the error messages in the context of the application (menus, color schemes, logos, etc.). The advantage of the approach shown here is that the error pages can still use the layouts you've defined for your controllers.

Catching UnknownAction and Routing Errors

These types of errors occur when Rails attempts to service a URL that maps onto a non-existent action (`ActionController::UnknownAction`) and/or non-existent controller (`ActionController::RoutingError`), or if the URL cannot be parsed at all (again, a `RoutingError`). As these cases are effectively equivalent to HTTP "Page not found" errors (with status code 404), a logical approach is to reproduce a "Page not found"-style error inside the application. We can actually just extend the error-catching code inside `rescue_action_in_public` to do this:

```
protected
def rescue_action_in_public(exception)
  if exception.is_a?(ActiveRecord::RecordNotFound)
```

```
      @message = "No record with that ID could not be found"
    elseif exception.is_a?(::ActionController::UnknownAction) or
    exception.is_a?(::ActionController::RoutingError)
      @message = "Page not found"
    end
    render :template => 'shared/exception'
  end
```

The only thing that's unusual about this is how the class of the exception is referenced: `::ActionControllerRoutingError`, with two colons at the beginning, before the module name. This is to do with Ruby **namespaces**: because we are sitting inside the `ApplicationController` class, we have to work up from this class to the `ActionController` module (think of '`::`' as similar to '`..`' when defining paths in the `href` attribute of an HTML `<a>` element).

Catching General Application-Level Errors

Occasionally, your application will throw errors that aren't due to user error, but down to bugs or parts of your infrastructure disappearing (e.g. the MySQL server breaking). Try stopping your MySQL server and see what happens to your application: because you've defined `rescue_action_in_public`, you will get a `Mysql::Error` in the development environment; or your exception template (`app/views/shared/exception.rhtml`) in the production environment, *sans* error message.

As we can't be sure of all the sundry error messages we might possibly suffer, we just need to apply a generic `else` to our current error catching code to handle all of them:

```
  protected
  def rescue_action_in_public(exception)
    if exception.is_a?(ActiveRecord::RecordNotFound)
      @message = "No record with that ID could not be found"
    elseif exception.is_a?(::ActionController::UnknownAction) or
    exception.is_a?(::ActionController::RoutingError)
      @message = "Page not found"
    else
      @message = "The application is not currently available"
    end
    render :template => 'shared/exception'
  end
```

Catching "Rails has Fallen Over" Errors

This type of error is a different kettle of fish, and requires a different approach. We're talking drastic errors: the kind where Rails itself implodes, and the application doesn't even raise its head above the parapet. This can happen if FastCGI is running your application and ties itself in knots, for example. The end user gets the dreaded "application error" as a response:

Application Error-

Rails application failed to start properly

These kinds of errors are unpredictable and hard to produce on demand. The response from the server also varies according to the type of server. For example, if you're running FastCGI under Apache, you will typically be seeing an error returned by Apache: the request never reaches Rails, as Rails itself isn't running properly.

The exact text rendered for this kind of error is defined at the bottom of the file `RAILS_ROOT/public/.htaccess`:

```
ErrorDocument 500 "<h2>Application error</h2>Rails application failed
to start properly"
```

This file is an Apache control file, which tells Apache what to do if an error occurs inside a Rails application running under CGI or FastCGI. If you want some text more in keeping with your application, you can either manually code some HTML here; or (better) create a custom HTML error page, styled in the same way as your application, and set the `ErrorDocument` directive to point at that. There is a template for this in `public/500.html` already, so you can edit that as a starting point; then, to set that as the error document, change the `ErrorDocument` directive to:

```
ErrorDocument 500 /500.html
```

If you are running an application under Mongrel, with Apache sitting in front of it acting as a proxy, the most likely error you'll get will be this one (a 503, rather than a 500 error):

Service Temporarily Unavailable

The server is temporarily unable to service your request due to maintenance downtime or capacity problems. Please try again later.

If you see this error, it means your Mongrel process needs restarting. See Chapter 9 for more information about keeping an Apache/Mongrel combination up and running.

Adding an Authentication System

When a web client makes requests to a web server, the server's default behavior is to treat each request in isolation from those around it. If the client makes three requests in a row, for example, there is no default sequencing information in those requests to tie them together: to all intents and purposes, they may as well come from different clients. This makes it very difficult to provide continuity between different responses: for example, if the client is filling a shopping basket, how does the server tell that the three requests relate to a single basket, rather than three separate ones?

This is where **cookies** come in. A cookie originates on the server and is sent to the client: the server is effectively saying, "I don't know who you are, but if you send this cookie back to me with your next request, I can keep track of you." Each time a client makes a request to a server it scans its stored cookies (typically held in text files) and sends back any that originated from that server. Effectively, the client is saying "Here's that cookie you sent me, which proves who I am. This request relates back to the other one I made a few seconds ago."

Cookies can store any type of textual information (including serialized objects), but their most common use is as an identifier for a **session**: a sequence of requests from a single client. On the first request from a client, the server responds by setting a session ID cookie on the client and reserving a "scratch pad" for data relating to the session, which could be a file on the server's file system or some space in a database table. As the client subsequently interacts with the server (e.g. adding items to a shopping basket), the server writes that information onto the scratch pad. It knows which pad to use, as each request from the client carries the identifying session ID. The data stored on the server is a part of the client session; but the only data passing between the client and the server is an identifier for that session: a pointer to the scratch pad.

This is important, because it is how most web applications implement authentication. The basic pattern is as follows:

1. The client requests a protected page in the application.
2. The server sends a session identifier (a cookie) to the client. This cookie should be sent back to the server with each subsequent request from the client. Plus, as the client requested a protected page, but hasn't logged in yet, the server redirects the client to the login page.

3. The client receives the redirection to the login form, as well as the Set-Cookie instruction from the server.

4. The client makes a new request for the login page, sending the session identifier cookie with it.

5. The server responds by sending an HTML form asking for the client's login credentials.

6. The client fills in the username and password fields and submits them back to the server. The session identifier cookie is again sent with the request.

7. The server tries to find a record in the user database with a username and password matching those submitted by the client:

   a. If a record exists, the server puts a mark in the client session to show that they have logged in successfully, and redirects the client to the protected page they requested.

   b. If the record doesn't exist, the server shows the login form again and denies access to the protected page.

This is the pattern we're going to follow for *Intranet*'s authentication system. Before we do that, though, we'll have a brief look at how sessions and cookies are implemented in Rails.

Cookies and Sessions in Rails

Session handling is turned on by default in Rails. This means that the session identifier cookies are already being transmitted automatically between the web browser and the *Intranet* application, even though we haven't done anything yet.

To see this happening, you'll need some kind of tool that can interrogate request and response headers (e.g. **LiveHTTPHeaders** in Firefox, from http://livehttpheaders.mozdev.org/). As an example, when the URL http://localhost:3000/people was requested from *Intranet*, the following Set-Cookie header came back in the response:

```
Set-Cookie: _Intranet_session_id=69289c7593407d1a5cadefd3de09a8e7;
path=/
```

Notice that this is a cookie which expires when the browser closes (there's no explicit expiry date set). Also, note that the cookie is called _Intranet_session_id. The name of this cookie comes from a setting in the ApplicationController class (in app/controllers/application.rb):

```
class ApplicationController < ActionController::Base
  session :session_key => '_Intranet_session_id'

  # ... other methods ...
end
```

Each application has its own :session_key setting, so that cookies for an application don't get mixed with cookies from unrelated applications on the same domain. You can change this name if you wish, but for our purposes we can leave it as it is.

On subsequent requests, the client sends back the session ID cookie:

```
Cookie: _Intranet_session_id=69289c7593407d1a5cadefd3de09a8e7
```

The Rails application can store data relating to this session via the session method on controllers. For example, if we wanted to store the date and the time when someone's session started, we might do this in the ApplicationController class:

```
class ApplicationController < ActionController::Base
  before_filter :track_login_time

  # Set the :login_time in the session if not already set
  protected
  def track_login_time
    session[:login_time] ||= Time.now
  end
end
```

Session data relating to the client is stored as a hash; the session method exposes this hash and enables the application to store values in it or retrieve values from it. If you want to destroy a session at any time, use:

```
reset_session
```

Similarly, we can set and retrieve cookies using the cookies method on a controller. For example, we might do something like record a user's font size preference in a cookie, which expires in two years' time:

```
def set_preference
  cookies[:font_size] = {:value => 'small',
  :expires => 2.years.from_now}
end
```

Note that the hash can also contain other standard cookie options, such as `:secure`, `:path`, and `:domain`: see the documentation for the `ActionController::Cookies` module for more details.

The preceding code sends this header in the response:

```
Set-Cookie: font_size=small; path=/; expires=Fri, 20 Feb 2009 08:03:27
GMT
```

Each time the client comes back to the application, providing the cookie hasn't expired, the preference is sent as a request header:

```
Cookie: font_size=small
```

And Rails can pick up the font size preference from the cookies inside a controller:

```
font_size = cookies[:font_size]
```

Building the Authentication System

Now that we've seen how to manage sessions in Rails, we are ready to start putting together the components required for the authentication system. These are:

1. A `User` model, which stores usernames and passwords in the `users` table in the database.

2. An `index` action to display the login form. To keep things simple, we'll add a dedicated `login_controller.rb` to manage this and other login-related actions.

3. A `check_credentials` action, to check submitted credentials and either redirect the user back to the protected page they requested (if they logged in successfully), or show the login form.

4. A `logout` action to reset the user's session and log them out. This is also useful during testing.

5. A `before_filter` on our controllers to authenticate the user before permitting them to perform certain actions. In the case of our application, we want to protect any action that can modify the database, i.e. `create`, `update`, and `delete`. The `employees'` action on `CompaniesController` is a trickier one, as it both displays and allows editing of employees: in this case, it makes sense to disable the editing buttons where the user isn't logged in, rather than deny access to the action altogether.

The User Model

First generate the User model from the command line (inside RAILS_ROOT):

```
$ ruby script/generate model User
```

Edit db/migrate/004_create_users.rb to set up the columns for the users table:

```
class CreateUsers < ActiveRecord::Migration
  def self.up
    create_table :users do |t|
      t.column :username, :string, :null => false
      t.column :passwd, :string, :null => false
      t.column :last_login, :datetime
    end
  end

  def self.down
    drop_table :users
  end
end
```

Note the column name passwd (instead of password) as "password" is a reserved word in MySQL, and can create problems when you're working with the MySQL console.

Apply the migration to the database:

```
$ rake db:migrate
```

A few simple modifications to the User class itself will also improve security and reliability. Firstly, some validation to make sure a username only exists once within the users table; secondly, validation to ensure a user has both a username and a password; and finally, application of a one-way digest to passwords stored in the database.

The first two of these measures are self-explanatory. The final measure, using a digest of the password, means that passwords are stored in a form that prevents them from being read from the database directly: instead of being stored as plain text, they will be stored as an SHA1 digest. SHA1 is a hash algorithm that converts a text string into a longer, random-looking string; retrieving the original string from the digested version of the string is nigh-on impossible. For example, for the plain text 'elliot', the SHA1 digest is:

```
dee6300e151043f915cc24dbc1409935bc4ae592
```

The advantage of this approach is in protecting passwords from people who might read the users table in the database (e.g. administrators, or people who've stolen it). Even with access to the table, the user's password is not visible.

Here's how the `User` class is implemented (in `app/models/user.rb`) to perform the required validations and to implement digested passwords:

```
require 'digest/sha1'
class User < ActiveRecord::Base
  validates_presence_of :username
  validates_uniqueness_of :username
  validates_presence_of :passwd

  def passwd=(pwd)
    write_attribute('passwd', Digest::SHA1.hexdigest(pwd))
  end
end
```

The unusual parts of this is the `require 'digest/sha1'` statement at the top, which pulls in the SHA1 digest library, and the `passwd=` method. This method overrides the default mutator method for the `passwd` field, as supplied by ActiveRecord. Instead, the custom method intercepts the `passwd` attribute before it reaches the database, applying an SHA1 digest to it as it is set.

While some kind of management interface for users would make life easier in the long term, the console provides an acceptable temporary measure for adding users. Add at least one for testing purposes:

```
$ ruby script/console
Loading development environment.
>> u = User.new :username => 'elliot', :passwd => 'police73'
=> #<User:0xb711f848 @attributes={"passwd"=>"bdbc07452121cfe2f35ff510b291
c09b2418d2db", "username"=>"elliot"}, @new_record=true>
>> u.save
=> true
```

Another alternative would be to add a migration to create the default system users, or maybe write a batch script to add them from a tab-separated file.

It's also possible to use something other than the database to store user credentials, e.g. an LDAP server, and interface with this from your Rails application.

Displaying the Login Form

The next component is the controller for managing the login process. Generate it first:

```
$ ruby script/generate controller login index logout
```

We passed both the name of the controller (`login`) and the names of the actions we want to define for it (`index`, `logout`). This adds empty method definitions for the actions to `app/controllers/login_controller.rb`, and creates an empty view template for each too.

The index action will just display a simple login form, which we define by modifying `app/views/login/index.rhtml`:

```
<h2>Please login to continue</h2>
<% form_tag :action => 'check_credentials' do -%>
<p><%= label :login, 'Username' %></p>
<p><%= text_field 'login', 'username'  %></p>
<p><%= label :login, 'Password' %></p>
<p><%= password_field 'login', 'passwd'  %></p>
<p><%= submit_tag "Submit" %></p>
<% end -%>
```

Note that the `action` attribute for the form is set to the `check_credentials` action on the `LoginController`: we'll write that next.

Checking Submitted Credentials

The `check_credentials` action will retrieve the username and password from the submitted form and use them to look up a record in the `users` table with matching username and password. If a record exists, the credentials submitted correctly identify a user, and they can be logged in; if not, access is denied.

As the action will be needed to perform a database lookup, we'll need some code to perform the query. This code should be a part of the model. (Recall that the model implements the business logic of the application. Controllers should be lightweight, with as little involvement in the database as possible, so we don't want the database query code in the `LoginController`.) So the first step is to write a method for the `User` model, which can look up a user by his/her username and (hashed) password:

```
class User < ActiveRecord::Base
  # ... other methods, validation etc.
  def self.authenticate(username, passwd)
    hashed_passwd = Digest::SHA1.hexdigest(passwd)
    user = self.find_by_username_and_passwd(username, hashed_passwd)
    return user
  end
end
```

The authenticate method takes a username and password, hashes the password, then uses a dynamic finder (see: *Finding Records Using Attribute-Based Finders* in Chapter 4) to search for a matching record. The return value is a User instance if one was retrieved, or nil if the finder fails to retrieve a record. We can write a unit test to check if the method works correctly (in test/unit/user_test.rb):

```
require File.dirname(__FILE__) + '/../test_helper'

class UserTest < Test::Unit::TestCase
  def setup
    User.new(:username => 'elliot', :passwd => 'police73').save
  end

  def test_authenticate
    assert User.authenticate('elliot', 'police73')
    assert !(User.authenticate('elliot', 'bilbo'))
    assert !(User.authenticate('frank', 'police73'))
  end
end
```

and run it with:

```
$ rake test:units
```

Now that this method is in place, we can add a first version of the check_credentials action:

```
class LoginController < ApplicationController
  def index
  end
  def logout
  end
  def check_credentials
    username = params[:login][:username]
    passwd = params[:login][:passwd]
    user = User.authenticate(username, passwd)
    redirect_to_index "Logged in OK? " + (!(user.nil?)).to_s
  end
end
```

For now, this action just redirects to the login page, displaying **Logged in OK? true** if the login was successful, or **false** otherwise. Try it by going to http://localhost:3000/login and entering some valid/invalid credentials, making sure that the controller responds correctly.

To start transforming this simple outline into a full-fledged authentication system, we'll do several things:

1. Set a session variable called :logged_in to true when the user successfully logs in. Otherwise, set it to false.

2. When a user logs in successfully, store their User object in the session. This is useful for personalization. We'll also set the date and time of the login in their user record.

3. When the user requests a protected page, store its URL in the session as :destination before redirecting them to the login page. If the user successfully logs in, redirect them back to that original page; if they fail to login, redirect back to the login form again.

Here's the implementation:

```
class LoginController < ApplicationController
  def index
  end

  def check_credentials
    username = params[:login][:username]
    passwd = params[:login][:passwd]

    # Default state is NOT to be logged in.
    session[:logged_in] = false

    user = User.authenticate(username, passwd)
    unless user.nil?
      # Set a marker in the session to show user is logged in.
      session[:logged_in] = true

      # Set a login success notice.
      flash[:notice] = "You have logged in successfully"

      # Store the login date and time.
      user.last_login = Time.now
      user.save

      # Store the user in the session.
      session[:user] = user

      # Set the destination to the protected page originally
      # requested, or to the list of people if coming in fresh.
      destination = session[:destination] ||
        {:controller => 'people'}
    else
      # Redirect back to the login form.
      destination = {:controller => 'login'}

      # Set a login failure notice.
```

```
    flash[:notice] = "Your username and/or password were not
recognised"
    end

    redirect_to destination
  end
end
```

Logging Out

The `logout` action on the `LoginController` is simple; it resets the user's session and redirects them back to the home page for the application:

```
class LoginController < ApplicationController
  # ... other actions
  def logout
    reset_session
    flash[:notice] = "You have logged out"
    redirect_to :controller => 'people'
  end
end
```

With these components in place, you can now test the login process. Log in at `http://localhost:3000/login`; you should be redirected to the people list. Now logout at `http://localhost:3000/logout`; you should see a **You have logged out** message.

It's hard to tell whether you are logged in or logged out at the moment, but a small addition to the menu (in `app/views/layouts/application.rhtml`) can help here:

```
<div id="menu">
...
</ul>
<p>
<% if session[:logged_in] -%>
Logged in as <strong><%= session[:user].username %></strong>;
<%= link_to 'Logout', :controller => 'login', :action => 'logout' %>
<% else -%>
<%= link_to 'Login', :controller => 'login' %>
<% end -%>
</p>
</div>
```

This displays the user's username and a logout link if they are already logged in; otherwise, it shows a login link.

Protecting Actions

The final step is to protect some actions on controllers to prevent access by users who aren't logged in. Firstly, write a private method called `authorize` on the `ApplicationController` class, which checks whether a user has the `:logged_in` variable set to `true` in their session:

- If they haven't, the URL of the current page is stored in the session (under the `:destination` key, as used in the `check_credentials` action) and the user is immediately redirected to the login form.

- If they have, no action is taken, and the rest of the page can be displayed.

Here's the method (in, `app/controllers/application.rb`):

```
class ApplicationController < ActionController::Base
  # ... other methods ...
  protected
  def authorize
    unless (true == session[:logged_in])
      session[:destination] = request.request_uri
      redirect_to :controller => 'login'
      return false
    end
  end
end
```

Note that the method explicitly returns `false`: this ensures that the filter chain halts at this point, no other filters are executed, and the user is immediately redirected.

To apply this method, we'll use a `before_filter` assigned to the actions we want to protect. For example, we can put it inside the `PeopleController` to protect any destructive actions:

```
class PeopleController < ApplicationController
  before_filter :authorize, :except => [:index, :search, :show]
  # ... other before_filter settings ...
  # ... other methods ...
end
```

Note that `authorize` is the first `before_filter` (they are applied in the same order as listed within the class definition). We use an `:except` option rather than `:only` so that the default is to authorize every action. If we add new actions, this ensures that the default is to protect them; if we want them to be public; we have to explicitly expose them.

To test this, log out and browse around the index, search, and show pages for people. You should be able to see them fine. Now, try to edit a person: you should be redirected to the login form. Once you log in, you should be redirected back to the original edit page you requested and be able to modify the person's details.

You can set a similar filter on the `CompaniesController` to protect that too:

```
class CompaniesController < ApplicationController
  before_filter :authorize, :except => [:index]
  # ... other before_filter settings ...
  # ... other methods ...
end
```

Finally, we need to protect `AddressesController`. Recall that this just uses the scaffold, so we need to enable the scaffold actions that list all addresses or show a single record: `index` and `show`, respectively:

```
class AddressesController < ApplicationController
  before_filter :authorize, :except => [:index, :show]
  scaffold :address
end
```

Adding Simple Task Tracking

The next feature requested for *Intranet* is a simple task-tracking module. This will enable users of the system to record activities they carry out with clients. Acme staff tend to work on an individual basis with other companies, and therefore would prefer to track activity with people rather than the companies they represent. (However, as people are associated with companies, all the activity related to a company can be aggregated from the tasks carried out with its employees.)

Rory and Jenny decide to implement a task list, which is displayed in a read-only mode alongside a person's record when in the "show" view, arranged in reverse chronological order (newest at the top). That person's tasks will also become editable by clicking on a link next to the task.

The Task Model

As always, the first step is to create a model to represent a task. A task will need the following fields:

- `title`: The title of the task
- `description`: A description of the task (optional)

- `user_id`: The member of Acme staff who "owns" the task
- `person_id`: The person (client) the task is associated with
- `complete`: Whether the task is complete (true/false)
- `start`: The start date and time for the task
- `end`: The end date and time for the task (optional)

Note that Rory and Jenny aren't aiming to produce a full-fledged project management system. They are just aiming at a tool for recording activity with clients. Eventually, it might grow into or be replaced by a full project management tool; for now, they have limited time, and want to provide as much functionality as simply as possible.

Generate a model from the command line:

```
$ ruby script/generate model Task
```

Write the migration to build the tasks table (in db/migrate/006_create_tasks.rb):

```ruby
class CreateTasks < ActiveRecord::Migration
  def self.up
    create_table :tasks do |t|
      t.column :title, :string, :null => false
      t.column :description, :text
      t.column :user_id, :integer
      t.column :person_id, :integer
      t.column :complete, :boolean, :null => false,
        :default => false
      t.column :start, :datetime, :null => false
      t.column :end, :datetime
    end
  end

  def self.down
    drop_table :tasks
  end
end
```

As tasks have relationships to both a `Person` and a `User`, these relationships must be specified in the `Task` model (app/models/task.rb). We also need to validate the fields:

```ruby
class Task < ActiveRecord::Base
  belongs_to :person
  belongs_to :user
  validates_presence_of :title, :message => 'Please supply a title'
  validates_associated :person, :message => 'The specified person is
invalid'
```

```
  validates_associated :user, :message => 'The specified owner is
invalid'
  validates_presence_of :start,
    :message => 'Please set a start date and time for the task'
end
```

The other side of the relationship to `Person` also needs to be specified
(in `app/models/person.rb`), as we'd like to be able to show all the tasks relating
to a person. This requires a `has_many` method call (highlighted below) inside the
`Person` class definition:

```
class Person < ActiveRecord::Base
  include AddressHandler

  belongs_to :company
  belongs_to :address
  has_many :tasks, :order => 'complete ASC, start DESC',
    :dependent => :nullify

  # ... other methods ...
end
```

Notice that the relationship includes the option `:order => 'complete ASC, start
DESC'`, to ensure that the associated tasks are retrieved in ascending order of whether
they are complete (incomplete tasks first), then descending order of their start date-
times. This is the desired order for displaying tasks alongside a person's full details.
We also include a `:dependent => :nullify` option, so that if a person's record is
destroyed, any of their dependent tasks have their `person_id` set to NULL.

We can also specify a `has_many` association in the `User` model:

```
class User < ActiveRecord::Base
  has_many :tasks, :order => 'complete ASC, start DESC',
    :dependent => :nullify

  # ... other methods ...
end
```

Again, the `:dependent => :nullify` option is specified, so that any tasks associated
with a user have their `user_id` attribute set to NULL, if that user is deleted.

The Tasks Controller

Next, generate the controller that will handle CRUD operations for tasks:

```
$ ruby script/generate controller tasks
```

The CRUD actions themselves are simple to add into the controller: as they only have to deal with a single model (Task) in isolation, they don't have the complexity of the previous controllers we've created. The actions look like this:

```
class TasksController < ApplicationController
  before_filter :authorize, :except => [:index, :show]
  before_filter :get_task, :only => [:show, :edit, :update,
    :confirm, :delete]
  def index
    @page_title = "All tasks"
    @tasks = Task.find(:all, :order => 'title')
  end
  def show
    @page_title = "Task: " + @task.title
  end
  def new
    @page_title = "Adding new task"
    @task = Task.new
  end
  def create
    @task = Task.new(params[:task])
    if @task.save
      redirect_to_index "Task added successfully"
    else
      @page_title = "Adding new task"
      render :action => 'new'
    end
  end
  def edit
    @page_title = "Edit " + @task.title
  end
  def update
    if @task.update_attributes(params[:task])
      redirect_to_index "Task updated successfully"
    else
      @page_title = "Edit " + @task.title
      render :action => 'edit'
    end
  end
  def confirm
    confirm_delete(@task,
      "Are you sure you want to delete " + @task.title + "?")
```

```
  end
  def delete
    do_delete(@task)
  end
  private
  def get_task
    @task = Task.find(params[:id])
  end
end
```

We're starting to see the code we've written previously paying off now: the highlighted sections show the use of authentication via the `authorize` method; application of a `before_filter` to fetch a task if the user is showing, editing or deleting it; use of the generic `confirm_delete` and `do_delete` methods to delete a task; and use of our generic `redirect_to_index` method. This demonstrates the advantages of constant refactoring, and how Rails enables us to create our own powerful macros for common patterns.

Task Views

We now need some view templates to go with the actions defined in the previous section.

Here's `index.rhtml` (to display a table of all tasks):

```
<h1><%= @page_title %></h1>
<table>
<tr>
<th>Title</th><th>Actions</th>
</tr>
<% @tasks.each do |task| -%>
<tr>
<td>
<%= link_to task.title, :action => 'show', :id => task.id %>
</td>
<td>
<%= link_to 'Edit', :action => 'edit', :id => task.id %> |
<%= link_to 'Delete', :action => 'confirm', :id => task.id %>
</td>
</tr>
<% end -%>
</table>
```

Here's `show.rhtml` (to display one task):

```
<h1><%= @page_title %></h1>
<p>(<%= datetime_span(@task.start, @task.end) %>)</p>
<%= content_tag('p', @task.description) if @task.description %>
<p><%= show_complete(@task) %> |
Owner: <%= @task.user.username %></p>
<p><%= link_to 'Edit', :action => 'update', :id => @task %> |
<%= link_to 'Delete', :action => 'delete', :id => @task %> |
<%= link_to 'Back to index', :action => 'index' %></p>
```

Note that the above template calls a helper method in `app/helpers/application_helper.rb` called `datetime_span` (first highlighted section). This helper displays a start and (optionally) an end date/time in human-readable form; if both are present," to " is placed between them:

```
module ApplicationHelper
  # ... other helpers ...
  # Display a start/end datetime span in human readable form. If
  # both are given, ' to ' is placed in the middle of the string.
  #
  # +start_datetime+ is a Datetime instance,
  # +end_datetime+ is optional.
  def datetime_span(start_datetime, end_datetime=nil)
    str = start_datetime.strftime('%Y-%m-%d@%H:%M')
    if end_datetime
      str += ' to ' + end_datetime.strftime('%Y-%m-%d@%H:%M')
    end
    str
  end
end
```

Another helper, `show_complete` (from `app/helpers/tasks_helper.rb`, as it works with a task's `complete` attribute and is thus specific to tasks) is used to display the `complete` status of the task. If the task is complete, this helper returns the string "Complete"; if it is incomplete, the helper returns a `<span>` tag with a `class` attribute set to "exception" and content "Incomplete". When rendered in the browser, any incomplete tasks appear with a red "Incomplete" message:

```
module TasksHelper
  def show_complete(task)
    if task.complete?
      'Complete'
    else
      content_tag('span', 'Incomplete', :class => 'exception')
    end
  end
end
```

Here's the new.rhtml template:

```
<% form_for :task, @task, :url => {:action => 'create'} do |f| %>
<%= render :partial => 'form', :locals => {:f => f} %>
<% end %>
```

And the template for edit.rhtml:

```
<% form_for :task, @task, :url => {:action => 'update', :id => @task.
id} do |f| %>
<%= render :partial => 'form', :locals => {:f => f} %>
<% end %>
```

Finally, the most complicated template is _form.rhtml (called by both edit.rhtml and new.rhtml). This follows the pattern of previous forms, like the one we created for people in Chapter 5 (*Creating a Person*). As the form needs to show both the owner of the task and the person associated with the task, we first need to retrieve the system users and people to populate the two drop-downs in the TaskController. We achieve this with get_users and get_people methods, which are called using a before_filter:

```
class TasksController < ApplicationController
  before_filter :get_people, :only => [:edit, :update, :new,
    :create]
  before_filter :get_users, :only => [:edit, :update, :new, :create]
  # ... other methods ...
  private
  def get_people
    @people = Person.find_all_ordered
  end
  private
  def get_users
    @users = User.find(:all, :order => 'username')
  end
end
```

With all the required data made available by the controller, we can now create the form itself in _form.rhtml:

```
<h1><%= @page_title %></h1>
<p>Required fields are marked with &quot;*&quot;.</p>

<p><%= label :task, 'Title', :required => true %>
<%= f.text_field :title %>
<%= error_message_on :task, :title %></p>
<p><%= label :task, 'Description' %><br/>
```

```
<%= f.text_area :description, :rows => 5, :cols => 30 %></p>
<p><%= label :task, 'Owned by user', :field_name => 'user' %>
<select name="task[user_id]">
<%= options_from_collection_for_select @users, :id, :username,
session[:user].id %>
</select>
<%= error_message_on :task, :user %></p>
<p><%= label :task, 'Associated with person', :field_name => 'person'
%>
<%= f.collection_select :person_id, @people, :id, :full_name,
:include_blank => true %>
<%= error_message_on :task, :person %></p>
<p><%= label :task, 'Complete' %> <%= f.check_box :complete %></p>
<% this_year = Time.now.year -%>
<p><%= label :task, 'Start', :required => true %>
<%= f.datetime_select :start, :start_year => this_year - 5,
:end_year => this_year + 5 %>
<%= error_message_on :task, :start %></p>
<p><%= label :task, 'End' %>
<%= f.datetime_select :end, :start_year => this_year - 5,
:end_year => this_year + 5, :include_blank => true, :default => nil
%></p>
<p><%= submit_tag 'Save' %> |
<%= link_to 'Cancel', :action => 'index' %></p>
```

Most of this should be self-explanatory (if a little dense). Two areas of code, which may be unfamiliar, are highlighted:

1. The first highlighted section shows the use of `options_from_collection_for_select` method to create the options for the owner drop-down. As we want to specify a default selected option for the owner attributed (set to the logged-in user), we can't use `collection_select`, as this method does not allow a default selected option to be supplied.

2. The `check_box` method creates an HTML `<input type="checkbox" ...>` element, which can be set using a Boolean attribute on a model (in our case, the `complete` attribute).

This completes the basic CRUD controller and views for tasks. To try them out, navigate to: `http://localhost:3000/tasks`, create a few tasks, then show, edit, and delete them, to test out all of the actions. Finally, ensure that you add a few tasks to the database so that you have some data to work with in the next section.

To be really useful, *Intranet* should go beyond these simple views and show tasks attached to a person. This is the context in which tasks are going to be used, so it makes sense to show them with a person's details, rather in an isolated "task administration" area. To accomplish this with whom we need to embed a list of records (tasks) inside their "parent" record's display (the person, the tasks are associated). This is slightly different from what we've done previously, where we've showed a parent record and one associated record simultaneously: for example, in our form, which enabled editing a person and their address at once (see: *Editing Multiple Models Simultaneously* in Chapter 5). Instead, we now need a way to show *multiple* tasks associated with a person, and enable users to easily add new tasks or edit/delete the existing ones in the list. The next section describes how to do this.

Showing Tasks for a Person

As tasks are managed in the context of a person, the obvious thing to do is to display them alongside a person's details in app/views/people/show.rhtml. We'll do this by separating the template into two <div> elements: one containing the person's details (the current content of the show.rhtml template), and the other containing the list of tasks associated with them.

First, wrap the entire content of the app/views/people/show.rhtml template in a <div> element with id="left_panel":

```
<div id="left_panel">
<h1><%= @page_title %></h1>
<p><strong>Job title:</strong> <%=d @person.job_title %></p>
. . .
<p><%= link_to 'Edit', :action => 'update', :id => @person %> |
<%= link_to 'Delete', :action => 'delete', :id => @person %></p>
</div>
```

Next, add the new <div> element (to hold the task list) at the bottom of the template with id="right_panel":

```
. . .
<%= link_to 'Delete', :action => 'delete', :id => @person %></p>
</div>

<div id="right_panel">
<h1>Tasks</h1>
</div>
```

Now we add some CSS styling (in `public/stylesheets/base.css`) to position the two `<div>` elements alongside each other:

```
#left_panel {
  float: left;
  width: 60%;
}
#right_panel {
  float: right;
  width: 39%;
  top: 0em;
  position: relative;
  background-color: #EEE;
  padding-left: 1%;
}
```

Browse to the details for a person to check that the layout is as expected. For example, in Firefox the page looks like this:

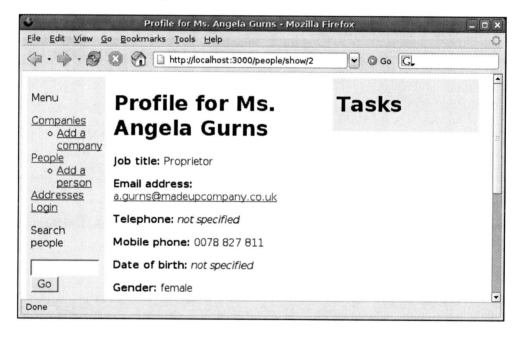

Notice the area on the right for listing tasks. Now, create a partial `app/views/tasks/_task.rhtml` to show a single task for a person. (As a starting point, you can copy the full `show.rhtml` template.) We'll use this partial once for each task associated with a person, and render the results inside the `<div id="right_panel">` element of the person's show template. Here's what the task partial looks like:

```
<div class="task">
<p><strong><%= task.title %></strong></p>
<p>(<%= datetime_span(task.start, task.end) %>)</p>
<%= content_tag('p', task.description) if task.description %>
<p><%= show_complete(task) %> |
Owner: <%= task.user.username %></p>
<p><%= link_to 'Edit', :controller => 'tasks', :action => 'edit',
:id => task.id %> |
<%= link_to 'Delete', :controller => 'tasks', :action => 'confirm',
:id => task.id %></p>
</div>
```

The main changes were:

1. Place the whole task inside a `<div>` element with `class="task"`. This will make it easy to style each task when displayed in a list.

2. Convert references to the `@task` instance variable into references to a local `task` variable. This is because we're going to be calling the partial from inside the `show.rhtml` template for the `PeopleController`, and setting the `task` variable once for each of the person's tasks.

3. Replace the heading with a `<p>` element containing the task title.

4. Remove the **Back to index** link (irrelevant in the context of a partial).

5. When creating the **Edit** and **Delete** links with `link_to`, pass a `:controller => 'tasks'` option, as deletions and updates will be managed by the `TasksController` (not the `PeopleController`, which is the context in which the template is rendered).

To render a person's tasks inside `app/views/people/show.rhtml`, edit the bottom few lines of the template to look like this:

```
<div id="left_panel">
<h1>Tasks</h1>
<p><%= link_to 'Add a new task', :controller => 'tasks', :action =>
'new', :default_person_id => @person.id %>
<% tasks = @person.tasks -%>
<% if tasks.empty? -%>
<p><strong>No tasks are associated with this person</strong></p>
<% else -%>
<% for task in tasks -%>
<%= render :partial => 'tasks/task', :locals => {:task => task} %>
<% end -%>
<% end -%>
</div>
```

Points to note:

- A link to add a new task is shown in a paragraph just under the **Tasks** heading. Note that this link includes the person's ID as the default_person_id option. This means that when creating a new task, we can associate the person with it by default.

- If a person has no associated tasks, an explanatory message is displayed; if the person does have associated tasks, they are rendered by a loop, which runs the _task.rhtml partial once for each task.

- The _task.rhtml partial is referenced using 'tasks/task', as we are rendering it from within the PeopleController. Therefore, we need to specify the "absolute" path of the partial (relative to app/views).

- On each iteration, the current task is passed into the rendered partial.

However, if you try to display a person's details at this point, you get this error:

```
undefined method 'show_complete' for #<#<Class:0xb72309f8>:0xb72309d0>
```

(NB you will get a different <Class> string.) Why is our show_complete helper causing this error to be thrown? Remember, we are trying to render a task in the context of PeopleController. By default, the PeopleController class only knows about application-level helpers (defined in app/helpers/application.rb) and its own helpers (defined in app/helpers/people_helper.rb); and show_complete is a task helper (in app/helpers/tasks_helper.rb), making it inaccessible to PeopleController.

To use the task helpers inside the PeopleController, simply add a line to the class definition (in app/controllers/people_controller.rb) to include the TasksHelper module in the controller:

```
class PeopleController < ApplicationController
  helper TasksHelper

  # ... other methods ...
end
```

Now, when you display a person's details (provided they have an associated task), you should see something like:

This is close to what we want. One remaining issue is that the tasks are a bit spread out: we can afford to style them in a more compact way, so add a few more lines to `public/stylesheets/base.css` to reduce the white space between the paragraphs:

```
.task {
  padding: 0.5em 1em 0.5em 1em;
  margin-top: 0.5em;
  font-size: 0.9em;
}
.task p {
  margin: 0em;
}
```

This gives us a slightly better layout (notice how the tasks list is more compact):

Redirecting to a Person after Adding or Editing a Task

The application now lists the tasks associated with a person alongside the person's details. When a user clicks on an **Edit** link for a task, or **Add a new task**, they are taken through to the tasks controller and the appropriate action. However, once their edits are completed, they are redirected back to the tasks index, rather than to the person associated with the task.

What we need to do instead is redirect the user back to the show action for the person associated with the task instead of to the list action. To do this, we first need to alter the create and update methods in the TasksController class, which otherwise just redirect to the TasksController index page:

```
class TasksController < ApplicationController
  # ... other methods ...

  def create
    @task = Task.new(params[:task])
    if @task.save
      flash[:notice] = "Task added successfully"
```

```
      redirect_to_person @task.person_id
    else
      @page_title = "Adding new task"
      render :action => 'new'
    end
  end
  def update
    if @task.update_attributes(params[:task])
      flash[:notice] = "Task added successfully"
      redirect_to_person @task.person_id
    else
      @page_title = "Edit " + @task.title
      render :action => 'edit'
    end
  end
  private
  def redirect_to_person(person_id)
    if person_id
      redirect_to :controller => 'people', :action => 'show',
        :id => person_id
    else
      redirect_to :action => 'index'
    end
  end
end
```

Rather than redirecting to the index action, these two actions now call the
redirect_to_person method, defined as a private method on this controller.
If a person has been assigned to the task, a redirect to that person's record is
performed; if not, the tasks index is displayed instead. Now, if you create or update
a task, you will be redirected back to the associated person's record when the save
completes. If the task doesn't validate, you'll see the form again with validation
errors, as per usual.

In the next few sections, we'll see how to really polish up the redirections, including
redirecting correctly after deletions, handling the **Cancel** link, and setting a default
person for new tasks.

Alternatives to the "external edit with redirect" approach

While we took the approach of editing a person's tasks on a separate page then redirecting back to the person's details, there are a couple of other approaches we could have taken instead.

Integrated forms

This is the approach we took with addresses: we incorporated the address form into the person (and company) form. However, we were only dealing with a single address at a time there. In the case of people and tasks, we could potentially have multiple tasks to edit, and we don't want to display an editing form for each individual task.

In-place editors

We could attach an in-place editor to each task so that it becomes editable in the page when clicked (see Chapter 7 *Improving the User Experience* for examples of in-place editing). This is an elegant solution, as the user never leaves the page, so there are no lengthy round-trips to the server. However, it only works if AJAX is available.

The advantages of the external edit with redirect approach (used here) are that it requires no JavaScript, but remains reasonably clean to implement, as we don't need a separate edit form for each task.

Redirecting after a Deletion

Recall the actions we added to `ApplicationController`, to manage generic deletions for any controller (see *A Shared View to Confirm Deletions* in Chapter 5). While they work fine, they assume that after a deletion we want to return to the `index` action of the controller. In the current case, we would prefer to redirect back to the `PeopleController`'s `show` action, for the person whose task we just deleted.

The solution is to make the `do_delete` (in `app/controllers/application.rb`) action more generic, so that it will accept a hash which specifies a URL to redirect to:

```
class ApplicationController < ActionController::Base
  # ... other methods ...
  private
  def do_delete(object, redirect_options=nil)
    if 'yes' == params[:confirm]
      object.destroy
      object_name = object.class.name.humanize
      flash[:notice] = object_name + ' deleted successfully'
      redirect_options ||= {:action => 'index'}
      redirect_to redirect_options
    end
  end
end
```

The changes are highlighted. Note how we can now pass in a `redirect_options` argument, which defaults to `nil`. Within the method, we set `redirect_options` to a hash just containing `{:action => 'index'}` if it hasn't been passed in as an argument (that's what `||=` does). Finally, we use `redirect_to` and pass it this hash. Note that this change doesn't break any of the previous calls to this method in other controllers, as we set a default for the `redirect_options` parameter (`nil`) in the method definition.

To use this in the `TasksController`, we just modify the delete action so that it redirects back to the person associated with the task just deleted:

```
class TasksController < ApplicationController
  # ... other methods ...
  def delete
    redirect_options = { :controller => 'people',
    :action => 'show', :id => @task.person_id }
    do_delete(@task, redirect_options)
  end
end
```

Handling the Cancel Link

The **Cancel** link available when creating or updating a task should return the user to that person's details. We can manage this by redirecting to a person's details if the task has been assigned to a person, or to the tasks index if not. Edit the **Cancel** link in `app/views/tasks/_form.rhtml`:

```
<p><%= submit_tag 'Save' %> |
<%
if @task.person_id
  cancel_url_options = {:controller => 'people', :action => 'show',
  :id => @task.person_id}
else
  cancel_url_options = {:action => 'index'}
end
-%>
<%= link_to 'Cancel', cancel_url_options %></p>
```

Setting a Default Person for a New Task

The last step is a small one, but can make quite a difference to usability. What we'll do is set a default person for new tasks, based on the ID of the person whose tasks we're editing.

This is actually very simple, and just requires a small change to the TasksController's new action (highlighted):

```
class TasksController < ApplicationController
  # ... other methods ...
  def new
    @page_title = "Adding new task"
    @task = Task.new
    if params[:default_person_id]
      @task.person = Person.find(params[:default_person_id])
    end
  end
end
```

If a `default_person_id` has been supplied in the querystring, the appropriate `Person` instance is retrieved from the database and assigned to `@task` (via the `person=` method). Then, when the form for creating a task is displayed, the person is pre-selected from the **Associated with person** drop-down box, as the person has already been assigned to the task. If a task is being created without a person ID specified, the drop-down box for selecting the person defaults to the blank option at the top.

Summary

This solution is still not perfect. For example, if you update a person's details, their tasks aren't even mentioned. It may be necessary to include the task listing in the `edit.rhtml` template, as well as in `show.rhtml`. Also, every time we edit, delete, or add a task we are redirected back to the record of the person associated with the task: in some cases, we may just want to bulk-edit tasks, and redirect back to the task index instead. These refinements are possible, but the system we've built so far covers the common case, where tasks are edited in the context of a person.

However, the simple task manager we've built is fairly flexible and intuitive for users. More importantly, writing it has enabled us to explore techniques for managing a list of child objects from inside their parent, without adding too much complexity and retaining cross-browser compatibility. This is a common use case, and one for which there is little guidance elsewhere.

Uploading and Attaching Files

The final feature request for *Intranet* is a facility for uploading files and associating them with tasks. Rails provides some simple, PHP-like wrappers around standard HTML file upload forms, which you can use in their raw form. For example, here's a simple upload form:

```
<h1><%= @page_title %></h1>
<% form_tag({:action => 'receive'}, {:multipart => true}) do -%>
<p>Select a file to upload:<br />
<%= file_field_tag('file_to_upload', :size => 40) %></p>
<p><%= submit_tag 'Upload' %></p>
<% end -%>
```

Note that this generates an HTML form with a file field for browsing to a local file. The important part is the `:multipart => true` option passed to `form_tag`: this sets the form's `enctype` attribute to `"multipart/form-data"`, the encoding required when posting files over HTTP.

The next step is to write a controller, which will render this form with its `index` action, and handle uploads via the `receive` action (at which the above form points). This can be placed into `app/controllers/upload_controller.rb` (and the view above can go into `app/views/upload/index.rhtml`):

```
class UploadController < ApplicationController
  def index
    @page_title = 'Upload a file'
  end

  def receive
    # Get the uploaded file as an object.
    file_to_upload = params[:file_to_upload]
    # The full path to the file on the original filesystem.
    full_filename = file_to_upload.original_filename
    # Get the last part of the filename.
    short_filename = File.basename(full_filename)
    # Retrieve the content of the file.
    file_data = file_to_upload.read
    # Append a timestamp to the filename to ensure it's unique
    # and set the path to somewhere inside public/files.
    new_filename = File.join(RAILS_ROOT, 'public/files',
      Time.now.to_i.to_s + '_' + short_filename)
    # Save the file into a folder inside the Rails app.
    File.open(new_filename, 'w') { |f| f.write(file_data) }
    # Set the flash and direct back to index.
    redirect_to_index 'File uploaded successfully'
  end
end
```

The last step is to create a `files` directory inside `RAILS_ROOT/public`, to hold the uploaded files. Now, browse to `http://localhost:3000/upload`, and you should be able to upload files to your heart's content.

This is a rough and ready file upload system. It doesn't handle multiple versions of the same file, or attach files to other records in the database, or display the uploaded files in any kind of list; but it does demonstrate the basic principles.

But there is a better way: by using a **plugin**.

Using Plugins

Rails **plugins** are a mechanism to embed chunks of functionality inside your applications, extending and overlaying the basic Rails framework. Their role is similar to a Firefox add-on, or a Drupal module: they can add new views, controllers, helpers, migrations, generators, etc.; in fact, any Rails "component" can be bundled inside a plugin.

Plugins are useful as they can provide you with functionality which might take days to write, in a matter of seconds. There are dozens (hundreds?) of plugins available, with functionality ranging from UK postcode validation (`validates_as_uk_postcode`) to methods for easily building SQL queries (`where`) to integration with other systems (`s3`, `mint`). They can also be useful for packaging your own code, turning it into an easily-distributable bundle. However, for our purposes, we'll just be using other people's plugins in this chapter.

The first step in using plugins is to find them. Repositories are typically accessible via HTTP, but some use HTTPS or Subversion (svn). In most cases, the repository is actually a Subversion repository exposed over HTTP, HTTPS or the Subversion protocol; when you are installing a plugin, you are actually exporting or checking out code from a repository (see Chapter 3 *Laying the Foundations* for an explanation of Subversion concepts).

 To access `svn://` URLs on Windows, you will need to install the command-line Subversion client (see Chapter 3 *Laying the Foundations*).

By default, Rails ships with access to the official Ruby on Rails plugins repository (`http://dev.rubyonrails.com/svn/rails/plugins/`). To see a full list of the repositories available, use the `script/plugin` script from the command line and pass the `discover` command:

```
$ ruby script/plugin discover
Add http://www.agilewebdevelopment.com/plugins/? [Y/n] y
Add svn://rubyforge.org/var/svn/expressica/plugins/? [Y/n] y
Add http://soen.ca/svn/projects/rails/plugins/? [Y/n] y
...
```

Answer **Y** (or press return) to each line, adding as many repositories as you like. The list of repositories is stored in a file called `.rails_plugin_sources` in your home directory (`Documents and Settings` on Windows, or `/home/username` on *nix). Each time you use the `plugin` script from now on, the repositories recorded in that file are accessed to build a list of plugins available for you to install.

If you want to add a single repository to your preferences, or manually add a repository not in the list returned by the `discover` command, you can do it with:

```
$ ruby script/plugin source <URL for repository>
```

To see a list of available plugins in the repositories you've selected:

```
$ ruby script/plugin list
```

This might take a while, as the script will interrogate all the new repositories and list the plugins they are offering (unfortunately, not alphabetically). Here's a short fragment of a full list:

```
account_location            http://dev.rubyonrails.com/svn/rails/plugins/
                                account_location/
acts_as_taggable            http://dev.rubyonrails.com/svn/rails/plugins/
                                acts_as_taggable/
browser_filters             http://dev.rubyonrails.com/svn/rails/plugins/
                                browser_filters/
continuous_builder          http://dev.rubyonrails.com/svn/rails/plugins/
                                continuous_builder/
deadlock_retry              http://dev.rubyonrails.com/svn/rails/plugins/
                                deadlock_retry/

. . .
```

To install a plugin available from one of your preferred repositories:

```
$ ruby script/plugin install <name of plugin>
```

So, to install `acts_as_taggable` from the list above, you would do:

```
$ ruby script/plugin install acts_as_taggable
+ ./acts_as_taggable/init.rb
+ ./acts_as_taggable/lib/README
+ ./acts_as_taggable/lib/acts_as_taggable.rb
+ ./acts_as_taggable/lib/tag.rb
+ ./acts_as_taggable/lib/tagging.rb
+ ./acts_as_taggable/test/acts_as_taggable_test.rb
```

You can see here that the plugin is downloaded a file at a time, via a svn export (i.e. a download which disassociates the files from the repository). It ends up being installed into the RAILS_ROOT/vendor/plugins directory, under a directory with the same name as the plugin: in this case, RAILS_ROOT/vendor/plugins/acts_as_taggable.

A plugin can be removed with:

```
$ ruby script/plugin remove <name of plugin>
```

which deletes the plugin's directory from vendor/plugins.

An alternative to this approach is to svn checkout the plugin. This leaves the association between the plugin and its origin Subversion repository intact, which means that you can upgrade it easily. Install a plugin this way with:

```
$ ruby script/plugin install -x <name of plugin>
```

Passing the -x flag to the install command uses a feature of Subversion called **externals**, which associates the plugin with *your* application's Subversion repository. This means that each time someone checks out *your* application, they will also check out the plugin from *its* repository (which is *external* to yours). It also means that each time someone does an svn up on your application to update it, they will also update any external plugins (installed with the -x flag) from *their* repositories. Note that the plugin itself is not included in your repository: just a reference to its origin repository.

In cases where a project is going to be widely distributed (e.g. to a team or to the public) and is already in its own Subversion repository, using the -x flag when installing plugins is recommended.

> If your application isn't itself associated with a Subversion repository, using the -x flag when installing a plugin will throw this error message:
>
> Cannot install using externals because this project is not under subversion.
>
> In this case, your only option is to install without the -x flag.

The plugin script can run a number of other commands, such as directly installing a plugin from a URL, or listing all the plugins in a given repository. Run the plugin script without a command specification (ruby script/plugin) to see what's available.

Using acts_as_attachment for File Uploads

Back to the file upload functionality we want to add to *Intranet*. We'll be using `acts_as_attachment`, a widely-used plugin with rich functionality, for our file upload management. This is provided by the *techno weenie* site (`http://techno-weenie.net/`), and is written by one of the core Rails developers (Rick Olson). Using it saves a lot of time, as the plugin provides generators and extra options for forms, which make is easier to process uploaded files. To get at it we have to add the *techno weenie* repository to our plugin sources:

```
$ ruby script/plugin source http://svn.techno-weenie.net/projects/plugins
```

Next, install the `acts_as_attachment` plugin using the `-x` flag:

```
$ ruby script/plugin install -x acts_as_attachment
```

This pulls the plugin into our application, as well as creating an externals definition in our Subversion repository, which links the plugin into *Intranet*.

 At the time of writing, `acts_as_attachment` was in the process of being deprecated in favor of `attachment_fu`. However, the beta state of `attachment_fu` meant that we went with the tried-and-tested plugin instead.

With the plugin installed, we can generate a model to represent files uploaded to *Intranet*. `acts_as_attachment` provides a handy generator for this:

```
$ ruby script/generate attachment_model file_attachment
```

This creates a `FileAttachment` model and migration for us, and each file we upload will be represented by a record in the `file_attachments` table in the database.

`acts_as_attachment` can either store uploaded files in the database or on the file system. What's the difference?

- If you store files in the **database**, the data for the file is stored in a field in the specified table. This can make your database enormous, but can simplify access and backups.

- If the **filesystem** method is used for file storage, a physical file is written to the file system, while its location and metadata are stored in the database table. This is more economical and intuitive, so it's the approach we'll be taking.

`acts_as_attachment` can also manage image files, producing thumbnails from them and resizing them. However, this functionality is dependent on having a Ruby graphics library available (e.g. **RMagick**). This is not important for *Intranet*, as most of the files are likely to be text or PDFs. For now, we'll just deal with the simple case, and ignore parts of the plugin only relevant to images.

Before creating the `file_attachments` table, take a minute to edit the migration in `db/migrate/006_create_file_attachments.rb`. The edited version of the file is shown below:

```
class CreateFileAttachments < ActiveRecord::Migration
  def self.up
    create_table :file_attachments do |t|
      t.column "content_type", :string
      t.column "filename", :string
      t.column "size", :integer
      t.column "task_id", :integer
      t.column "parent_id", :integer
    end
  end
  def self.down
    drop_table :file_attachments
  end
end
```

We've specified a `task_id` field (highlighted) to associate the uploaded file with a task. However, it is also necessary to specify a `parent_id` field, which mirrors the parent record ID (in this case, the ID of the parent task): this is because `acts_as_attachment` uses this internally to decide which records and files need to be deleted from the file system when a parent record is deleted (and a dependency has been specified). Unfortunately, in this version of `acts_as_attachment`, both are needed, even though this introduces duplication and confusion.

Run the migration to add the new table to the database:

$ rake db:migrate

We also need to edit the `FileAttachment` model to associate a file with a task, set up storage on the file system, set a maximum size for uploaded files, and tell the model where uploaded files should be stored:

```
class FileAttachment < ActiveRecord::Base
  belongs_to :task
  acts_as_attachment :storage => :file_system,
```

```
        :max_size => 10.megabytes,
        :file_system_path => 'public/files'
    validates_as_attachment
  end
```

The :filesystem_path option (highlighted) sets RAILS_ROOT/public/files as the location for uploaded files. If you haven't already created the public/files directory, do so now. On *nix, this directory must be writable by the user who owns the Rails process (in our case, by the owner of the Mongrel process, which is running the application). When a file is uploaded, it is stored in a subdirectory of the :filesystem_path; the name of the subdirectory corresponds to the parent_id of the record in the file_attachments table. For example, if a file in the file_attachments table has the filename confused.jpg and a parent_id of 12, it will end up being stored in RAILS_ROOT/public/files/12/confused.jpg.

The final step is to mark the other side of the tasks to file_attachments relationship, specifying that tasks can have many files attached:

```
class Task < ActiveRecord::Base
  belongs_to :person
  belongs_to :user
  has_many :file_attachments, :dependent => :destroy,
    :order => 'filename'
  # ... other methods ...
end
```

The has_many relationship (highlighted) has the :dependent option set to :destroy, to ensure that when a task is deleted, all the associated records in the file_attachments table are also deleted. When an instance of FileAttachment is deleted, acts_as_attachment will also simultaneously remove related files from the file system. We also specify that attachments should be ordered by filename when retrieved through this association.

Managing File Attachments for a Task

Each file has a task with which it is associated. The controller must therefore act in the same way as the TasksController we saw earlier in this Chapter: each time we add or delete an attachment, we need to redirect back to the task associated with the attachment when the action completes.

 We won't provide any advanced versioning or editing capabilities, so there is no need for an update action in this development iteration.

As with the views we wrote for the `TasksController`, we'll display file attachments in a separate area next to the task when editing it. When we're displaying a task, we'll just list its associated files as hyperlinks.

Unlike tasks, we won't provide a page that enables a file attachment to be uploaded and arbitrarily associated with a task. Instead, all file uploads will be explicitly associated with a task, and only listed or edited in that context. At a later date, it will still be possible to list all the files that have been uploaded in an "*über* file attachments list", but we'll keep things simple for now.

To sum up, here's the extra functionality we need:

- In the task edit form (`app/views/tasks/edit.rhtml`), show a secondary file attachment form (`app/views/file_attachments/_form.rhtml`), which enables file attachments to be added for the task. We'll write this first, as the other functionality is hard to add and debug without having any file attachments to experiment with.

  Note that we're not going to enable file attachments on *new* tasks: the task must first be saved to the database and then edited again to add file attachments to it.

- Create a `FileAttachmentsController` that can add a single file for a specified task. As each file is associated with a task, when a file is added by the `FileAttachmentsController`, redirect back to the `TasksController` to update the associated task.

- Amend the task partial (`app/views/tasks/_task.rhtml`) to list file attachments.

- Extend the attachments form and the controller to manage file attachment deletions.

- Protect the actions on the `FileAttachmentsController` so they are only accessible to logged in users.

Adding a Form for Attaching a File to a Task

First, create a form that enables a new file to be uploaded and associated with a task (in `app/views/file_attachments/_form.rhtml` — you'll need to create the `file_attachments` directory in `app/views` first). This form is similar to the one we created at the beginning of this section, requiring the correct form encoding and a file field:

```
<h2>File attachments</h2>

<% form_for 'new_attachment', :url => {:controller => 'file_
attachments',
```

```
    :action => 'receive', :task_id => task.id},
    :html => {:multipart => true} do |f| %>
    <p>Upload a new attachment:<br />
    <%= f.file_field(:uploaded_data, :size => 20) %></p>

    <p><%= submit_tag 'Save' %></p>
    <% end %>
```

This template expects to be handed a `task` parameter (first highlighted line) representing the `Task` instance with which newly-uploaded files should be associated.

The second highlighted line creates the file upload field, giving it the special name `'uploaded_data'`. If you use this name for a file field, `acts_as_attachment` knows that the file uploaded with it is to be saved as an instance of your file model (in our case, as an instance of `FileAttachment`). Although there is only a single field containing the file data, the special `'uploaded_data'` name means that `acts_as_attachment` decomposes it into `content_type`, `size`, `filename`, etc. The decomposed data is then used to set the corresponding attributes on the model instance.

We want to make this form available when a task is being edited, so edit `app/views/tasks/edit.rhtml` to look like this (the changes are highlighted):

```
    <div id="left_panel">
    <% form_for :task, @task, :url => {:action => 'update', :id => @task.
    id}
    do |f| %>
    <%= render :partial => 'form', :locals => {:f => f} %>
    <% end %>
    </div>

    <div id="right_panel">
    <%= render :partial => 'file_attachments/form',
    :locals => {:task => @task} %>
    </div>
```

Notice how the `@task` variable is passed as a local variable when rendering the `file_attachments/form` partial. We also created two `<div>` elements, one for the task and the other for the file attachment management panel, then reused the `"left_panel"` and `"right_panel"` IDs (used earlier to style the person view and show their tasks alongside their details) to make the two `<div>` elements sit next to each other.

You should end up with a task update form that looks like this:

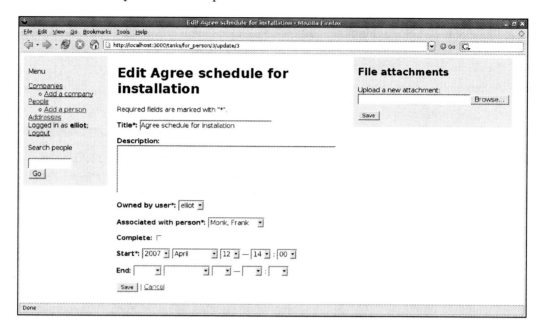

Adding a File Attachment to a Task

Now we can add the `FileAttachments` controller and `receive` action, which the form in the previous section posts to. First, we need a controller. From the command line, run the generator:

```
$ ruby script/generate controller file_attachments
```

Now add the `receive` action:

```
class FileAttachmentsController < ApplicationController
  def receive
    # Get the task the file is to be attached to.
    task = Task.find(params[:task_id])
    task_id = task.id

    # Get the ID of the person associated with the task;
    # we'll use this to redirect back to the task update view
    # for the person.
    person_id = task.person_id

    # Create the attachment.
    @new_attachment = FileAttachment.new(:task_id => task_id,
    :parent_id => task_id)
    @new_attachment.attributes = params[:new_attachment]
```

```
@new_attachment.save
  # Set the flash and direct back to update action
  # for task/person.
  flash[:notice] = 'File uploaded successfully'
  redirect_to :controller => 'tasks', :action => 'edit',
    :id => task_id, :person_id => person_id
end
end
```

The action pulls the `task_id` from the request parameters and uses this to get a `Task` instance to associate this attachment with. It also gets the associated `person_id` from the task, so that once the action completes, the controller redirects back to the task edit page.

When creating the attachment, we first get a fresh instance of `FileAttachment`; setting its `parent_id` and `task_id` attributes to the the ID of the task. The remainder of the attributes are set from the `:new_attachment` parameters in the request: this includes a special `uploaded_data` field (discussed earlier, see: *Adding a Form for Attaching a File to a Task*), which sets attributes specific to `acts_as_attachment` (i.e. `content_type`, `size`, and `filename`).

Listing File Attachments for a Task

As we've specified an association between a task and its file attachments, adding a listing is simple. Edit the bottom part of `app/views/tasks/_task.rhtml` like this:

```
. . .
Owner: <%= task.user.username %></p>
<div class="file_attachments_for_task">
<p><strong>File attachments</strong></p>
<% unless task.file_attachments.empty? -%>
<% for attachment in task.file_attachments -%>
<p>
<%= link_to attachment.filename, attachment.public_filename %>
</p>
<% end -%>
<% else -%>
<p>None</p>
<% end -%>
</div>
. . .
```

The important part of this template is how we create the link, using two methods added to the model instances by `acts_as_attachment`: `filename` gives us the plain file name for the attachment (e.g. `quotation.doc`), while `public_filename` gives the publicly-accessible path to the file (e.g. `/public/files/10/quotation.doc`).

Finally, style the attachments area to make it stand out a bit more (in `public/stylesheets/base.css`):

```
.file_attachments_for_task {
  background-color: #DDD;
  padding: 0.5em;
}
```

You should now be able to add a few attachments to a task and view them, e.g.:

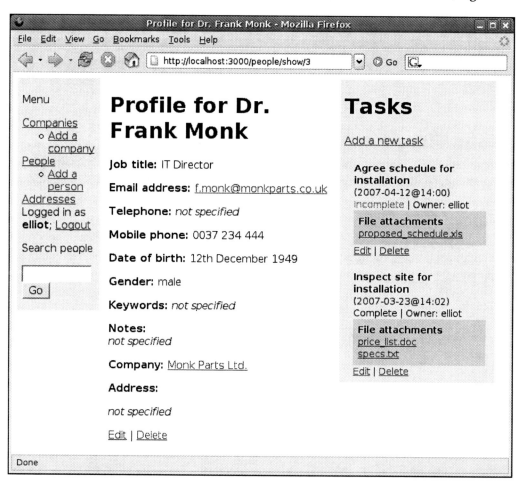

Deleting File Attachments for a Task

Now that the layouts are in place, and we are able to see the attachments for a
task, we can extend the attachment management panel to handle deletions as well
as additions.

First, when we display app/views/file_attachments/_form.rhtml, we'll display
each existing attachment with a check box next to it: if the form is submitted and any
check boxes have been selected, the associated attachments are removed. As well
as deleting the record from the file_attachments table in database, the associated
physical file will also be removed. Here's the new form appended to the top of
the template:

```
<h2>File attachments</h2>
<% form_tag :controller => 'file_attachments',
:action => 'remove', :task_id => task.id do %>
<% unless task.file_attachments.empty? -%>
<p><em>Tick boxes to select attachments to delete</em></p>
<% for attachment in task.file_attachments -%>
<p>
<%= check_box_tag 'attachments_to_remove[]', attachment.id, false,
:id => 'attachments_to_remove_' + attachment.id.to_s %>
<%= link_to attachment.filename, attachment.public_filename %>
</p>
<% end -%>
<%= submit_tag 'Delete' %>
<% else -%>
<p><strong>No attachments</strong></p>
<% end -%>
<% end -%>
<p><strong>OR</strong></p>
<% form_for 'new_attachment', :url => {:controller => 'file_
attachments',
:action => 'receive', :task_id => task.id},
:html => {:multipart => true} do |f| %>
. . .
```

An interesting point to note here is that we can build traditional forms with Rails,
without having to resort to using form_for. We've used the check_box_tag helper
here to create a series of check boxes all called attachments_to_remove[]. As
the name of the form element ends with ' [] ', Rails will automatically gather the
parameters into an array when the form is submitted (as it happens in PHP with the
form elements named this way).

Here's what the page looks like when rendered:

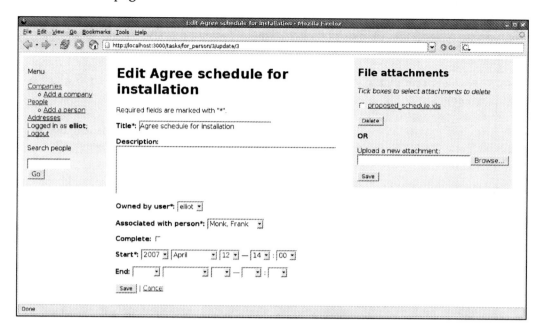

Next, we add a new `remove` action to `FileAttachmentsController` to handle deletion of file attachments. This action will redirect back to the task edit form (as the `receive` action does). We can also take this opportunity to do a bit of refactoring: the redirection is the same for both `receive` and `remove` actions, so we can move that into a separate `redirect_to_person_task` method; and we need to retrieve a `Task` instance, `task_id`, and `person_id` to run both actions; so we can move those operations into a `prepare` method and use a `before_filter` to call it. Here's the resulting controller class definition:

```
class FileAttachmentsController < ApplicationController
  before_filter :prepare
  def receive
    @new_attachment = FileAttachment.new(:task_id => @task_id,
    :parent_id => @task_id)
    @new_attachment.attributes = params[:new_attachment]
    @new_attachment.save
    # Set the flash and direct back to update action for task.
    flash[:notice] = 'File uploaded successfully'
    redirect_to_person_task
  end
  def remove
    FileAttachment.destroy params[:attachments_to_remove]
```

```
    flash[:notice] = 'Attachments removed'
    redirect_to_person_task
  end

  private
  def redirect_to_person_task
    redirect_to :controller => 'tasks', :action => 'edit',
    :id => @task_id, :person_id => @person_id
  end

  private
  def prepare
    task = Task.find(params[:task_id])
    @task_id = task.id
    @person_id = task.person_id
  end
end
```

The new `remove` action is highlighted: it destroys an array of `FileAttachment` IDs retrieved from the `attachments_to_remove` request parameter.

Protecting File Attachment Actions

The last step is to secure the `FileAttachmentsController` so that only logged-in users are able to manage attachments. This is as simple as adding one line to the top of the class definition, to protect every action on the controller (see the section *Protecting Actions* earlier in this chapter):

```
class FileAttachmentsController < ApplicationController
  before_filter :authorize

  # ... other methods ...
end
```

Finally, the file attachment functionality is complete!

Summary

The aim of this chapter has been to show more of the depth and usefulness of Rails, while at the same time demonstrate how to extend an existing application with new functionality. The beauty of Rails is that it is easy to tack new functionality on with extra components, whether new actions for existing controllers, new actions for all controllers, or new models and plugins.

This chapter has hopefully given you the confidence to grow your application to meet new requirements and some guidance about how to go about adding new functionality.

In the next chapter, we'll see how to improve the efficiency and performance of a Rails application: making use of caching, using **Capistrano** for automating repetitive tasks, and setting up the infrastructure for large scale deployment.

9

Advanced Deployment

So far, we've dealt with a simple deployment situation—a single production machine running *Intranet* as a Mongrel instance, backed by a MySQL database. This will be able to cope with a fair amount of traffic, and it may be that in your situation, there will be no need for anything more complex.

Having said this, one issue that will definitely arise is how to roll out new versions of the application. This introduces several challenges, such as ensuring the application is compatible with new versions of Rails, upgrading the database, and so on. **Capistrano**, a tool for simplifying and automating deployment of applications, was designed to ease multiple deployments, and we'll be seeing how it can help us meet these challenges. We'll also cover common deployment issues and their solutions, plus other housekeeping that an application requires, such as clearing out stale sessions and managing log files.

If you have a lot of users connecting to the application concurrently, you may find that things start to slow down. In this chapter, we'll cover how to keep up your application's speed using some simple techniques, such as **caching**. If things are still too slow, the next option may be to add more hardware to cope with the load. We'll see how to scale a Rails application using **Apache**, as well as by adding more servers.

This chapter is slightly trickier to follow than previous ones, as we're now considering two machines—one for development and a second for production (called the **development machine** and **production server** respectively in this chapter). *Intranet* is being deployed from the former to the latter. You can still follow the tutorial on a single machine by treating it as both the development machine and production server: simply ensure that you can login to it via SSH. If you want to test the Apache deployment tips, ensure you have Apache installed (see Chapter 6 for some instructions). The section on large-scale deployments is harder to simulate with a single machine, so we'll just be covering some of the concepts to give you an idea of the issues and solutions.

Deployment with Capistrano

Capistrano is designed to make your life easier by automating the repetitive tasks associated with application deployment. Typically, to get a Rails application into production, we would log in to the production server using SSH, and perform the following actions:

- Check out the latest version of our code from the repository into the correct directory on the server.

- Update the production database using migrations. If the database is significantly altered, it may be necessary to stop the Mongrel process first, to prevent any errors from occurring. If the database structure changes, but the application code is still expecting the old structure, there could be a disastrous mismatch.

- Restart the Mongrel process so that it is serving the latest version of the code (remember that in production, changes to the code are not dynamically loaded by Rails, so we have to restart the server process to make changes live).

In fact, this is how we did our first production deployment. However, if we have to repeat deployment several times, we need to remember each step and the order in which they should be applied every time, which can be tedious and error-prone.

An alternative is to use Capistrano, which eases the deployment process by automating the above tasks for us. When we trigger it, it will log in to the server, check out the latest code from the Subversion repository, update the database, and restart Mongrel, all using a handful of simple commands. We don't even have to leave our development machine. Even better, it will also make it easy for us to roll back to a previous version of the application if something goes wrong with the deployment. This can of course be done manually, but this requires a precise sequence of steps to be followed — something at which people are inherently bad, but at which computers excel.

 While Capistrano can be used to deploy *from* Windows, it is not designed to deploy *to* a Windows production server. It is best used for deployment to *nix or Mac servers.

In the following sections, we'll see how to set up the deployment environment and deploy *Intranet* onto the production Linux server. For more details on installation of each component, refer to Chapter 3 *Laying the Foundations*.

Getting Started with Capistrano

The first step in using Capistrano is to apply it to a Rails application. For example, if the application were in /home/demo/Intranet you would do:

```
$ cap --apply-to /home/demo/Intranet
```

This command adds two files to the application:

- lib/tasks/capistrano.rake: Applying Capistrano to your application makes some extra Rake tasks available (see *Running a Migration* in Chapter 4). However, these tasks are now deprecated, and Capistrano has its own command-line tool (cap, as used above) to run tasks, so the file can be ignored or deleted.

- config/deploy.rb: This file contains the configuration for Capistrano and should not be deleted. It specifies where your Subversion repository is, where your servers (web, application, database) are, how to log in to them via SSH, which directory to deploy the application to, etc. It is also the place where you put custom tasks specific to your application; we'll see some of these later.

The next step is to customize the configuration file (config/deploy.rb) to tell Capistrano where the production server is and how to log in to it. Here are the lines that need to be configured, along with some sample data:

```
set :application, "Intranet"
role :web, "192.168.13.129"
role :app, "192.168.13.129"
role :db,  "192.168.13.129", :primary => true
```

Capistrano can cope with setups where an application is to be deployed to multiple servers, with each server having a different role. The roles available by default in Capistrano (you can define your own on top of these) are:

- app: An application server, running the Rails application. Typically, this will be a machine running Rails under one or more Mongrel processes.

- web: A web server serving static files. Some applications serve JavaScripts, stylesheets, and static HTML files from a web server like Apache, running on a completely separate machine from the Rails processes proper.

- db: A database server, storing the back-end data for the application. You need to set the :primary => true option for a role if you want to be able to run migrations automatically through Capistrano.

In our case, we're using a single server, which acts as the web server, application server, and database server, as well as the Subversion server. That's why we removed this line from the generated Capistrano file:

```
role :db,    "db02.example.com", "db03.example.com"
```

You only need multiple `role :db` lines if you are using multiple database servers. The default `deploy.rb` file also contains multiple specifications for both `:web` and `:app` servers. As we only have a single server, we can trim those settings down to leave a single host specification `192.168.13.129` (the IP address of our server), as in the example on the previous page. You could use a domain name instead of an IP address here; so, if the IP address `192.168.13.129` were registered with the domain name `server.company.local`, we could have configured `deploy.rb` with:

```
set :application, "Intranet"
role :web, "server.company.local"
role :app, "server.company.local"
role :db,  "server.company.local", :primary => true
```

When you ask Capistrano to deploy your application, it will attempt to log in via SSH to the `:web`, `:app` and `:db` servers to do the necessary code check out and command-line actions (e.g. run migrations, restart Mongrel) to get your application running. Our recommendation would be to create one user account on each server specifically for Capistrano. The home directory of this account can be used as the deployment location for Rails applications, and the same user account can be used to check out code from the local Subversion repository.

Log in to the server and set up an account specifically for deploying Rails applications (e.g. I called mine `captain`). On a Linux server, you can do this as follows:

```
$ sudo groupadd captain
$ sudo useradd --create-home -g captain captain
$ sudo passwd captain
Enter new UNIX password:
Retype new UNIX password:
passwd: password updated successfully
$ sudo mkdir /home/captain/apps
$ sudo chown captain.users /home/captain/apps
```

The final command creates a directory called `apps` inside `captain`'s home directory. This is where we will deploy our Rails applications to.

It's worth checking that you can log in over SSH to the production server from the development machine using the account you've just created, before attempting a deployment with Capistrano. This will ensure that the account is set up correctly.

Once you have a Capistrano user on the production server, you need to add its username and password to the deployment recipe (`deploy.rb`):

```
set :user, "captain"
set :password, "police73"
```

If you have the expertise, you can set up SSH public key authentication for logins from developer machines to the server instead of using usernames and passwords. This is more secure, as it means you don't need to put usernames and passwords in your deployment recipes. See `http://sial.org/howto/openssh/publickey-auth/` for some instructions.

Once Capistrano has logged in via SSH, it will need to check out the code from the Subversion repository. As we are using Subversion over an SSH tunnel (via an `svn+ssh` URL), we specify the username as part of the repository URL:

```
svn+ssh://captain@server.company.local/repository/#{application}/trunk
```

Each time we deploy the application, we will be prompted for the password of the `captain` user. This is because Capistrano has no mechanism for caching passwords between SSH sessions, or for allowing you to specify an `svn+ssh` password in the configuration file.

If you get annoyed with continually being prompted by Subversion for passwords, investigate an SSH password-caching tool like **Pageant** for Windows (`http://www.chiark.greenend.org.uk/~sgtatham/putty/download.html`), or **ssh-agent** for *nix and Mac systems (included with the OpenSSH tools). Alternatively, you can use the even simpler method of setting up a password-less public key on the client, and registering that key with the server. See the previous tip box for more information.

Another alternative is to enable access to the Subversion repository over HTTP for checkouts. If you're using this configuration, you can add the Subversion credentials directly to `deploy.rb`:

```
set :svn_username, "captain"
set :svn_password, "police73"
```

Capistrano will then be able to automatically log in to the repository over HTTP and check out the code, without requiring you to enter a password.

Finally, set the directory on the server into which the Rails application code should be checked out. This will depend on how your application server is set up and the permissions of the person who is deploying the application. As we have a `captain` account specifically for our Rails applications, we can use the `apps` directory inside that user's home directory as our deployment destination:

```
set :deploy_to, "/home/captain/apps/#{application}"
```

This references the `application` variable set earlier in the recipe (`"Intranet"`), specifying that the application is deployed to `/home/captain/apps/Intranet`.

A Complete Deployment Recipe

The final deployment recipe looks like this:

```
ip_address = "192.168.13.129"
set :application, "Intranet"
role :web, ip_address
role :app, ip_address
role :db,  ip_address, :primary => true
set :user, "captain"
set :password, "police73"
set :repository, "svn+ssh://captain@#{ip_address}/repository/#{application}/
trunk"
set :deploy_to, "/home/captain/apps/#{application}"
```

We've created a variable `ip_address` to store the IP address of our single server, to help prevent typos. We've then referenced it in several places in the recipe.

Preparing the Production Database

We are also going to need a production database on the server. Creating a database and user was discussed in Chapter 4 *Creating a Database and System Account*, and configuring the production environment in the `database.yml` file was covered in Chapter 6 *The Production Database*.

As a quick reminder: in the case of MySQL, we can create the database and user on the server with the `mysql` command-line client:

$ mysql -uroot -p

Once into the client, do:

mysql> CREATE DATABASE intranet_production;

**mysql> GRANT ALL ON intranet_production.* TO intranet@localhost
IDENTIFIED BY 'police73';**

mysql> FLUSH PRIVILEGES;

(Replace `police73` with the password you want to give to the `intranet` user.)

Then we can configure the `database.yml` file for the production database like this:

```
production:
  adapter: mysql
  database: 'intranet_production'
  username: intranet
  password: police73
  host: localhost
```

First Deployment

With the configuration file edited to the deployment environment, we are ready to set up the required directories on the server. Connect into the RAILS_ROOT for the *Intranet* application and run the `cap setup` command:

```
$ cap setup
  * executing task setup
  * executing "umask 02 &&\n    mkdir -p /home/captain/apps/Intranet /
home/captain/apps/Intranet/releases /home/captain/apps/Intranet/shared /
home/captain/apps/Intranet/shared/system &&\n    mkdir -p /home/captain/
apps/Intranet/shared/log &&\n    mkdir -p /home/captain/apps/Intranet/
shared/pids"
    servers: ["192.168.13.129"]
    [192.168.13.129] executing command
    command finished
```

As you can see, this logs into the application server(s) and creates several directories, which will store releases of the application and related temporary files (logs, pids). The directories (inside `/home/captain/apps`) are:

- `Intranet`: The main directory for the application.

- `Intranet/releases`: Individual releases of the application end up in here. Each time you deploy the application via Capistrano, you add a new directory for that release inside this directory.

- `Intranet/shared`: Each release of the application shares the files in here, which means you have a shared set of `log` files, a single location for Mongrel `pid` files, etc.

- `Intranet/shared/log`: All releases of the application put their logs into this directory.

- `Intranet/shared/pids`: When the application is running under Mongrel, the Mongrel `pid` file should go in this directory.

- `Intranet/shared/system`: This can be used to house files and directories that need to remain constant across releases. We'll be using it shortly as a place to store file uploads (see the previous chapter, where we added this functionality).

We can now deploy the application into this directory structure:

```
$ cap cold_deploy
```

You should get feedback on the task's progress like this:

```
  * executing task deploy
  * executing task update
 ** transaction: start
  * executing task update_code
  * querying latest revision...
captain@192.168.13.129's password:

...

  * executing task spinner
  * executing "sudo  -u app /home/captain/apps/Intranet/current/
    script/spin"
    servers: ["192.168.13.129"]
    [192.168.13.129] executing command
 ** [out :: 192.168.13.129] sudo:
 ** [out :: 192.168.13.129] no passwd entry for app!
    command finished
command "sudo  -u app /home/captain/apps/Intranet/current/script/spin"
failed on 192.168.13.129
```

You will be prompted for `captain`'s password at some point; this will be used to log in to the Subversion repository and check out the code.

This almost looks OK. However, an error occurred towards the end of the command's execution, during the `spinner` task:

```
no passwd entry for app!
```

This is because Capistrano logged in as `captain` and tried to run a script inside the deployed Rails application (`script/spin`) as the `:app` user; but the `:app` user doesn't exist on the production server. It turns out, this error is irrelevant for our case, as we don't want to start the server using `script/spin`; we want to override this behavior to start Mongrel instead (see the section *Managing Mongrel from Capistrano*). So, we can ignore this error for now. The important thing is that our code has been deployed to the production server. Where is it?

Look inside the apps/Intranet directory and you'll see that some new files and directories have been created:

- current: This is a symlink (a shortcut in Windows parlance) to the latest release in the releases directory.

- revisions.log: This file contains a record of when releases were made and who made them.

- releases/yyyymmddhhnnss: Each sub-directory of the releases directory contains a version of our application. When a new release of the application is deployed, a new sub-directory is added under the releases directory. Note that each sub-directory is timestamped with the date and time when the release was deployed.

  While the releases are independent of each other, each contains more symlinks that point up to the shared directory (see the previous section). This ensures that different releases all share a single set of log files, pid files, etc.

 If you want to see the full set of tasks made available by Capistrano, execute the following on the command line:

cap show_tasks

Migrating the Production Database

The cold_deploy task doesn't run the database migrations. So, while our code is deployed, there is no database for it to work with. We can apply our migrations to the production database with another Capistrano task, migrate:

```
$ cap migrate
  * executing task migrate
  * executing "cd /home/captain/apps/Intranet/current && rake
    RAILS_ENV=production  db:migrate"
    servers: ["192.168.13.129"]
    [192.168.13.129] executing command
 ** [out :: 192.168.13.129] (in /home/captain/apps/Intranet/
releases/20070413171324)
 ** [out :: 192.168.13.129] == CreatePeople: migrating ==================
==================================
 ** [out :: 192.168.13.129] -- create_table(:people)
 ** [out :: 192.168.13.129] -> 0.0831s
 ** [out :: 192.168.13.129] == CreatePeople: migrated (0.0837s) =========
==================================
  . . .
```

If this works, you should see something like the output on the previous page (truncated for brevity). Note that the production database was used as the target for migrations (Capistrano's default environment).

Running Other Commands on the Server with invoke

There is no default Capistrano task for starting Mongrel (but we'll be writing one shortly). However, we can run any arbitrary task on the server using `cap invoke`. The `invoke` command logs into the server using the username and password set in `deploy.rb`; then, on the remote machine, it executes the command passed to it. For example, to start our application, we can do:

```
$ export COMMAND="cd /home/captain/apps/Intranet/current; \
mongrel_rails start -d -e production -p 4000 \
-P /home/captain/apps/Intranet/shared/pids/mongrel.pid"
$ export ROLES=app
$ cap invoke
```

First, we set up the command we want to execute by specifying a COMMAND environment variable. Here, the command we're setting up will run `mongrel_rails` to start a Mongrel instance to serve a Rails application; next, we specify the group of machines where we want to run the command using a ROLES environment variable. To specify multiple roles, place commas between them (e.g. ROLES=web, app). Finally we invoke COMMAND on the remote machines.

Hopefully, you'll see the `mongrel_rails` command being executed:

```
  * executing task invoke
  * executing "mongrel_rails start -d -e production -p 4000 -P
    /home/captain/apps/Intranet/shared/pids/mongrel.pid"
    servers: ["192.168.13.129"]
    [192.168.13.129] executing command
    command finished
```

With the database migrated and Mongrel started, the application is now in production. Use a browser to confirm it is up and running; if not, see the section later in this chapter for some hints about how to troubleshoot your deployment.

In the next section, we'll write a new Capistrano task that encapsulates the manual Mongrel command above.

Managing Mongrel from Capistrano

In the previous section we saw how to do a cold deployment of our code to the
server; we also saw that the command threw an error, as Capistrano tried to run
the `script/spin` command to start the application. This is because Capistrano is
running its `spinner` task as a sub-task of the `cold_deploy` task, which in turn calls
`script/spin` inside the application.

However, we can override any of Capistrano's default tasks with our own by
defining appropriate methods in the deployment recipe. In our case, we want to
override the `spinner` task, which will be used to cold start a Mongrel instance for
the application, and we'll also need to override the `restart` task, which stops the
application and starts it again (so that any changes to the code are reflected in the
production instances). For good measure, we can add our own `stop` task (sometimes
it's useful to be able to just stop Mongrel) and add an alias, `start`, for the spinner
task. To define these tasks, add the following into the section commented with TASKS
in `config/deploy.rb`:

```
# Where to store Mongrel PID file
mongrel_pid = "#{shared_path}/pids/mongrel.pid"
# Port to run on
port = 4000
desc "Override the spinner task with one which starts Mongrel"
task :spinner, :roles => :app do
  run <<-CMD
    mongrel_rails start -e production -p #{port}
    -P #{mongrel_pid} -c #{current_path} -d
  CMD
end
desc "Alias for spinner"
task :start do
  spinner
end
desc "Override the restart task with one which restarts Mongrel"
task :restart, :roles => :app do
  run "mongrel_rails restart -P #{mongrel_pid}"
end
desc "Stop Mongrel"
task :stop, :roles => :app do
  run "mongrel_rails stop -P #{mongrel_pid}"
end
```

We now have `spinner` and `restart` tasks that override the defaults provided by Capistrano, plus a `start` alias for the `spinner` task, and a new `stop` task. A few points to note:

- The `run` method can be used to execute a command-line string on the server; here we're executing our custom `mongrel_rails` command (see previous section), passing the environment to run in, the port to use, where to place the `pid` file, and which application to run. You can use `run` to execute any valid command on a deployment server.

- Inside our custom tasks, we can reference the Capistrano variables `release_path` and `shared_path`. These refer to the absolute path to the latest release of the application and to the shared directory respectively.

- We're scoping our two tasks to particular roles using the `:roles => :app` option, meaning, we only run them on the application server, where Mongrel is running; if you need to specify multiple roles, pass an array of role names into this option, e.g. `:roles => [:app, :web]`.

- In case you're not familiar with the `<<-CMD ... CMD` syntax: this is known as **heredoc**, and can be used to create multi-line strings without the necessity of inserting newline characters and escaping quote marks.

Adding these tasks means that Capistrano will call the correct commands when we cold deploy or deploy a new version of the application. We can also run our tasks manually to get "remote control" of our Mongrel servers with:

```
$ cap start
$ cap stop
$ cap restart
```

Centralizing File Uploads

One other issue that isn't immediately obvious is that *Intranet*'s file upload functionality complicates the picture. Currently, uploaded files are stored in the `public/files` directory. However, when we upgrade the application, we effectively start from a clean slate again: we get a new `public/files` directory which is empty. What we really want is to keep file uploads in a central location available to every release—each time we upgrade, we still reference the same file uploads directory.

Capistrano provides a `shared/system` directory for exactly this scenario. Data that is part of the back-end store for the application is used by every release (similar to how we have a single database instances for all releases). In our case, we'll create a `files` sub-directory inside `shared/system`; then we'll create a symbolic link (like a Windows shortcut) from the `public/files` directory of the application to the `shared/system/files` directory.

First we define a task in `config/deploy.rb`, which will set up the required directories and symlinks. The task creates the directory `shared/system/files` with the appropriate permissions (read, write, execute for the `captain` user; read and execute for everyone else), removes the existing `public/files` directory in the newly deployed release, and creates a symlink from `public/files` to `shared/system/files`:

```
task :symlink_for_file_uploads, :roles => :app do
  run <<-CMD
    mkdir -p -m 775 #{shared_path}/system/files &&
    rm -Rf #{release_path}/public/files &&
    ln -s #{shared_path}/system/files #{release_path}/public/files
  CMD
end
```

We can now make use of Capistrano's callback mechanism to hook into the execution of tasks, before or after they run. This enables us to layer our tasks over the existing Capistrano default tasks, adding functionality to them without having to fiddle with Capistrano's core code.

To hook into a task, we provide a callback handler. This is a custom task which has a special name, significant to Capistrano. The name should consist of `before_` or `after_`, followed by the name of the task we want to attach our handler to. In this case, we want to create the directories and symlinks after the new version of the application has been retrieved from Subversion. The task that updates the application code from Subversion is called `update_code`; therefore, our callback handler should be called `after_update_code`. It is defined like this:

```
task :after_update_code do
  symlink_for_file_uploads
end
```

Now when you deploy the application again, you should see the `symlink_for_file_uploads` task being executed after the code for the release has been updated from Subversion, e.g.:

```
$ cap deploy

  . . .

  * executing task after_update_code

  * executing task symlink_for_file_uploads

  * executing "mkdir -p -m 775 /home/captain/apps/Intranet/shared/system/
files &&\n    rm -Rf /home/captain/apps/Intranet/releases/20070428155358/
public/files &&\n    ln -s /home/captain/apps/Intranet/shared/system/
files /home/captain/apps/Intranet/releases/20070428155358/public/files"

  . . .
```

You can verify that the symlink has been created correctly by connecting to the current release directory, then going to the `public` directory and listing the directory contents (notice the italicised `files` entry in the listing below):

```
$ ls -go
total 44
-rw-rw-r-- 1   235 2007-04-28 16:50 404.html
-rw-rw-r-- 1   309 2007-04-28 16:50 500.html
-rwxrwxr-x 1   477 2007-04-28 16:50 dispatch.cgi
-rwxrwxr-x 1   859 2007-04-28 16:50 dispatch.fcgi
-rwxrwxr-x 1   476 2007-04-28 16:50 dispatch.rb
-rw-rw-r-- 1     0 2007-04-28 16:50 favicon.ico
lrwxrwxrwx 1    47 2007-04-28 16:50 files -> /home/captain/apps/Intranet/
shared/system/files
drwxrwxr-x 3  4096 2007-04-28 16:43 images
-rw-rw-r-- 1  7552 2007-04-28 16:50 index.html
drwxrwxr-x 3  4096 2007-04-28 16:43 javascripts
-rw-rw-r-- 1    99 2007-04-28 16:50 robots.txt
drwxrwxr-x 3  4096 2007-04-28 16:43 stylesheets
lrwxrwxrwx 1    41 2007-04-28 16:50 system -> /home/captain/apps/Intranet/
shared/system
```

Upgrading the Application

Capistrano really shows its character when you want to easily upgrade an application: with a single command, deploy a new version from the repository and migrate the database, far more easily than the old-fashioned way of doing each step in the deployment manually. To see this in action, we'll add a new migration to the application, which will set up a default administrator account. First create the skeleton for the migration (on the development machine):

```
$ ruby script/generate migration default_admin_user
```

Then edit `db/migrate/008_default_admin_user.rb` and add this content:

```
class DefaultAdminUser < ActiveRecord::Migration
  def self.up
    u = User.new(:username => 'admin', :passwd => 'admin').save
  end
  def self.down
    User.find_by_username('admin').destroy
  end
end
```

When the migration is applied, a default administrative user with username *admin* and password *admin* is added to the `users` table. (The highlighted section of the code shows where the credentials are set.). Ensure that the migration is added to the Subversion repository, so it is available when you next deploy to the production server.

The command to check out the latest version of the code and apply any new migrations is:

```
$ cap deploy_with_migrations
```

This will also restart the Mongrel instance, and you can now test that the new *admin* account has been correctly added to the database.

Cleaning Up Obsolete Releases

After you've deployed several new releases, your production server will get cluttered with obsolete entries in the `releases` directory. To clear out all of the releases except for the most recent five, do:

```
$ cap cleanup
```

Note that by default this Capistrano task will attempt to use `sudo` when deleting the obsolete files and directories. However, if the account Capistrano uses to log in (in our case, `captain`) is unable to use `sudo` on the production server, you'll get this error message when you run the task:

```
$ cap cleanup
    ...
    * executing "sudo  rm -rf /home/captain/apps/Intranet/
releases/20070428153649"    servers: ["192.168.13.129"]
      [192.168.13.129] executing command
  ** [out :: 192.168.13.129] captain is not in the sudoers file.  This
incident will be reported.
    ...
```

To turn off this behavior, you have to tell Capistrano that it doesn't need to use `sudo` to perform tasks on the production server. Add this line near the top of `config/deploy.rb`:

```
    set :use_sudo, false
```

This should fix the problem and allow the `cleanup` task to run correctly.

> In our case, it's safe to turn off `sudo`, as the `captain` user owns the directory into which we're deploying the application, and is also the owner of the Mongrel process that is running the application. In situations where this is not the case (for example, if you are running Mongrel under one user account and the application files are owned by a different account), you may not have the option to turn off `sudo`. In this case, you may need to add the Capistrano user to the `sudoers` file instead. How to do this is beyond the scope of this book; but the sudo website (http://www.gratisoft.us/sudo/) has plenty of documentation that should help.

Downgrading the Application

The final situation that we need to deal with is what happens when deployment of a new version of the application goes wrong: perhaps once it's on the production server, some unexpected fault brings the whole site down. In this situation, you need to be able to go back to the last known good version of the application, which will usually be the previous release. Capistrano provides a task to do this:

```
$ cap rollback
```

This command actually rolls back the application code, shifting the `current` symlink to point at the previous version of the application in the `releases` directory. However, it doesn't automatically roll back the database: potentially you could roll back to version 1 of your application while retaining a database structure that only works with version 2.

Capistrano can be used to work around this issue, and run migrations up or down to bring the database back in line with the application version. Currently this has to be done manually after you've run `cap rollback`.

For example, say we roll back to the version of the *application* before the migration (of the previous section) was added. We also want to roll back to the version of the *database* before the migration was applied. To find the latest migration in the application, take a look in the `current/db/migrate` directory (this is the "rolled back" application directory). In our case, the highest numbered migration in that directory is `007_create_file_attachments.rb`; so, we need to migrate the database down to version 7. The command for doing this is:

```
$ cap -s migrate_env="VERSION=7" migrate
  * executing task migrate
   * executing "cd /home/captain/apps/Intranet/current && rake RAILS_
ENV=production VERSION=7 db:migrate"
```

```
    servers: ["192.168.13.129"]
    [192.168.13.129] executing command
 ** [out :: 192.168.13.129] (in /home/captain/apps/Intranet/
releases/20070502221404)
 ** [out :: 192.168.13.129] == DefaultAdminUser: reverting ==============
===================================
 ** [out :: 192.168.13.129] == DefaultAdminUser: reverted (0.2761s) =====
===================================
    command finished
```

(Replace the number 7 in the command with the appropriate version to migrate to.)

Troubleshooting Deployment

Rails deployment is complex, involving Subversion checkouts, web, database and application servers, multiple user accounts, and a variety of permissions. With so many variables in the mix, things can go wrong and often do. On top of that, Capistrano is a complex beast, doing a complex job, which makes things even worse. Consequently, you will run across deployment errors. To help you work out what's happening when these occur, here are some examples of the kinds of error you might have to face, and fixes for them.

Incompatible Rails Versions

If the version of Rails on the production server mismatches the one required by the application, you may get this error message when you run `cap deploy_with_migrations`:

```
 ** [out :: 192.168.13.129] Cannot find gem for Rails ~>1.2.3.0:
 ** [out :: 192.168.13.129] Install the missing gem with 'gem install -
v=1.2.3 rails', or
 ** [out :: 192.168.13.129] change environment.rb to define RAILS_GEM_
VERSION with your desired version.
```

The error is being thrown because of this line in `config/environment.rb`:

```
    RAILS_GEM_VERSION = '1.2.3' unless defined? RAILS_GEM_VERSION
```

This states the version of Rails required by the application. As the version of Rails on the production server and the version on the development server are different, Rails will refuse to start the application. There are three ways to fix this:

1. **Remove the offending line from environment.rb**: This is the simplest fix, but it means that your Rails application won't check the version of Rails that it is running under. If the application relies on specific Rails features that are absent from old versions of Rails (for example), and you deploy to a server lacking those features, the application may not work correctly.

2. **Freeze gems into the application**: Rails provides a facility that enables you to take Rails with the application. This technique is known as "freezing" Rails, and is accomplished by running the following `rake` task:

   ```
   rake rails:freeze:gems
   ```

   What this does is copy the current Rails gems (`rails`, `activerecord`, `activesupport`, `actionpack`, `actionmailer`, `actionwebservice`) into the `vendors/rails` directory inside the application. Rails will now use the gems in that directory instead of the centrally-installed gems when running the application. Note that this technique is only useful if the version of Rails you need isn't installed on the production server.

   If you'd rather freeze a specific Rails version into your application (rather than the one installed on the development machine) you can do:

   ```
   rake rails:freeze:edge TAG=rel_1-2-3
   ```

   where `rel_1-2-3` is a Subversion tag representing release 1.2.3 of Rails (see Chapter 3 for coverage of what Subversion tags are). You can get a full list of Rails tags by visiting `http://svn.rubyonrails.org/rails/tags/`.

   The down side to using the `rake` tasks to freeze Rails gems is that they export the specified version of Rails into the `vendor/rails` directory. This means that you will need to store the whole of Rails in your application's Subversion repository too, which isn't ideal. A better approach is to manually create a link in your application that references the Rails Subversion repository using the `svn:externals` property (discussed in Chapter 8 in the context of plugins). You can do this by editing this property via Eclipse (editing Subversion properties is covered in the section *Ignoring Temporary Files* in Chapter 4) and setting its value to one of the Rails version tags, e.g.:

   ```
   vendor/rails
   http://svn.rubyonrails.org/rails/tags/rel_1-2-3/
   ```

   If you now do an `svn up` to update your application, Rails will be fetched into `vendor/rails`; however, you no longer need to store Rails in *your* repository. Instead it will be automatically fetched from the Rails repository proper each time your application is checked out, as your application now just references the external repository.

The only other issue with this approach is that you are reliant on the Rails Subversion repository being available to perform your deployment. If you don't want this dependency, don't use the `svn:externals` approach.

3. **Upgrade Rails on the server**: Ensure that the production server is using the same version of Rails as the application by ensuring the correct version is installed, e.g.

```
gem install rails -v 1.2.3
```

Missing Libraries

One other more obscure situation you may run across is where the version of Ruby on the server is different from the one on the development machine(s). For example, imagine your application uses the **libxml-ruby** library (an alternative Ruby XML library, which is faster than Ruby's default REXML library). **libxml-ruby** is installed on the developer machines but not on the production server; the gem is pulled into the application in `environment.rb` with:

```
require 'libxml-ruby'
```

On the production server, the **libxml-ruby** gem is not available. When you try to start Mongrel (e.g. with `cap spinner`), the command fails; however, no indication of this is given by Capistrano, and when you try to browse to the application, it is unavailable.

Mongrel logs its activity into a file inside the application's log directory; in the case of an application deployed under Capistrano, this file is `shared/log/mongrel.log`; it should hopefully give you more insights into any errors that occur while Mongrel is starting, e.g.:

```
** Starting Mongrel listening at 0.0.0.0:4000
** Starting Rails with production environment...
/usr/local/lib/site_ruby/1.8/rubygems.rb:251:in 'report_activate_
error': Could not find RubyGem libxml-ruby (>= 0.0.0) (Gem::LoadError)
        from /usr/local/lib/site_ruby/1.8/rubygems.rb:188:in
'activate'
        from /usr/local/lib/site_ruby/1.8/rubygems.rb:66:in 'active_
gem_with_options'
...
```

In any situation where Capistrano doesn't report any errors but your application has failed to start, check this log first.

Incorrect Subversion Password or Repository Permissions

In cases where Capistrano is trying to check out code from the Subversion repository and you type in the wrong password, you may see this error message:

```
captain@192.168.13.129's password:
Permission denied, please try again.
```

Run the task again and type in the correct password.

User Doesn't Have SSH Access to the Server

If Capistrano tries to log in to a server using the username and password credentials you supplied, and those credentials are incorrect, you may see this error message:

```
 ** [update_code] exception while rolling back: Net::SSH::
AuthenticationFailed, captain
authentication failed for 'captain'
```

Fix the user and password settings in `config/deploy.rb`.

Inaccessible Application Server

If you get the IP address or domain name of an application or web server wrong in `config/deploy.rb`, you are likely to see this error message:

```
** [update_code] exception while rolling back: Errno::EHOSTUNREACH, No
route to host - connect(2)
/opt/lampp/lib/ruby/gems/1.8/gems/net-ssh-1.0.10/lib/net/ssh/transport/
session.rb:88:in 'initialize': No route to host - connect(2) (Errno::
EHOSTUNREACH)
```

This indicates that Capistrano is unable to log in to the server. Fix the IP addresses and/or host names assigned to any `role` settings in `config/deploy.rb`.

Inaccessible Database Server

If you spell the database host name incorrectly, you will get an `Unknown MySQL server` error when running `cap migrate` (see below, where the host name is "localhosti" instead of "localhost").

```
$ cap migrate
  * executing task migrate
  * executing "cd /home/captain/apps/Intranet/current && rake RAILS_
```

```
ENV=production  db:migrate"
    servers: ["192.168.13.129"]
    [192.168.13.129] executing command
 ** [out :: 192.168.13.129] (in /home/captain/apps/Intranet/
releases/20070413171324)
 ** [out :: 192.168.13.129] rake aborted!
 ** [out :: 192.168.13.129] Unknown MySQL server host 'localhosti' (1)
 ** [out :: 192.168.13.129] (See full trace by running task with --trace)
    command finished
command "cd /home/captain/apps/Intranet/current && rake RAILS_
ENV=production  db:migrate" failed on 192.168.13.129
```

Fix the `host` property in `config/database.yml` to make this go away.

Dealing with the Inexplicable

When everything else fails, you may need to do some more significant debugging. In Chapter 6: *Errors in Production*, we covered some of the common errors and fixes. Other approaches:

1. Check the log files: `mongrel.log` and `production.log` should give you some clues; the MySQL log files might also help.

2. Run the application in the development environment on the production server. This should give you more immediate error reporting in the browser, which makes life easier when you are trying to unravel knotty problems.

3. Run the test suite on the production server. This is usually worth doing anyway, but can be particularly useful when trying to track down obscure errors.

Getting Back to a Clean Slate

If you get really stuck, the only thing left to do may be to completely wipe the application off the production server and start from scratch. With any luck, this shouldn't be necessary too often. Here are some instructions for completely rebuilding your application on the production server:

1. Log onto the production server.

2. Back up the production database using `mysqldump` (see *Back Up Rails* in Chapter 6).

3. Copy the `shared/system` directory somewhere safe.

4. Kill all the Mongrel processes on the server. To manually stop Mongrel, do:
   `$ mongrel_rails stop -P apps/Intranet/shared/pids/mongrel.pid`
   (passing the path to your Mongrel PID file as the `-P` option)

5. Check all the Mongrel processes are dead:

   `$ killall mongrel_rails`

6. Rewind the database back to version 0:

   `$ rake db:migrate VERSION=0`

7. Remove the directory containing all deployed versions of the application. (In the Acme case, this is the entire `Intranet` directory).

This puts you back to a clean slate. You can now go back to the development machine and run:

```
$ cap setup
$ cap cold_deploy
$ cap migrate
```

Once this finishes, the code and database are back to the latest version. You can now import the MySQL backup into the production database, and move the contents of `shared/system` back into the appropriate directory inside the deployed application.

Housekeeping

There are a few techniques that are rarely covered in the Rails printed literature, even though they are essential to keeping Rails applications in good working order. This section covers these bits and pieces.

Starting Mongrel Automatically

Currently, Mongrel has to be started and stopped manually from the development machine. If the production server is rebooted, someone will have to remember to restart the application too. A better solution is to add a start/stop script to the production server to run Mongrel automatically with the server.

First, create a *nix script to control the application in `script/mongrel_init`. Here's an example for Ubuntu:

```
#!/bin/bash
# Ubuntu Linux init script for Rails application
# set these variables to your production environment
APP_USER=captain
APP_NAME=Intranet
```

```
APP_PORT=4000
APP_HOME=/home/captain/apps/Intranet
# more variables - you don't need to set these
CURRENT=$APP_HOME/current
PID=$APP_HOME/shared/pids/mongrel.pid
MONGREL="sudo -u $APP_USER /usr/bin/mongrel_rails"
ENVIRONMENT=production
# load library functions
. /lib/lsb/init-functions
case "$1" in
  start)
    log_begin_msg "Starting Rails application $APP_NAME"
    $MONGREL start -c $CURRENT -e $ENVIRONMENT -p $APP_PORT -P $PID -d
    log_end_msg 0
    ;;
  stop)
    log_begin_msg "Stopping Rails application $APP_NAME"
    $MONGREL stop -P $PID
    log_end_msg 0
    ;;
  restart)
    log_begin_msg "Restarting Rails application $APP_NAME"
    $MONGREL restart -P $PID
    log_end_msg 0
    ;;
  *)
    echo "Usage: $0 {start|stop|restart}"
    exit 1
    ;;
esac
exit 0
```

You'll need to set the variables prefixed with APP_ in the above script to values appropriate to your production server.

This script is in a format that can be used by the *nix initialization (init) system to control Mongrel during server starts, stops, and reboots. For more about *nix init scripts, see http://www.linux.com/article.pl?sid=06/01/03/1728227.

Next, make the script executable:

```
$ chmod +x script/mongrel_init
```

This script can now be executed with a `start`, `stop`, or `restart` option, e.g.

```
$ ./mongrel_init start
```

```
$ ./mongrel_init stop
```

```
$ ./mongrel_init restart
```

Deploy the application to the server. Then, on the production server, copy the script from `script/mongrel_init` into the `/etc/init.d` directory:

```
$ sudo cp script/mongrel_init /etc/init.d/mongrel_intranet
```

Finally, you need to add the script to the initialization sequence for the production server. On Ubuntu Linux, you can do this with:

```
$ sudo update-rc.d mongrel_intranet defaults
```

Now Mongrel should start and stop with the server.

Clearing Out Stale Sessions

One other common task you need to perform is clearing out stale session files (i.e. sessions associated with clients who are no longer connecting to the application). Rails doesn't do this automatically for you. If you are using file system sessions (see the section *Cookies and Sessions in Rails* in Chapter 8) and have a busy site, the `RAILS_ROOT/tmp/sessions` directory for your application can rapidly fill up with session files as a result.

Rails provides a simple Rake task to clear out stale session files:

```
$ rake tmp:sessions:clear
```

This script just does a blanket clean-up of session files, regardless of whether they are still in use. However, it's simple enough to write a script that will clear out any session files in a time-sensitive fashion, which should leave behind those still being actively used. For example, here's one to clear sessions that were last accessed more than 6 hours ago, which you can add to `script/clear_sessions`:

```bash
#!/bin/bash
# Clear out stale sessions (last accessed more than 6 hours ago)
/usr/bin/find /home/captain/apps/Intranet/current/tmp/sessions \
-name "ruby_sess*" -amin +360 -exec rm {} \;
```

The session files for the application are all prefixed with `"ruby_sess"`. This script finds all of the files in the sessions directory (`RAILS_ROOT/tmp/sessions`), matching this file name pattern (the `-name` switch) that were last accessed (the `-amin` switch) more than 6 hours (360 minutes) ago (`+360`). Each matching file is passed to the `rm` command (via the `-exec` switch), which removes it.

Make the script executable:

```
$ chmod +x script/clear_sessions
```

Deploy the script to the production server. Make sure it is still executable once deployed.

To call the script on a schedule, set up a **cron job** to run every hour on the production server, using whatever cron tools you have available. You should do this as the captain user, who has permission to write into the sessions directory. For example:

```
$ su - captain
Password:
$ crontab -e
```

will open up captain's crontab for editing. Add this line:

```
0 * * * * /home/captain/apps/Intranet/current/script/clear_sessions
```

which schedules the clear_sessions.sh script to run at 0 minutes past every hour of every day. If things are working correctly, you should see entries like this in /var/log/syslog, indicating that the command ran:

```
May  9 00:00:41 demo-server /USR/SBIN/CRON[7079]: (captain) CMD (/
home/captain/apps/Intranet/current/script/clear_sessions)
```

If the script fails to run correctly, you'll get error messages sent to the standard Linux mail spool; for the captain user on Ubuntu, this goes to /var/mail/captain. An individual error email looks something like this:

```
From captain@demo-server Wed May 09 00:00:41 2007
...
From: root@demo-server (Cron Daemon)
To: captain@demo-server
Subject: Cron <captain@demo-server> /home/captain/apps/Intranet/
current/script/clear_sessions
...
Date: Wed, 09 May 2007 00:00:41 +0100
/bin/sh: /home/captain/apps/Intranet/current/script/clear_sessions:
Permission denied
```

Emailed errors can be useful in helping track down problems with a cron job. If you have an email server correctly configured for email, you could forward the output from cron jobs to an arbitrary administrator email address instead.

Keeping Log Files Manageable

The Rails log files are essential for tracking down issues with your application. However, after a few weeks or months of operation, those files start to get big. As well as taking up disk space, this can make them slow to open with a text editor for viewing.

The solution is to **rotate** the logs; that is, periodically rename the current log, and archive it, and open a fresh empty file for storing new log entries. Here's a sample Ruby script for doing this, which you could place in script/rotate_logs:

```ruby
#!/usr/bin/env ruby
# Rotate logs on production server; call via cron
LOG_ROOT = File.join(File.dirname(__FILE__), '../log')
suffix = Time.now.strftime('%Y-%m-%d')

['mongrel', 'production'].each do |log_for|
  log_file = File.join(LOG_ROOT, log_for + '.log')
  archived_log_file = log_file + '.' + suffix
  File.rename(log_file, archived_log_file)
  File.new(log_file, 'w')
end
```

This script takes the current mongrel.log and production.log script and renames them, appending the date in YYYY-MM-DD format to each filename as a new suffix. It then creates new empty log files, mongrel.log and production.log, which the application can continue logging into. Make sure you deploy the new script to the server (using cap deploy).

To run the script periodically, add it to the captain user's crontab (see the previous section for instructions on editing crontab). For example, adding this line to the crontab will run the script at seven minutes past midnight every day:

```
7 0 * * * /usr/bin/ruby \ /home/captain/apps/Intranet/current/script/
rotate_logs
```

A final nicety is to ensure that all the custom scripts we're adding are made executable when deployed to the production server. (I found myself doing this manually each time I deployed new scripts, as the correct permissions weren't being stored in the Subversion repository.) You can do this by adding a new Capistrano task to config/deploy.rb called make_scripts_executable, and then by including this script as part of the after_update_code task (see the earlier section *Centralizing File Uploads*):

```ruby
desc "Make all custom scripts (in script directory) executable"
task :make_scripts_executable, :roles => :app do
  run "chmod -R u+x #{release_path}/script"
```

```
end
task :after_update_code do
  symlink_for_file_uploads
  make_scripts_executable
end
```

Note that you could go even further than this, and add a handler to `cold_deploy` to create the cron jobs for you. That task is left as an exercise for you.

Reducing Log Detail

One other way of managing logs more effectively is to reduce the amount of detail they contain. Rails supports different so-called **log levels**. The best way to imagine these is as representing different levels of sensitivity; the lower the log level, the less sensitive the logging system is; the less sensitive it is, the less it reports on what the application is doing. The log levels available are:

- `:debug` (most sensitive)
- `:info`
- `:warn`
- `:error`
- `:fatal` (least sensitive)

The log level can be configured as per environment. The default log levels for each environment are as follows:

- **test**: log level = `:debug`
- **development**: log level = `:debug`
- **production**: log level = `:info`

I'd recommend leaving the log levels for test and development as they are, at their most sensitive. However, for production, you may find that you don't want such verbose logging (the `:info` log level includes details of every controller/action invocation, templates rendered, time for rendering etc., which can result in large log files very quickly).

To reduce the sensitivity of logging, edit `config/environments/production.rb` and set the `config.log_level` directive as follows:

```
config.log_level = :error
```

You'll need to restart Mongrel for the new log level to take effect.

Setting the log level to :error tells Rails to ignore warnings and only report on errors (serious and fatal). In turn, this reduces the amount of data written into the logs, which means they don't grow so rapidly. If you find that reducing logging in this way makes it hard for you to track down errors when they occur, you can always turn up the sensitivity again.

Optimizing a Rails Application

There comes a point in the life of most applications when the people using it complain about it. Sometimes this is down to the usability of the application's front end—buttons in the wrong place, tortuous workflow, bad color choices, small fonts, etc. This is largely down to interface design, an enormous topic outside the scope of this book.

Other times, an application may have a great interface but still be unusable. Often, this is because it's just too slow. In the case of Rails, this problem might arise sooner than you expect. The Ruby interpreters available at present (mid 2007) are quite slow themselves; coupled with that, all the clever meta-programming that makes Rails such a pleasure for developers turns it into a resource-hogging nightmare for system administrators.

Slowness is something you can deal with, requiring minimal artistry and resources. This section covers how to track down particular issues with your application, and what to do about them once you've found them. We'll be looking at several aspects of this:

1. Finding bottlenecks in the application
2. Using caching to increase performance
3. Scaling up the infrastructure to improve performance in general

Finding Bottlenecks

If users complain that a Rails application "feels slow", they might not give you much to work with. Some may give you more useful clues, like mentioning certain screens that render slowly, but end users are often unable to provide the kind of detailed information you need to make improvements. You need to be able to home right in on suspect lines of code. It may be that a mere handful of controllers, actions, helpers or methods are causing the problems, giving an overall impression of slowness. You need to know where those lines of code are.

The first step is to gather some solid usage data from the application logs, to use for further analysis. Rails logs are a rich seam of data waiting to be mined, including details of requests made and how long each response took. In addition, the response times are further decomposed into the time taken to run queries against the database and the time taken to render the response body (e.g. the HTML page). This is invaluable when hunting for the causes of problems.

> In the previous section, we discussed turning down the log sensitivity to reduce the size of log files. However, to get enough useful data to identify slow parts of the application, you will need to switch the log level to `:info` or `:debug`.

Here is an example from *Intranet*'s `production.log` running at `:info` logging level; the example below was produced by the `PeopleController`'s show action:

```
Processing PeopleController#show (for 127.0.0.1 at 2007-05-23
22:46:28) [GET]
  Session ID: 12ea4dfe55a2ba103cdb14587b702411
  Parameters: {"action"=>"show", "id"=>"4", "controller"=>"people"}
Rendering  within layouts/application
Rendering people/show
Completed in 0.04771 (20 reqs/sec) | Rendering: 0.01422 (29%) | DB:
0.03226 (67%) | 200 OK [http://localhost/people/show/4]
```

The last line (highlighted) is the one we're interested in. There are three figures here we can use for analysis:

1. The response was completed in 0.04771 seconds

2. The time spent on rendering was 0.01422 seconds (29%)

3. The time spent on database activities (DB) was 0.03226 seconds (67%)

While this is interesting, on its own it doesn't help identify which controller/action combinations are slowest. We need comparative data across all controller/action responses, and a decent mass of it, to produce meaningful statistics.

Mocking up data for analysis

The best logs for analysis are those from a version of the application running in production, after it's been in use for (at least) several days. This will give you the most realistic data to work with.

If you don't have this sort of data, you can use a tool like **Apache Bench** (ab), included with the Apache web server distribution, to create some mock data instead. Apache Bench enables you to run a mass of concurrent HTTP requests against a website, emulating access by web browsers. See `http://httpd.apache.org/docs/2.2/programs/ab.html` for details.

Alternatively, you could write your own spidering program to randomly visit pages on your site and recursively follow links from each page. This can be used to build a reasonable mass of data very quickly. A sample Ruby script that does this, `script/spider.rb`, is available from the book's Subversion repository. The script starts from the path `/people`, visiting that page 10-100 times; parses links out of each visited page, adding any URLs found to the queue of paths to visit; then visits each of those pages 10-100 times; and so on. Note that this doesn't send any "post" requests or log in as an adminstrator; but this capability could easily be added.

As the format of Rails logs is entirely predictable, it's straightforward to write a summarizer to analyze log file data. An example is available in the book's Subversion repository as `script/quick_logfile_analyzer.rb`. The script parses the log file, grouping requests by controller/action; it then averages out the requests and orders them, listing the controller/action pairs visited and the associated response times; the fastest-responding ones are at the top and the slowest ones at the bottom. Here's an example of the bottom of its output for some sample log data:

```
...

*****************************
PeopleController#show completed in an average time of 0.181 seconds
(5.5 requests per second)
(times based on 659 requests)
Rendering took on average 0.131 seconds (72%)
Database queries took on average 0.012 seconds (6%)
*****************************
TasksController#create completed in an average time of 0.198 seconds
(5.1 requests per second)
(times based on 1 request)
Rendering took on average 0.134 seconds (67%)
Database queries took on average 0.007 seconds (3%)
*****************************
CompaniesController#employees completed in an average time of 0.203
seconds (4.9 requests per second)
```

```
(times based on 10 requests)
Rendering took on average 0.058 seconds (28%)
Database queries took on average 0.024 seconds (11%)
******************************
AddressesController#index completed in an average time of 0.467
seconds (2.1 requests per second)
(times based on 8 requests)
Rendering took on average 0.136 seconds (29%)
Database queries took on average 0.011 seconds (2%)
*****************************
AddressesController#show completed in an average time of 1.044 seconds
(1.0 requests per second)
(times based on 2 requests)
Rendering took on average 0.365 seconds (34%)
Database queries took on average 0.005 seconds (0%)
*****************************
TasksController#update completed in an average time of 3.048 seconds
(0.3 requests per second)
(times based on 3 requests)
Rendering took on average 2.498 seconds (81%)
Database queries took on average 0.040 seconds (1%)
```

As you would expect, `update` and `create` actions are slowest: typically, SQL UPDATE and INSERT operations are slower in MySQL databases (as evidenced by the slower database query times for those actions in the log extract above). However, the slowest action that simply retrieves data is the `PeopleController`'s `show` action. This is to be expected, as this action potentially involves every table in the database, pulling in a `Person` object, an associated `Address` for that person, the `Company` they work for, a set of `Tasks` associated with that person, and `FileAttachment` objects attached to the tasks. If any action is going to be slow, it's likely to be this one.

> **Is it worth it?**
>
> Before you go any further, consider whether it's worth the effort to optimize your application. You now have some firm data from which to estimate the number of requests per second your application should be able to field. In our case, our slowest action has the capacity to handle approximately 25 requests per second. If your application is not likely to reach the estimated capacity, the effort of optimizing may not be worth it. Don't optimize for the sake of it; only do so if you really need to.

So, we now know which controller and action we might consider optimizing. However, we don't know why it's slow. At this point, we need to be able to see what's going on when we call the `PeopleController`'s `show` action, and identify which parts of the action are slow.

To get right inside actions, you can use Ruby's profiling mechanism to get a very low-level view of what's going on inside your application. This approach is covered in the next section.

If you can, cache

The biggest bottleneck in most Rails application is page rendering; as you can see from the sample data on the previous page, for our slowest retrieve action (`PeopleController#show`), rendering takes 76% of the total response time. Judicious use of caching can dramatically improve the performance of most Rails applications. If your application is slow, it may not even be necessary to go to the extent of profiling your actions: just use caching on the slowest controller/action pairs and you will frequently see a marked improvement. We'll take a look at caching shortly.

Controller Action Profiling Using around_filter

Ruby provides classes for profiling running code. These can be employed as a wrapper around controller actions to find out exactly what's going on when they're called. For example, you can manually run the profiler inside the Rails console (`script/console`) to watch method calls. Below is an example of using the console to profile the `Person.find` method:

```
$ script/console
Loading development environment.
>> require 'profile'
>> Profiler__.start_profile
>> Person.find 1
>> Profiler__.stop_profile
>> Profiler__.print_profile(STDOUT)
```

% time	cumulative seconds	self seconds	calls	self ms/call	total ms/call	name
10.66	0.13	0.13	1	130.00	160.00	Mysql::Result#each
10.66	0.26	0.13	52	2.50	6.54	RubyLex#getc
9.02	0.37	0.11	27	4.07	6.30	Module#module_eval
5.74	0.44	0.07	1846	0.04	0.04	String#==
3.28	0.48	0.04	34	1.18	3.24	Array#include?

. . .

I've taken out some of the return values for brevity. The start_profile and
stop_profile class methods are the key; they bracket the code to be profiled,
Person.find 1, and start/stop the profiling mechanism. The profile itself is printed
using the print_profile class method; in this case, it is printed to standard
output (STDOUT).

To put the profiling around an individual controller action directly inside Rails
(instead of manually, as above), we can apply an around_filter to the methods
we want to profile. We saw examples of before_filter and after_filter in the
section *Using Filters* in Chapter 5; around_filter can similarly be used to run some
code before an action (to start the profiler) and again after the action (to stop the
profiler and print its results). By creating a class and giving it a class method called
filter, we can specify that class itself as the filter. The filter method should
accept a controller and an action block as arguments; it should also call the action,
otherwise around_filter will just block it.

Following is an example filter class that does the job—starting the profiler, calling
the action, then stopping the profiler and writing the profile results into a file.
Add it inside the ApplicationController class definition (in app/controllers/
application.rb):

```
class ApplicationController < ActionController::Base
  # ... other methods ...

  if DEFINE_PROFILER
    # A class which can be used as an around_filter for a controller,
    # to profile actions on that controller; profiles get
    # written into the profile directory with the
    # filename '<controller>_<action>.txt'
    class ProfileFilter
      require 'profile'

      # Extend the ProfileFilter class with methods from the
      # Profiler__ class
      extend Profiler__

      # The filter class method must be implemented to
      # employ this class as a filter
      private
      def self.filter(controller, &action)
        start_profile
        action.call
        stop_profile
        profile_file_name = controller.controller_name.to_s + '_' \
          + controller.action_name.to_s + '.txt'
        out = File.open(
```

```
            File.join(RAILS_ROOT, 'profile', profile_file_name), 'w'
        )
        print_profile(out)
      end
    end
  end
end
```

Why is this class definition wrapped in an `if...end` statement? It turns out that just having the class defined inside the controller slows it down the immensely. By making definition of the class conditional, we can easily switch it off when not needed by setting `DEFINE_PROFILER` to `false`, which prevents the controller from being slowed down.

So where do we set the `DEFINE_PROFILER` variable? We can add it to the bottom of the `environment.rb` file to set it in every environment:

```
DEFINE_PROFILER = true
```

If we want to have a different setting for each environment, we could instead specify this for individual environments inside their configuration files (`config/environments/production.rb` etc.).

Next, create a directory for storing profiles called `profile`; each controller/action profile gets its own file in that directory.

An `around_filter` can now be applied to any controller you want to profile by amending the controller's class definition. You can also apply `:except` and `:only` options, as for other types of filter, e.g.:

```
class PeopleController < ApplicationController
  around_filter ProfileFilter, :only => [:show]
  # ... other methods ...
end
```

Note that this makes the application considerably slower; but it can help you identify which parts of an action are absorbing the most time. Here's a sample of the output (from `profile/people_show.txt`):

```
  %   cumulative   self              self    total
 time   seconds   seconds   calls  ms/call  ms/call  name
15.08     0.84      0.84       3   280.00   400.00  ERB::Compiler::ExplicitScanner#scan
 5.03     1.12      0.28     269     1.04    13.31  Array#each
 5.03     1.40      0.28       7    40.00    42.86  Kernel.sleep
 4.31     1.64      0.24     269     0.89     0.93  Object#method_added
 3.05     1.81      0.17      73     2.33     2.74  ActiveRecord::Base#connection
```

2.69	1.96	0.15	9	16.67	218.89	Dependencies.new_constants_in
2.33	2.09	0.13	24	5.42	6.25	ActiveRecord::Base#define_read_method
2.15	2.21	0.12	19	6.32	18.95	ActionController::Routing::
						RouteSet#generate
2.15	2.33	0.12	400	0.30	0.30	String#<<
1.97	2.44	0.11	432	0.25	0.25	Module#===
1.80	2.54	0.10	74	1.35	1.35	Array#include?
1.80	2.64	0.10	19	5.26	5.26	Mysql#query

. . .

Note that by far the slowest part of the action is the `ERB::Compiler::ExplicitScanner#scan` method, whose three calls take 15% of the total time of the action. This method is invoked during view rendering; looking back at the output from the simple log analyzer of the previous section, rendering accounts for 72% of the execution time for this action, on average; so calls to this method account for 15% of that. By contrast, database methods take 6% of the action's execution time.

To reiterate the tip from the end of the previous section: caching is likely to improve performance here, taking a bite out of that 72%. In most cases, it is more likely to improve your application's performance, and do so more simply, than any other optimization. But it's nice to have data from the profiler to back up this assertion.

 The example above uses the standard, slow built-in Ruby profiler, which makes testing lots of actions very time-consuming. If you need a faster profiler, take a look at **ruby-prof** (`http://rubyforge.org/projects/ruby-prof/`). It seemed a bit buggy when I used it with Rails, sometimes producing incomplete profiles, but you may have better luck with it.

Profiling Everything

If you want to profile everything, it is possible to run the whole Mongrel process, along with any actions carried out by the application, under the profiler. To do this, run the following from the command line (on *nix):

```
$ ruby -r profile script/server 2> profile/everything_profiled.txt
```

This loads the profiling library (`-r profile`), starts the server, and redirects any profiling output into the `profile/everything_profiled.txt` file. This produces a great deal of output, and is harder to decipher than the individual action profiles shown above. However, you can always search through the output for the actions you are interested in, and the extra detail may be useful on occasion.

The Rails Profiler

Rails contains its own profiler script, in `script/performance/profiler`. It can be used to test individual methods inside your application and help you identify what they are doing. I personally don't tend to use it very often, as I think it's more useful to profile controller actions (see previous section). The Rails profiler can't do that by default. But the built-in profiler can be useful where you have inexplicably slow methods and want to find out why.

To use the profiler, pass it a code fragment and a number of times to run that fragment, e.g.:

```
$ script/performance/profiler "Person.find :all" 10
```

You get standard Ruby profiler output, which you can then use to identify the slowest parts of the method call.

Improving Application Performance with Caching

As mentioned in the previous sections, using caching is the quickest and easiest way to improve the performance of a Rails application. Rails provides several types of caching, each of which provides speed benefits. However, they are not all equal in terms of speed benefit, and have different areas of application. The table below summarizes the types of caching available.

Type of caching	Speed	Description
Page	Fastest	Caches whole views for a particular route, storing each as a full HTML page*.
		Can only be used for pages where every client gets the same content; e.g. a public home page, which looks the same for every visitor.
		As the action isn't invoked (Rails delivers the HTML file directly), filters aren't activated, so it is not suitable for pages which require authentication or other use of filters.
		As the whole HTML page is cached, Apache can be used to serve the cached page directly if it is available.
Action	Second fastest	Caches individual controller actions as whole HTML pages, like page caching*.
		BUT the action and any filters still run, so it is possible to use authentication etc.
		Can only be used where an action produces the same output for all clients.

Type of caching	Speed	Description
Fragment	Slowest	Caches parts of views, e.g. a menu or a content area*.
		A fragment can be as small as a single paragraph, so this technique is very flexible and fine grained.
		Can be used to cache different content for different users.

* See notes on how cache elements are named, in the following section

How Cache Elements are Named

Caching stores cache elements (entire HTML pages or HTML fragments) under keys; the base key for a cached element is the path of the *visited* page minus the querystring. For example, these paths would each produce a different cache key:

- `people`
- `people/index` (even though it refers to the same page as `people`)
- `people/show/5`

While the following two paths would produce the same cache key:

- `people/index?page=1`
- `people/index?page=2`

The three different types of caching take the base cache key produced by the path and append other pieces of information to get the full location, as shown in the table below.

Type of caching	Cache key prefix [1]	Cache key suffix	Example cache key for path /people/show/5	Default location when caching to file_store on localhost:4000 [2]
Page	-	.html	people/show/5.html	public/people/show/5.html
Action	<host: port>/	.cache	localhost:4000/ people/show/5.cache	tmp/cache/localhost:4000/ people/show/5.cache
Fragment	<host: port>/	.cache	localhost:4000/ people/show/5.cache	tmp/cache/localhost:4000/ people/show/5.cache

1 Action and fragment caching uses the host name and port number as part of the cache key. This makes it possible for a single Rails application to be served under multiple domain names, while allowing each to have its own isolated cache.

The default cache store is `file_store`: the cache elements are kept on the local filesystem. The table shows where each type of cache element is kept when this cache store is used: page cache elements go into the `public` directory, while action and fragment cache elements go into `tmp/cache`. Other cache stores are available, as we'll see in the section *Advanced Scaling*, later this chapter.

If you need to change the location for cached page elements, set the following directive in `config/environment.rb`:

```
# Set page cache location to public/cached_pages
ActionController::Base.page_cache_directory = "public/cached_pages"
```

To change the location of the fragment (and action) cache, set this directive in `config/environment.rb`:

```
# Set fragment (and action) cache store type to :file_store
# and store cached fragments in tmp/fragments
ActionController::Base.fragment_cache_store = :file_store, "tmp/
fragments"
```

Deciding What to Cache

The first step when using caching is to decide which types of caching can be used in your application. The table in the previous section gave some idea of the situations where different types of caching are applicable; let's see whether any of them apply to *Intranet*:

- **Page caching**: This can only be used where every client visiting a given path gets the same view. If there are any differences based on the client's status, you can't use page caching effectively. In the case of *Intranet*, each page contains a link to the login page for anonymous users, or displays the user's username once they have logged in. This means that page caching isn't feasible.

- **Action caching**: Like page caching, action caching stores a whole page of HTML for each path. Unlike page caching, the action is still invoked by Rails, so authentication filters can run. This makes it possible to do something like show cached pages to anonymous users, but show the same pages dynamically when the user is logged in. However, this would be a slightly complicated solution, and one that is not worth pursuing in our context.

- **Fragment caching**: In the case of *Intranet*, this is the most flexible and useful of options. It can be used at several points in our code to cache parts of the page that remain stable between requests, while enabling us to retain the flexibility to show different views to different users.

Looking at the options available, it seems clear that fragment caching is best suited to our needs. We'll briefly look at page and action caching in the following sections, but concentrate on wringing most of our performance improvements out of fragment caching.

Caching vs. static HTML pages

If you have a page that changes once in a blue moon and that doesn't need to be generated by Rails, another option is available—create an HTML file and serve it direct from the web server, bypassing Rails entirely. Examples might be a terms and conditions page, an "about us" page, or contact information: all of these pages rarely change but are usually an essential part of a public web application.

If you are using Apache as a front-end for your Rails application, you can use conditional URL rewriting (available in Apache's `mod_rewrite` module) to serve static pages where they are available; this leaves any URLs that can't be mapped to files to be served dynamically by Rails instead. The section *Using Apache to Serve Static Assets* (later this chapter) covers how to use this technique to serve static files, such as JavaScripts and stylesheets, as well as cached pages and actions.

Preparing for Caching

Before you can start using caching, you need to enable it for the environment you're running under. By default, the production environment has caching enabled, but the development environment does not.

Set whether caching is on or off by editing the appropriate environment file (`config/environments/production.rb`, `config/environments/development.rb`) and setting this directive:

```
config.action_controller.perform_caching  = true
```

Page Caching

Page caching is very simple to implement. Inside a controller's class definition you simply specify the names of actions to which you want to apply page caching, e.g.

```
class PeopleController < ApplicationController
  caches_page :index, :show
  # ... other methods ...
end
```

With this in place, visiting /people will create an HTML file, public/people.html. If you look in the log file, you should see something like this:

```
Cached page: /people.html (0.00065)
```

This indicates that Rails has cached the page into a file called people.html; the path /people.html indicates that this file is stored inside the public directory. Note that Rails doesn't create a people directory, as there is only a forward slash at the start of the path, not anywhere within it. If we visited the path /people/index, Rails would actually create a new file in public/people/index.html, with the same content as public/people.html. Even though both paths point to the same controller and action, caching considers the two paths in isolation and creates one cached HTML file for each.

The next time the /people path is requested, Rails will deliver the public/people.html file and not run the index action at all. You won't even get an indication in the log file that this has happened as Rails isn't even invoked. Great! We're already saving time.

Similarly, if we visit the show action for a particular person (e.g. people/show/5), we'll get another HTML file in public/people/show/5.html, containing the cached HTML for that person's detail page. The next time we visit that same path, we'll see the cached page. As the person's ID is part of the path, each person's detail page gets its own element in the cache and its own HTML file in public/people/show.

However, it's not all roses. What happens if there are several pages of people to list using the index action? Recall that we created some pagination links at the bottom of the people#show view (in app/views/people/show.rhtml) to enable clicking through the list of people 10 at a time (see the section *Pagination* in Chapter 5). Each pagination link contains a page variable in the querystring, like this:

```
/people?page=2
```

The index action uses this to decide which page of results to show. However, if you click on these pagination links and the /people path has a cached element in public/people.html, each link just displays the first page of results that was cached. This is because caching ignores the querystring; so each page of results is treated as a request for /people and mapped onto the public/people.html cache element.

The solution is to include the page number as part of the path (which caching doesn't ignore) instead of as a querystring variable (which caching does ignore). In config/routes.rb, add a rule to do this, just above the default routing rule for controllers and actions (highlighted):

```
ActionController::Routing::Routes.draw do |map|
    # ... other routes ...
    # Enable caching of paginating index pages for PeopleController
    map.connect 'people/index/:page', :controller => 'people',
    :action => 'index'
    # Install the default route as the lowest priority.
    map.connect ':controller/:action/:id'
end
```

Now the pagination links have URLs like this:

```
people/index/2
```

Each page gets cached into `public/people/index/X.html`, where X is the page number (and value of the `page` parameter). This solves the problem. Anywhere where you want to cache a page that changes based on request parameters, those request parameters need to be part of the cache key; the simplest way to ensure this is to fold required parameters into the path using the routing configuration, as shown above.

While page caching is fast, once a cached element for a `controller#action` has been generated, Rails is no longer invoked when its path is requested. This means that even if a cached page required authentication the first time it was cached, once it exists in the cache it will be delivered to everyone, ignoring authentication. If you have pages that are the same for every logged in user that you want to cache, but still want to exclude unauthenticated users, you need to use **action caching** instead, as described in the next section.

 Keep in mind that the page caching above is for demonstration purposes only. The pages in *Intranet* change depending on the user, and whether they are logged in or not; page caching is not feasible in our case. If we used page caching, the first-cached version of a page might contain a logged-in user's username. This could then become the cached page that all subsequent users see, causing confusion when they apparently see themselves logged in under a different username.

Action Caching

Action caching caches entire HTML pages, like page caching; but cached elements are delivered via Rails, rather than directly from the cache. This means that you can still use filters for authentication (and other tasks). So if you have a page that you want only logged in users to see, and the page is the same for all of those users (e.g. a message of the day page), action caching is the answer.

The cache elements created by action caching are still keyed by path: this means that any querystring parameters that alter the page output need to be part of the path, as described for paging parameters in the previous section.

There are few places in *Intranet* where action caching is applicable. But for the purposes of explication, here's how to cache the `PeopleController`'s index and show actions, as hilighted in the following code:

```
class PeopleController < ApplicationController
  helper TasksHelper

  before_filter :authorize, :except => [:index, :search, :show]
  before_filter :get_person, :only => [:update, :delete]
  before_filter :all_addresses, :only => [:update, :create]

  caches_action :index, :show

  # ... other methods ...
end
```

The `caches_action` method in the class definition can be passed the names of one or more actions to cache. Note that this method should be called after any filter definitions to ensure that the filters are applied before caching is carried out.

The first visit to the path `/people` generates a cache file in `tmp/cache/localhost:4000/people.cache` (not in the `public` directory). (Note how the host name and port are part of the cache key.) You should see a line like this in the log:

```
Cached fragment: localhost:4000/people (0.00038)
```

Subsequent visits to the page receive the content of the cache file. However, unlike page caching, the log will record this, as Rails is invoked to retrieve the page from the cache:

```
Fragment read: localhost:4000/people (0.00023)
```

As both requests are logged, we can compare the before-caching and after-caching requests. In my case, here are the times for rendering the page on the first visit, before a cached action is available (16 requests per second):

```
Completed in 0.06197 (16 reqs/sec) | Rendering: 0.01825 (29%) | DB:
0.00812 (13%)
```

These are the times when the request is served from the cache (230 requests per second):

```
Completed in 0.00433 (230 reqs/sec) | DB: 0.00129 (29%)
```

In the second case, statistics for Rendering are absent; the templating engine isn't invoked as the HTML for the page is retrieved from the cache, not generated. Even taking into account the slight slow-down caused by writing into the cache during the first request, the request served from the cache is an order of magnitude faster.

> Again, action caching is not really suitable for *Intranet*, for the reasons described at the end of the section on page caching; each page is different for every user.
>
> However, this raises an interesting point; if we took the username out of the HTML for the page, we could cache pages for all users (e.g. /people, /people/show/X). In cases where you need to do page or action caching, but the page content prevents you from doing so, it might be worth making pages generic so they can be cached.

Fragment Caching

Fragment caching is the most useful caching option where you have an application with no generic pages (i.e. pages that stay the same for all users). However, even in these types of application, there will still be large parts of the page that *are* the same for all users; for example, a menu, a header, or footer may be entirely static. But these elements may still be generated using Rails; for example, the menu may be constructed using the link_to helper, as is the case with *Intranet*'s menu.

Caching static fragments can remove the load caused by calling helper methods continually. Rather than caching a whole page, we just cache part of a view and store the generated HTML fragment. This is done directly inside view templates, rather than inside the controller as is done for page and action caching. For example, here's how we might cache the menu in app/views/layouts/application.rhtml:

```
...
<body>
<% cache(:controller => 'menu') do -%>
<div id="menu">
<p>Menu</p>
<ul>
<li><%= link_to 'Companies', :controller => 'companies' %>
<ul>
<li><%= link_to 'Add a company', :controller => 'companies',
:action => 'create' %></li>
</ul>
</li>
<li><%= link_to 'People', :controller => 'people' %>
<ul>
```

```
<li><%= link_to 'Add a person', :controller => 'people',
:action => 'create' %></li>
</ul>
</li>
<li><%= link_to 'Addresses', :controller => 'addresses' %></li>
<li>
<% end -%>
...
</body>
</html>
```

The start of the HTML fragment to cache is marked with `<% cache(<options>)` `do -%>`, where `<options>` is a hash passed to Rails' `url_for` method. `<options>` is converted into a path (using the routing configuration) to generate the cache key for the fragment. Note that the path doesn't have to exist in this case; there is no `menu` controller, but we are still passing it as part of the path specification. The end of the fragment is marked with `<% end -%>`. The resulting fragment is stored in `tmp/cache/` `localhost:4000/menu.cache`.

Fragment caching can even be used to store different views for different users. For example, we could cache the login link or logged-in username by passing the username as a component of the cache key:

```
<%
# start caching
user = session[:user]
username = (user.nil? ? nil : user.username)
cache(:controller => 'login_panel', :username => username) do
-%>
<% if session[:logged_in] -%>
Logged in as <strong><%= session[:user].username %></strong>;
<%= link_to 'Logout', :controller => 'login', :action => 'logout' %>
<% else -%>
<%= link_to 'Login', :controller => 'login' %>
<% end -%>
</li>
</ul>
<% end # end caching -%>
```

Each logged in user now gets a personalised fragment in the cache store. For example, if the *admin* user is logged in, their menu is cached in `tmp/cache/` `localhost:4000/login_panel.username=admin.cache`. Users who aren't logged in get the version of the menu cached in `tmp/cache/localhost:4000/login_` `panel.cache` (note there's no `username` parameter in the filename).

Fragment Caching for Actions

The fragment cache can be used to store any generated HTML, including the entire output from the template for an action. Good candidates for this are templates for actions that display data; in our case, `show` and `index` actions on any controller.

As an example, we'll cache the output from the `show` action for `PeopleController`. To do this, edit the `app/views/people/show.rhtml` template, putting:

```
<% cache do -%>
```

above the first line and:

```
<% end -%>
```

as the very last line, wrapping all of the template's RHTML. As we've specified no options to the cache method call, the cache key for the fragment will be `localhost:4000/people/show/X`, where X is the ID of the person. Visit a person's detail page in your browser and check that the cache file is being generated (in `tmp/cache/localhost:4000/people/show/X.cache`). You can also check the log file for a line like this:

```
Cached fragment: localhost:4000/people/show/2 (0.00238)
```

On the next visit to the same page, the cached fragment is used instead of the HTML for the page being generated. To give a rough idea of the speed difference (in the production environment), consider the initial generation of the cached version, as follows:

```
Completed in 0.19671 (5 reqs/sec) | Rendering: 0.11522 (58%) | DB:
0.05368 (27%)
```

A subsequent request answered by reading from the cache, is recorded as follows:

```
Completed in 0.00615 (162 reqs/sec) | Rendering: 0.00288 (46%) | DB:
0.00255 (41%)
```

Much faster! However, one point to note is that, unlike page or action caching, fragment caching still runs the code inside the action. This means that for the `show` action, the database call to retrieve the person's record from the database still runs. This is despite the fact that we are not using the person's record to generate the HTML for the page any more, as it is being pulled from the cache. In the next section, we'll look at some techniques for avoiding these redundant database queries.

Avoiding Database Calls for Cached Fragments

Usually, an action will retrieve one or more records to service a request; for example, the show action in the PeopleController pulls in the person's record from the database (using the get_person method, triggered as a before_filter). When you cache a fragment for a controller, the action will carry on running these database actions, even though they may have become redundant. Once a fragment has been cached, Rails no longer needs the database retrieval to generate the fragment's HTML, as it is retrieved from the cache instead.

The usual technique is to skip the retrieval of the database record if a fragment for the page exists. In our case, we can edit the show method so that it only retrieves a person's record if there is no cached fragment for it. To check for the existence of a fragment, you can use the read_fragment method:

```
def show
  get_person unless read_fragment({})
  # NB NEXT LINE DOESN'T WORK PROPERLY ANY MORE - see text!
  @page_title = 'Person profile for ' + @person.full_name
end
```

Note that read_fragment is passed an empty hash ({}) as an argument. Here, if you do this, Rails uses the path of the current page as the key to search for in the fragment cache. read_fragment works in a similar way to the cache helper we saw in the previous section. You give it a set of options suitable for passing to url_for, and those options are used to generate the key for a cache element to read.

As we are now only calling get_person if a fragment doesn't exist, we can remove it from the PeopleController's before_filters:

```
before_filter :get_person, :only => [:update, :delete]
```

Here's what happens the first time a path like /person/show/5 is requested:

1. The show action is invoked.
2. As read_fragment returns nil (no cached element for person/show/5), get_person is called.
3. get_person sets the @person instance variable via a database query.

However, if the same path is requested again, the following happens:

```
You have a nil object when you didn't expect it!
The error occurred while evaluating nil.full_name
```

What's going on here? The problem is that this time round, the cache fragment does exist, so Rails doesn't perform the database query. This means that the `@person` instance variable is not set. Recall that the show action sets the `@page_title` by referencing the `@person` variable:

```
def show
  get_person unless read_fragment({})
  @page_title = 'Person profile for ' + @person.full_name
end
```

Now that there is no `@person` variable set, `@person` returns `nil`; so when the template tries to call `@person.full_name` (i.e. `nil.full_name`), we get the error message.

To work around this, we need to be able to cache some content for the `@page_title` variable when we first cache the `show` action, then check for a cached title when we run the `show` action, instead of assuming `@person` has been set.

We can work round this by employing the full power of the Rails caching mechanism. When the `show` action is invoked, we check for a page title fragment in the cache; if it's there, we retrieve it and set the `@page_title` instance variable; if not, we generate it from the `@person` object then store it in the cache. Here's the rewritten `show` action that implements this behavior:

```
def show
  get_person unless read_fragment({})
  title_cache_key = fragment_cache_key({}) + '.title'
  @page_title = read_fragment(title_cache_key)
  unless @page_title
    @page_title = 'Person profile for ' + @person.full_name
    write_fragment(title_cache_key, @page_title)
  end
end
```

The highlighted lines include a couple of calls to Rails methods we've not seen before:

- `fragment_cache_key` generates a key for an element in the fragment cache. In the case of the title, we use the cache key for the path plus a suffix `".title"`. This means that the title for the page `/people/show/5` will get the cache key `people/show/5.title`; and when using a filesystem cache (as we are here) will end up in the file `RAILS_ROOT/tmp/cache/people/show/5.title.cache`. You can use this to generate your own custom cache keys for any type of fragment you like.

- `write_fragment(title_cache_key, @page_title)` writes the `@page_title` instance variable into the cache, under the generated key.

As we're likely to need to do this kind of custom caching in several places, it is useful to make this into a generic method available to all controllers by adding it to the `ApplicationController` class:

```
class ApplicationController < ActionController::Base
  # ... other methods ...

  # Store a fragment in the cache; "." + fragment_suffix is
  # appended to the standard cache key for this
  # controller/action; if a fragment with this key exists,
  # return it; if not, call the block &generator to create
  # the value, store it in the cache, and return it
  private
  def handle_text_fragment(fragment_suffix, &generator)
    text_fragment_name = fragment_cache_key({}) + "." +
                         fragment_suffix
    value = read_fragment(text_fragment_name)
    unless value
      begin
        value = generator.call
        write_fragment(text_fragment_name, value)
      rescue
        value = ''
      end
    end
    return value
  end
end
```

To use this to set the `@page_title` variable in the `show` action:

```
def show
  get_person unless read_fragment({})
  fragment = handle_text_fragment("title") { @person.full_name }
  @page_title = "Profile for " + fragment
end
```

What we're doing here is calling `handle_text_fragment` with `title` as the suffix for the fragment cache key; this means the method will work with a cache fragment called `people/show/X.title` (where `X` is the ID of the person to show). If the fragment exists, the `fragment` variable is set to its value; if not, the block { `@person.full_name` } is executed to generate the value instead, and that value stored in the cache. Finally, `@page_title` is constructed from the string `"Profile for "` with whatever `handle_text_fragment` returned appended to it.

This means that we can now remove the database query altogether, as both the person's details and the page title are cached in step with each other. This produces phenomenal speedups. Before caching:

```
Completed in 0.12266 (8 reqs/sec) | Rendering: 0.03310 (26%) |
DB: 0.08563 (69%) | 200 OK [http://localhost/people/show/4]
```

When the same page is rendered from the cache:

```
Completed in 0.00718 (139 reqs/sec) | Rendering: 0.00537 (74%) | DB:
0.00000 (0%) | 200 OK [http://localhost/people/show/4]
```

From 8 requests per second to 139! Also note that there are now no database queries (DB: 0.00000 (0%) in the log entry).

The only downside to this approach is that the fragment for the page content and its title have to stay in sync. If the page title fragment is deleted but the page content fragment remains, Rails will always try to run the generator block to create the new fragment; but as the database fetch is being skipped, the generator block has no @person variable to work with, and returns the empty string (that's why the begin...rescue block is there: to capture situations where the block code causes an error). However, this is a small price to pay for the performance benefits gained.

Clearing out the Cache

Up until now we've happily been caching the output of what were previously dynamic pages. However, we've done nothing to ensure that the cache doesn't become **stale** (i.e. displaying data that is no longer correct or may not even exist any more). What if a person's record is updated? At the moment, the application knows nothing about this and the show action continues to deliver stale data from the cache.

What we need is a way of **expiring** elements in the cache when data changes. For example, if a person's record is updated, we will need the cached show page to expire for that person; similarly, if we cache the index page (which lists all people on the system) we need to expire it if new people are added, to keep the list up to date.

It is possible to manually expire the cache using one of the Rails built-in Rake tasks:

```
$ rake tmp:cache:clear
```

This can be useful if you have generated pages that very rarely change and don't rely on the database; in the case of *Intranet*, the menu may occasionally change, but any changes aren't connected to database actions and are difficult to detect. In this case, the easiest thing is to clear the cache when you make a change to the RHTML file containing the menu (app/views/layouts/application.rhtml).

But this technique is laborious where you have cached pages that should expire when data in the database changes. A better technique here is to automatically detect changes in the database and expire the cached fragments associated with those changes.

Rails provides a special `ActionController::Caching::Sweeper` class for exactly this purpose. Create a new file in `app/controllers/people_sweeper.rb` with this content:

```
class PeopleSweeper < ActionController::Caching::Sweeper
  observe Person

  def after_update(record)
    clear_people_fragments(record)
  end

  def after_destroy(record)
    clear_people_fragments(record)
  end

  def clear_people_fragments(record)
    key = fragment_cache_key(:controller => 'people',
    :action => 'show', :id => record.id)
    expire_fragment(key)
    expire_fragment(key + ".title")
  end
end
```

A sweeper is a combination filter (which runs some code before or after a controller action is invoked) and observer (which watches the database for changes). Inside it, you define callback handlers that respond to actions on the observed models. In this case, `observe Person` specifies that the sweeper will only respond to changes to the `Person` model. When the sweeper responds to a database change, its callback handlers (`before_*`, `after_*`) can then be used to expire cache elements. Here, we're expiring the cached view for the `show` action.

A sweeper is activated by attaching it to a controller, as follows (highlighted):

```
class PeopleController < ApplicationController
  helper TasksHelper

  before_filter :authorize, :except => [:index, :search, :show]
  before_filter :get_person, :only => [:show, :update, :delete]
  before_filter :all_addresses, :only => [:update, :create]

  cache_sweeper :people_sweeper, :only => [:update, :delete]

  # ... other methods ...
end
```

When the `update` or `delete` actions are invoked on the `PeopleController`, the appropriate sweeper handler (one of its `after_*` methods) is called, with the modified `record` (`Person` instance) being passed in as an argument. Each of these methods in turn calls `clear_people_fragments`, which expires the appropriate fragments from the cache using the `expire_fragment` method.

Note that if we were caching the output of the `people/index` page, the sweeper should expire its associated cache elements when `update` or `delete` actions occur. Also note that there are additional `expire_page` and `expire_action` methods available to the sweeper if you are using page or action caching.

Optimizing How Rails Uses the Database

One other easy optimization you can perform is to reduce the load Rails puts on the database. By default, ActiveRecord is quite wasteful of resources. To demonstrate, consider the case where we have a person with associated address, company, and three tasks. If you call the `PeopleController`'s show action for this person (with an ID of 1), the following four SQL queries are executed (along with a few others – see the logs):

1. Load details from the people table: `SELECT * FROM people WHERE (people.'id' = 1)`
2. Load the person's associated company: `SELECT * FROM companies WHERE (companies.'id' = 1)`
3. Load the person's associated address details: `SELECT * FROM addresses WHERE (addresses.'id' = 1)`
4. Load the person's tasks: `SELECT * FROM tasks WHERE (tasks.person_id = 1) ORDER BY complete ASC, start DESC`

This issue is sometimes termed the **1+N query problem** (`http://www.infoq.com/articles/Rails-Performance`). When Rails retrieves an object (like a person) that has an association to other objects (like companies, addresses, and tasks), it runs one query for the person, plus another query to retrieve the data for each association (N more queries).

The reason this is wasteful is that a knowledgeable SQL programmer would be able to convert this into a single **left outer join** query (a.k.a. a **left join**), pulling the required data from the four tables in one pass. The `companies`, `addresses`, and `tasks` tables have associations with the `people` table, so our programmer could construct this single query to pull all the data out via shared keys:

```
SELECT * FROM people
LEFT OUTER JOIN companies ON people.company_id = companies.id
LEFT OUTER JOIN addresses ON people.address_id = addresses.id
LEFT OUTER JOIN tasks ON people.id = tasks.person_id
```

If you've done any PHP programming with SQL, you are probably familiar with this syntax. This statement retrieves data from all four tables, joining the rows in the different tables together using the shared keys. The downside to this approach is that it returns one row for each task, along with copies of the person, company, and address records resulting in each task carrying several fields of redundant data. In a traditional language, it would be the programmer's job to loop through the rows, ignoring the repeated data and picking out the individual tasks.

Fortunately, Rails provides functionality to avoid both the multiple queries and the pain of manually sifting the redundant data. ActiveRecord enables **eager loading of associations**, which, like an expert SQL programmer, performs the necessary left join operations to load all the data in one pass. As a bonus, it also manages the result set and converts it into objects without the programmer having to do any work.

It's very simple to implement, too. In our case, we can change the `PeopleController` to load the person plus their company, address, and tasks in one pass. We'll do this by editing the private `get_person` method in the `PeopleController`, which loads a person's record for subsequent display or editing:

```
class PeopleController < ApplicationController
  # ... other methods ...
  private
  def get_person
    @person = Person.find(params[:id],
      :include => [:company, :address, :tasks])
  end
end
```

The important part of this is the new `:include` option, which is passed to `find` (highlighted). This tells ActiveRecord to create an SQL statement that includes left joins to the three associated tables. Note that you can do this from either side of an association; in our case, we're joining from the person through two `belongs_to` associations (to address and company) and a `has_many` association (to tasks).

If you run the `show` action for the person again, you shouldn't notice any difference in the browser (though see the next section for one caveat). But if you look in the logs, you'll see that the four separate queries we saw earlier have gone, to be replaced by one looking like this:

```
Person Load Including Associations (0.035309)  SELECT people.'id' AS
t0_r0, people.'title' AS t0_r1, people.'first_name' AS t0_r2,
...
addresses.'id' AS t2_r0, addresses.'street_1' AS t2_r1,
...
```

```
tasks.'id' AS t3_r0, tasks.'title' AS t3_r1, tasks.'description' AS
t3_r2,
...
FROM people LEFT OUTER JOIN companies ON companies.id = people.
company_id LEFT OUTER JOIN addresses ON addresses.id = people.
address_id LEFT OUTER JOIN tasks ON tasks.person_id = people.id WHERE
(people.'id' = 1)
```

We've taken a lot of the detail out to keep things brief, but you can hopefully see that Rails has constructed a left join SQL query similar to the one we hand-crafted earlier. This single query was run instead of four separate ones. The fact that the show action (when run via a browser) still renders the page correctly also shows that Rails has intelligently dissected the data into a Person instance and its associated objects (an Address, a Company, and one or more Task instances). Bear in mind, though, that although the number of queries has been reduced, construction of objects from the SQL result sets still has to be performed.

Ordering for Eager Loading

There is one small caveat to mention for eager loading. Note that the left join statement constructed by Rails doesn't order the results in any way. But remember that we specified ordering when we associated the person model with the task model:

```
has_many :tasks, :order => 'complete ASC, start DESC',
:dependent => :nullify
```

In our original version of the show action, the tasks shown are ordered, due to the ordering specified for the association. By contrast, when using eager loading, ordering on associations is ignored, so the tasks come out in ID order. The result is that the show action using eager loading has a different task order from our original show action. If you want to retain ordering for tasks (as we do), you need to attach an :order option to the find method call, e.g.

```
class PeopleController < ApplicationController
  # ... other methods ...
  private
  def get_person
    @person = Person.find(params[:id],
      :include => [:company, :address, :tasks],
      :order => 'tasks.complete ASC, tasks.start DESC')
  end
end
```

Tasks are now displayed in the same order as they were before we implemented eager loading.

> **Other Optimizations**
>
> Using caching is the most important optimization you can make, and can yield instant results. Trimming the number of database queries using eager loading can also help.
>
> However, the bottleneck may sometimes be in other parts of your application: perhaps a slow connection to a web service you are querying, a lag caused by parsing complex XML files, or a query to an enormous database table. The techniques covered earlier in this chapter should go some way to helping you find those bottlenecks. But as they can be fairly application specific, we have decided not to cover the gamut of possible solutions here.

Scaling Your Rails Infrastructure

In Chapter 6, we saw how to put a whole Rails application running on Mongrel behind Apache, so that any requests to the virtual host `http://intranet.company.local/` are proxied through to the Mongrel instance on port 4000 (via `mod_proxy`). This made it simple to present a Rails application via a user-friendly URL and without a port number.

In the remainder of this chapter, we'll extend this basic configuration to make the application perform more efficiently by applying the following techniques:

- **Setting up Apache to serve static assets**: This technique reduces the load on Mongrel, leaving it to concentrate on running Rails (what it's good at), and letting Apache serve static files like images, JavaScripts, and HTML (what Apache is good at).

- **Using Apache to load balance onto a Mongrel cluster**: Instead of using a single Mongrel instance to run the application, we can assemble a "pack" of Mongrels to handle the load. Apache sits in front of the pack, distributing requests evenly between the Mongrel instances.

- **Advanced techniques for scaling**: Going beyond a single machine, we'll discuss the de facto standard techniques for scaling a Rails application across multiple physical machines.

FastCGI

In the bad old days, the main approach for deploying Rails applications was FastCGI. These days, this approach is largely deprecated in fresh production environments in favor of Mongrel. However, you may still find that FastCGI is the only option offered by your shared hosting company; most hosting companies offering Rails hosting use the FastCGI approach.

If you have the option, go for Mongrel; if you are forced to use FastCGI, good luck! I have always found it flaky and resource-intensive, and won't be covering it here.

Using Apache to Serve Static Assets

The first performance improvement we can make to our infrastructure is to enable Apache to serve static files for our application (i.e. images, JavaScripts, and cached pages). In Chapter 6, we created a basic setup for putting a Mongrel instance behind Apache running `mod_proxy`; in this section, we will amend this basic setup, adding some rewrite rules to serve static files through Apache, bypassing Mongrel altogether.

The resulting configuration will look like this:

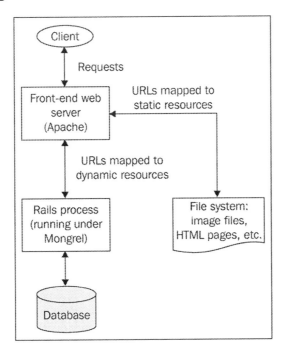

Any resources that exist on the filesystem are served directly by Apache; any remaining URLs are proxied through to the application running as a Mongrel instance.

Tweaking Our Basic mod_proxy Configuration

Our basic setup in Chapter 6 didn't deal with the shared directories we're now using with Capistrano; our application is in the captain's home directory (/home/captain/apps/Intranet), but Apache's log files are still going into their default location. The first thing we can do is edit httpd.conf to log the virtual host into /home/captain/apps/Intranet/shared/log. Then we'll tell Apache that the DocumentRoot for this virtual host is in the current/public directory; that way, we can configure Apache to serve static files directly from there and bypass Rails. Here is the amended VirtualHost entry for intranet.company.local:

```
<VirtualHost *:80>
  ServerName intranet.company.local
  ServerAlias www.intranet.company.local

  # Put the Apache logs in the shared Capistrano log directory
  ErrorLog /home/captain/apps/Intranet/shared/log/intranet-error.log
  CustomLog /home/captain/apps/Intranet/shared/log/intranet-access.log
common

  # Point the DocumentRoot into the current public directory
  DocumentRoot /home/captain/apps/Intranet/current/public

  # Proxy all requests through to Mongrel
  ProxyPass / http://127.0.0.1:4000/
  ProxyPassReverse / http://127.0.0.1:4000/
  ProxyPreserveHost On
  ProxyRequests Off
</VirtualHost>
```

Reload Apache to make the changes take, e.g. if you followed the Linux installation instructions in Chapter 6 you can do:

```
$ /etc/init.d/apache2.2 graceful
```

At the moment, Apache isn't doing anything other than proxying all requests, so the *Intranet* logs won't contain any hint that we've moved the Apache log files. In the next section, we'll get Apache to serve static files, which will add some entries to the logs.

Adding Rewrite Rules to Serve Static Files

To get Apache to serve static files, we first need to make some changes to the permissions on the directory where those files exist. We can do this using a standard `<Directory>` directive for the `public` directory of our Rails application in `httpd.conf`:

```
<Directory /home/captain/apps/Intranet/current/public>
  AllowOverride none
  Options FollowSymLinks
  Order allow,deny
  Allow from all
</Directory>
```

Next, we modify the `<VirtualHost>` entry, adding some directives which invoke the powerful features of Apache's `mod_rewrite` module (which we enabled while installing Apache in Chapter 6). The `mod_rewrite` module can be configured to change incoming request URLs into different ones, based on the conditions specified. Here's what the rewrite rules look like (highlighted):

```
<VirtualHost *:80>
  ServerName intranet.company.local
  ServerAlias www.intranet.company.local

  # Put the Apache logs in the shared Capistrano log directory
  ErrorLog /home/captain/apps/Intranet/shared/log/intranet-error.log
  CustomLog /home/captain/apps/Intranet/shared/log/intranet-access.log common

  # Point the DocumentRoot into the current public directory
  DocumentRoot /home/captain/apps/Intranet/current/public

  # Turn on the rewrite engine
  RewriteEngine on

  # Useful for debugging rewriting
  RewriteLog /home/captain/apps/Intranet/shared/log/intranet-rewrite.log
  RewriteLogLevel 9

  # 1. If you're using page or action caching,
  # this directive will serve cached files direct from Apache
  RewriteRule ^([^.]+)$ $1.html [QSA]

  # 2. Check whether there is a file matching the request path
  RewriteCond %{DOCUMENT_ROOT}%{REQUEST_FILENAME} !-f

  # 3. Only triggered if no matching file found; proxy through
  # to Mongrel
  RewriteRule ^/(.*)$ http://127.0.0.1:4000%{REQUEST_URI} [P,QSA,L]
</VirtualHost>
```

Note the use of `RewriteEngine on`, which makes `mod_rewrite` available for this virtual host; and a couple of directives to turn on verbose rewrite engine debugging, logged into a new log file (`intranet-rewrite.log`) alongside the Apache and Rails logs.

More complex are the `RewriteCond` and `RewriteRule` directives. Below, each of the numbered highlighted sections in the code is explained in more detail:

1. The first `RewriteRule` directive specifies that any request URLs matching the regular expression `^([^.]+)$` (i.e. any that don't contain a period character) are transformed using the substitution `$1.html`. In effect, this turns every request URL without a period character into a request for the same URL with `.html` appended. The odd-looking `[QSA]` flag states that any querystring attached to the original request URL should then be appended to the new `.html` URL too. (`QSA` stands for "Query String Attach".)

   For example, if the original request was for:

   `http://intranet.company.local/people/search?term=angela`

   This would get rewritten by this rule to:

   `http://intranet.company.local/people/search.html?term=angela`

   (Note the extra `.html`.)

2. The `RewriteCond` directive specifies that any `RewriteRule` directives that follow it should only be applied if there is no file at the location `%{DOCUMENT_ROOT}%{REQUEST_FILENAME}`. (`-f` is the mechanism for telling `mod_rewrite` to test for the existence of a file; `!-f` only returns true if the specified file doesn't exist).

   `%{DOCUMENT_ROOT}` returns the absolute path to the document root for the host: in this case, `/home/captain/apps/Intranet/current/public`.

   `%{REQUEST_FILENAME}` returns the path part of the URL, minus the querystring.

   When does this `RewriteCond` return true and trigger rewriting by the subsequent rules? As an example, take this URL: `http://intranet.company.local/people/search.html?term=angela`.

   Here, the `%{REQUEST_FILENAME}` variable contains: `/people/search.html`.

   So the `RewriteCond` only returns true if there is a file at the path: `/home/captain/apps/Intranet/current/public/people/search.html`.

3. The final `RewriteRule`, only triggered if there is no static file that can serve the request (see bullet point 2), proxies any remaining requests through to the Mongrel instance in the background. The [P, QSA, L] flags cause Apache to proxy the request (P), attach the querystring (QSA) and stop processing rewrite rules if this one is matched (L). (Note that using `mod_rewrite` enables us to remove the `mod_proxy` directives we used previously.)

To see this in action, we'll return to the request for the URL:
`http://intranet.company.local/people/search?term=angela`

This URL has the `REQUEST_URI`: `/people/search` and querystring:
`term=angela`

The rewrite rule would convert this URL to: `http://127.0.0.1:4000/people/search?term=angela`, which would be served by the Mongrel instance running on `localhost`, port 4000.

In the next section, we'll set up a load-balanced cluster of Mongrels and use rewrite rules to proxy dynamic requests to the cluster instead of to a single Mongrel instance.

Remember to reload Apache once you've edited the `httpd.conf` file:

```
$ /etc/init.d/apache2.2 graceful
```

Once we've set this up, how do we know it's working? That's what the rewrite log file, `intranet-rewrite.log`, is for.

For URLs proxied through to Mongrel you should see entries like this in the rewrite log:

```
192.168.13.1 - - [11/Jun/2007:17:08:16 +0100] [intranet.company.local/
sid#8126278] [rid#8185fe8/initial] (2) forcing proxy-throughput with
http://127.0.0.1:4000/companies
192.168.13.1 - - [11/Jun/2007:17:08:16 +0100] [intranet.company.local/
sid#8126278] [rid#8185fe8/initial] (1) go-ahead with proxy request
proxy:http://127.0.0.1:4000/companies [OK]
```

For static files in the public directory, served directly by Apache without rewriting, you should see entries like this in the rewrite log:

```
192.168.13.1 - - [11/Jun/2007:17:08:16 +0100]
[intranet.company.local/sid#8126278] [rid#818a668/initial]
(1) pass through /stylesheets/base.css
```

For cached pages and actions, where the URL is rewritten to one with `.html` on the end, you should see log entries like this in the rewrite log:

```
192.168.13.1 - - [11/Jun/2007:17:15:42 +0100] [intranet.company.local/
sid#8126278][rid#8185fe8/initial] (1) go-ahead with /home/captain/
apps/Intranet/current/public/people.html [OK]
```

 Once you are happy that your rewrite rules are working correctly, comment out the lines that enable rewrite logging in the `httpd.conf` file.

Proxying to a Mongrel Cluster

In the previous section, we saw how to serve static files from Apache while proxying requests for dynamic content through to a single Mongrel instance. In this section, we'll see how to scale this architecture by employing several Mongrel instances as the target for Apache to proxy dynamic requests onto.

The resulting configuration will look like this:

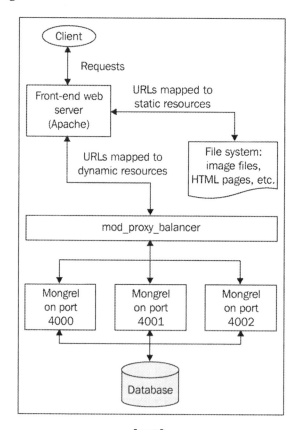

In our configuration, we'll use three Mongrel instances, running on ports 4000, 4001 and 4002, to serve dynamic requests. Three instances is a good figure to start out with when creating a Mongrel cluster, as it provides a decent amount of redundancy (you can lose two instances and the application will keep running) and performance (for example, this will help prevent the application from grinding to a halt during large file uploads).

> The setup we'll discuss here will still be serving data from a single database, files off a single file system, and session data from a single session store, all located on one server. Where you need to introduce multiple physical machines and possibly multiple domains, you'll need to think about using a distributed session store and/or database cluster. The section *Advanced Scaling* later in this chapter covers these techniques in overview.

There are two steps involved in setting up this arrangment:

1. Setting up the Mongrel cluster
2. Configuring Apache to proxy dynamic requests to the cluster (rather than the current arrangement, where requests go to a single Mongrel instance).

We'll cover each step in the following sections.

Setting up the Mongrel Cluster

The `mongrel_cluster` gem provides commands for configuring a cluster of Mongrel instances (see the section *Mongrel: a Better Way to Run Rails Applications* in Chapter 3). We'll use this to set up our cluster on the production server. Run this command to create a configuration file for our cluster:

```
$ mongrel_rails cluster::configure -e production -p 4000 -N 3 \
-c /home/captain/apps/Intranet/current/ -a 127.0.0.1 \
-C /home/captain/apps/Intranet/shared/system/intranet_cluster.yml \
-P /home/captain/apps/Intranet/shared/pids/mongrel.pid \
--user captain --group captain
```

The flags set the following elements of the configuration:

- `-e` = environment to run each instance under.
- `-p` = port number of the first Mongrel.
- `-N` = number of Mongrel instances to start in the cluster; the ports for the instances start from the one set using the `-p` flag, with the port number being incremented by 1 for each subsequent instance; in our case, we'll end up with instances on ports 4000, 4001, and 4002.

- -c = RAILS_ROOT directory of the application to serve.
- -a = run the instances only on the IP address specified; here we're restricting the Mongrel instances to only respond to requests originating on the same machine (localhost).
- -C = location of the generated configuration file.
- -P = where to put the pid file for the cluster; each instance gets its own pid at this location, with the port number inserted before the suffix; in our case, we'll get the PID files mongrel.4000.pid, mongrel.4001.pid and mongrel.4002.pid.
- --user = user to run the Mongrel instances as; note we've set it to the captain user.
- --group = group to run the Mongrel instances as.

Here's what the resulting configuration file (/home/captain/apps/Intranet/shared/system/intranet_cluster.yml) looks like:

```
user: captain
cwd: /home/captain/apps/Intranet/current/
port: "4000"
environment: production
group: captain
address: 127.0.0.1
pid_file: /home/captain/apps/Intranet/shared/pids/mongrel.pid
servers: 3
```

> You may also want this file in the Subversion repository (e.g. in the config directory) so it can be included the first time the application is deployed to a clean server.

Next, we need to add a script to the system that will start our cluster. Before we do this, though, we'll stop our existing Mongrel instance:

```
$ sudo /etc/init.d/mongrel_intranet stop
```

We can now edit our /etc/init.d/mongrel_intranet script to start the cluster, rather than an individual Mongrel instance:

```
#!/bin/bash
# Ubuntu Linux init script for Rails application in cluster

# set these variables to your production environment
CONF=/home/captain/apps/Intranet/shared/system/intranet_cluster.yml
APP_NAME="Intranet"

# more variables - you shouldn't need to change this
```

```
MONGREL="/usr/bin/mongrel_rails"
# load library functions
. /lib/lsb/init-functions
case "$1" in
  start)
    log_begin_msg "Starting Mongrel cluster: $APP_NAME"
    $MONGREL cluster::start -C $CONF
    log_end_msg 0
    ;;
  stop)
    log_begin_msg "Stopping Mongrel cluster: $APP_NAME"
    $MONGREL cluster::stop -C $CONF
    log_end_msg 0
    ;;
  restart)
    log_begin_msg "Restarting Mongrel cluster: $APP_NAME"
    $MONGREL cluster::restart -C $CONF
    log_end_msg 0
    ;;
  *)
    echo "Usage: $0 {start|stop|restart}"
    exit 1
    ;;
esac
exit 0
```

To start the cluster manually, do:

```
$ sudo /etc/init.d/mongrel_intranet start
```

You can also use `stop` and `restart` to control the cluster as a single entity.

Test the cluster by browsing to `http://localhost:4000/`, `http://localhost:4001/` and `http://localhost:4002/`. You should see the same Rails application at each location. Note that you won't be able to see these servers from any machine other than the one they're running on (i.e. on `localhost`), as we specified they should only serve on the `localhost` IP address.

We'll also need to use this new script inside our Capistrano recipe to start/stop/restart the cluster when we deploy a new version of the application (replacing our previous versions of these tasks in `config/deploy.rb`):

```
# Cluster config file location
cluster_config = "#{shared_path}/system/intranet_cluster.yml"
desc "Override the spinner task with one which starts Mongrel"
```

```
task :spinner, :roles => :app do
  run <<-CMD
    sudo mongrel_rails cluster::start -C #{cluster_config}
  CMD
end
desc "Alias for spinner"
task :start do
  spinner
end
desc "Override the restart task with one which restarts Mongrel"
task :restart, :roles => :app do
  run "sudo mongrel_rails cluster::restart -C #{cluster_config}"
end
desc "Stop Mongrel"
task :stop, :roles => :app do
  run "sudo mongrel_rails cluster::stop -C #{cluster_config}"
end
```

 Note how we had to use `sudo` in each of these commands so that the Mongrel instances are able to be run as the `captain` user and group.

The next section covers how to load-balance from Apache onto our new Mongrel cluster.

Load Balancing from Apache to the Mongrel Cluster

The `mod_proxy_balancer` module in Apache enables you to set up several **workers** (servers that received proxied requests from the load balancer) and distribute requests to a single virtual host across them. In our case, this means that each Mongrel is a worker, which gets a share of the requests coming into `http://intranet.company.local/` dished out to it; any requests for static files are still served directly by Apache, without touching the cluster. `mod_proxy_balancer` does its best to ensure that the load on each of the servers is evenly balanced; you have a choice of whether load is determined using the number of requests served, or the number of bytes. We'll use the number of requests (the default) and configure Apache to evenly distribute load across the cluster.

 Note that you must have Apache 2.2 installed to use `mod_proxy_balancer`. Earlier versions of Apache do not have support for this module.

The first step in configuring the proxying through to a cluster is to tell Apache where the workers are. This is done in the `httpd.conf` file as follows:

```
<Proxy balancer://intranet_cluster>
  BalancerMember http://127.0.0.1:4000
  BalancerMember http://127.0.0.1:4001
  BalancerMember http://127.0.0.1:4002
</Proxy>
```

This can go above the `VirtualHost` directive for `intranet.company.local`. We simply specify a `Proxy` directive with a special `balancer://` URL; then add a `BalancerMember` directive for each of our Mongrel instances.

Finally, you reference the balancer inside the rewrite rules for the `VirtualHost`, instead of `http://localhost:4000` (the URL of our old, singular Mongrel instance). The necessary change is highlighted below; note that I've also removed rewrite debugging and the directive for serving cached pages and actions, which aren't used in *Intranet*:

```
<VirtualHost *:80>
  ServerName intranet.company.local
  ServerAlias www.intranet.company.local
  # Put the Apache logs in the shared Capistrano log directory
  ErrorLog /home/captain/apps/Intranet/shared/log/intranet-error.log
  CustomLog /home/captain/apps/Intranet/shared/log/intranet-access.log common
  # Point the DocumentRoot into the current public directory
  DocumentRoot /home/captain/apps/Intranet/current/public
  # Turn on the rewrite engine
  RewriteEngine on
  # Static files can be served straight off the filesystem
  RewriteCond %{DOCUMENT_ROOT}%{REQUEST_FILENAME} !-f
  RewriteRule ^/(.*)$ balancer://intranet_cluster%{REQUEST_URI} [P,QSA,L]
</VirtualHost>
```

Reload Apache to make the changes take effect:

```
$ sudo /etc/init.d/apache2.2 graceful
```

If you now browse to `http://intranet.company.local/`, you are seeing dynamic pages being delivered by the Mongrel workers in the cluster. If you are one of those people (like me) who likes to see things in writing before you believe them, you can turn on debugging for your Mongrel cluster in the `intranet_cluster.yml` file like this:

```
user: captain
cwd: /home/captain/apps/Intranet/current/
port: "4000"
```

```
environment: production
group: captain
address: 127.0.0.1
pid_file: /home/captain/apps/Intranet/shared/pids/mongrel.pid
servers: 3
debug: true
```

This will create a directory, `shared/log/mongrel_debug`, containing more information than you are likely to need about what your Mongrel cluster is doing. For proof that the cluster is working, the `rails.log` file should contain entries like this:

```
Fri Jun 15 12:13:06 BST 2007 REQUEST /people
--- !map:Mongrel::HttpParams
SERVER_NAME: 127.0.0.1
HTTP_MAX_FORWARDS: "10"
PATH_INFO: /people
HTTP_X_FORWARDED_HOST: intranet.company.local
HTTP_USER_AGENT: ApacheBench/2.0.40-dev
SCRIPT_NAME: /
SERVER_PROTOCOL: HTTP/1.1
HTTP_HOST: 127.0.0.1:4002
REMOTE_ADDR: 192.168.13.1
...
HTTP_X_FORWARDED_SERVER: intranet.company.local
REQUEST_URI: /people
SERVER_PORT: "4002"
...
```

Browse a few pages across the application, have a check in the logs, and make sure that each port number in the cluster appears at least once in this file. That should be enough proof.

However, if you really need visible proof right before your very eyes, here's how you can see the actual host and port of the Mongrel instance serving each page of an application. First, add a `before_filter` to `app/controllers/application.rb`:

```
class ApplicationController < ActionController::Base
  # ... other methods ...
  before_filter do |controller|
    controller.instance_variable_set(:@host_and_port,
```

```
        controller.request.env['HTTP_HOST'])
    end
    #  ...
end
```

This sets an instance variable called `@host_and_port` for every action on every controller; this returns the true host and port of the Mongrel instance serving the request, rather than the one in the request URL.

Next, display that instance variable in the application layout (`app/views/layouts/application.rhtml`), e.g. in the page `<title>` element:

```
<!DOCTYPE html PUBLIC "-//W3C//DTD XHTML 1.0 Strict//EN" "http://www.
w3.org/TR/xhtml1/DTD/xhtml1-strict.dtd">
<html xmlns="http://www.w3.org/1999/xhtml" lang="en_GB" xml:lang="en_
GB">
<head>
<title><%= @page_title || 'Intranet' %> on
<%= @host_and_port %></title>

...
```

Now if you visit `http://intranet.company.local/`, you should notice that the host and port number are included in the title bar of the browser; if the cluster is working correctly, the port number should change occasionally between requests. That should satisfy even the hardest skeptic that the cluster is working and being proxied to correctly.

Advanced Scaling

Throughout this chapter, we've seen how to progressively improve the performance of a Rails application; first by identifying bottlenecks, then by improving performance using caching, and finally by scaling up using Apache and Mongrel clustering. The resulting configuration is strong enough to manage significant loads. If you are building applications to service an intranet (as we've been doing throughout this book), this configuration is likely to be sufficient.

However, if your application is on the public Internet and popular, you are likely to face other issues which this arrangement isn't able to cope with. Here are a few brief tips and pointers about improving performance by further scaling out your Rails infrastructure:

- **Use a faster session and cache store**: We've stuck with the file system for caching both session data and cached fragments. However, input-output (IO) to a hard disk can often prove a bottleneck for large applications. You can improve the IO speed by writing temporary data to more efficient types of store, rather than to the file system. The de facto standard way of doing this for large Rails application is **memcached** (`http://danga.com/memcached/`). Rather than storing data on the disk, memcached acts like a big "lookup table" in memory where you can store session and cache data. IO to memory is far faster than IO to disk, so expensive disk operations can be entirely eliminated by utilising it. See `http://wiki.rubyonrails.com/rails/pages/MemCached` for some links to useful tutorials and other information. While memcached isn't necessary in our case, you can use it to make impressive performance improvements to heavily-used Rails applications. Another less-heavyweight approach would be to use the database as a session store; see the Rails documentation for `ActionController::Base` for details.

- **Add more hardware**: In the configuration we've used here, everything is running on a single machine. Another option to scale out the infrastructure would be to add more hardware and distribute servers across it; for example, put the database server on one machine and the Mongrel instances plus Apache on another; or have a separate machine dedicated to Apache, for serving all your static assets like images, stylesheets, and JavaScripts (Rails out of the box can cope with this scenario, and has a `config.action_controller.asset_host` setting in `config/environments/production.rb` where you can specify a separate "asset server" for serving all static files).

- **Replicate or cluster the database**: If the database is the bottleneck in your application, you could split the database functionality across two machines, and replicate from the master to the slave. The slave could then be used for retrieval (e.g. for reporting or producing relatively-static parts of the website) while the master could be used to handle updates (e.g. taking customer orders). See the MySQL website for more details: `http://dev.mysql.com/doc/refman/5.1/en/replication.html`.

  Another approach might be to cluster MySQL (or whichever database you're using), to effectively turn multiple database servers across serveral machines into one or two "super" database servers. See the MySQL website for more details: `http://dev.mysql.com/doc/refman/5.1/en/mysql-cluster.html`.

- **Use a faster load balancer**: Apache is a general-purpose web server, not specifically optimized for load balancing. If you really just want a load balancer and not a large web server, you could potentially get more performance by using a smaller, more specialized tool. The current flavor of the month in the Rails community is **Nginx** (`http://nginx.net/`), an exceedingly fast, small web server and load balancer, which is relatively easy to configure for use with a Mongrel cluster. You could also try a dedicated load balancer like **Pound** (`http://www.apsis.ch/pound/`) or **Pen** (`http://siag.nu/pen/`). For the extreme Rails enthusiast, there is also the option of using a hardware load balancer across large numbers of Mongrel instances — see `http://tinyurl.com/gefp5` for a thorough round-up of the issues involved.

Summary

As we've seen in this chapter, building a Rails application is not just about coding using the framework; it also requires consideration of other issues around deployment. Capistrano can go a long way to making those issues less painful by making deployment much smoother.

Beyond deployment of the application itself, we also considered the environment around the application: the web server it is running on, the log files it accumulates, what happens when the machine is physically restarted, and so on. We've seen a few useful tips and techniques for making your applications run happily and indefinitely.

Even when your application is up and running, you need to stay tuned into its performance, listening to users and keeping an eye on any issues that arise. You also need to know how to identify and deal with those issues right down in the raw code; we put together a few useful scripts to help with this.

Finally, when issues arise, we saw that there are several highly effective things you can do to improve performance. We'd consider caching to be the simplest and most efficient of them. Beyond improvements to the code, the decoupled nature of Rails also makes it easy to improve performance by adding more servers (software and hardware).

10
Down the Track

Throughout this book, we have followed Rory in the construction of his first Ruby on Rails application. The process of building a basic application has been described using this example. From this straightforward starting point, the application has been developed and expanded allowing us to describe the techniques used to overcome problems and create working solutions that can be used in a variety of situations.

So where does a developer of a small business applications go from here? A simple answer to this is that a developer can improve their Rails and Ruby skills further and become an expert in the language and the framework. However, there is an alternative approach, which is to widen your skills. That is, to develop skills in the areas and systems that work with Rails and your applications in your environment. Therefore, in this chapter, we will cover both: how one can improve one's Rails skills further and suggest alternative skills that complement Ruby on Rails, thereby broadening your skill set. Rather than using Rory's solution to discuss the issues, we will use our own experiences to describe some paths that have led us beyond the ability to build straightforward Rails applications.

Going off the Rails

Convention is the strength of Rails. It makes it easier to use, and the resulting code is easier to read as well as modify. It is the convention that goes a long way to make Ruby on Rails such a good and agile development environment.

Yet, at some point while creating applications, you will need to break the basic conventions. The danger in this is that you can end up with a disorganized mess. However, in my experience the process of going beyond conventions has taught me more than any other process about how Rails works. It has given me a deeper understanding of how the different parts work together. I believe that going through this process has been an essential part of my Rails skill development.

When I was younger, I used to kayak canoe and the development of my canoeing skills gave a useful analogy to my skill development in Rails. I spent a couple of years learning the basic kayak skills: paddling straight, changing direction, sculling sideways, escaping from an over-turned kayak, preventing over-turning, and eventually the Eskimo roll. This initial maneuver allows a canoeist to right a capsized kayak without leaving their seat. Even after I had learnt the skill and practised it many-a-times in safe environments, it was some time before I used it to right a genuine capsize. That is, to restore to upright a capsized kayak that I had not deliberately over-turned. Then the day came: I was caught in a wave and flipped upside down. Previously, I would have bailed out, but on this occasion I held fast, adjusted my paddles, and flipped the kayak upright.

From that point on, my canoeing skill leaped up to a new level. Because, I no longer had to worry about capsizing the kayak, I was able to be more adventurous. And if I over did it, a quick twist of the torso and flick of the paddles, and I was upright again. I went from being a canoeist that kept to the quiet stretches of water to the one who thoroughly enjoyed the rough water.

The analogy is useful as it allows me to make the following points:

- The skill is not in being able to capsize a kayak (in fact, learners can be very good at capsizing), but rather the skill is in the ability to return back to the upright position. Similarly, any developer can break the standard Rails conventions: the skill is in being able to break the convention and then tidy up the result so that the rest of the application is not adversely affected.

- The Eskimo roll is not the first skill you learn as a canoeist. You should not start your Rails development by breaking the conventions. You need to be skilled at Rails to understand the effect of breaking a convention, and therefore limit its impact.

- Even after you master the Eskimo roll, the best position to be in a kayak is upright. Keeping to the Rails conventions makes the framework a joy to work with. Break conventions because you have to, not for any other reason.

The process of successfully breaking the Rails convention goes through the cycle described in figure 1.

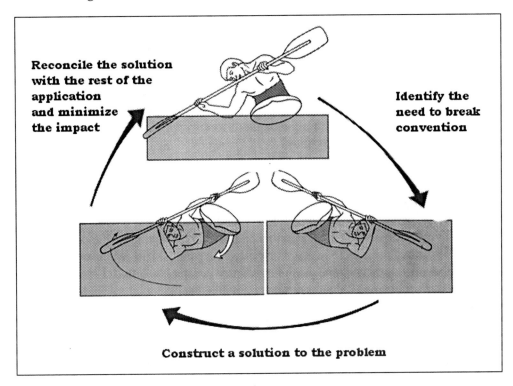

This cycle has three elements:

1. Identify the need to break convention: we find there is something we want the application to do, that we are unable to do within the standard Rails practice.

2. Construct a solution to the problem: following some research and testing a solution is found that allows us to achieve the desired solution.

3. Reconcile the solution with the rest of the application to minimize the impact: modifications are made to the application so the solution can be integrated. This is the hardest part of the process, but is the most important part for success to be achieved. It basically requires that our solution passes on to Rails resulting objects that behave as closely as possible to the standard Rails objects.

The key to success is in completing the whole cycle.

The point where I first went off the Rails was while working with an application that was relatively mature. It had been developed over a number of months and was already in daily use within the business. However, as its importance within the business grew, so did a requirement for it to be able to use data from an external source. In this case, it was a time-sheet application, the database for which was hosted on a Microsoft SQL server. My Rails application used a MySQL database. The structure of the time-sheet data was complex and it would be very complicated to create Rails models to match each table. Therefore, two basic conventions were being broken. The first, reasonably minor: data being spread across two databases. The second, more fundamental: the database data to model object relationship did not comply to what ActiveRecord expected.

My first attempt at a solution was difficult to maintain. It relied on a single model, a custom connection to the MS SQL database and multiple `find_by_sql` calls grabbing data via complex joins of views and tables in the time-sheet database. It worked, but each time I used objects that were created via the model, I had to customize the connection to other objects. The solution would not scale. The more I used it, the more modifications I needed to make. However, the process did teach me how to connect to a second database, and how I could use customized model methods to replicate the way a normal Rails model behaves.

I then discovered that MS **SQL Server Integration Services** (SSIS) can be used to pull the data I needed into a new database. Most of the joins could be managed within the SSIS data transfer. The resulting database would then have a simpler structure. I only needed to read information from the time-sheet system; no writing back to the time-sheet system was required. So, I did not have to maintain a link between the new database and the time-sheet system. Instead, a scheduled process passed new time-sheet data to the new database at midnight each night. With a simpler data structure, I was able to split the data across a small number of Rails models that more accurately matched the data structure. However, the structure was such that I still had to work differently with the model objects using the time-sheet data, than with the normal ActiveRecord objects. This build of the solution taught me how I could use the database tools to simplify the problem.

The third iteration of a solution came about when I realized that some fairly small modifications to the SSIS data transfer would allow me to structure the new database in a manner that was compliant with ActiveRecord. That is with table names being plurals of object names, each table having a primary key field called ID, and field names in lower case with underscores separating the words. Once I had done this, the deviation from Rails convention was reduced to a minimum—that minimum deviation being that some data was on a second database. The only problem then was to ensure that ActiveRecord did not try to access data across both databases with a single SQL call. To do this, custom methods were written that recreated the model connections normally generated by `belongs_to` and `has_many` relationships.

So, for example, in a projects model rather than using "has_many: tasks" to create a project.tasks relationship, a new project method called tasks would be created that returned an array of task objects. Similarly, a project method in the task model returned a project object that matched the project to which the task belonged. This, therefore, replicated the behavior that would have been achieved with "belongs_to: project" in a normal Rails application.

What I had done, in effect, was three Eskimo rolls; that is three rotations through the cycle of: identify the requirement to break convention; find a solution; reconcile the solution with the rest of the application. Each time I went through the cycle, the solution became simpler and the deviation away from the basic Rails practice became less.

A measure of the solution's success was that I was able to use the final solution to pull information from a third system: the company accounts. While going through the three cycles, I learned more about the interaction between model objects and their databases than I believe I could easily have if I had not had to fix my broken conventions.

In my experience, the most useful skills required to allow me to step outside the Rails conventions have been an understanding of the underlying Ruby language and SQL database tools. However, I have also used modifications to web servers to over come other Rails issues. To get the best from Rails, one must learn to get the best out of the supporting systems.

Better to go off the Rails than grind to a halt

The key point here is that success does not come from the breaking, but from the fixing. If you come to a point where you cannot proceed without breaking the standard conventions, then break them, but always carry out the whole cycle by reconciling and minimizing the impact. It is always better to find a solution and improve it, than to grind to a halt because you cannot find a solution within the standard tool set. Often, the process of stepping outside of Rails will help you find a better way to solve your problem within Rails.

SQL

I saw a posting in a Rails newsgroup asking for advice on the best administrative tool to use with the poster's SQL database. The majority of replies suggested that with the development of migrations a Rails developer should keep away from SQL. This newsgroup thread seems to reflect the views of a number of Rails developers. The more I develop Rails applications, the more I am confident that this view is mistaken. A developer who ignores SQL is tying one hand behind their back. SQL databases form the core of almost all Rails applications, and not using the free extra resources that SQL can provide, seems daft to me.

Migration is a splendid system that simplifies database table creation and modification. Migrations add order, structure, and ease to table development. However, creating tables is only a small part of what a SQL database engine can do. SQL tools provide a very efficient system to process, combine, and compare data. What is more, the SQL tools are installed when you install the database, so they are a free resource waiting to be used.

However, there is also the argument that ActiveRecord is already leveraging SQL within each Rails application, and usually makes a very good job of generating SQL calls from executing Rails code. This is a sound argument. So, if this is true, where is the need to create and use custom SQL code? The simple answer is, when standard Rails code and the resulting ActiveRecord generated SQL takes too long to process the data; or SQL offers a way to summarize, compare, or combine data in a simpler manner than what can be done within Ruby and Rails.

In my experience, ActiveRecord generated SQL works well when retrieving and processing data from one or two tables. When you start wanting to combine data from three or more tables, processing the data purely within Rails and ActiveRecord generated SQL can take many seconds. In these circumstances, a custom SQL call can greatly improve the performance.

A second area where an understanding of SQL is useful, is when you need to apply grouping to a data set. ActiveRecord supports grouping, however, it is not as simple as it might first appear. In my experience, it is often easiest to create the required grouping statement in SQL and then reverse engineer it back into an ActiveRecord find statement.

A detailed guide to SQL is beyond the scope of this book. So instead, I will describe here a couple of examples that show how a knowledge of SQL can help to create better, or at least faster, Rails applications.

Gathering Data from a Daughter Object's Daughter

In building a project management application, I needed to process data that was held within a daughter object that was itself a daughter object. That is, each project was represented by a **project** object. Each project had a number of daughter objects called **tasks**. Each Task could also have daughter objects called **budget**.

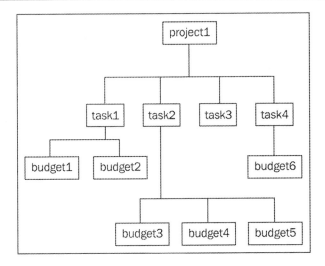

Within the model definition, for each model class, I was able to specify the relationship. So, a project has_many tasks, and a task has_many budgets. Also, budgets belong_to task, and tasks belong_to project.

I could also use :through option to create a project has_many budgets relationship in the Project model:

```
has_many :budgets, :though :tasks
```

And improve performance of retrieving Budget information when iterating through a project's tasks by using an :include option in the definition of the has_many tasks statement:

```
has_many :tasks, :include => :budgets
```

However, in my main project reporting tool, I needed to be able to output the final project budget value. This was not a simple task. If a task had three budgets, the final budget was not the sum of all the three budgets, but rather the value of the last budget. Also, I needed to be able to assign a budget to a task, but set a flag to prevent that budget from being used when calculating the total project budget.

So, to get the project budget, I needed to sum the last budget item in each task that had a flag set for it to be included in the project budget. I created a task method called final_project_budget that returned the value of a relevant budget object, if one existed. I was then able to use Project.tasks to return a collection of tasks assigned to the project and then iterate through them to calculate the sum of the values returned by the final_project_budget method.

The process worked fine. It accurately returned the correct figure each time. The code was fairly simple and therefore easy to modify and maintain. The problem was that the resulting report took eight seconds to render for one project. This was not apparent initially, when each project only had a couple of tasks, but as tasks were added the application slowed.

The main problem was that each-and-every retrieval of a budget data from a task involved a separate SQL call to the database. So, one SQL call would return the list of tasks relating to a project, and then a further SQL call would be called on each task to get the budget information. Then some processing in Ruby added the budgets together and returned the correct number.

My solution was to create a single SQL call that gathered and processed all the information in one go. This is the SQL statement used:

```
SELECT SUM([value]) as total_budget
FROM [Data_Warehouse].[dbo].[budgets] budget
INNER JOIN (
    SELECT MAX([target_on]) as date
      , [task_id]
    FROM [Data_Warehouse].[dbo].[budgets]
    WHERE [project_id] = 147 AND [part_of_parent] = 1
    GROUP BY [task_id]
) AS last_target_on
ON last_target_on.date = budget.target_on
AND last_target_on.task_id = budget.task_id
```

This is Transact SQL used on a MS SQL database, and therefore the syntax may not be correct for other databases. However, it is not the code itself that is important, but the fact that a single SQL call could be created that did all the processing required.

The code uses the SQL SUM function to add up the values assigned to a number of budget entries. Most of the work is carried out with a JOIN to a second SELECT statement. This second statement finds only the latest budgets assigned to each task, and that have the part_of_parent flag set (it is this flag that determines whether a budget is to be included in the project budget). This JOIN, therefore, ensures that only the correct last budgets for each task are passed to the initial SUM([value]) statement.

It was then a case of replacing 147, (the id for a particular project), with code that would insert the current project's ID, using the SQL statement with a find_by_sql call, and then processing the result to output the solution as required.

```
def total_budget
    sql = "SELECT SUM([value]) as total_budget
            FROM [HL_Data_Warehouse].[dbo].[budgets] budget
```

```
            INNER JOIN (
              SELECT MAX([target_on]) as date
                , [task_id]
              FROM [HL_Data_Warehouse].[dbo].[budgets]
              WHERE [project_id] = #{self.id} AND [part_of_parent] = 1
              GROUP BY [task_id]
            ) AS last_target_on
            ON last_target_on.date = budget.target_on
            AND last_target_on.task_id = budget.task_id"
    budget = Budget.find_by_sql(sql)
    return budget[0].total_budget
  end
```

This method was added to the Project model. Then, for a Project object called project, the application could call `project.total_budget` to return the total budget.

As a result of this modification, the page that had taken eight seconds to load now took eight tenths of a second to load; ten times faster to load than before the modification.

Using a model's ActiveRecord connection

There is a better technique to using `find_by_sql` for the `total_budget` method. The above example, while useful in that it shows a real world example of how an application was improved by adding some SQL magic, is also problematic. The issue is that it has forced the results of the SQL call into a collection of budget objects. This does not cause an error, but it would be neater if the objects returned using the SQL query formed a simple array of hashes whose properties were defined solely by the data returned from the database and did not inherit any of the properties from the parent model.

The solution is to use the parent's connection to the database, and then use one of two connection methods to return the data in a more suitable set of object. The options are:

```
connection.select_all(sql)
#returns data in an array of hashes where each hash corresponds to a
data row.
connection.select_one(sql)
#returns a single hash containing the first row of data from the sql
call
```

Therefore, a better version of the `total_budget` method using the connection object, would be as follows:

```
def total_budget
    sql = "SELECT SUM([value]) as total_budget
```

```
                FROM [HL_Data_Warehouse].[dbo].[budgets] budget
                INNER JOIN (
                  SELECT MAX([target_on]) as date
                    , [task_id]
                  FROM [HL_Data_Warehouse].[dbo].[budgets]
                  WHERE [project_id] = #{self.id} AND [part_of_parent] = 1
                  GROUP BY [task_id]
                ) AS last_target_on
                ON last_target_on.date = budget.target_on
                AND last_target_on.task_id = budget.task_id"
        budget = connection.select_one(sql)
        return budget.total_budget
      end
```

Using GROUP BY to Summarize Data

GROUP BY is a very useful SQL option that can be used to quickly generate summary reports. It can be used via an ActiveRecord `find` method using the `:group` option. However, its use is not as simple as it might appear from the Rails `api` pages. Consider this example:

We have an application that stores data on the contents of boxes of fruit. It contains a single MySQL table:

ID	fruit	quantity	source
1	Orange	50	Jaffa
2	Apple	110	UK
3	Orange	30	Jaffa
4	Apple	60	UK
5	Orange	90	Spain
6	Pear	40	UK
7	Orange	110	Spain
8	Orange	110	Spain
9	Apple	50	Belgium
10	Apple	20	France
11	Pear	110	UK

We want a summary report that details how many of each type of fruits you have in all the boxes. We can use GROUP BY to do this. However, it is not as simple as the following:

```
report = Boxes.find(:all, :group => 'fruit')
```

This would generate the following:

ID	fruit	quantity	source
2	Apple	110	UK
1	Orange	50	Jaffa
6	Pear	40	UK

This has not provided a summary, but rather has simply pulled out the first entry for each type of fruit.

So, what is missing?

Let us start by looking at the SQL that generated the group data:

```
SELECT * FROM boxes b GROUP BY fruit
```

The problem is that by using the short-hand * in the SELECT part of the statement, the job of selecting what is to be returned has been handed over to SQL. As the example above demonstrates, SQL's best effort will usually not give us the desired result. Instead, we must specify, which fields are to be included in the output. However, the following would generate an error:

```
SELECT fruit, quantity FROM boxes b GROUP BY fruit
```

We also need to specify an aggregate function for each field that is not being grouped. Here are some of the commonly used aggregate functions:

- AVG — Average value for those in the field.
- COUNT — Number of items in the group.
- MAX — Maximum value in group. If used on a MySQL varchar field, it returns the last value in an alphabetical order.
- MIN — Minimum value in group. If used on a MySQL varchar field, it returns the first value in an alphabetical order.
- SUM — adds together the values held in the field.

The field fruit is being grouped, so it can stay as it is in the SQL statement. An aggregate function needs to be applied to the quantity field, as this field is not being grouped. That is, there will be a number of quantity values in each group, but only one fruit value. So, all we need to tell SQL is, which quantity value should be returned for a group; the fruit value is automatically returned.

```
SELECT fruit, sum(quantity) AS 'total_quantity' FROM boxes b GROUP BY
fruit
```

This will produce the desired result:

fruit	total_quantity
Apple	240
Orange	390
Pear	150

Notice that AS was needed to specify a meaningful name for the quantity output.

To generate the desired result set in Rails, the following code can be used.

```
report = Boxes.find(:all,
                :select => "fruit, sum(quantity) AS 'total_quantity'",
                :group => 'fruit')
```

By using the select option in the find statement, the output was controlled and the desired results obtained.

It is also possible to group on multiple fields. For example:

```
SELECT fruit,
       source,
       sum(quantity) as 'quantity',
       count(*) as 'boxes'
FROM boxes b
GROUP BY fruit, source
```

This will produce a report showing how many fruits there are from each source and in how many boxes:

fruit	source	quantity	boxes
Apple	France	20	1
Apple	Belgium	50	1
Apple	UK	170	2
Orange	Jaffa	80	2
Orange	Spain	310	3
Pear	UK	150	2

From this, we can see there are three boxes of Spanish oranges containing 310 fruits in total. The Rails code would look like this:

```
report = Boxes.find(:all,
                    :select => "fruit,
                       source,
                       sum(quantity) AS 'total_quantity',
                       count(*) as 'boxes'"
                    :group => 'fruit, source')
```

Simple, don't you think! Well not really.....

A Deeper Look at Aggregate Functions

Aggregate functions need to be used carefully. Consider how you would find the source of the boxes with the least fruit of each type. Your first stab at a solution may be:

```
SELECT fruit,
       MIN(quantity) AS 'quantity',
       MIN(source) AS 'source'
FROM boxes
GROUP BY fruit
```

This would return the record set below, which at first glance looks correct:

fruit	quantity	source
Apple	20	Belgium
Orange	30	Jaffa
Pear	40	UK

However, the source of the box with the least apples is France and not Belgium. In fact, it is only by chance that the other two records match the correct result. MIN (source) has returned the first source in alphabetical order—not the source that matches the minimum quantity.

To get the correct result, we first need to find the minimum quantities for each fruit and then use that data to pull out the records that match that information. The following code does that:

```
SELECT b.fruit, b.quantity, b.source
FROM boxes b
JOIN (SELECT fruit, MIN(quantity) AS 'quantity'
      FROM boxes
```

```
        GROUP BY fruit
      ) AS s
ON b.fruit = s.fruit AND b.quantity = s.quantity
```

The result is shown below.

fruit	quantity	source
Orange	30	Jaffa
Pear	40	UK
Apple	20	France

ActiveRecord's `find` method has a `:joins` option and can be used to construct this query. A `:from` option is also needed so that an alias of 'b' can be specified for the boxes table. However, the resulting code is more complex than the original SQL code:

```
report = Boxes.find(:all,
                 :select => 'b.fruit, b.quantity, b.source'
                 :from => 'boxes b'
                 :join => "(SELECT fruit, MIN(quantity) AS 'quantity'
                   FROM boxes
                   GROUP BY fruit
                   ) AS s
                   ON b.fruit = s.fruit AND b.quantity = s.quantity)"
```

Personally, I would use a `find_by_sql` method as it would be easier to maintain:

```
sql = "SELECT b.fruit, b.quantity, b.source
      FROM boxes b
      JOIN (SELECT fruit, MIN(quantity) AS 'quantity'
            FROM boxes
            GROUP BY fruit
           ) AS s
      ON b.fruit = s.fruit AND b.quantity = s.quantity"
report = Boxes.find_by_sql(sql)
```

Knowledge of SQL makes it easier to get the most of the `:group` option in ActiveRecord's `finds` method and also makes it easier to extend further SQL's GROUP BY options.

A little SELECT goes a long way

In both of these examples, refining the SQL SELECT statement sent to the database greatly improved the efficiency with which Rails was able to obtain the data required for the application. Mastering this one, SQL command can provide many dividends. SELECT statements simply read data and therefore do not alter the data in the database. Therefore, you can safely experiment with them to find the statement that achieves what you need. Time spent mastering this SQL command will give you a simple way to improve the performance of Rails applications.

Business Processes

In building business applications, a developer is endeavoring to model or support a business process. With large applications, the job of identifying and then analyzing the business process is usually carried out by a different person or team than those who write and develop the resultant application. With small business applications, this is less likely to be the case. Either, the size of the project or the team working on the application, prohibits the use of specialists to study the business process.

Therefore, to realize the maximum potential for small business application development, it is usually the case that the developer will also need to take on the role of analyzing the business process. It may even be the case that to keep up a supply of new work, the developer themselves will need to identify potential new projects and development opportunities.

The key skill to being able to identify opportunities for new applications is an understanding of how businesses work. In fact, I would go so far as to say that once you are reasonably competent at building applications, time spent studying business processes is more important to a small application developer, than perfecting coding skills.

I would highly recommend that anyone wanting to make a career in this field takes time to study business processes. Two of the most valuable courses I have taken part in recently were on *business management* and *management accounts*. The skills and knowledge gained during those courses has made me much more successful at identifying the best opportunities to improve business processes. Since completing those courses, I am confident that I now make more successful applications.

To Be Successful, Build Successful Business Applications

What is it that makes a business application successful? The answer is simple: an application that generates profit.

Forget clever design, efficient use of processors, elegant interface. All of these are desirable, but if your applications do not provide a demonstrable benefit to the business, you might as well have stayed at home. The benefits that all businesses need are those that improve the bottom line: *they increase profits*. There is no better hook to catch the interest of people who will pay you to create applications for them, than for you to demonstrate that you can increase their profits.

So, how do small applications generate profit? There are three ways to generate more profit within a business:

- Increase sales by either increasing the number of sales or increasing the revenue from each sale (or less easily, both).

- Reduce what it costs you to sell.

- Spend as little as you can on the parts of the business that generate the least profit, and minimize any resources given over to loss making activities.

Business applications can address all of these profit opportunities. For example, when we choose an elegant programming framework like Rail to create business applications, to be successful we do so because:

- It allows us to create applications more quickly and therefore increase the number of applications we can produce at the same cost.

- The resulting code is easy to maintain, so it costs us less to support the application.

- The framework conventions allow us to spend more time on the aspects of the application that are unique to the project, and spend minimal time on the less productive routine tasks.

If you ask most people how a business increases profits, they will usually reply that the business increases sales. However, it is usually far easier to increase profits by reducing costs and minimizing the time spent on loss making activities. It is in these areas that most opportunities for small business applications arise.

A full insight into business processes is beyond the scope of this book; it is a large area of study. Instead, below are a number of examples of areas where opportunities for small applications commonly arise.

Automate Simple Repetitive Jobs

A simple way to reduce costs is to reduce the time it takes to carry out repetitive tasks. One of my most successful applications is an *Excel macro*. A colleague was processing the output from a series of data loggers. This output was in the form of comma-delimited text files. He had to open each one, carry out some processing to normalize the data, and then reformat it to create a graphical report. The process took him a couple of hours for each set of data (the data was broken down into many subsections and each had to be normalized separately). It took me a few hours to write an Excel VBA macro that would input the data, normalize it, and reformat it for the graphical report. The result was that a process that had taken a couple of hours manually could be completed in a second or two. The macro was written five

years ago and is still in constant use — perhaps two or three times a week. That single, simple application has saved hundreds of hours of work, thereby freeing up my colleague to do more revenue generating work than he previously had the time to do.

Rapid and Detailed Reporting

Rapid: One of the main difficulties in managing a business is the speed at which information on current activities becomes available. It is common for a business not to know the full cost of a project until after the project has completed and long after the time when there was any opportunity to address any excess in expenditure. Also, that information may become available in a central accounting department reasonably rapidly, but take some time to filter down to the people who could use that information to improve the way they work.

Therefore, applications that gather and analyze cost information rapidly and present it in easy to understand and relevant reports are a boon to any business. They allow managers to identify where the costs are being generated and react in time to cut down costs spent on non-profit making activities, and divert resources to successful parts of the business.

Detailed: It is a common mistake of unsuccessful small businesses not to analyze their costs properly and repeatedly sell their services too cheaply. In this situation, a common trap is to think that all that is needed to correct the situation is to work harder. Sales teams try harder to sell more of the same loss making services and people work longer hours to satisfy the extra orders. The result is a lot of people working very hard to make a loss!

Often, it is not a lack of effort that puts a company out of business. They fail because they do not have the information available that tells them their costs have in fact outstripped the revenue their activity raises.

A time-sheet system is a typical application that addresses these types of problem. Imagine a paper based time-sheet system whereby sheets are submitted at the end of each week or month. All these sheets then have to be approved by supervisors before being passed to a clerk to input into a central system where the data on the sheets can be analyzed. This process takes days. Reports can themselves take time to generate. The result can be that the reports, on time spent on a project, reach the managers weeks after the time was actually committed. Also, because of the effort required in processing these time-sheets, the level of details is often reduced to simplify the process. However, this makes the system less useful and can lead to over-sights into areas where resources are being wasted. This type of paper based time-sheet system is not uncommon in small businesses.

An online time-sheet system can allow an employee to submit time-sheet information soon after they have carried out the work. As soon as the data has been submitted, the data is available to analyze. A central database system can analyze varied data very rapidly, so more detailed information can be gathered. Managers can have reports on activity within days, if not hours, of it happening and can use that information to improve the way their current activities are developing. In that way, they can use the resources intelligently to maximize profits.

Ensure Customers Pay for the Goods and Services that the Business Provides

When people think of customers obtaining goods without paying for them, their first thought is usually theft. Unfortunately, over-sight is a far easier way for customers to obtain goods or services without paying for them. The project manager who forgets to sign off a project as complete, the well intentioned technician who upgrades one part of a customer's system while repairing another, the accountant who puts an instruction to invoice in their "completed" tray instead of their "to-do" tray, the warehouse worker who puts two items in a carton when there should have been only one. All of these can lead to a customer receiving goods for free and the effect is that the total cost of getting the goods to the customer becomes a loss to the business. Such over-sights are very expensive to a business.

Therefore, systems are required that track orders for goods and services, and the paths of items through the business. Reports on completion, and more importantly lack of completion, of each sale are important to every successful business. For example, a sales process system can track a sale from the initial order right through to payment of invoice. It can provide reports on the status of all items and highlight orders that have not yet been invoiced. Such a system would help minimize the likelihood that customers receive goods without paying for them.

Review of Business Activity Examples

The examples above are just three areas where business activity can be enhanced with the addition of small applications. As I stated at the start of this section, this is not a comprehensive list or set of descriptions, but rather examples that demonstrate there are many areas where small applications can benefit a business.

My key point is that all businesses have systems and processes that can be improved, and we as application developers have the tools to make those improvements. Yet, as you complete this book, you may be surprised to find there is not a queue of business leaders beating at your door. Every town has a multitude of businesses. If each has processes that can be improved with the addition of small applications, why are business managers not scrambling for your services? In my experience, the answer is simple; managers often do not understand the capabilities of simple computer applications and fail to recognize their potential benefits.

Therefore, as a small application developer we have two choices: either to wait for the relatively small number of opportunities that others will bring to us; or actively go out and identify the multitude of opportunities that can be found within any business.

Small business applications do not come to he who waits

If you wish to work full time on small business applications, you cannot rely on others to bring you new projects. You need to develop the skills to identify opportunities for new applications. To do that successfully and repeatedly, you must learn to identify business processes that can be simplified, made more effective, and/or efficient via a small application.

Dealing with Success

Unfortunately, there is a flip side (why are things never easy). Once we develop the skills to identify the potential areas where the applications will improve the way a business works, the problem can become one of the volume and time available. There can be just too many applications for a small team to develop. In addition to this, once senior managers start to realize the benefits our applications provide, the pressure to provide even more solutions in shorter time scales can become almost oppressive.

In many ways, being a successful developer in demand is a good position to be in, but it does bring its own problems. Here are a few strategies to help in this situation:

Just Because You Can, Doesn't Mean You Should

I expect that you got into application development because you enjoy it and find it rewarding. That is certainly why I develop applications. However, the desire to develop, and one's own pride in the work we do can lead to developers taking on projects that they do not have the time or resources to complete satisfactorily. This is especially the case for larger projects or in periods when the demand is high. In such cases, a better option is to buy an off-the-shelf solution. Also, there is no point in reinventing the wheel—if an application is readily available that will satisfy the requirement and is within budget, it is almost always a mistake to develop your own solution instead, unless you have a very good reason to do so.

Therefore, when we identify a potential new project, we should always ask the question "Is there an application readily available that would satisfy the project requirements?" If we identify such an application, we then need to analyze the costs and benefits of using that application, then compare those with a similar analysis of an application we would build ourselves. If such analysis demonstrates that buying the application is more beneficial, buy the solution.

Bought in solutions Provide their Own Opportunities

However, just because an application is bought in, does not mean that we cannot use our own skills to improve the way the application works within the target business.

In fact, developing an infrastructure, whereby one application's data is used by another application throughout the business can be a demanding and rewarding task. Some very useful small business applications simply allow one off-the-shelf system to use data from another system. It is another potential area for development. Although Rails was not designed to work with multiple data sources, it is fairly straightforward to allow it to. Also, Ruby is able to handle this sort of work. Using Ruby without Rails is a small leap once we understand how the systems underlying Rails work.

Ensure There is Time to Complete Each Task

Application development often hits unexpected complications and the time required to create a new application is notoriously difficult to predict. Therefore, always include time to deal with unforeseen problems, while setting and agreeing to deadlines. In fact, if you are really finding it difficult to judge how long a project will take to complete, it is surprising how well taking your best estimate and doubling it works. It can make a very good starting point for your first projects. Once you have a few under your belt, you should be able to make more sophisticated scheduling estimates.

Taking the time to review how long it took to complete a task will be very useful as it will allow us to improve our projected completion schedules. The better we can make our own projections, the less likely it is that we will find ourselves working to other people's unrealistic deadlines.

The Final Destination

Within this book, we hope to have provided you with the information you need to move from Rails novice to confident small business application developer. By considering the development environment as a whole, rather than code in isolation, we have described not only how to put an application together, but also how to bring together all the parts that are required to build a working solution.

One may wish to spend as much time as possible writing good Rails code, but successful application development cannot be carried out in a bubble. At some point, it must integrate with its environment. To do so in a Rails environment, the application must work well on the platform hosting it. Data needs to be retrieved from databases efficiently, processed, and handed on to web servers. As this reliance on other systems is so important to the final product, we have taken time to describe how to set up the environment, and most importantly the integration between services.

Like most people, we like an easy life. In development that means making use of the tools available to simplify the job. It means, using an integrated development environment that simplifies and helps organize the creation and editing of code. Just as important is having a source control system that reliably and simply stores version information to facilitate backup and collaboration. Therefore, these topics have also been covered.

In this final chapter, we have moved beyond Rails by considering the skills one can use to broaden a developer's skill set. we have also, in the clichéd language of business, considered applications as solutions to business problems, rather than simply collections of code. In this, we hope we have highlighted that there is more to writing successful applications than good coding skills. The applications have to work well, but they also need to satisfy a businesses requirement.

However, as important as all of the above is, there is one overriding message that we hope this book passes on:

[Ruby on Rails is an excellent system to build small business applications.]

It provides the tools to build scalable, easily maintained applications that are simple to distribute throughout a business. The code is flexible and can be transferred to many different environments. Its structure is portable and easy to back up. Most importantly, it does so many of the routine tasks for the developer that they are left to concentrate on the parts of the application that matter. That is, the unique attributes that will allow each application to closely match the requirements of the project that spawned it.

Ruby on Rails has provided us with the tools to most efficiently fill our working days building small business applications; a task we get great satisfaction from. Our hope is that the contents of this book helps you gain as much satisfaction from using this excellent framework to solve the problems that arise within the businesses you work for and with.

A
Running Your Own Gem Server

Rubygems is a great system for maintaining libraries for use with Ruby. It makes it simple to upgrade to new versions of Rails, Capistrano, Mongrel, etc. with a single command.

However, if you use a default Rubygems configuration, each time a developer installs a gem they fetch it from a repository on the Internet. This could result in different developers ending up with different versions of a single gem, depending on which was available when they performed the installation. While this might not make a difference in some cases, with gems like Rails (which change radically between versions), it could result in an application working on one machine and not on another.

Another issue is finding the more obscure gems, which reside in non-standard repositories. In this case, configuring the developers' machines for each non-standard repository can be painful, particularly if you use several such repositories.

The simplest way to give developers access to a consistent repository with all the gems they require is to *set up your own gem server*. There are two methods for doing this:

1. If you have a machine with all the required gems installed, you can use the built-in `gem_server` command on that machine to serve up its gems to others.

2. You can serve gems out of Apache by manually setting up a gem repository. This gives you more control over which gems are presented to client machines, but is harder to maintain.

Both techniques are covered in the next two sections.

Serving Installed Gems

To explain how this technique is applied, let's remind ourselves of Acme's setup. They have a production machine to which their applications are deployed, which contains *most* of the gems required by the developers (see, Chapter 3). Note that I said *most*, as Capistrano is not installed: technically, it is only required on the developer machines. However, to be able to serve it from the production machine, it needs to be installed on that machine too. (The gem_server command only offers up gems installed on the machine where it is running.) They install Capistrano (and its dependencies) with the following:

```
$ gem install capistrano -y
```

Next, they can make the gems on the production machine available via HTTP using this simple command:

```
$ gem_server
[2007-07-03 21:34:38] INFO  WEBrick 1.3.1
[2007-07-03 21:34:38] INFO  ruby 1.8.4 (2005-12-24) [i486-linux]
[2007-07-03 21:34:38] INFO  WEBrick::HTTPServer#start: pid=7543 port=8808
```

As you can see from the output, this starts a WEBrick server on the default port 8808 (gem_server -p N can be used to start the server on port N). Browsing to http://<server address>:8808/ (replacing <server address> with the IP address or domain name of the production machine) will now yield the documentation for the gems on the server. We had a brief look at this feature in the section: *A Note on Rails Documentation* in Chapter 3. If the gems were installed without documentation (using the --no-rdoc switch), you will just get a list of the installed gems without documentation links.

But there is another hidden aspect to the gem server: if you browse to the same address with the path /gems/, i.e. to http://<server address>:8808/gems/, you'll see the gems installed on the server displayed as links.

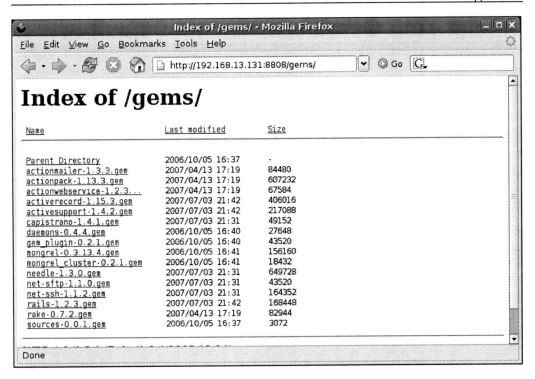

This indicates that the gem server is presenting its installed gems over HTTP. Once this is up and running, you can now use the gem command line tool on a developer machine to list the gems on the gem server:

```
$ gem list --remote --source http://192.168.13.131:8808

Bulk updating Gem source index for: http://192.168.13.131:8808

*** REMOTE GEMS ***

actionmailer (1.3.3)
    Service layer for easy email delivery and testing.
... etc. ...
```

(Replacing the IP address of the --source URL with the one for your server, of course.)

You can also install a gem from your own gem server with:

```
$ sudo gem install rails -y --source http://192.168.13.131:8808
Password:
Bulk updating Gem source index for: http://192.168.13.131:8808
Successfully installed rails-1.2.3
```

Setting Your Gem Server as the Default

If you want to configure gem to use your gem server as the default repository, create a file called .gemrc in your home directory (/home/username on Linux, Documents and Settings\Username on Windows). Next, add this single line (it's a YAML file):

```
gem: --source http://192.168.13.131:8808 -y
```

Remember to replace the --source URL with the one appropriate to your server. Note that I also added the -y switch to ensure that all dependencies are installed each time you install a gem. Now, each time you install a gem, your intranet gem server will be used as the default repository, rather than the public Internet gem repository.

Creating a Gem Server Manually

While the approach of the previous section is simple to set up, it doesn't give you much control over which gems are offered on the server. If you want to offer gems without installing them, you have the option to create a gem server manually. In the case of Acme, where they already have Apache installed on the production machine, it makes sense to make use of that to present the gems over HTTP. This also has the advantage that Apache starts and stops with the physical machine, due to its incorporation into the init sequence (see, Apache on Linux and Mac OS X in Chapter 4); with the gem_server command, you would have to write your own start/stop script to get this happen.

To set up a gem server using Apache on Linux, follow these steps:

First, create a directory to use as the base for the gem server. To keep things simple, I created this as a sub-directory inside Apache's htdocs directory (as root):

```
$ mkdir /opt/apache2.2/htdocs/gemserver
```

Next, create the directory, which will hold the gems:

```
$ mkdir /opt/apache2.2/htdocs/gemserver/gems
```

Gems are typically available for download from Rubyforge, though they may be offered from non-standard repositories. For example, you can get the Rails gems from http://gems.rubyforge.org/gems/. We'll start by getting the Rake gem to demonstrate:

```
$ cd /opt/apache2.2/htdocs/gemserver/gems/
$ wget http://gems.rubyforge.org/gems/rake-0.7.3.gem
```

A gem is just a zip file with a nonstandard suffix (.gem). Put all the gem files you want to serve into the gems directory.

Configure Apache to serve the new directory as a virtual host by adding the following directive to /opt/apache2.2/conf/httpd.conf:

```
<VirtualHost *:80>
  ServerName gems.company.local
  DocumentRoot /opt/apache2.2/htdocs/gemserver
</VirtualHost>
```

You will need to add the new domain name to the DNS as appropriate: see Chapter 6, *Into Production* for details. Reload Apache:

```
$ /etc/init.d/apache2.2 graceful
```

The final step to enable your repository is to index the gems it contains:

```
$ index_gem_repository.rb -d /opt/apache2.2/htdocs/gemserver
```

Note that the -d switch should reference the directory above the gems directory. This adds two files, yaml and yaml.Z, and a directory, quick, to the gemserver directory. These are used by clients (like the gem command line tool) to discover gems in the repository.

Now, test that the repository responds correctly to gem from a remote machine:

```
$ gem list --remote --source http://gems.company.local/

*** REMOTE GEMS ***

Need to update 1 gems from http://gems.company.local/

.

complete

rake (0.7.3)
    Ruby based make-like utility.
```

Using this technique, you can make a precise set of gems available to developers. The down side is that you need to run the index_gem_server.rb command each time you add or change gems, to update the index (or you could use cron to do this automatically); you have to maintain the repository and ensure that the dependencies between gems are satisfied; and the documentation isn't displayed if you visit http://gems.company.local/ (the gems aren't necessarily installed, so may not have documentation available).

You can set up developer machines to use the repository, as their default, as outlined in the section: *Setting Your Gem Server as the Default* on the previous page.

Index

Thank you for buying
Ruby on Rails Enterprise Application Development

Packt Open Source Project Royalties

When we sell a book written on an Open Source project, we pay a royalty directly to that project. Therefore by purchasing Ruby on Rails Enterprise Application Development, Packt will have given some of the money received to the Ruby on Rails project.

In the long term, we see ourselves and you—customers and readers of our books—as part of the Open Source ecosystem, providing sustainable revenue for the projects we publish on. Our aim at Packt is to establish publishing royalties as an essential part of the service and support a business model that sustains Open Source.

If you're working with an Open Source project that you would like us to publish on, and subsequently pay royalties to, please get in touch with us.

Writing for Packt

We welcome all inquiries from people who are interested in authoring. Book proposals should be sent to authors@packtpub.com. If your book idea is still at an early stage and you would like to discuss it first before writing a formal book proposal, contact us; one of our commissioning editors will get in touch with you.

We're not just looking for published authors; if you have strong technical skills but no writing experience, our experienced editors can help you develop a writing career, or simply get some additional reward for your expertise.

About Packt Publishing

Packt, pronounced 'packed', published its first book "Mastering phpMyAdmin for Effective MySQL Management" in April 2004 and subsequently continued to specialize in publishing highly focused books on specific technologies and solutions.

Our books and publications share the experiences of your fellow IT professionals in adapting and customizing today's systems, applications, and frameworks. Our solution-based books give you the knowledge and power to customize the software and technologies you're using to get the job done. Packt books are more specific and less general than the IT books you have seen in the past. Our unique business model allows us to bring you more focused information, giving you more of what you need to know, and less of what you don't.

Packt is a modern, yet unique publishing company, which focuses on producing quality, cutting-edge books for communities of developers, administrators, and newbies alike. For more information, please visit our website: www.PacktPub.com.

PUBLISHING

Learning jQuery

ISBN: 978-1-847192-50-9   Paperback: 380 pages

Better Interaction Design and Web Development with
Simple JavaScript Techniques

1. Create better, cross-platform JavaScript code

2. Detailed solutions to specific
    client-side problems

jQuery Reference Guide

ISBN: 978-1-847193-81-0   Paperback: 225 pages

A Comprehensive Exploration of the Popular
JavaScript Library

1. Organized menu to every method, function,
    and selector in the jQuery library

2. Quickly look up features of the jQuery library

3. Understand the anatomy of a jQuery script

4. Extend jQuery's built-in capabilities with plug-
    ins, and even write your own

Please check **www.PacktPub.com** for information on our titles

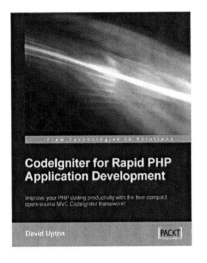

CodeIgniter for Rapid PHP Application Development

ISBN: 978-1-847191-74-8   Paperback: 220 pages

Improve your PHP coding productivity with the free compact open-source MVC CodeIgniter framework!

1. Clear, structured tutorial on working with CodeIgniter

2. Careful explanation of the basic concepts of CodeIgniter and its MVC architecture

3. Using CodeIgniter with databases, HTML forms, files, images, sessions, and email

4. Building a dynamic website quickly and easily using CodeIgniter's prepared code

CherryPy Essentials

ISBN: 978-1-904811-84-8   Paperback: 272 pages

Design, develop, test, and deploy your Python web applications easily

1. Walks through building a complete Python web application using CherryPy 3

2. The CherryPy HTTP:Python interface

3. Use CherryPy with other Python libraries

4. Design, security, testing, and deployment

Please check **www.PacktPub.com** for information on our titles

Printed in the United Kingdom
by Lightning Source UK Ltd.
124457UK00002B/191-214/A